# FANTASY WORLD-BUILDING

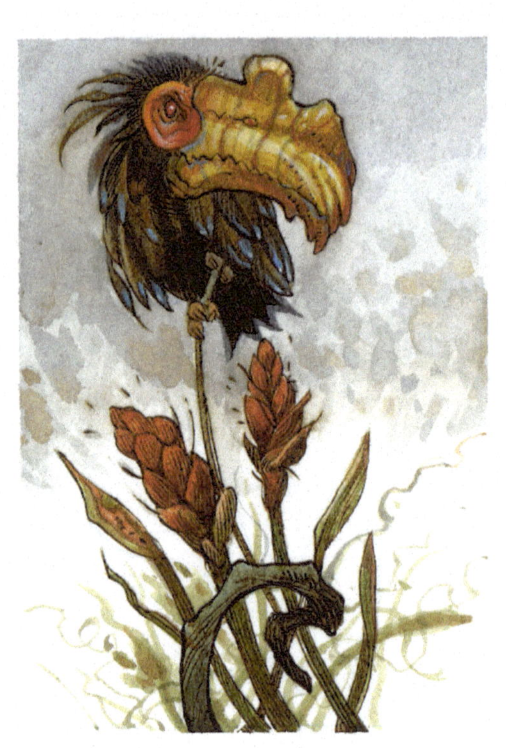

# FANTASY WORLD-BUILDING

## A Guide to Developing Mythic Worlds and Legendary Creatures

## MARK A. NELSON

*Foreword by*
## TODD LOCKWOOD

DOVER PUBLICATIONS
Garden City, New York

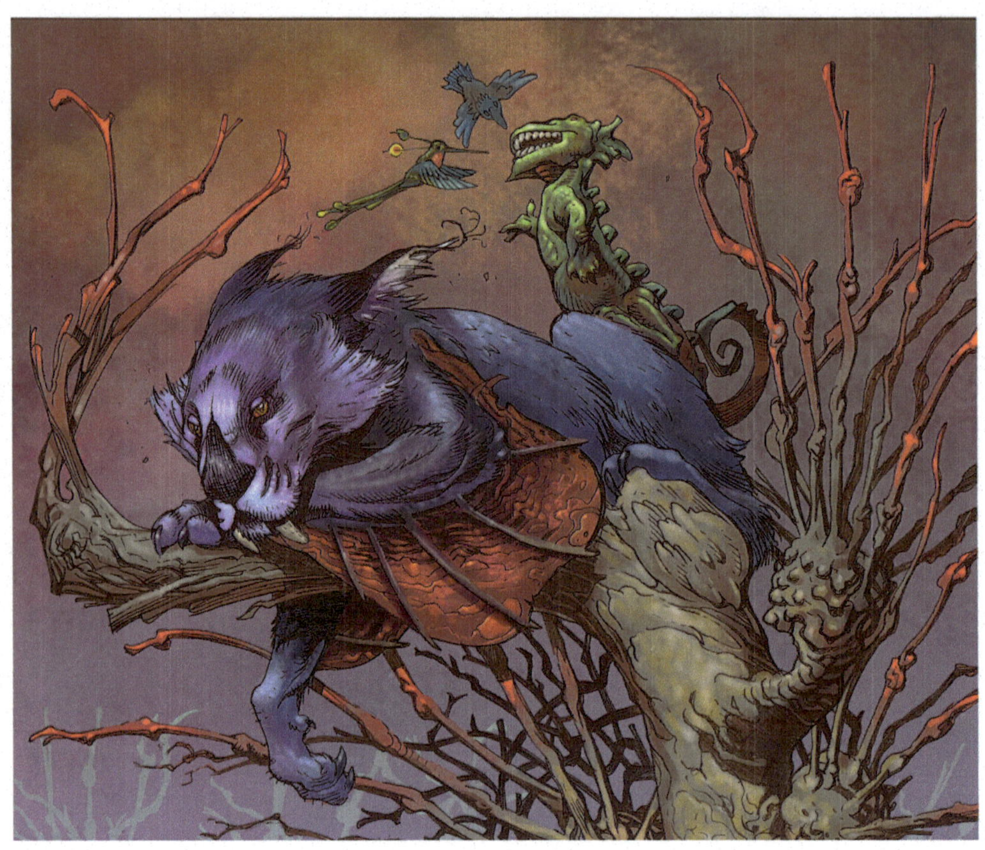



*Fantasy World-Building: A Guide to Developing Mythic Worlds and Legendary Creatures* is a new work, first published
by Dover Publications in 2019.

Edited by Stephanie Castillo Samoy
Designed by Marie Zaczkiewicz

ISBN-13: 978-0-486-82865-7
ISBN-10: 0-486-82865-4

Printed in the United States of America
82865405    2025
www.doverpublications.com

# CONTENTS

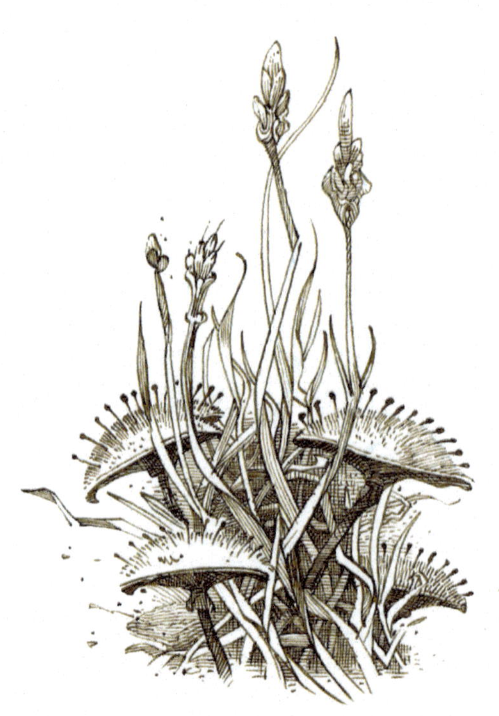

# FOREWORD

There is a monster in the heart of Texas.

I first met this beast in 1996, shortly after joining the art staff at TSR, makers of the role-playing game *Dungeons & Dragons*. I was surrounded by luminaries in the field of fantastic illustration; they all knew and admired him. He visited once or twice, and I was struck by his gigantic personality and enormous good cheer. I quickly learned that his outsize presence and sense of humor are dwarfed only by the immensity of his talent.

I speak, of course, of Mark A. Nelson. He taught illustration at the time at Northern Illinois University in DeKalb, not far from the TSR offices. There he helped to launch the careers of a great many notable illustrators: Tom Baxa, Jeff Laubenstein, Jim Nelson, rk post, Armand Balthazar, Mike Sutfin, and many, many more. It's a long list. All were touched by his glorious madness. Suffice it to say that his influence on the industry has been gargantuan.

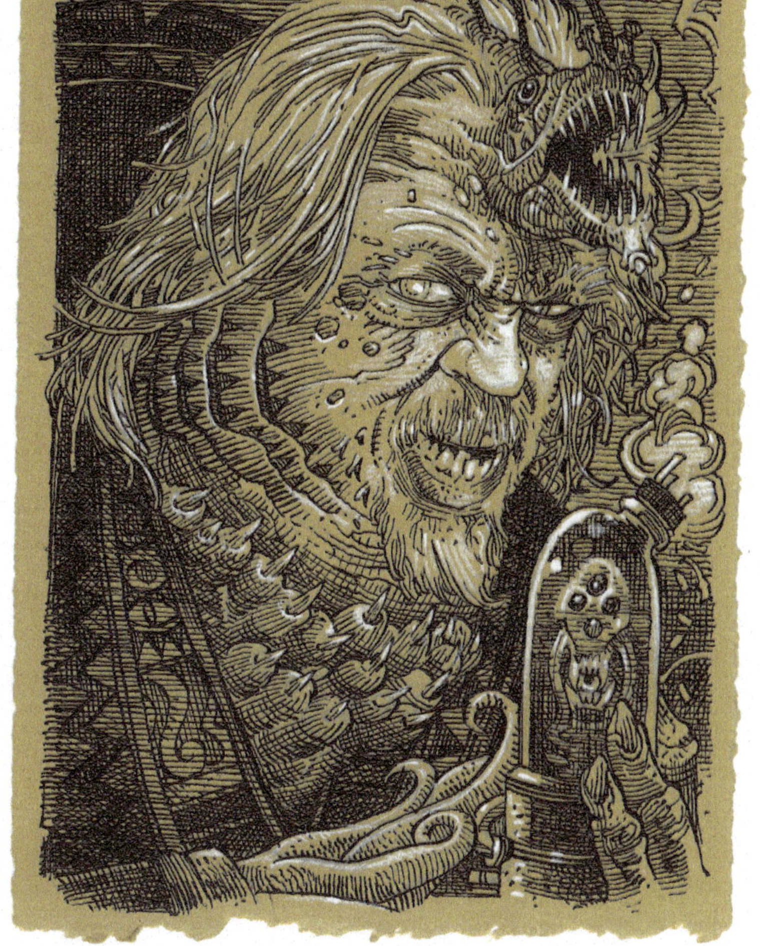

He invited us to his expansive home one time. It was like walking into the treasure hoard of a dragon. We drooled over countless flat files full of art—his own and others'—and his massive collection of amazing memorabilia. I recall, in particular, the skull of a saber-toothed lion, which I covet to this day.

Eventually, the university and the monster parted ways. He found himself in the Lone Star State, where he still resides, like an "ogre-mage" determined to populate the world with all manner of monsters, demons, primordial behemoths, fairies, dragons, and maidens fair and foul. His particular alchemy draws on a bottomless well of anatomical knowledge, creative energy, and diabolical wit. He is easily the most prolific artist I know. He's unstoppable. And that's a good thing. He makes the universe a bigger, scarier, more mysterious, funnier place.

You hold in your hands a link to his special magic. Enter, sharpen your claws, file your teeth, and prepare to unleash monsters of your own on the world.

Todd Lockwood
Naples, Italy
November 2018

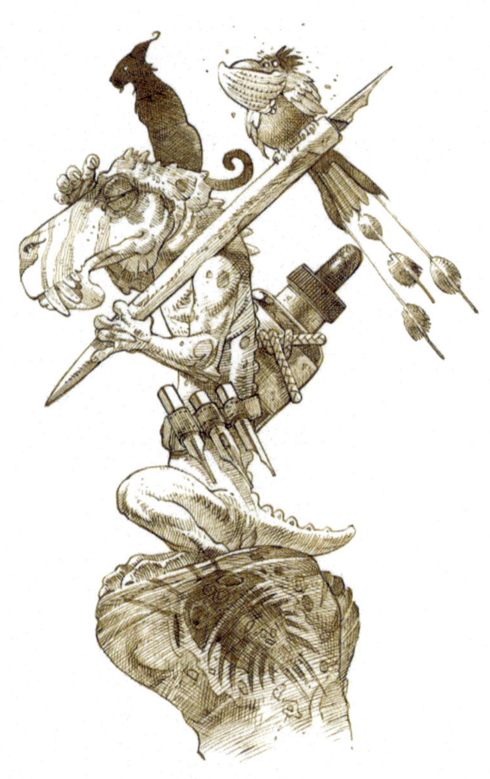

# 1

# VISUAL PROBLEM SOLVER

**W**orking as a visual problem solver is what most artists do. We develop or are presented with a series of descriptions and ideas to create worlds, characters, and stories. It is our hope that we do this in believable scenarios in the form of finished artwork.

Sometimes you work within a set of parameters set by the project. Other times you set these considerations yourself. When you are dealing with licensed properties, you have to work within provided guidelines. This by no means should stifle your creativity. In fact, you can find many ways of working and creating outlooks within these guidelines.

I have worked on many licensed properties and have designed buildings, creatures, spaceships, rooms, interiors, and costumes that ranged from the humorous to the dark. I have drawn funny animals to terrifying ones, hard sci-fi to horror, and realistic settings to the fantastic. Each represented a new answer within this world, an avenue for me to conquer as an artist and grow my skill set. I try to look at it all as a challenge. What can I do to bring it to life with a set of visuals in an interesting way, a new way, or build upon the existing world and add my personal touch? When do we start talking worlds? You get to fill them with everything, and I do mean everything! This includes your favorite habitats, rocks, grass, trees, critters, buildings. . . . The list goes on and on. It is a rather daunting challenge, but here is where the seeds of this book came from.

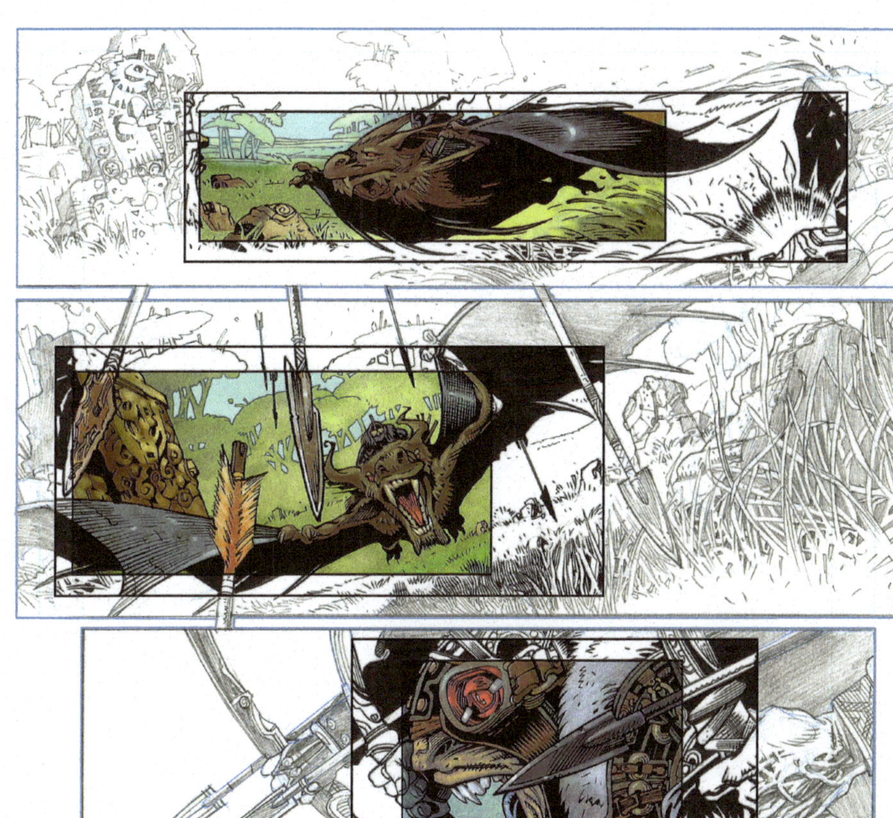

## SOMEONE SETS A PROBLEM: A SWORD.

Just what does this mean?

The mind starts: short sword, broadsword, two-handed battle sword, more than one blade, etc.

What type of pommel? Grip? Cross guard or rain guard? Leather grip or bone grip?

Type of metal? The finish? Damascus steel? Engraved? Flutes? Is it old and rusty? New and highly polished? Does it have decorations or engraving? And so on.

And if the character has a very well-defined sword, you can always practice your skills in drawing and/or painting metal and researching the method of how it was made, with the hope of adding more believability to your finished product.

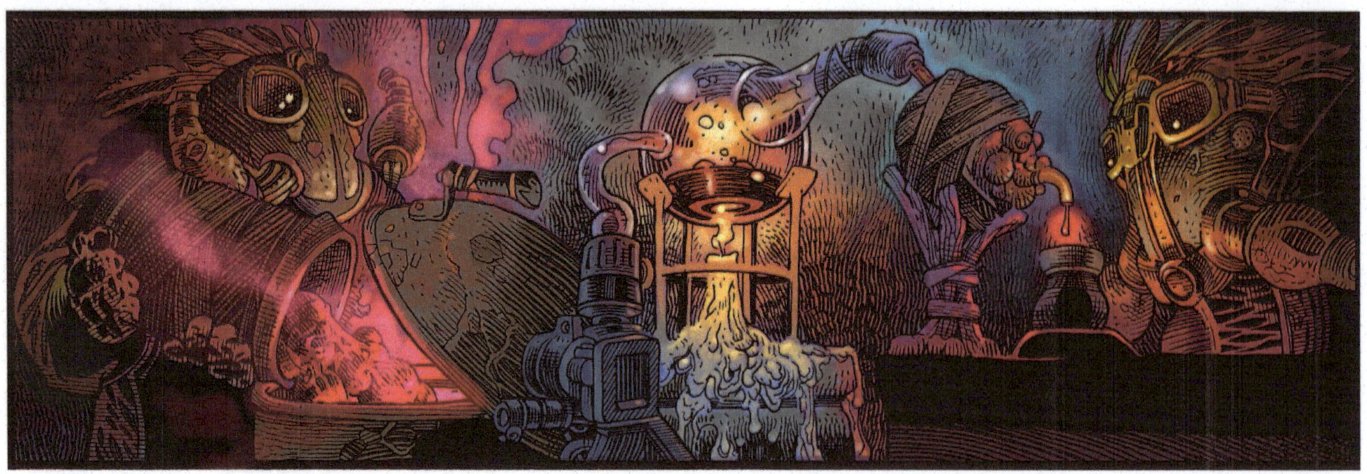

## RESEARCH, RESEARCH, RESEARCH

I am a huge proponent of research. When I started doing illustration, there was no Internet. If you wanted to find things, you went to the library, checked out books, pored over magazines and other periodicals for reference. As you collected images, you put them into file folders and labeled them. You created what was called a "morgue." When illustrators died, their morgues often were passed on or sold. They were rich depictions of periods in time, examples of work by other illustrators, and amazing collections of images. Needless to say, it was a lot of paper, file cabinets, and weight to move.

Nowadays, the Internet has given us a worldwide morgue of images, but I still have reference files on my hard drive. The digital camera has added another file-gathering tool. I have shot many different references with my camera and smartphone. The information highway is just a touch away, and your information gathering has never been easier. The morgue is an old habitat. It allows you to place materials where you need them, find images quickly, and forces you to organize photos and references.

## CHARACTER

Model sheets, FBS (front-back-side), or character design sheets is where we start. Everything is worked out by height, body shape, and clothing. Then the character is rotated to the side and back, and the drawing is finished. Sometimes a three-quarter shot is added for a mild action pose. Occasionally, when deadlines are imminent, I will do a three-quarter shot of a spaceship or other element and the modeler will finish the 3-D sculpture of it.

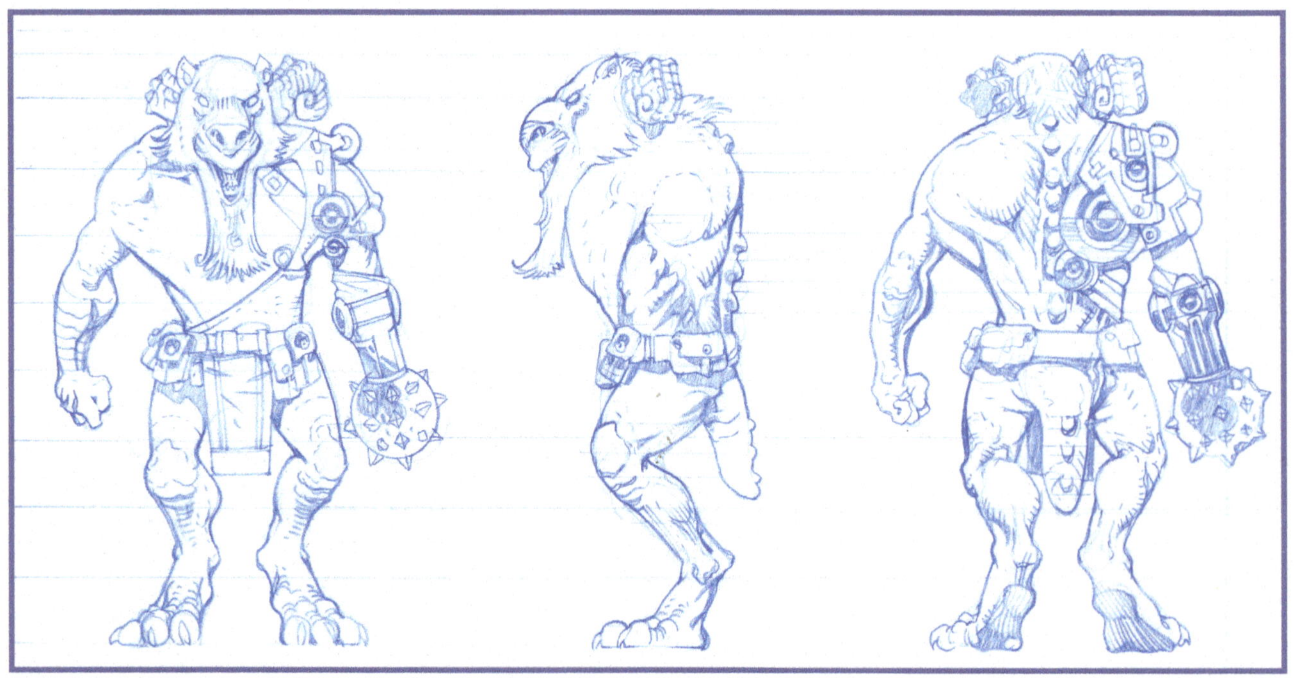

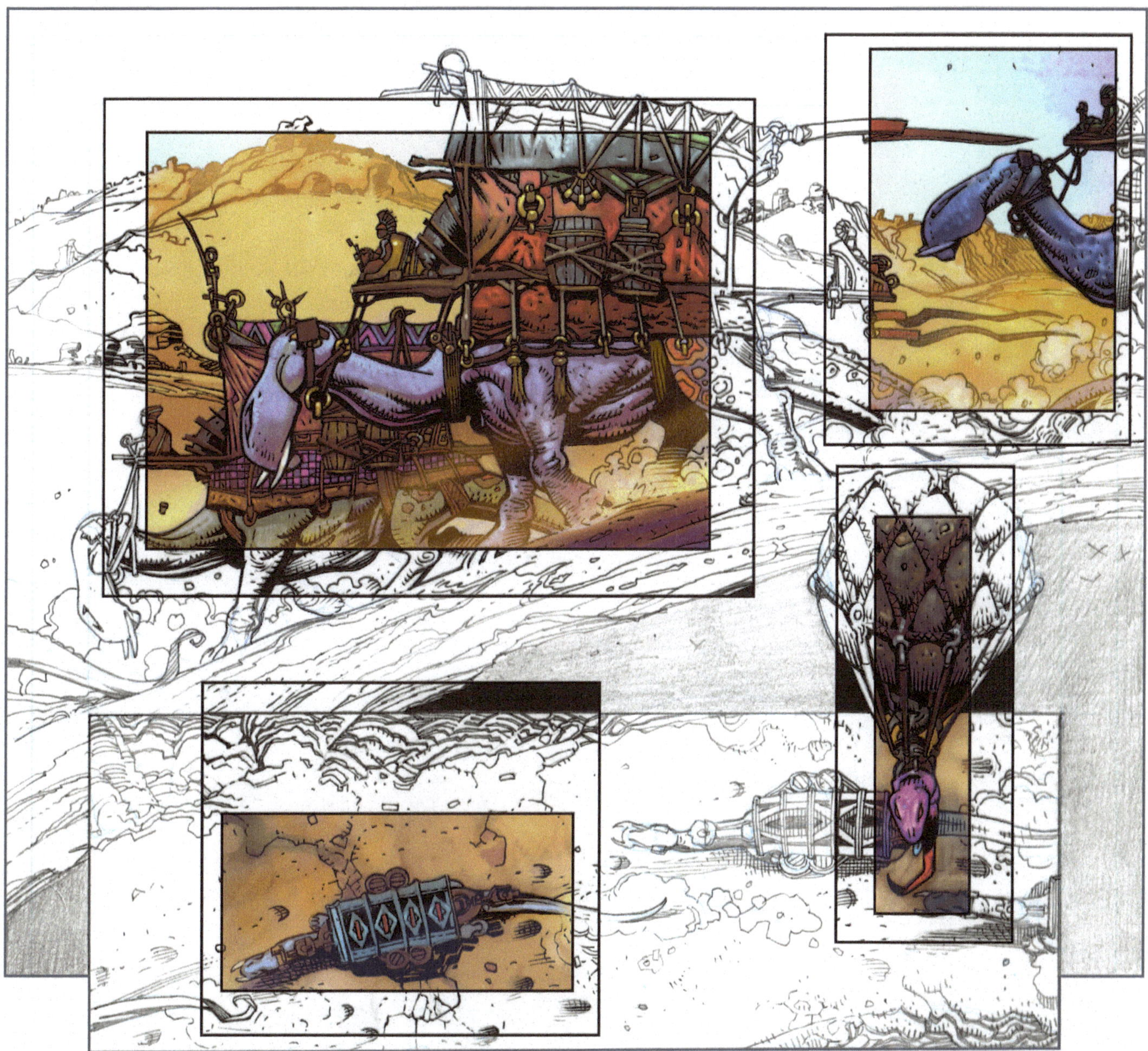

## THE STORY

Whether you are working on a single page, a series of images, or a sequential set of pages, the story is the main driving factor. It can be as simple as drinking a cup of tea or as complex as the battlefield of life. You, as the artist, have many tools at your disposal. How do you use your camera? How are you going to establish the space, character introductions, reactions to one another, action scenes, quiet moments, mood, time of day?

When I was working on a comic series, I used a model to portray a major character and shot a whole series of her as I tried to capture her unique body language: holding a coffee cup; leaning forward and talking; cradling the cup with one hand, then two; looking over the top of the cup. Storyboards for movies and comics share common terms and visuals. The difference is movie storyboards stay within a horizontal orientation and comics are vertical. But all the principles and terms of establishing a close-up shot, medium shot, long shot, POV (point of view), eye level, horizon line, birds-eye, and worms-eye are the same.

When I am watching a movie, there are many ideas running through my head:

1. Entertainment
2. Storytelling and how the camera is being used
3. Body language and the reactions of characters
4. Does the story hold together?
5. Is it believable within the parameters established by the director/editor/writers?

Idea: The story can be told partially by a tapestry on the wall and the reaction of the character.

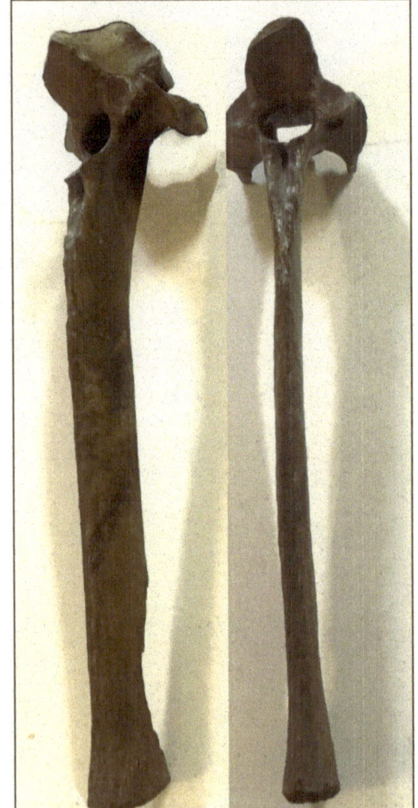

Here are several pictures of my bison bone.

# 2
# IDEAS

Ideas can come from anywhere. They can be simple, complex, or fill any conceptual need. They are the foundation to build upon.

So let's look at the creation of an idea from an object. I have bones and skulls in my studio. One of my favorite bones is a vertebra from a bison hump. The vertebra has the usual hole for the spinal cord, and one of its transverse processes (a small bony projection off the right and left sides of the vertebra) helps support the fat hump. So the two transverse processes are short, and the spinal cord hole is extended at different lengths as you move along the length of the spine.

First thought: Could this be a formation that we adapt for residing in? The Great Backbone City? The residents could add on structures like tents for more room as the family grows.

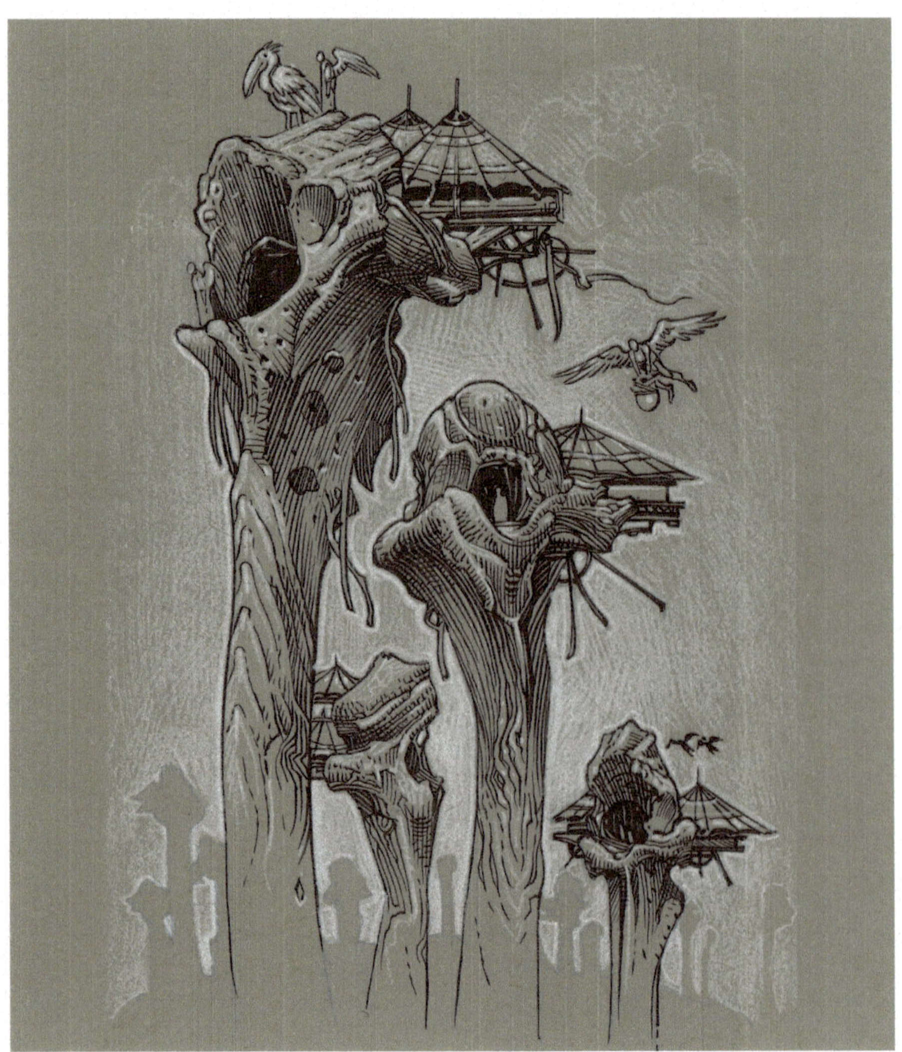

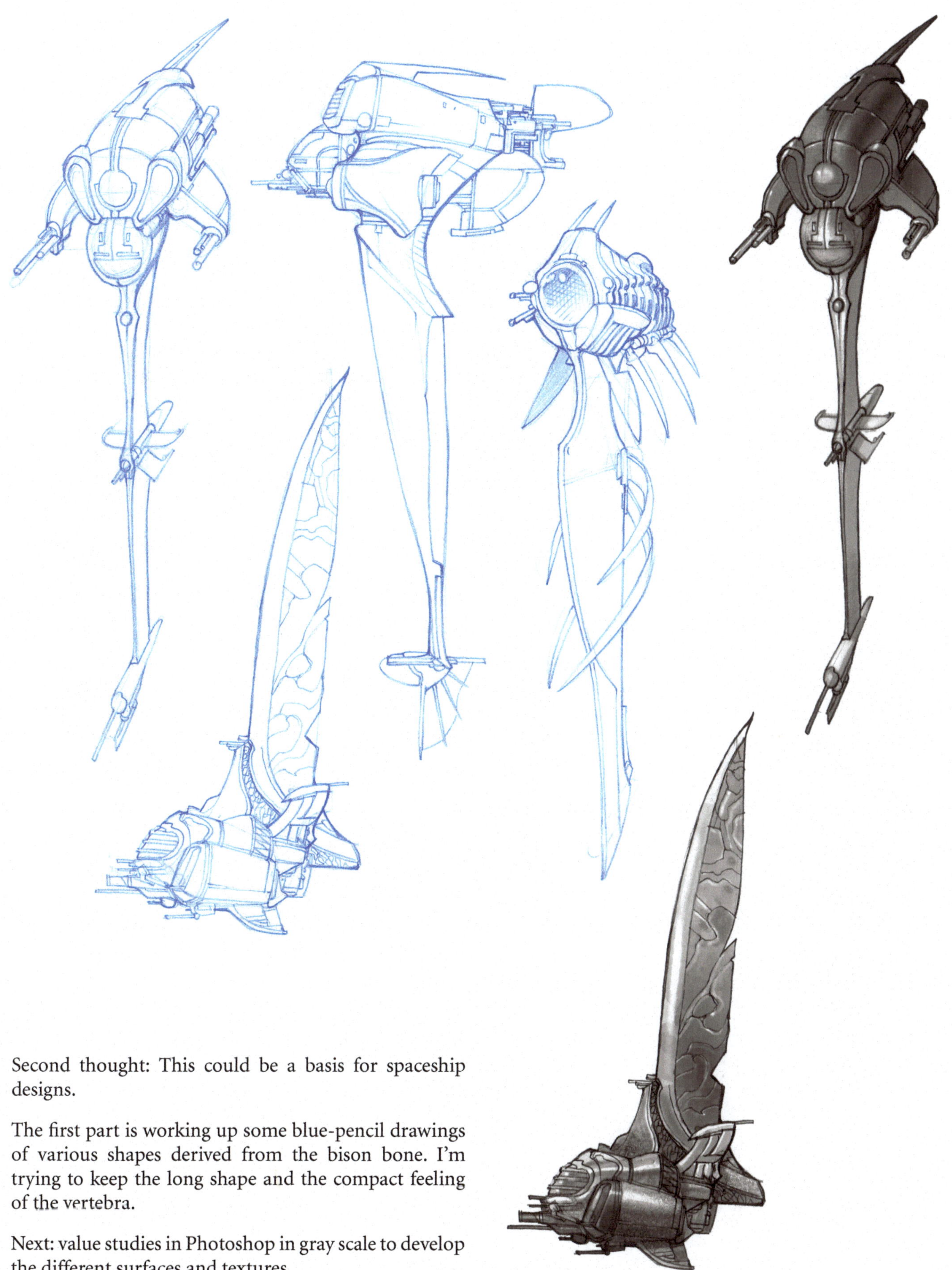

Second thought: This could be a basis for spaceship designs.

The first part is working up some blue-pencil drawings of various shapes derived from the bison bone. I'm trying to keep the long shape and the compact feeling of the vertebra.

Next: value studies in Photoshop in gray scale to develop the different surfaces and textures.

Finally: color studies to create the final look.

At this point, I try as many different things and variations as time allows. You can make a clean ship or one that is rusted and worn, brightly colored or subtle. It really is decided by how you want each one to look.

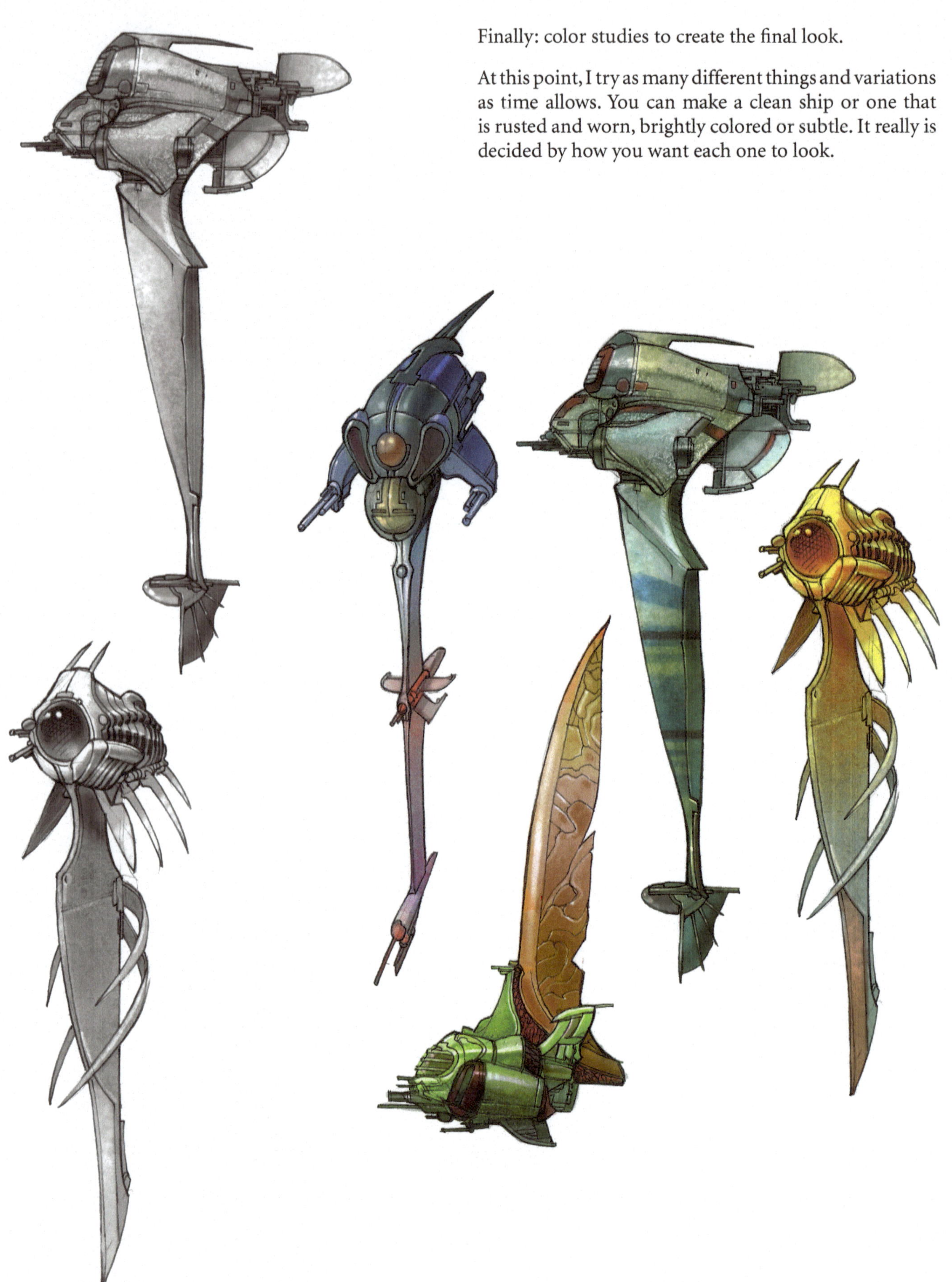

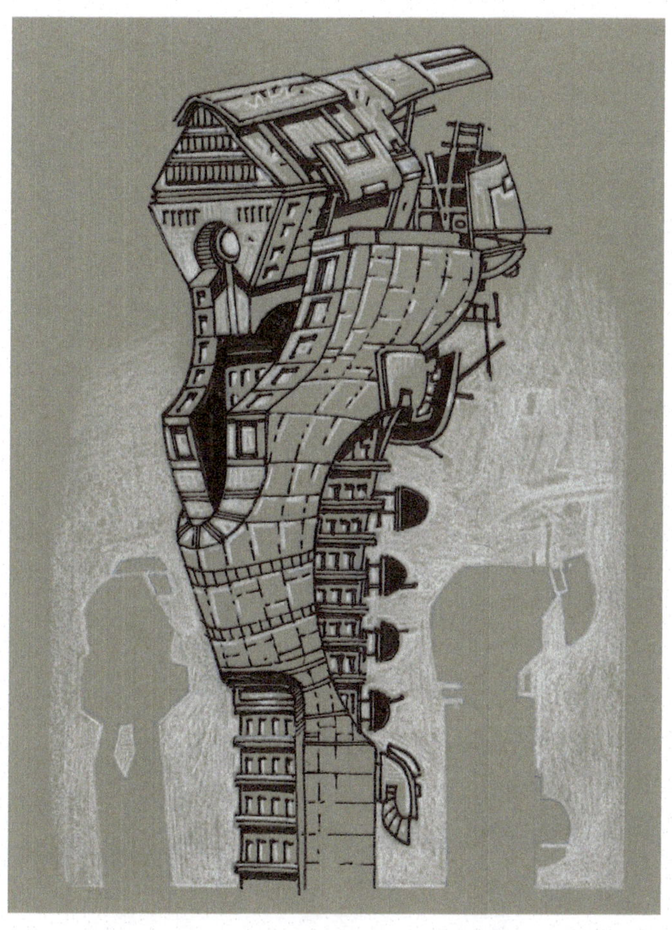

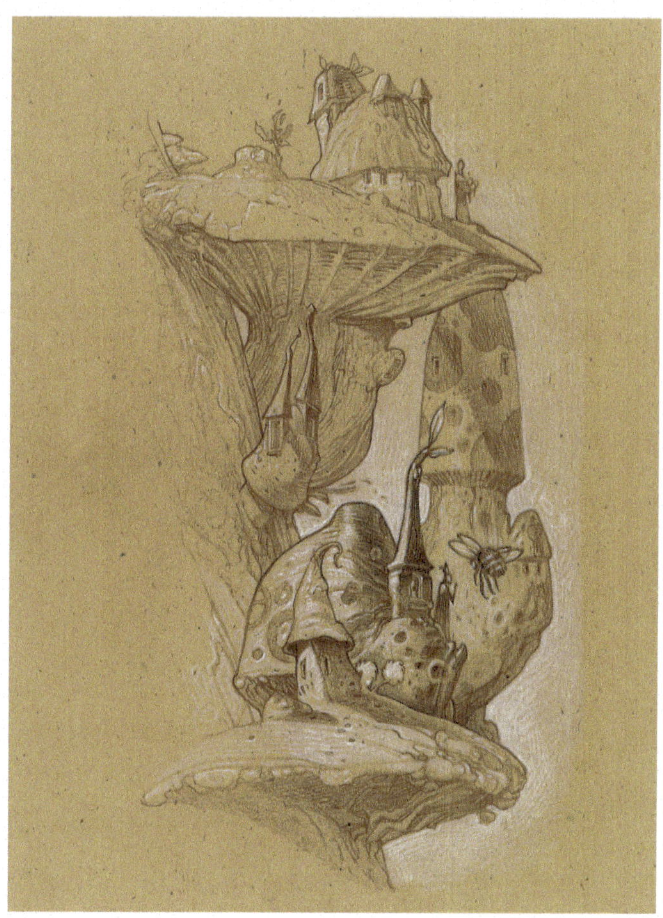

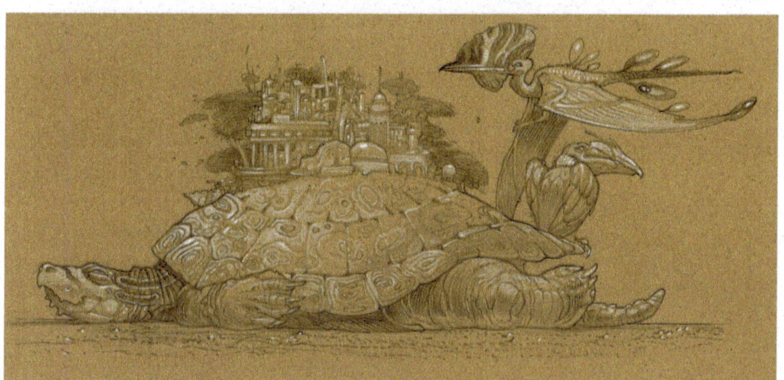

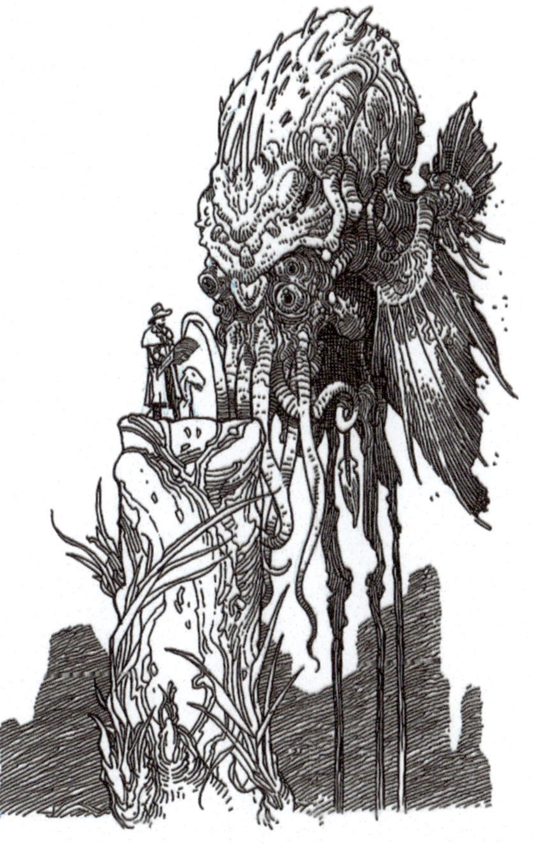

Third thought: high-tech building. A skyscraper made with panels, interior rooms, and wind fans.

So this can become a springboard. What about a mushroom city? A city built on the back of a large animal?

Or, perhaps, all the answers lay with the Giant Shelled Cephalopod.

A note: Bones have incredible shapes and provide for us an interior structure to support our muscles and organs. They need to have ridges, bends, and valleys into which the tendons and muscles fit. Each bone has a unique shape and function. The main difference between us and insects is our skeleton is on the inside covered with muscles and flesh (endoskeleton) and their skeleton is on the outside (exoskeleton), like a suit of armor, and all the muscles are inside.

# HISTORY

My grandmother was born in 1904 and died in 1997, just before her ninety-third birthday. She told me of how she rode a horse to school and lived on a farm. To think about what she experienced is amazing! World War I and World War II, the Korean War, the Vietnam War, and all the other wars. She saw the development of the phonograph, the record player, mono and stereo sound, and the radio; the evolution of film from the silents to the talkies and from black-and-white to color; and the invention of cassette tapes, CDs, DVDs, the television, remote control, flat screens, and computers. She witnessed numerous medical advances: the cure for polio, heart transplants, mechanical hearts, the growth of microsurgery, cataract surgery, hip and knee replacements, and more. The Chicago area was her home, so she was there in the time of Prohibition and gangsters, along with the rise of the museums, the Art Institute, and all the other huge cultural features. And that's just the tip of the iceberg.

History is a giant smorgasbord. It has everything. You want appetizers, salads, main courses, and dessert? It is all there! From spicy to bland, sweet to sour, happy to sad, and any other composition you want to make.

Pick a time frame and look at everything in and around it. What interests you? The Civil War did not have lasers, but what it did have was just as deadly. Over 51,000 people died at Gettysburg in two days of conflict. As a world culture, we have designed tools to kill and others to save lives. We have shown great compassion and total disregard. We are complex yet simple. We have a single or group dynamic constantly at odds or getting along. There are so many stories within all these factors. We can have stories about invention, growth, or outlook to new worlds, or we can stay here and live life in a ten-by-ten-foot cube.

History gives us stories. Not to be aware of them and not to research means you miss out on life. You can become the world builder.

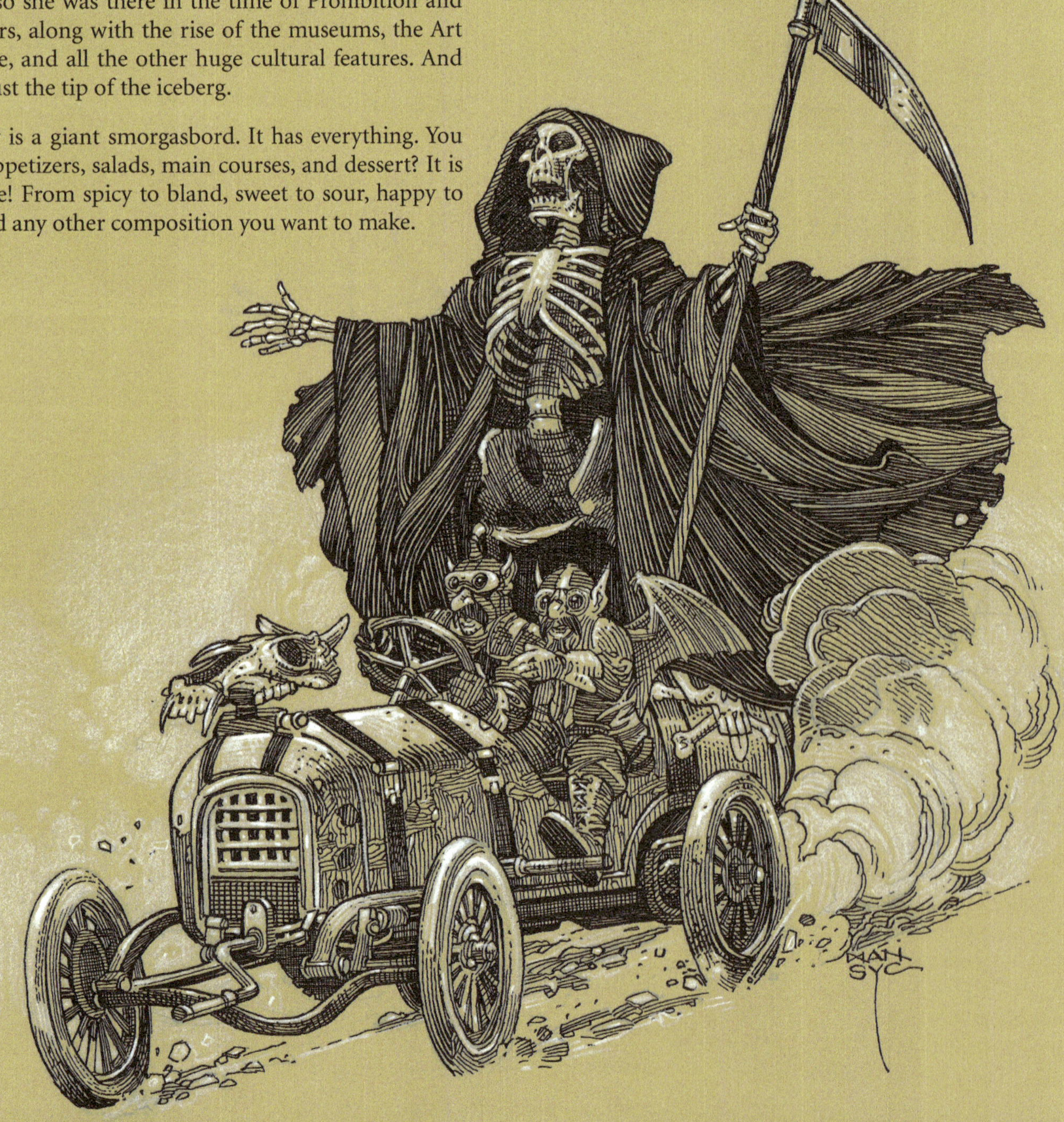

# HABITATS

One of the first key elements is to think of the habitat or environment. In what part of this world are we? Each area has its distinct characteristics and comes with a range of plant life, animal inhabitants, and geology that will become the raw material for creating our own environments and cultures. This includes building materials, metals and ores for weapons, farming, hunter-gathering, nomadic lifestyles, clothing, and goods for trade.

Habitats may blend into one another and can have a range of soils, vegetation, altitudes, and temperatures. Example: plains to mountains.

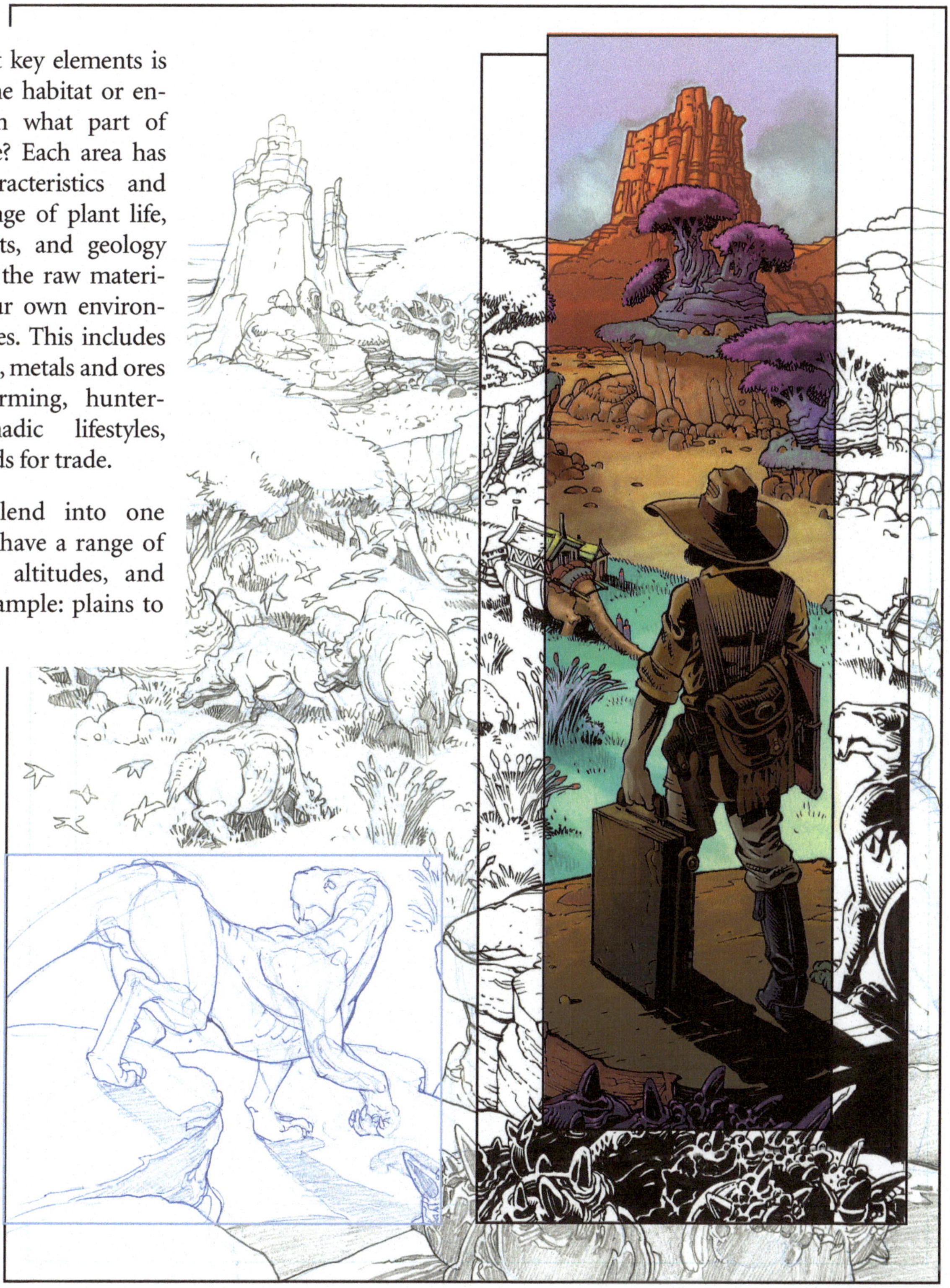

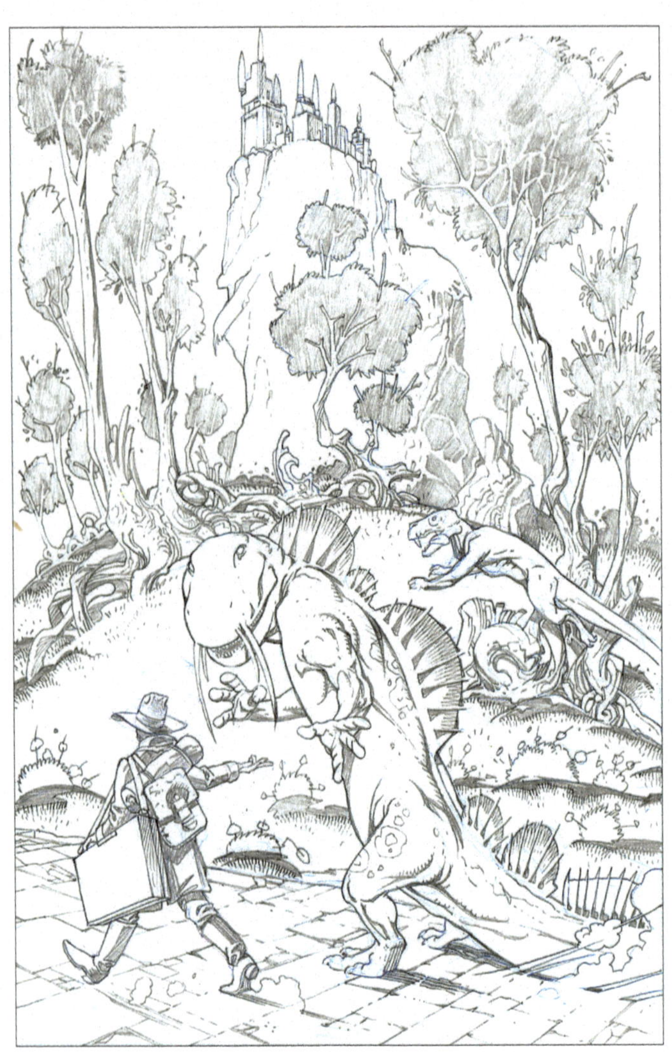

## HABITAT TYPES

Temperate, subtropical, tropical, polar

## TERRESTRIAL VEGETATION TYPES

Forest, steppe, grassland, semiarid, or desert

## FRESHWATER HABITATS

Marshes, streams, rivers, lakes, ponds, and estuaries

## MARINE HABITATS

Salt marshes, the coast, the intertidal zone, reefs, bays, the open sea, the seabed, deepwater and submarine vents

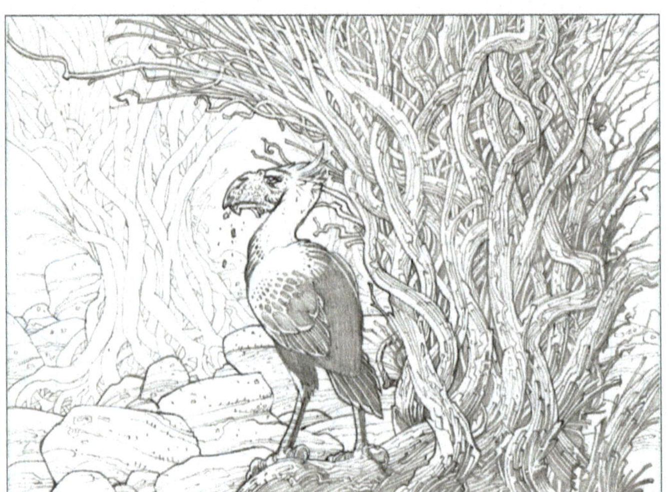

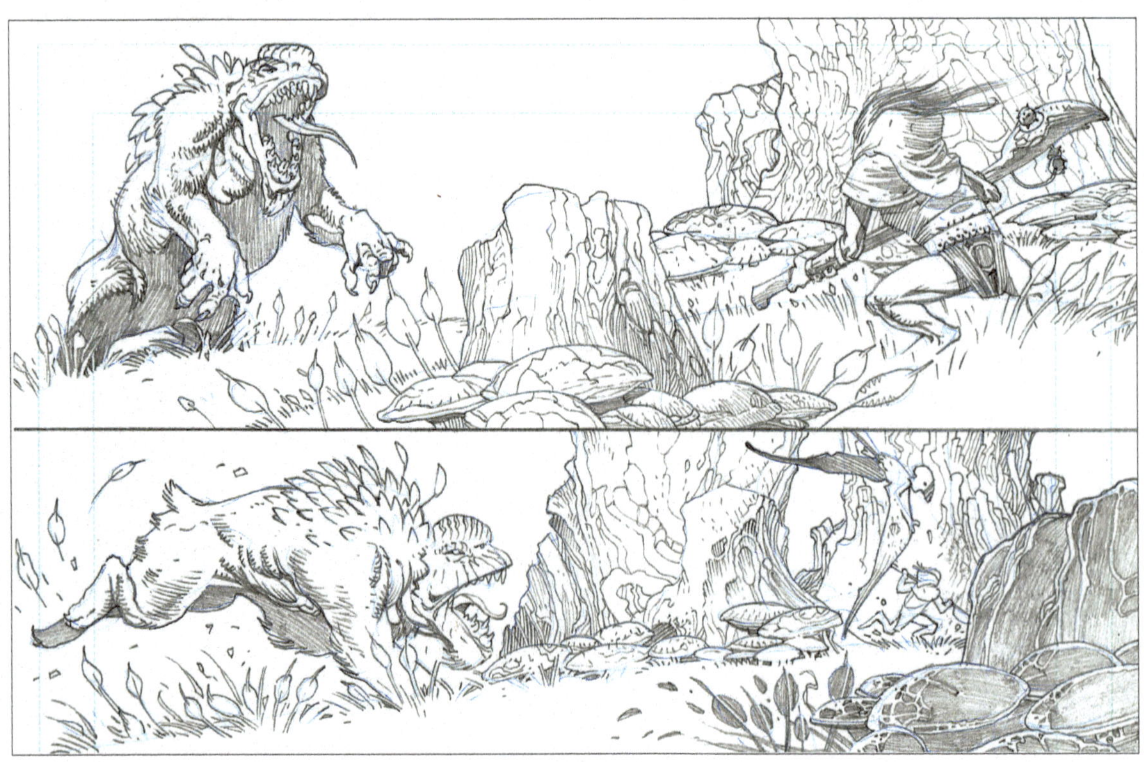

The geology of an area can be incredibly varied. You can have soft strata that wear away when they are windblown, creating arches and curving pathways. Sometimes the underlying stratum is harder and is left behind. This leaves cooled molten shapes to create another range of forms and surfaces. Crystalline forms created by saturation and dripping can have wonderful geometric shapes with softer edges.

Strata also can range in color. The Badlands in South Dakota have a color range from soft ocher to purple. The Petrified Forest in Arizona has trees that absorbed different materials and became crystal. Here, the range of color and translucency is stunning. The red earth in the Carolinas versus the green of the vegetation and trees is another wonderful contrast.

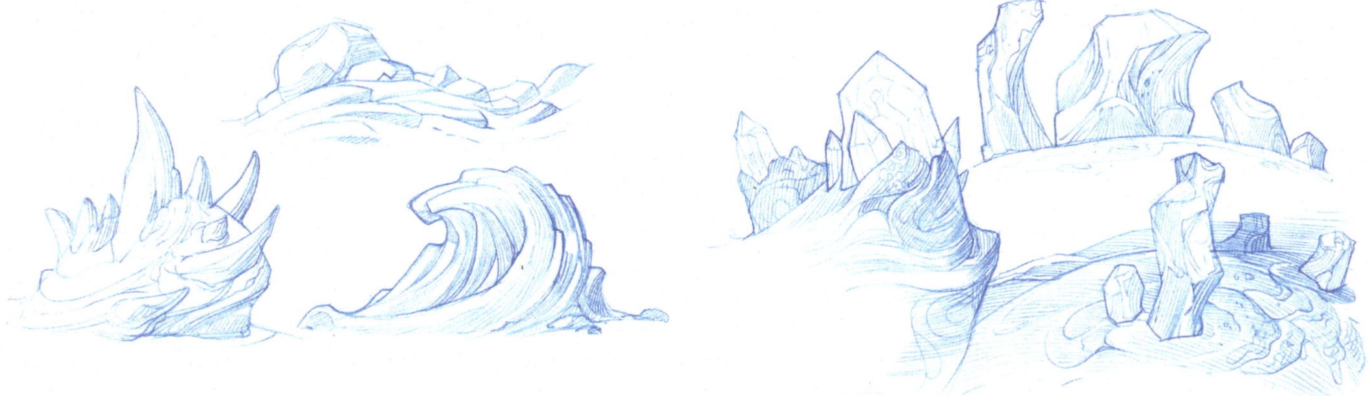

Sketchbook: thinking about rock shapes and forms (blue pencil).

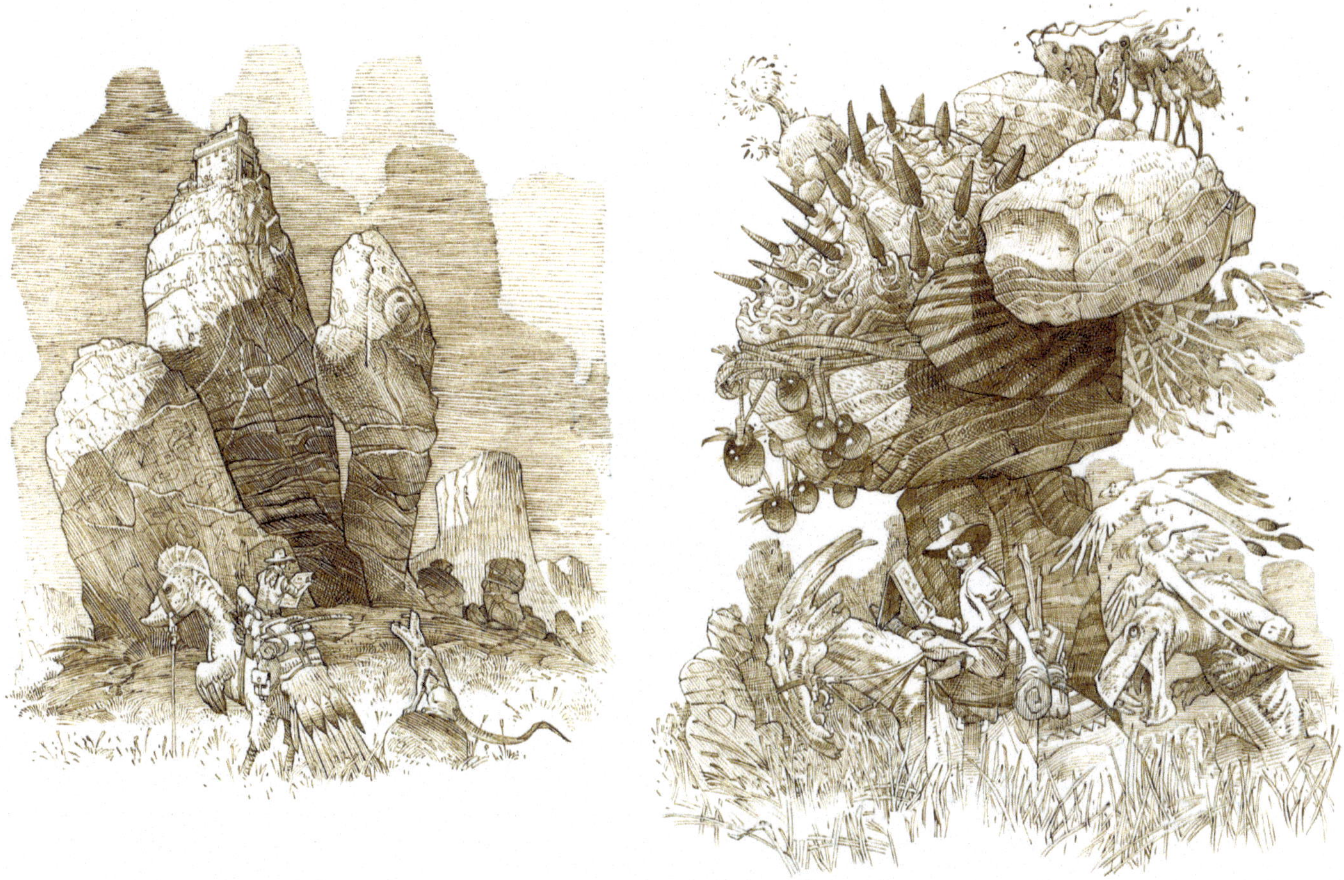

Drawings: rock in an environment of tall grass, with the possibility of nest builders that could have gathered some rocks. Or is it a leftover windblown form?

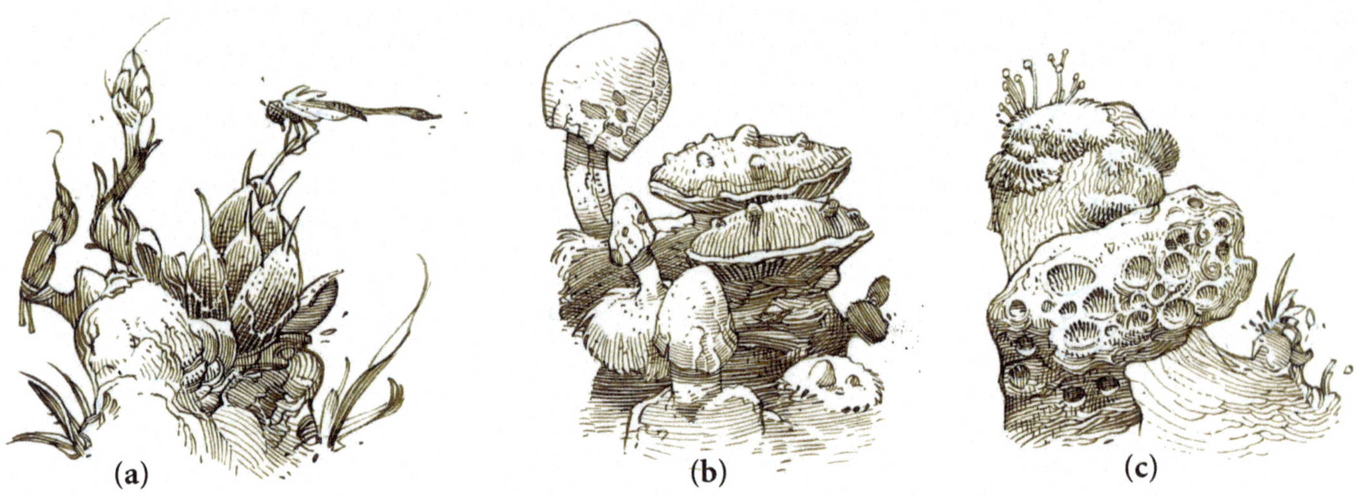

(a)        (b)        (c)

## FLORA

Plant life also can be varied. This includes types of (a) cacti, (b) mushrooms, (c) mosses, (d) bushes, (e) pod shapes, and (f) fruit-bearing bushes or trees. Each could have its own miniuniverse or symbiotic relationships with other life forms. They can have their own means of protection: spikes, poisonous fruit, or excreted irritants (such as poison ivy and oak).

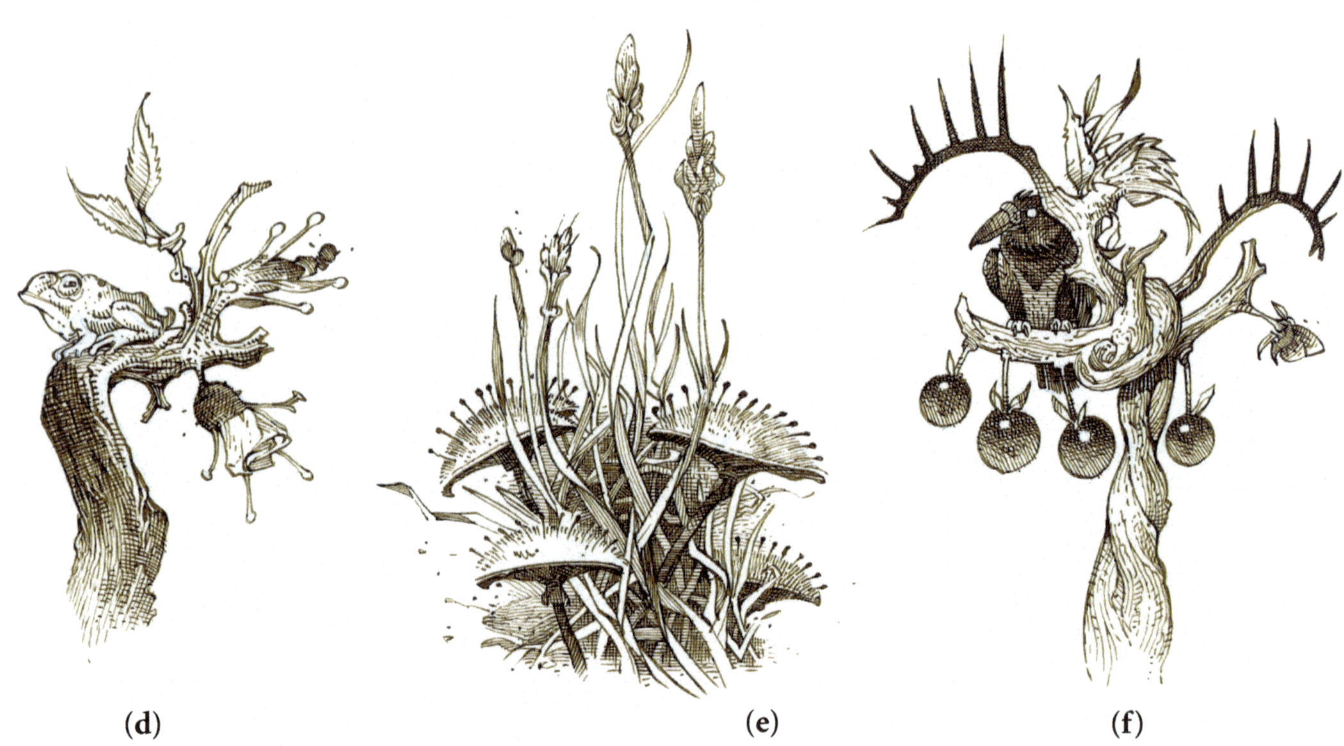

(d)        (e)        (f)

## WHAT ARE THEY USED FOR?

Food: vegetables, spices, and livestock feed.

Raw material: plant fibers woven into clothing, healing herbs, poisonous herbs, wind barriers, and protective barriers. They can and have played a huge part in stopping conquests. The plains of the Midwest were known as the green sea. They were flat and had very few distinguishing elements. The Spanish conquistadores wrote that it was just a green field for as far as the eye could see.

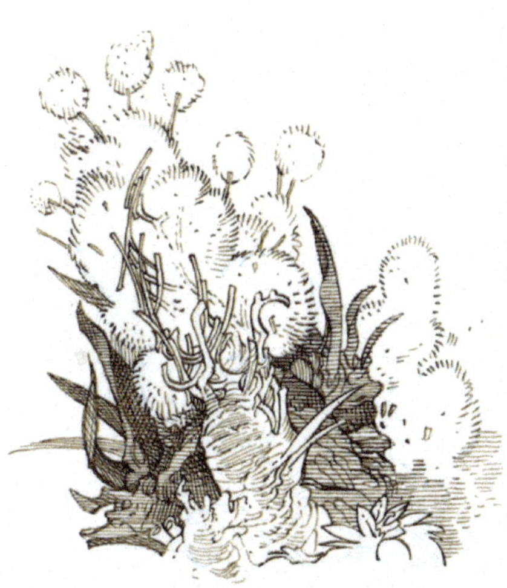 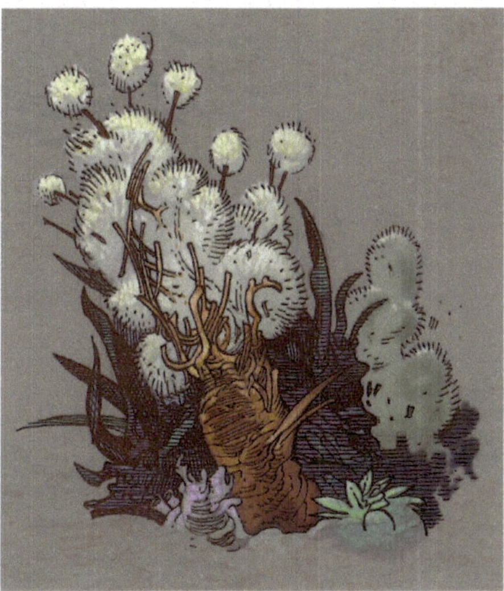 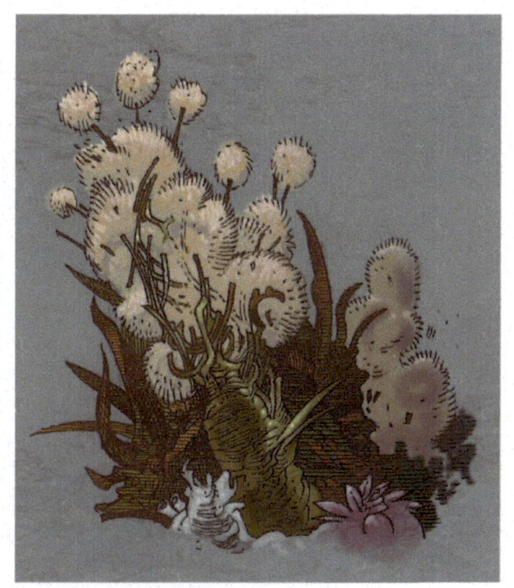

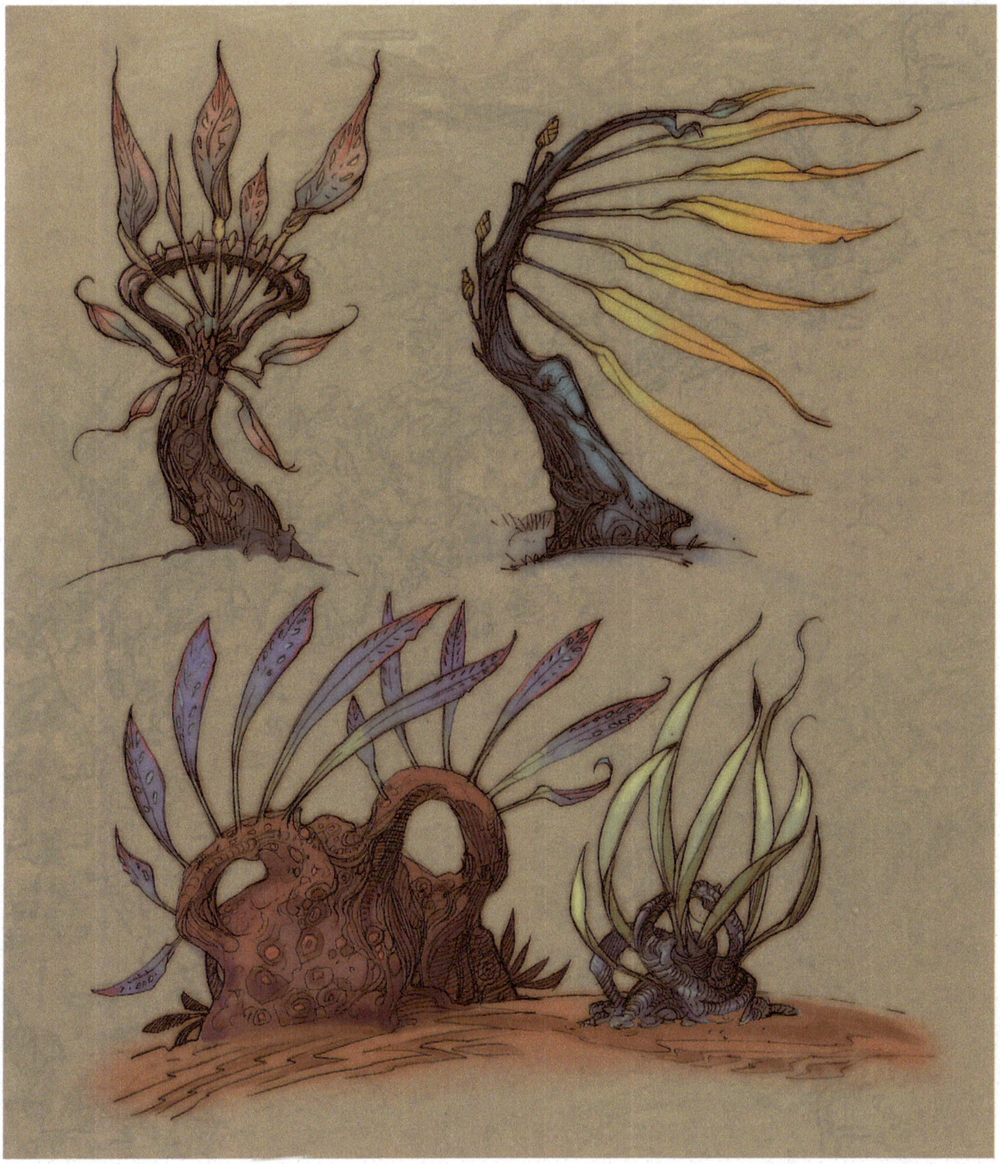

Here are studies of soft cottonlike plants with some color variations and a feather grass that grows in clumps or on various types of stalks.

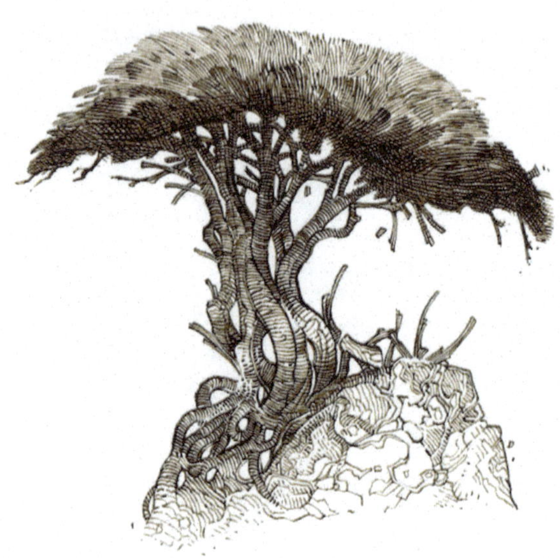

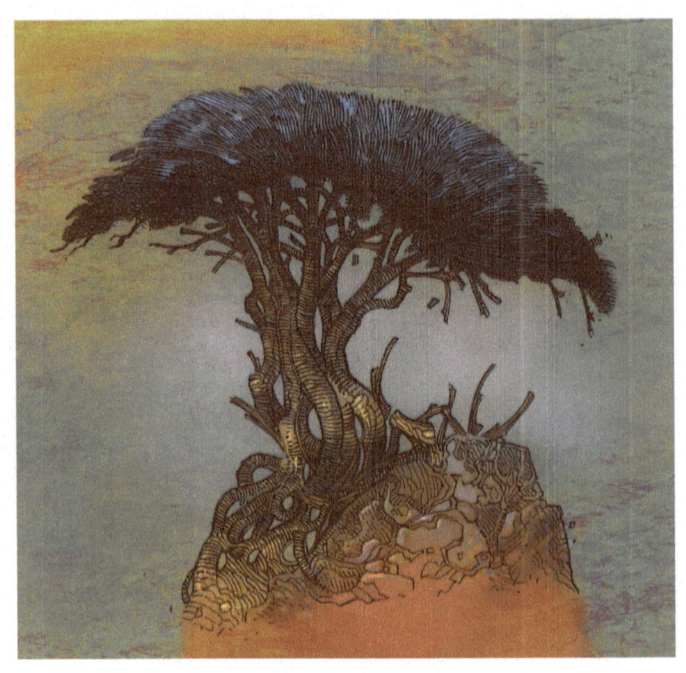

Trees have wonderful canopies and shapes. I've included some sketchbook studies (blue), which always get the process started. But I do like canopy trees. In the top drawings, there is a vine-wrapped stalk. The bottom left ink drawing is derived from the African baobab tree, but the trunk is thin and straight. The last ink drawing on the bottom right is a bat-wing canopy, complete with a cactus and a giant lizard.

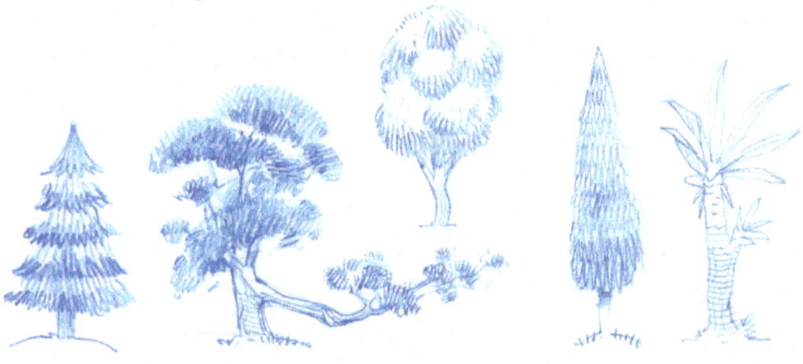

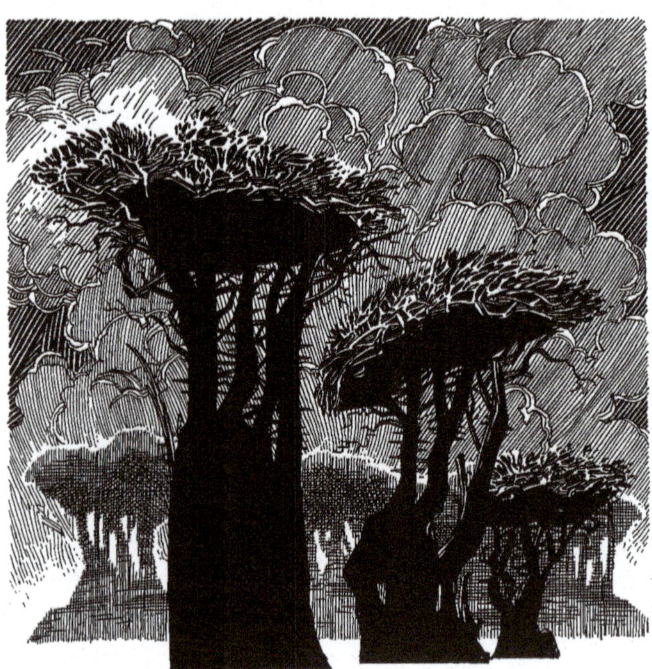

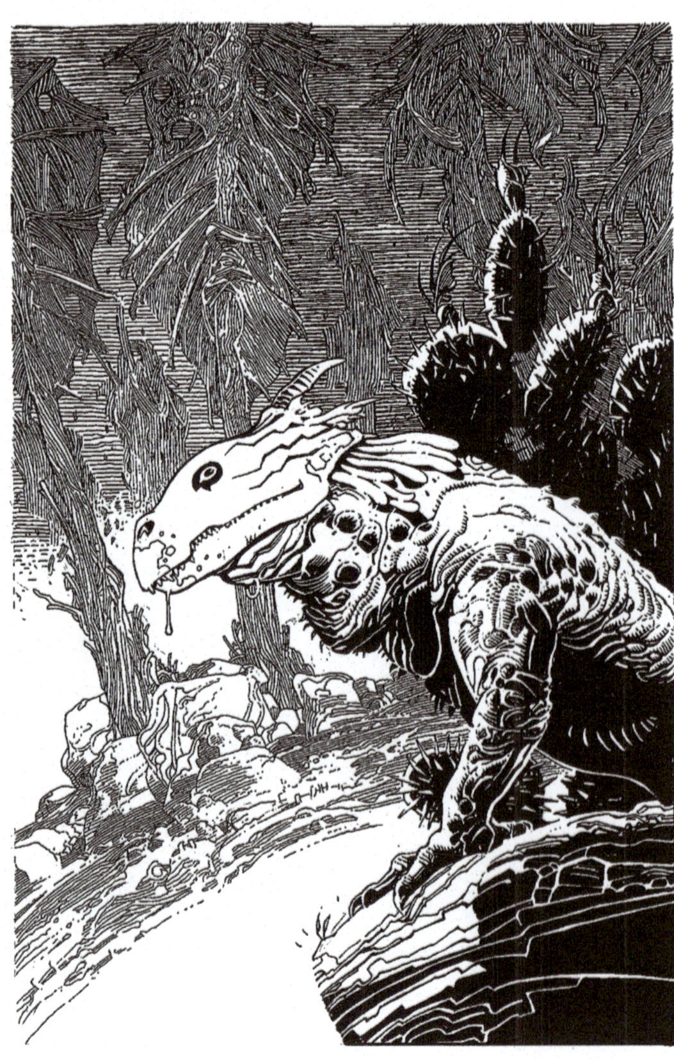

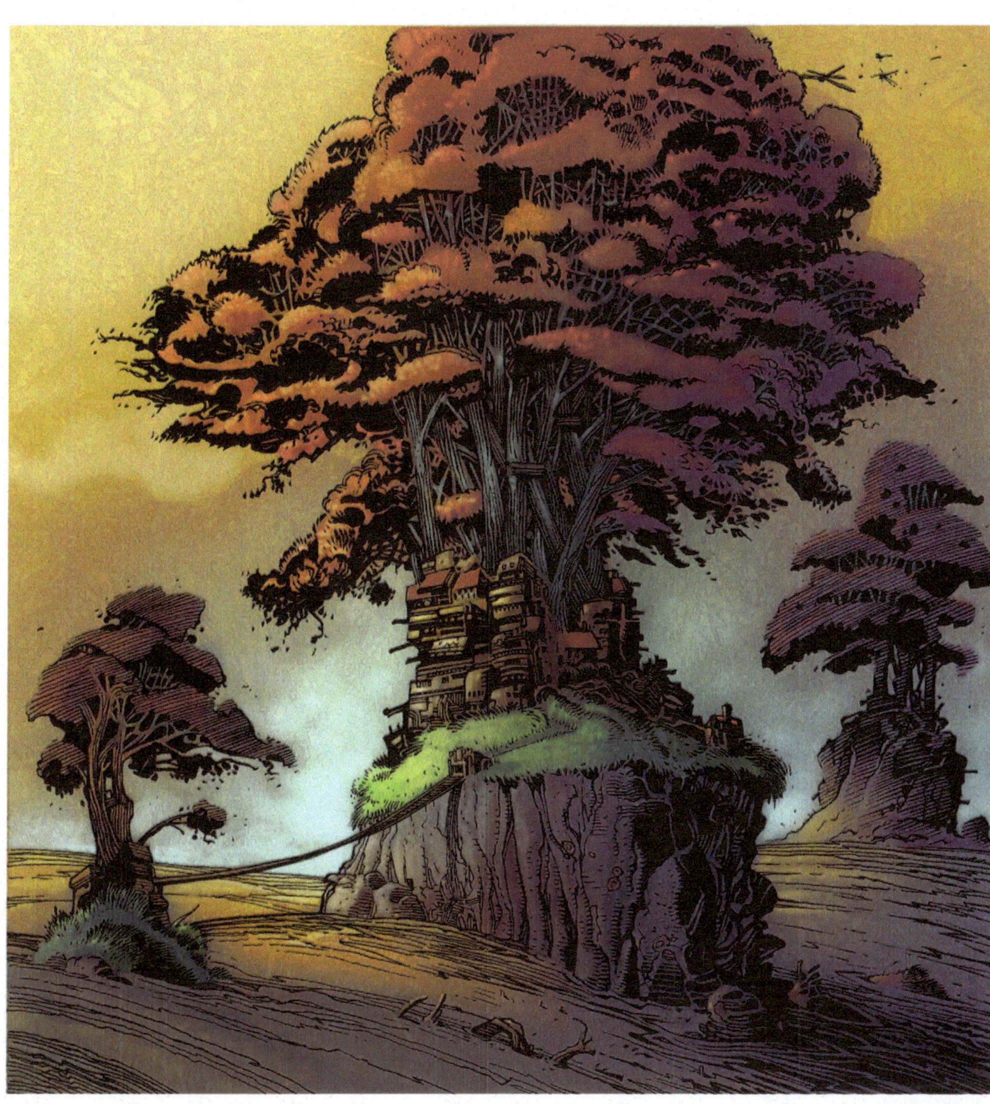

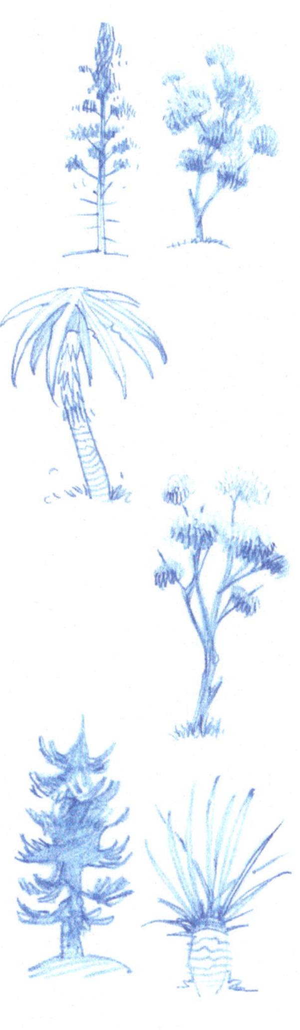

The idea here is a desert sea of moving sand, where there are islands of hard rock and tree roots that life has inhabited. Living in this one tree forest is a race that captures giant dragonflies. This tribe can travel to different areas of the desert, creating trade routes within this world.

The top right images show more sketchbook doodles (blue).

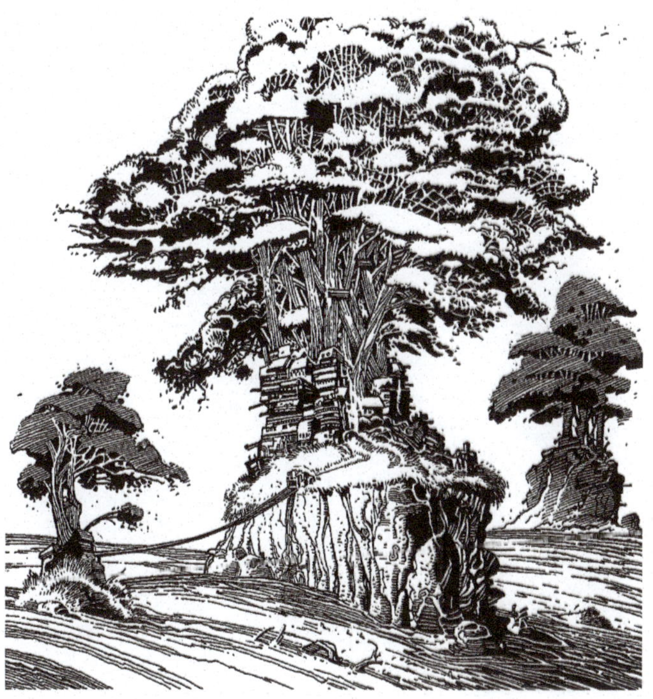

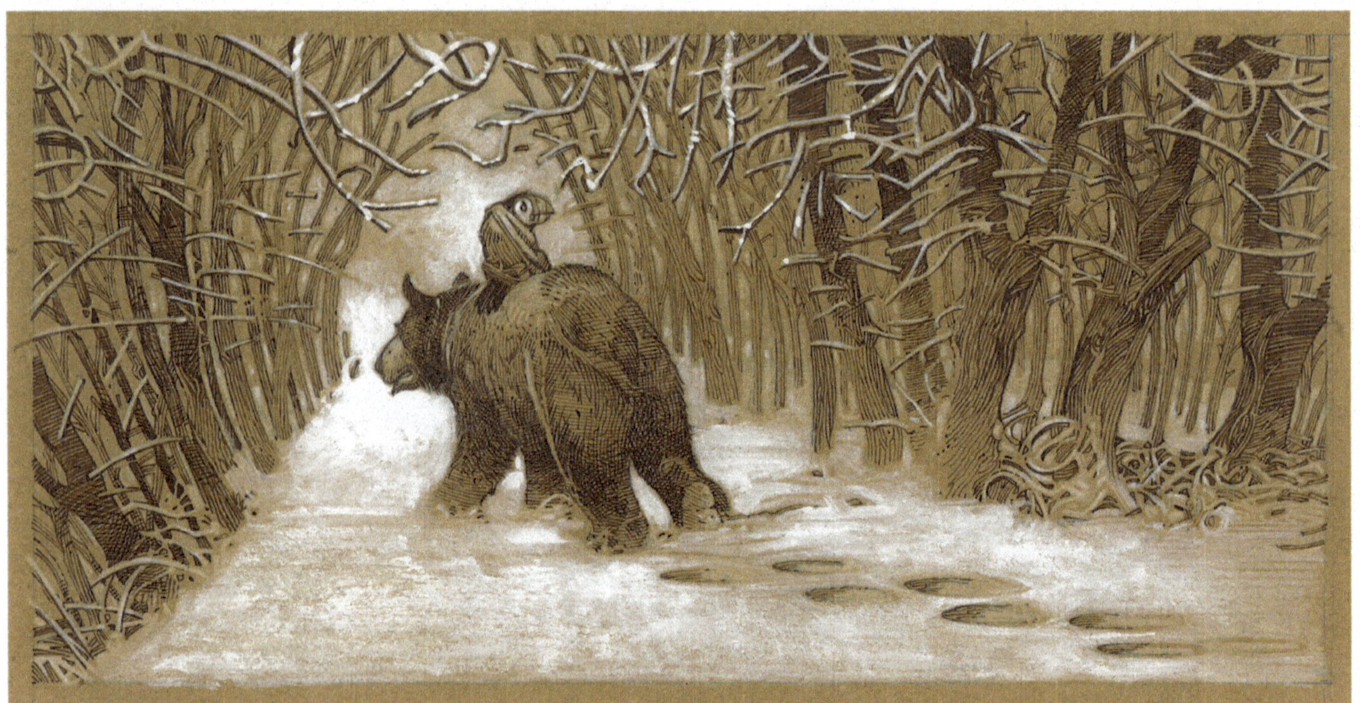

## POLAR HABITAT

Here, cold would reign supreme. Snowfall would cover the trees and the ground. Spring and summer may be short.

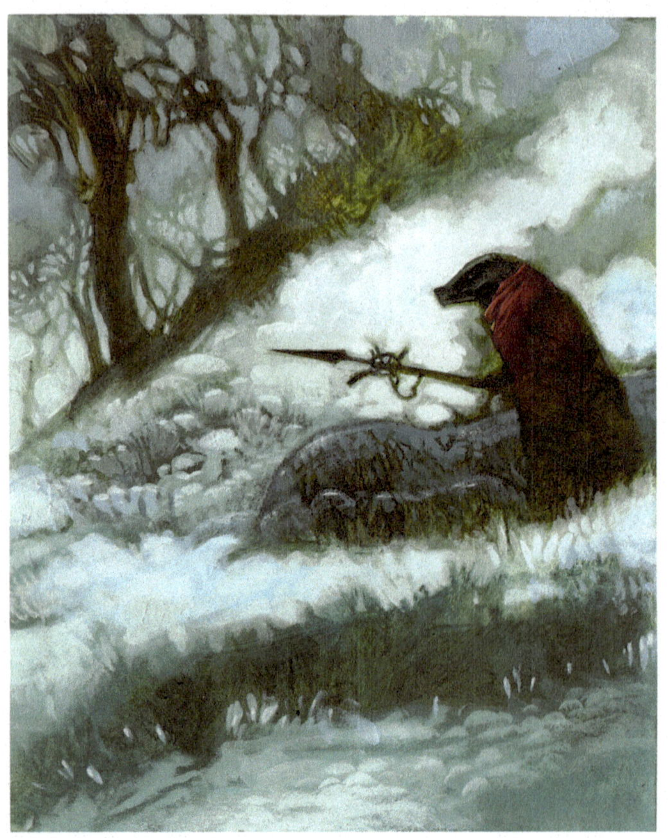

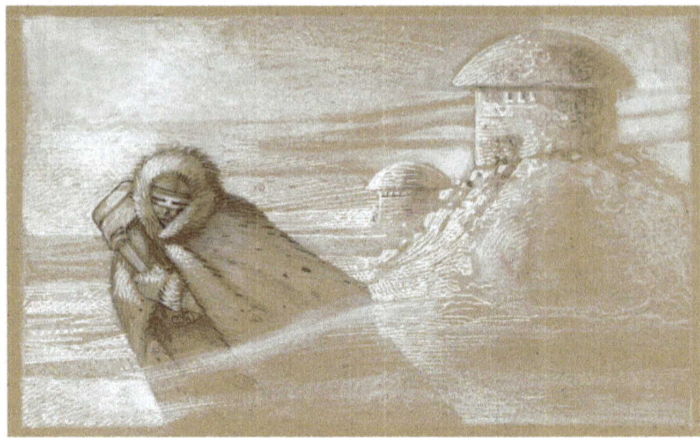

Houses could be built of snow, ice, or materials brought in. You would need to have protection from the weather, a way to store food, and a means to get food. Fishing through the ice? Local beasts? A short time to gather plants?

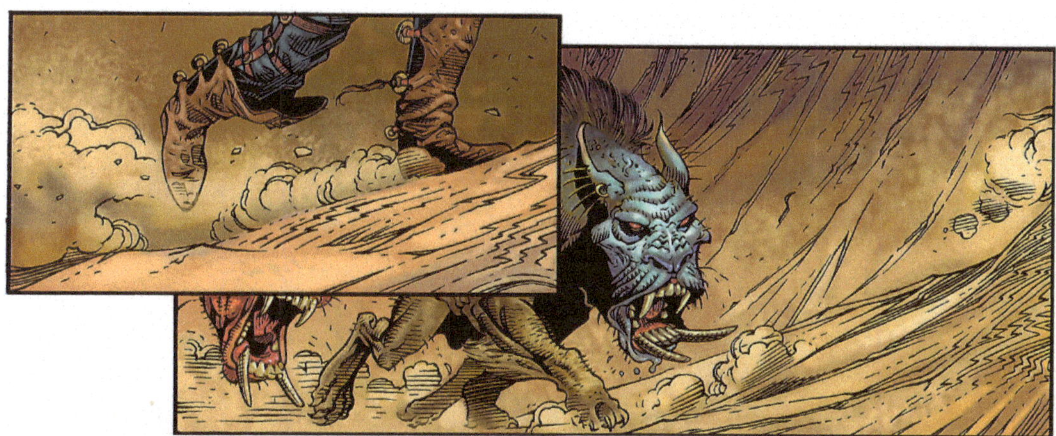

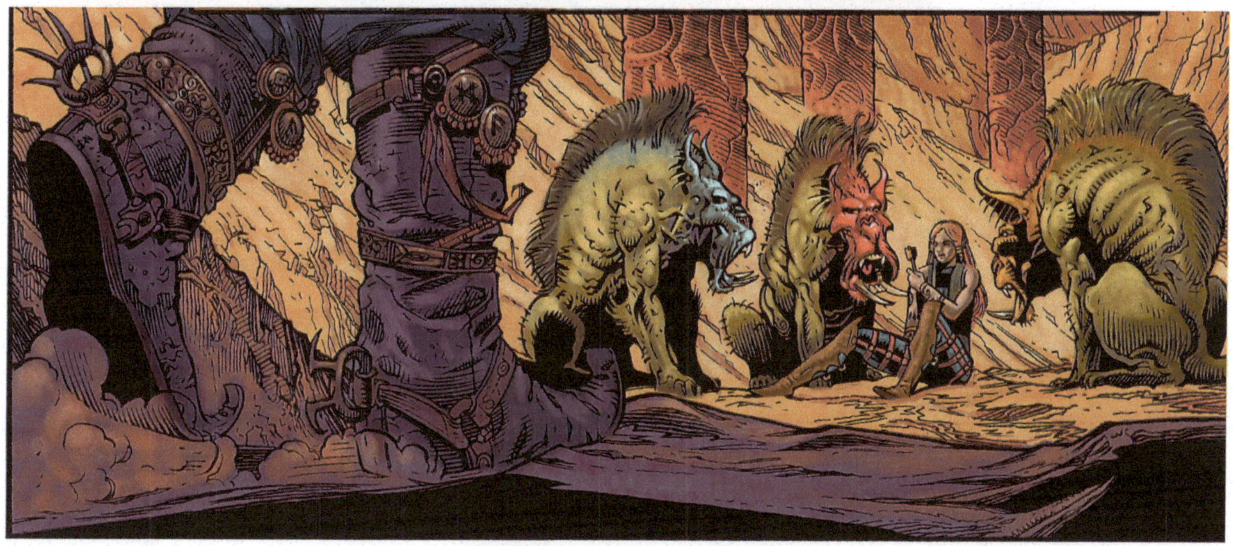

## DESERT HABITAT

The desert can be very hot *and* very cold. During the day, the heat is unbearable, and at night it cools quickly. Shaded areas will be cooler than sunny spots. Here in Texas where I live, the shadowed area of my porch is almost ten degrees cooler than in the sun.

The top panels show the heat and dusty feel of the desert. The third panel was colored to show the coolness in the shade and the transition into the hotness of the day.

The bottom drawing shows the start of sunset with the coolness creeping in. But the heat still burns on the horizon.

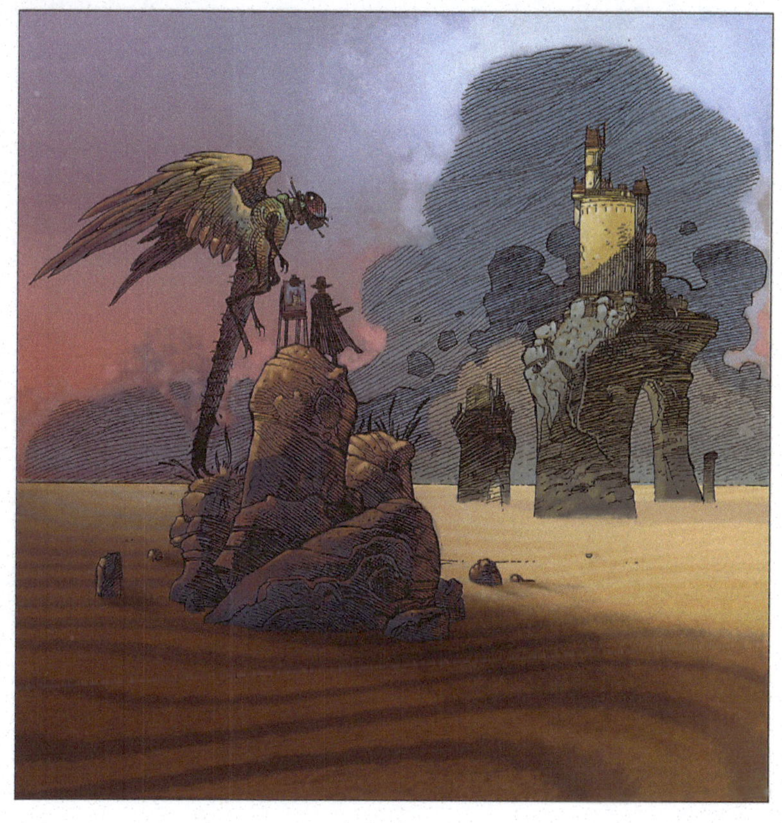

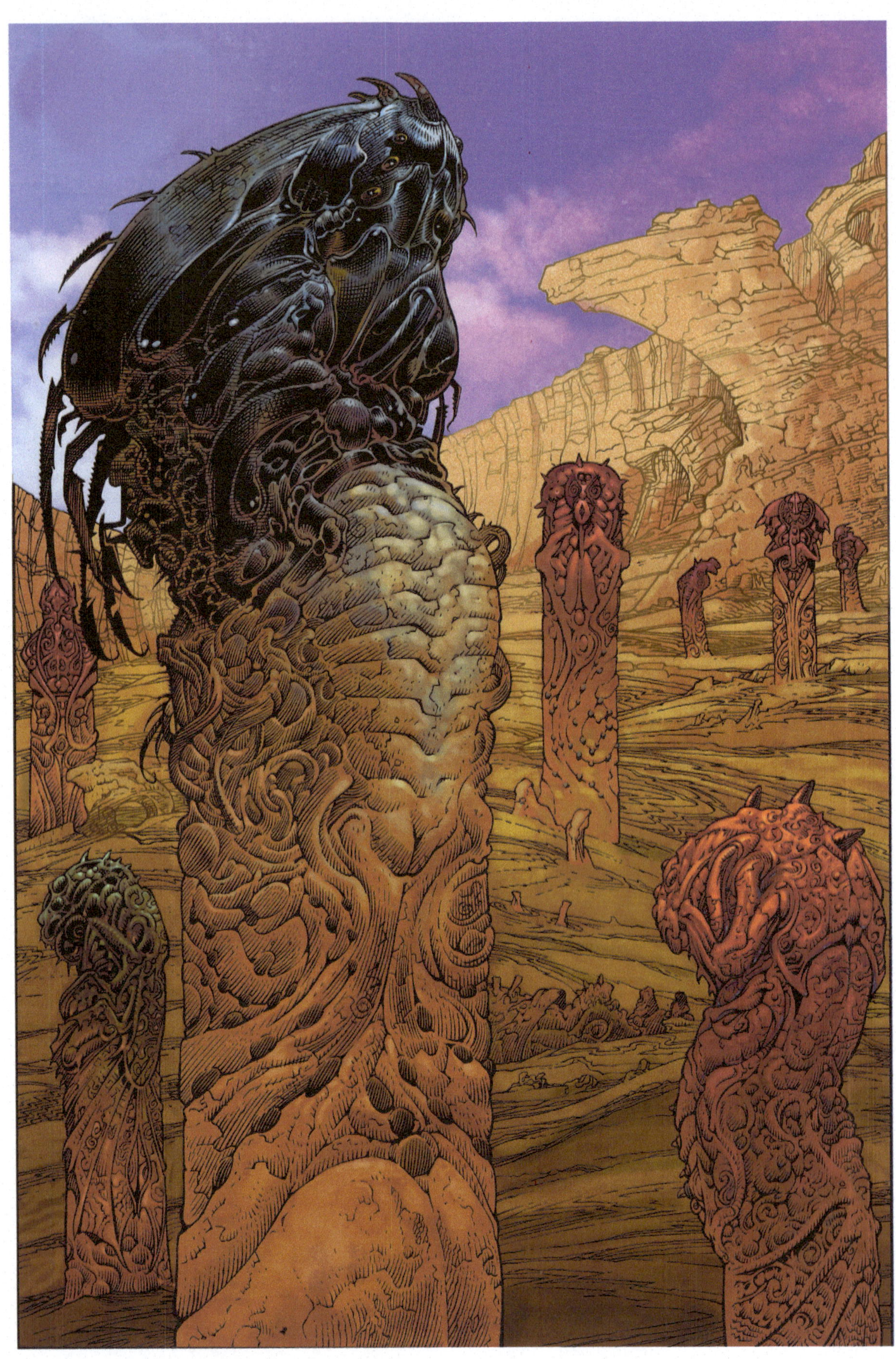

A windswept valley in the desert with strange rocklike plant forms.

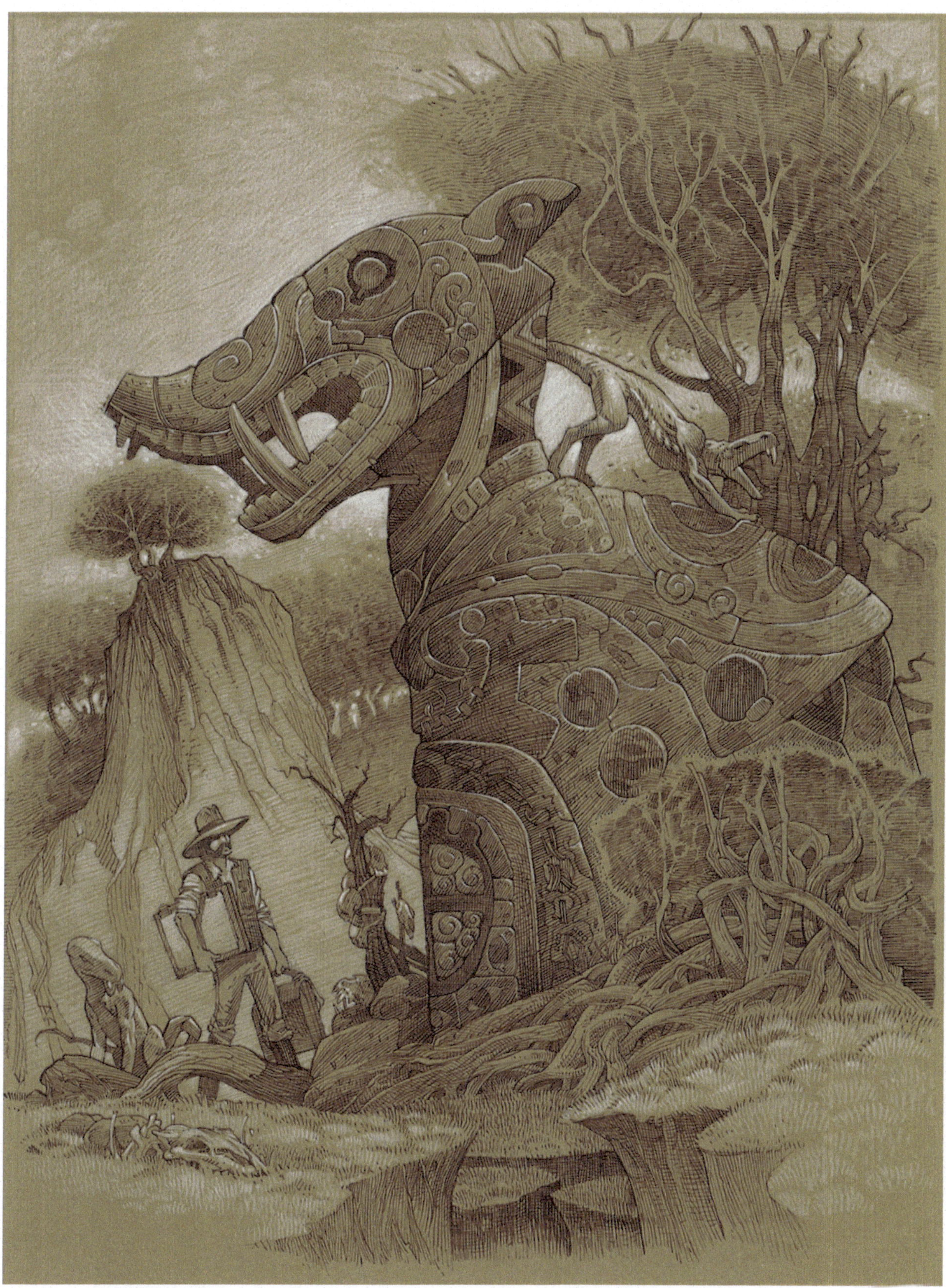

I fell in love with the old photographs of A. P. Maudslay, the archaeologist who uncovered many pre–Columbian ruins in Central America from 1888 to 1902. The period is at the end of the Victorian Era and right up against the Industrial Revolution. It was a time of exploration into the unknown. We really didn't know much about other cultures, and they were, for all intents and purposes, mysteries.

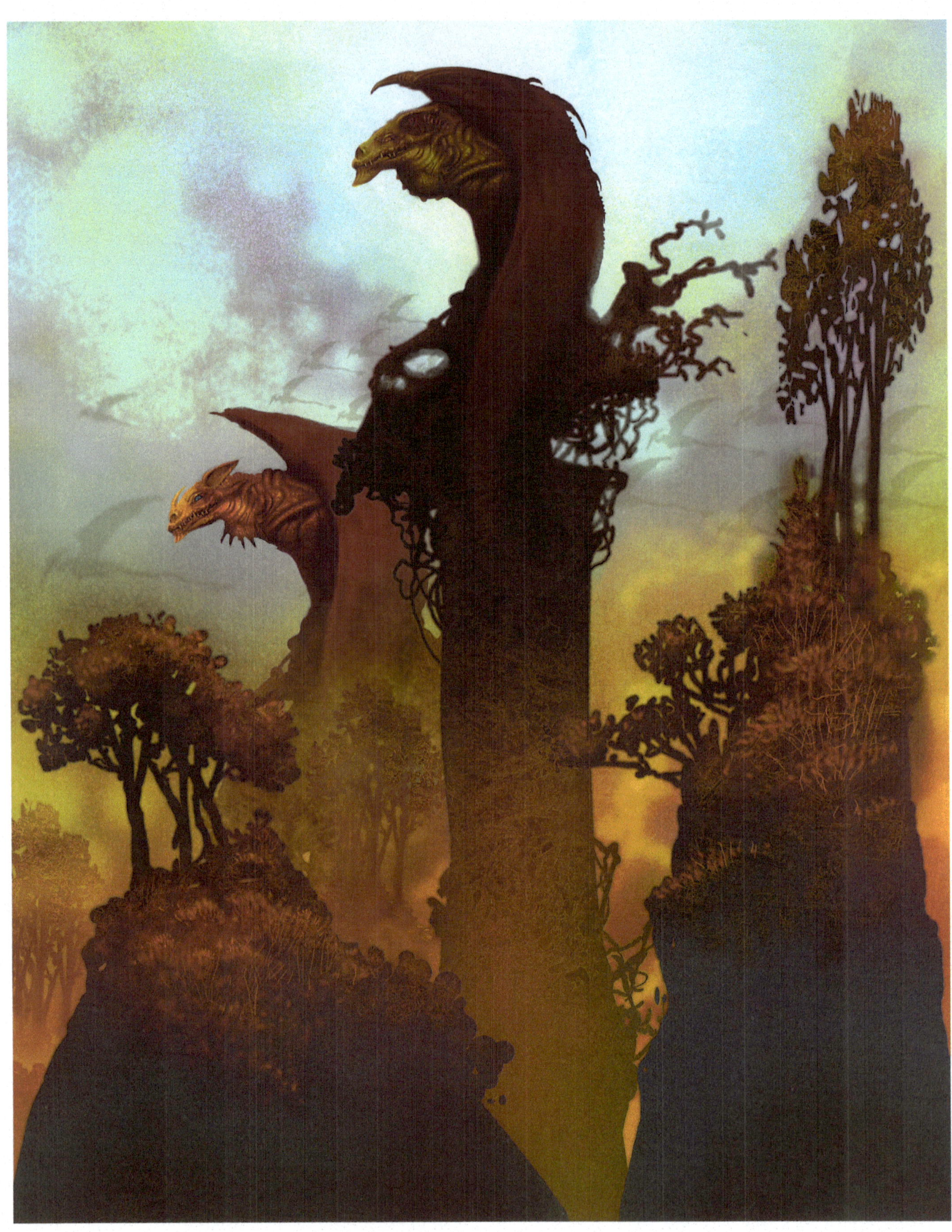

Moving in a completely different direction, this is derived from the mists and rock towers of China, working with a flat-looking space that in reality is very deep.

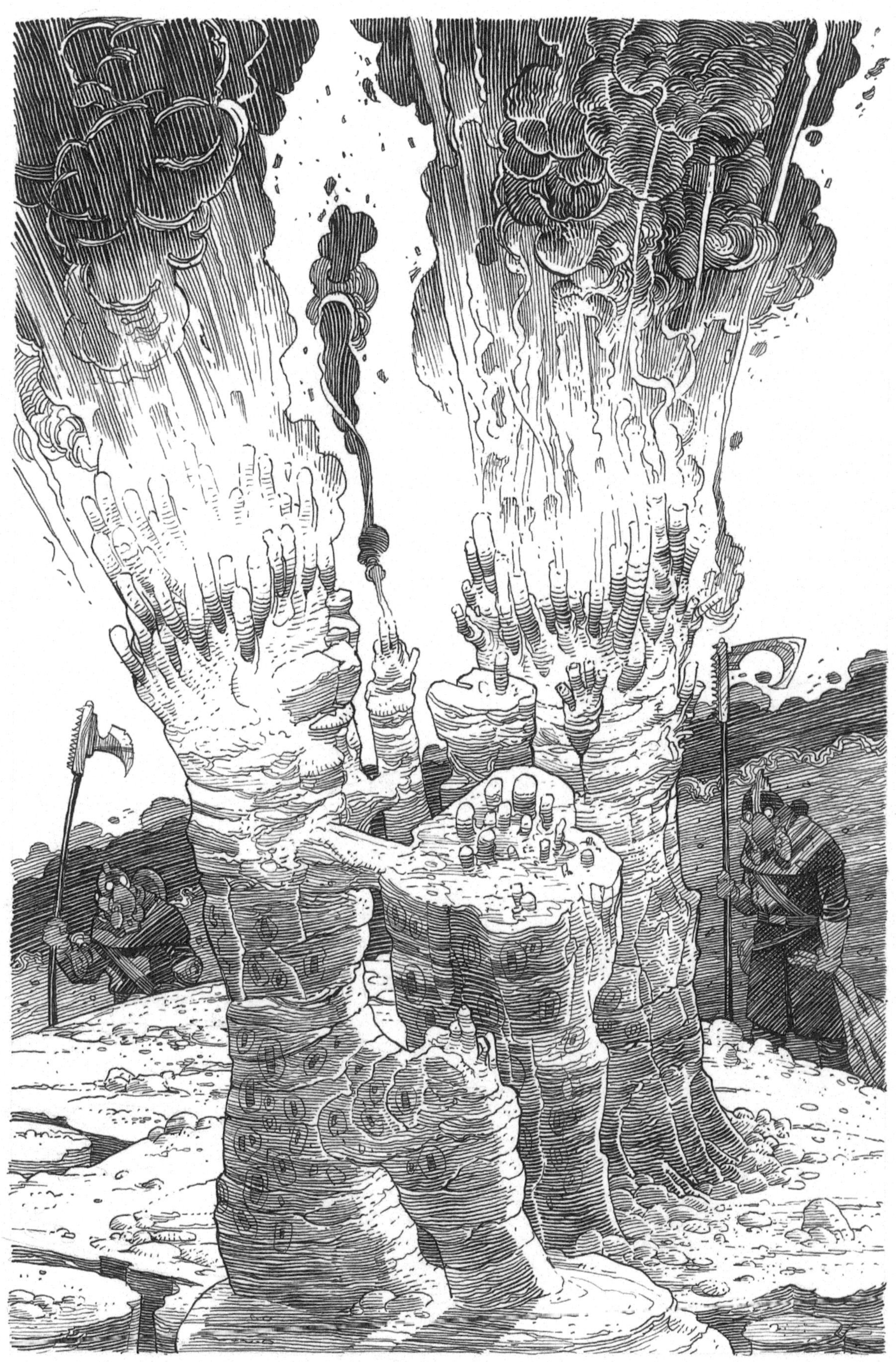

The geothermal vents under the sea were the inspiration for this drawing.
The farmers have to collect materials from the poisonous gas-filled area.

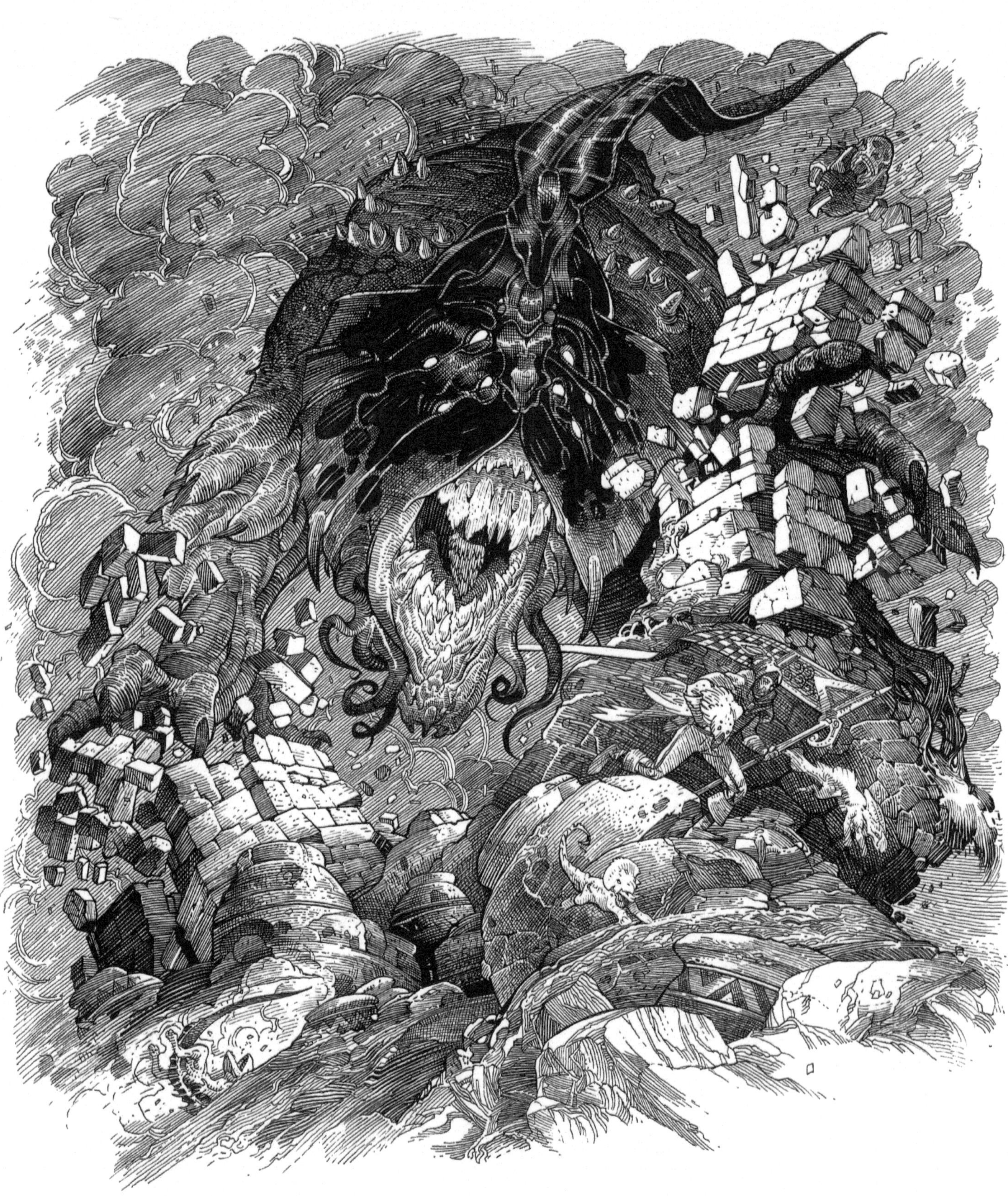

Stealing the White Owl of Wunderlich will lead to all sorts of trouble. Here is where the fun of placing artifacts adds to the richness of the environment. The towers are now gone as the structures are being destroyed, but there are parts of statues and pots that will remain. So later, as we come along and unearth this site, we put conjecture to what has happened.

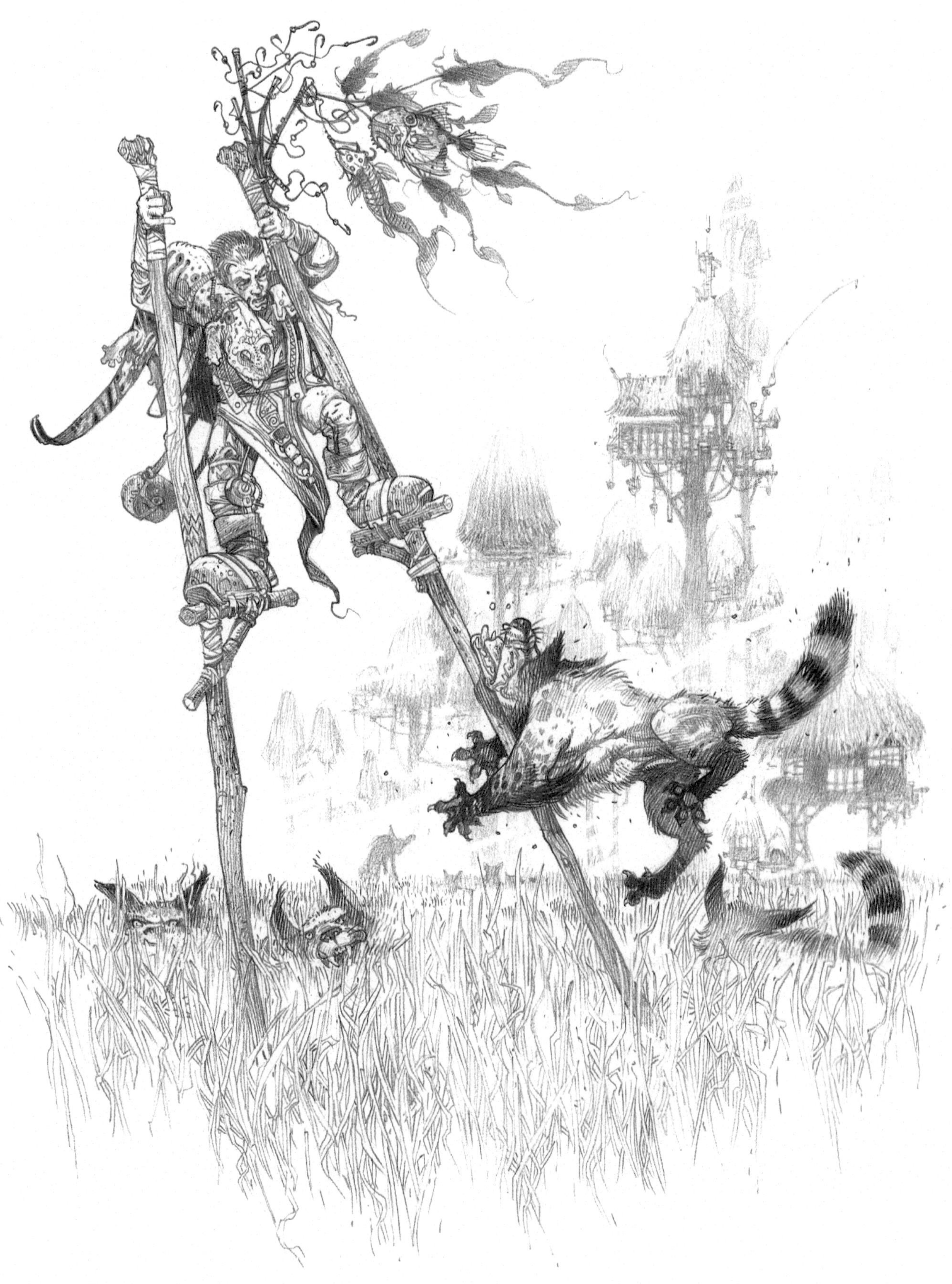

How do you move around in a marshy area? Here is the local fisherman protecting his catch from a pack of swamp dawgs. Would you live in tree houses? How do you get up and down?

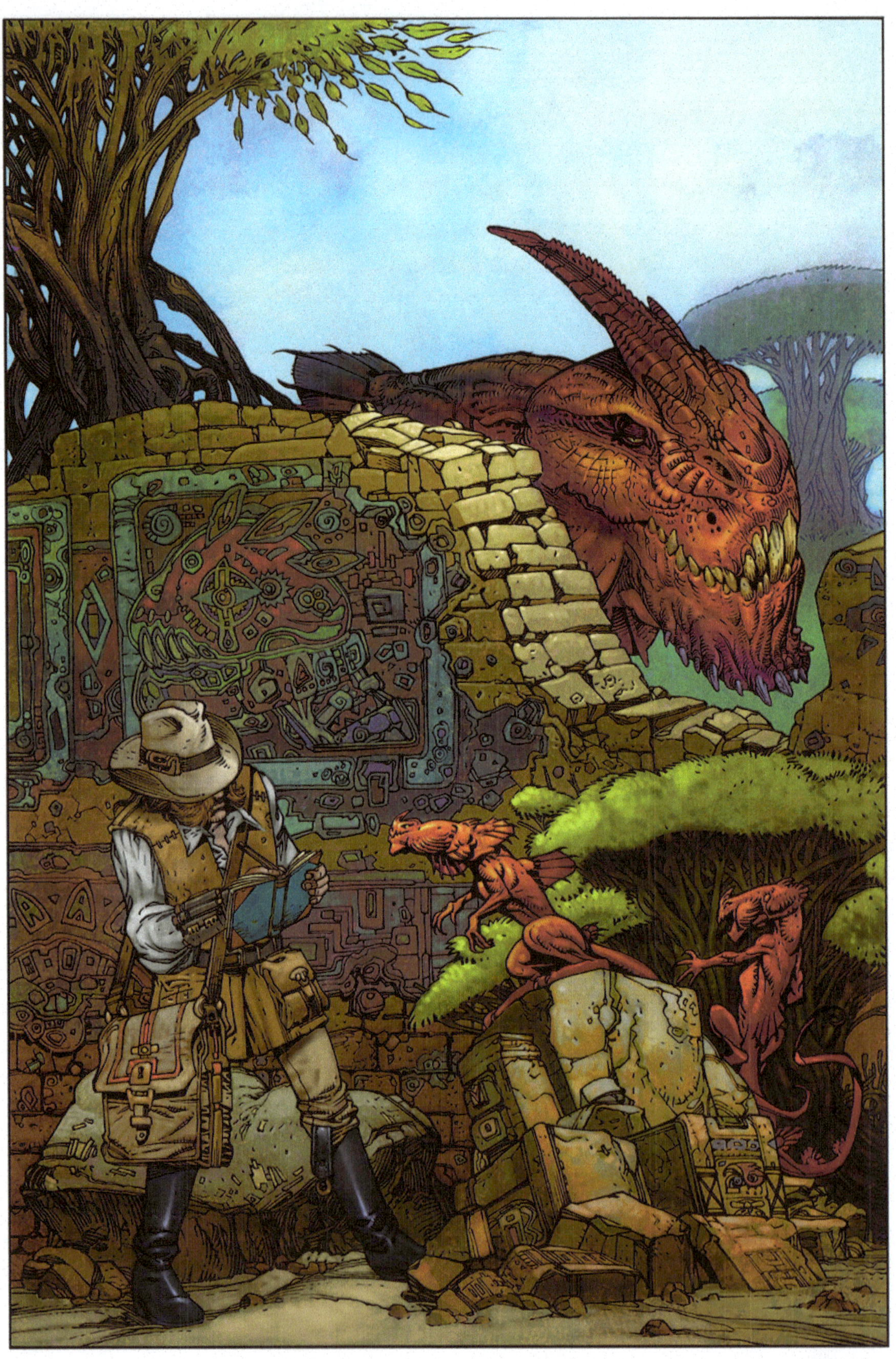

J. V. Holbrook is a naturalist making drawings of the local reptilian inhabitants. The ruins are covered with designs and glyphs that tell a story in a dead language. Canopied trees and soft, warm mists push the background and add depth. "Mom" is arriving, and the kids are having way too much fun.

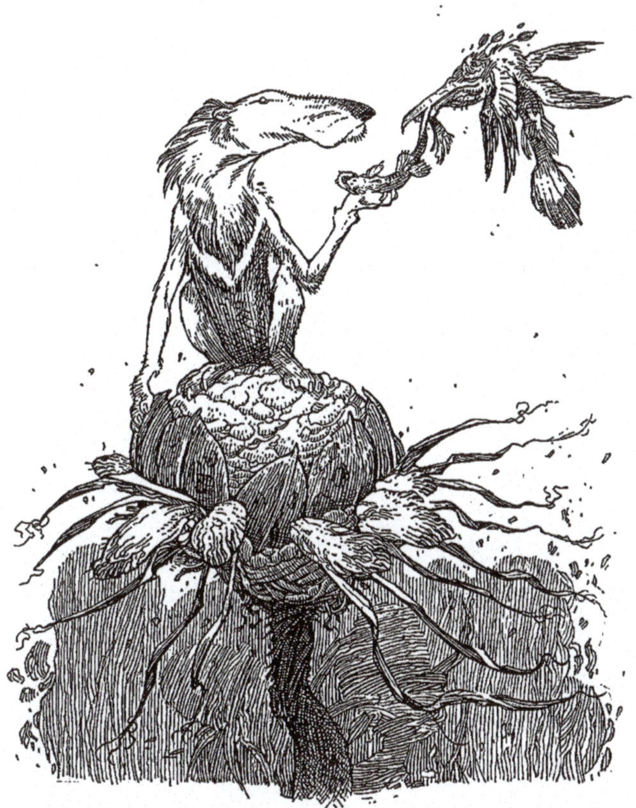

"The Bribe." What makes this fun for me is the strange plant that Dixie is sitting on.

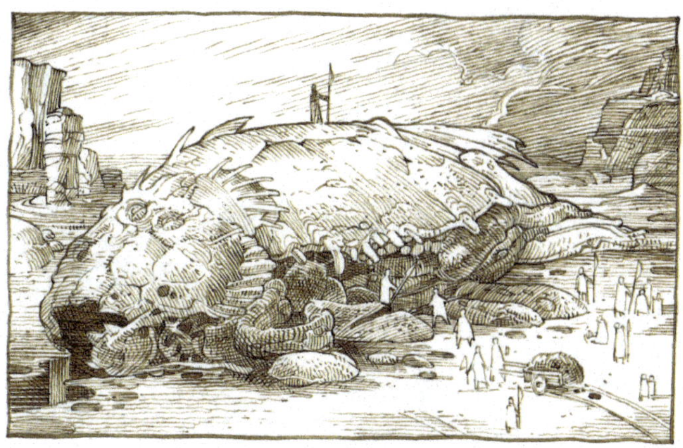

The fish becomes an environment within an environment in this study.

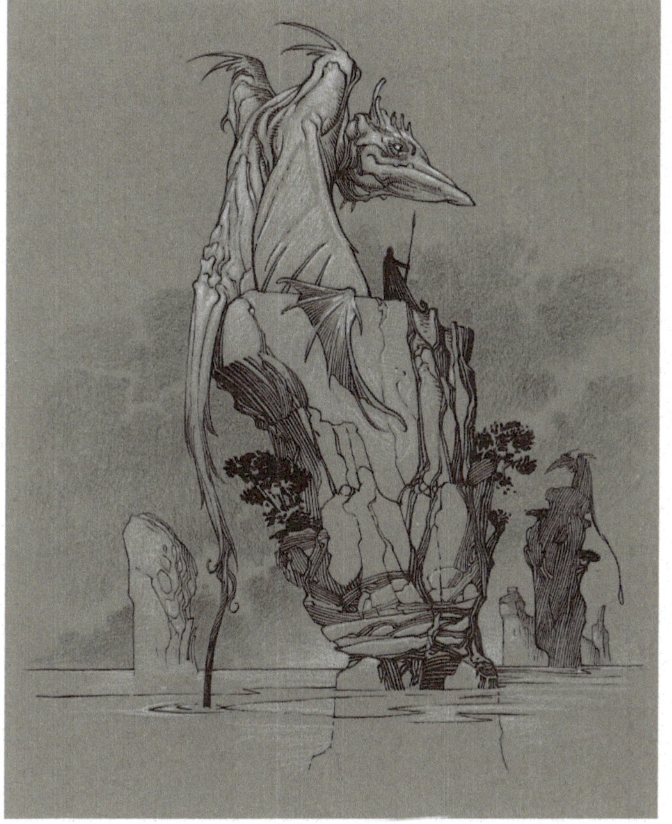

Shorebirds along the coast help the locals fish and gather from the sea.

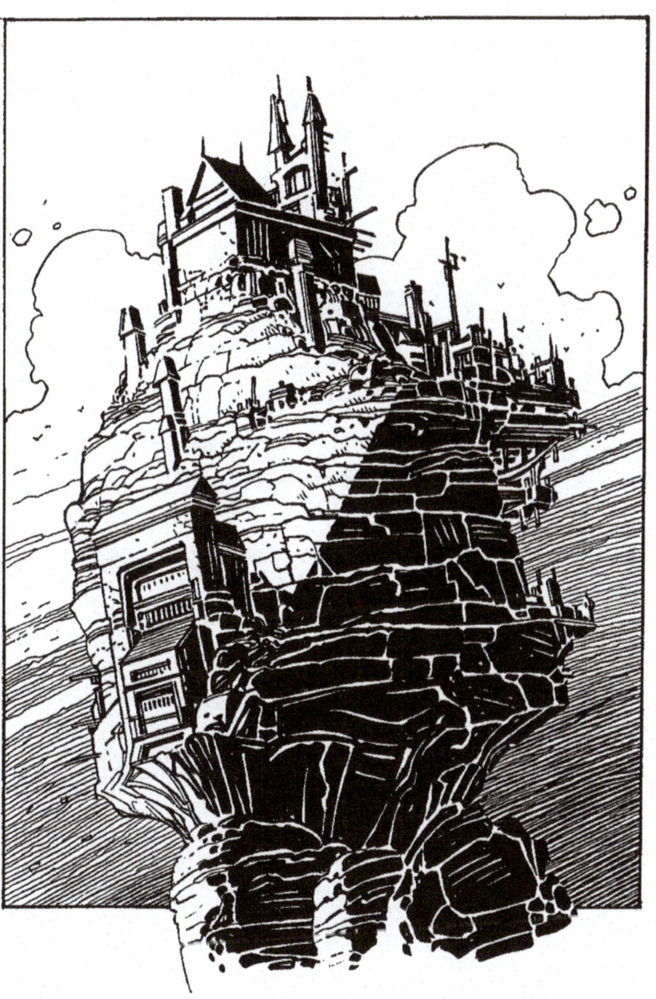

The tower city, high in the mountains, awaits the zeppelin's return.

# WEATHER AND SEASONS

Weather and seasons will affect your work.

Here I took the same scene and colored it in three different ways.

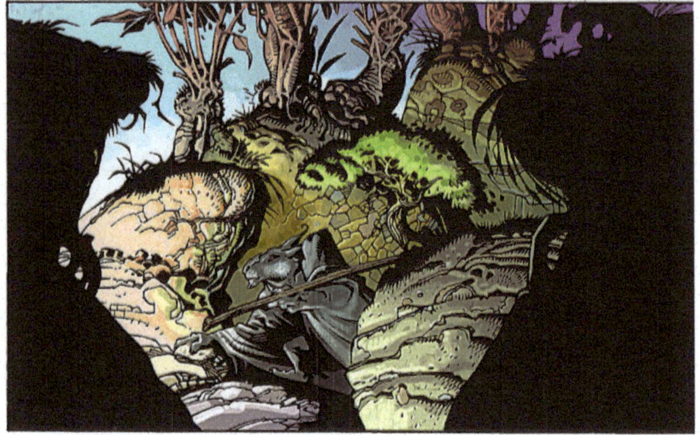

Version 1 is close to sunset, with the light coming from the left. But the colors are still within daylight values.

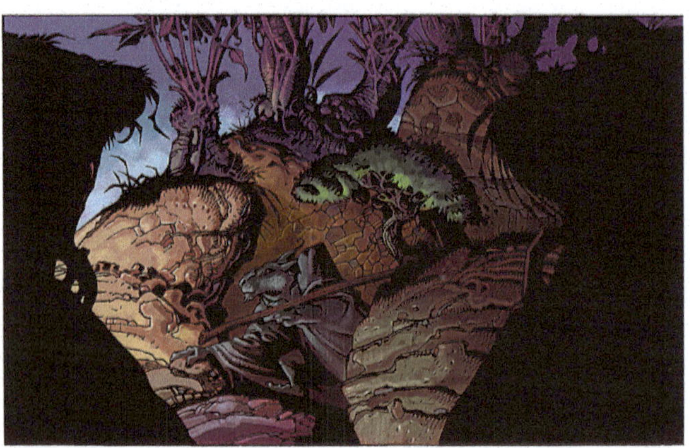

Version 2 is closer to sunset, with the cool colors moving in. The values become closer, and there is more of a purple haze to fill it in.

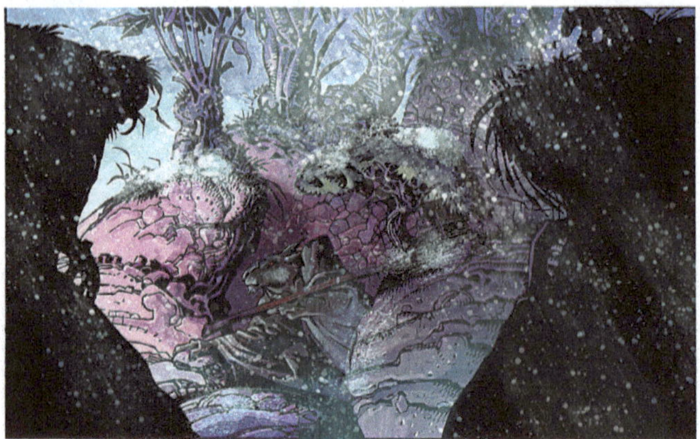

Version 3 is the winter snow, and the flurries obliterate details and soften the forms. Values get lighter and closer together as we move back into the storm.

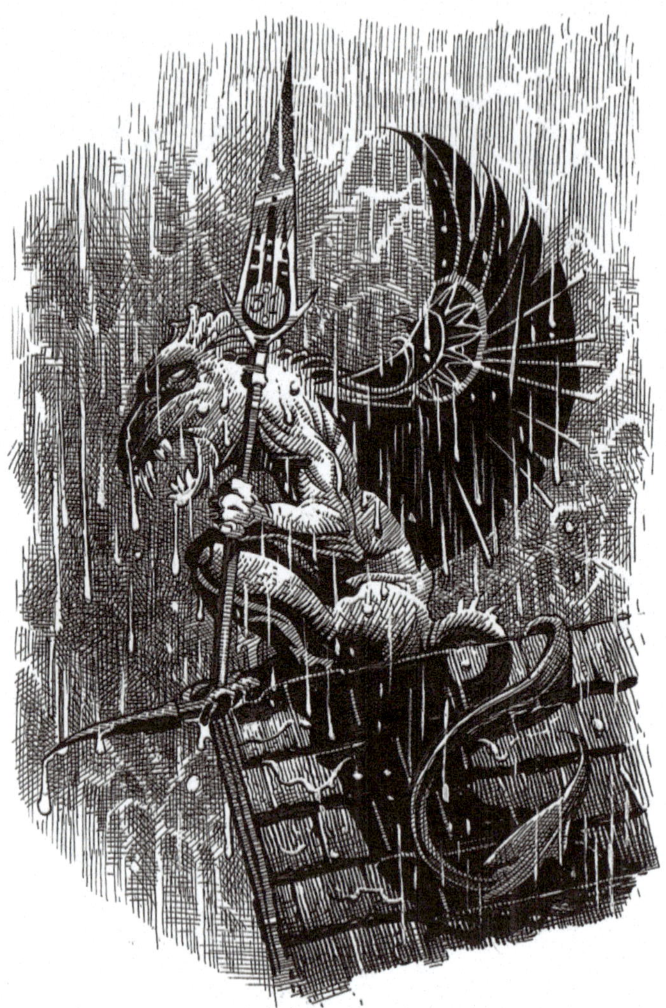

Rain can create mood and hide forms, making the background not as distinct. It's also fun to push the raindrops and drips to give our gargoyle a rather dreary environment.

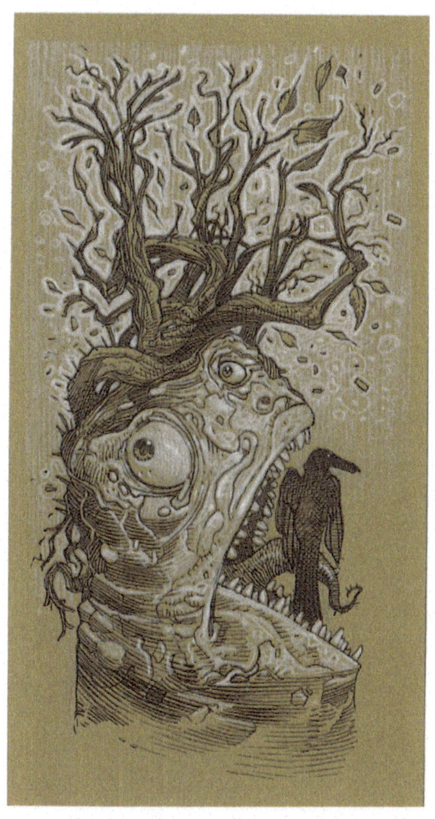 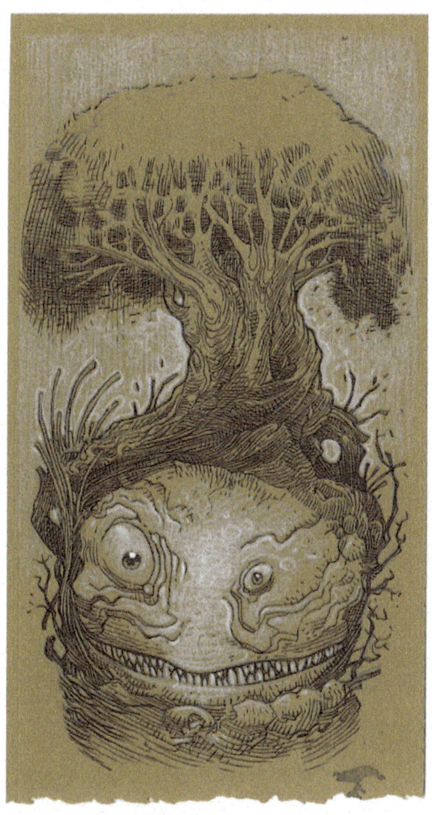 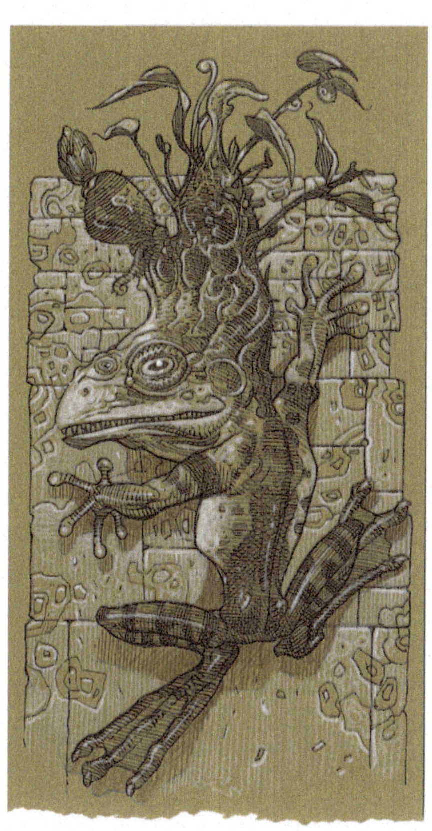

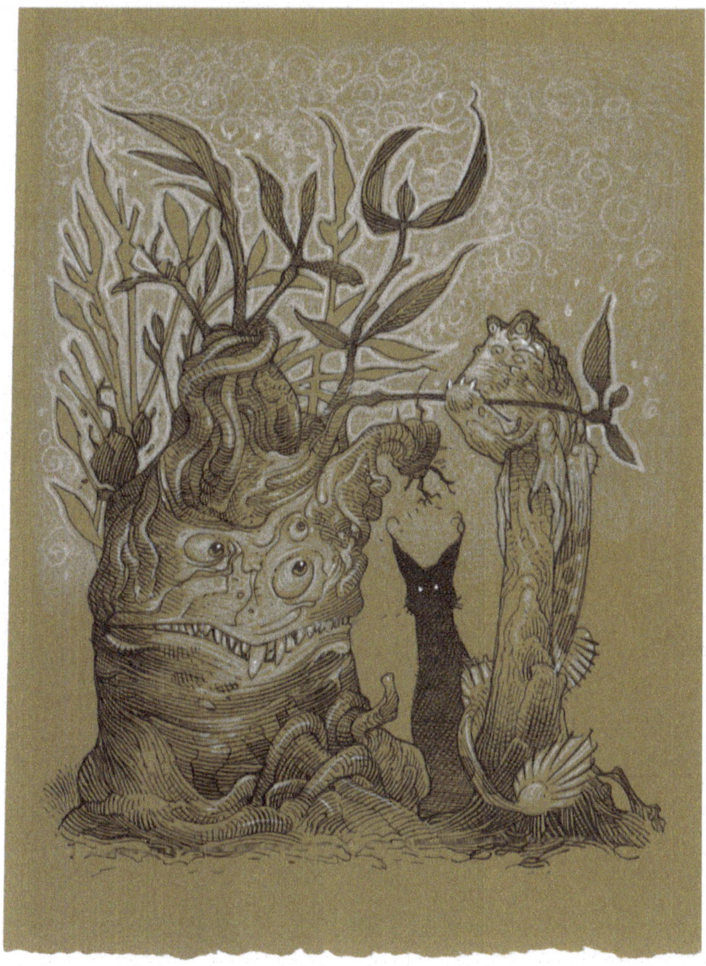

## IDEA

Let's mix things up. Here is a mash-up of environmental elements.

Trees and land become animated objects, the frog wears its forest, and the forest can eat, share, and talk with other animals. The living forest is a myth that goes way back in the history of many cultures. It hearkens to a time when animals talked to one another and weather gods played games with humans. (But that is another story.)

When you look around, do you ask where certain things come from? Spices are from around the world. Some grow in arid areas; others in swampy places, heavily temperate forests, tropical forests, mountains, and low grassland prairies. The spice trade was a huge business. What other things do we pay for that come from other parts of the world?

Economies were built up in Holland around the tulip trade. So how do the riches of one area account for the growth of industry, trade, and interaction with other countries and cultures? Many interlocking elements have pulled cultures together and pushed them apart.

# 4
# ANIMALS

Creatures are my favorite things to design and draw. Here, the smorgasbord is unending.

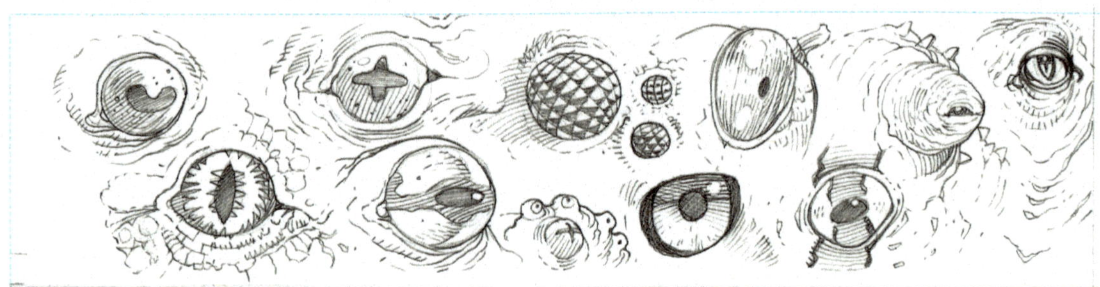

What type of eyes? Cuttlefish, gecko, insect, mammal, or chameleon? Most life forms have some type of ocular organ.

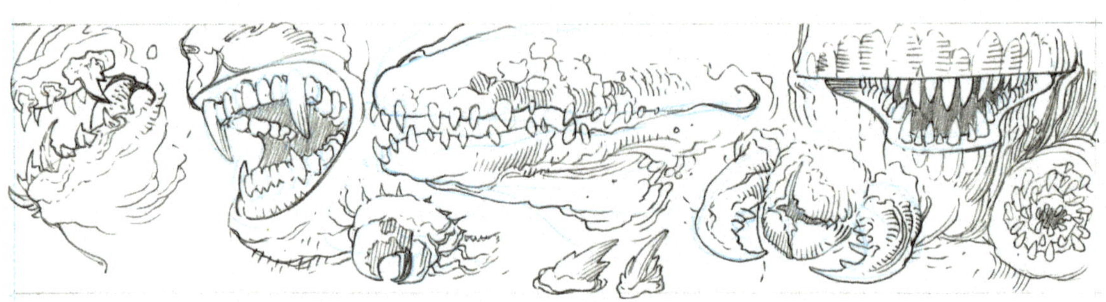

Teeth, beaks, mandibles, jawless mouths, and there are many more.

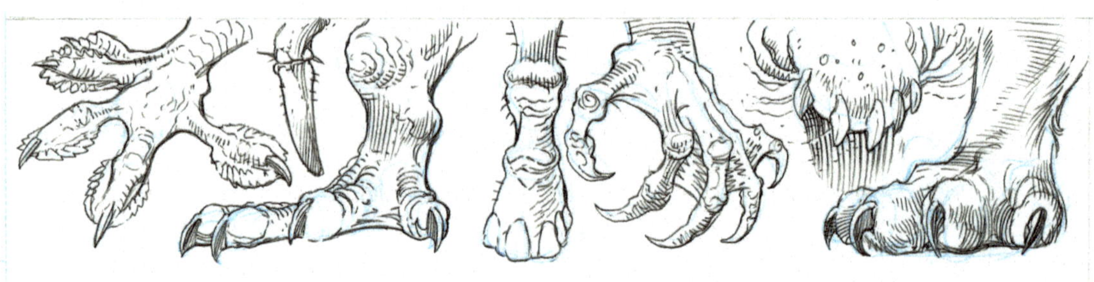

Claws, feet, insectoid claws, hooves, paws, and whatever else you can put together.

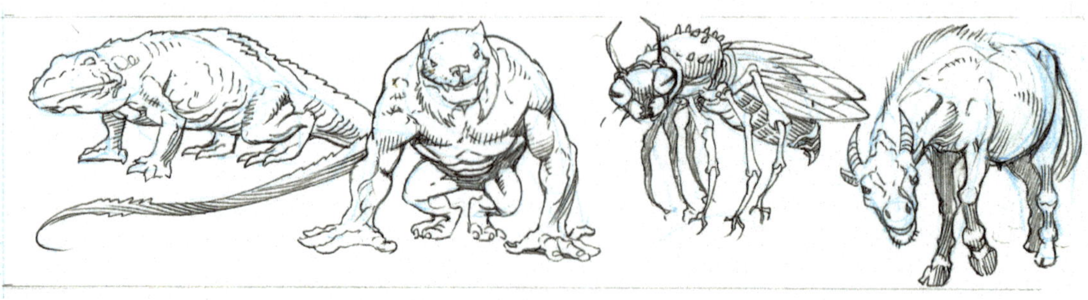

So reptilian, humanoid, insectoid, mammalian, or . . . ?

My drawing process starts with a simple gesture line. I think of it as a wire frame to get the interior skeleton structure. The second stage is to build up the basic forms. This includes the shape of the head, rib cage, legs, arms, and feet. Third, I tighten up the line work, clean up the forms, and add some details. Now I can refine the roughs and do a finished pencil.

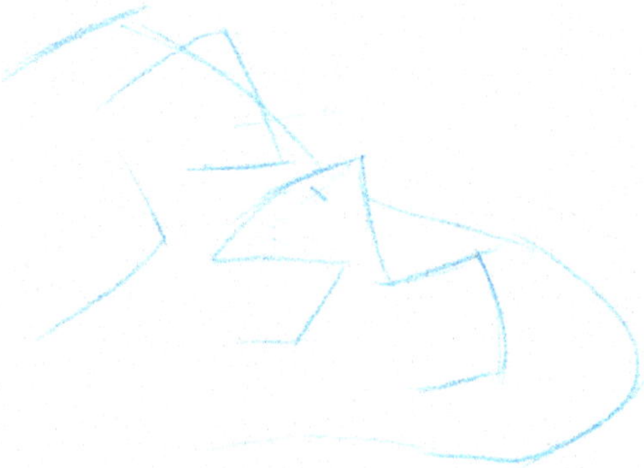

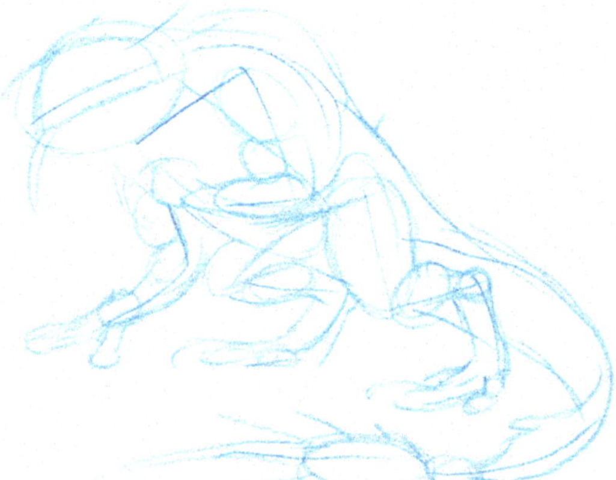

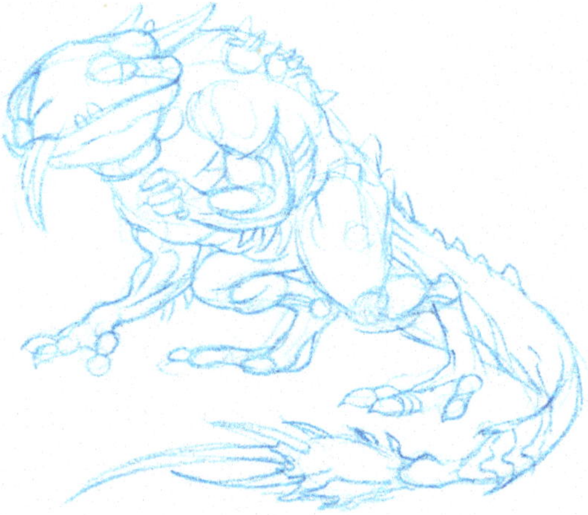

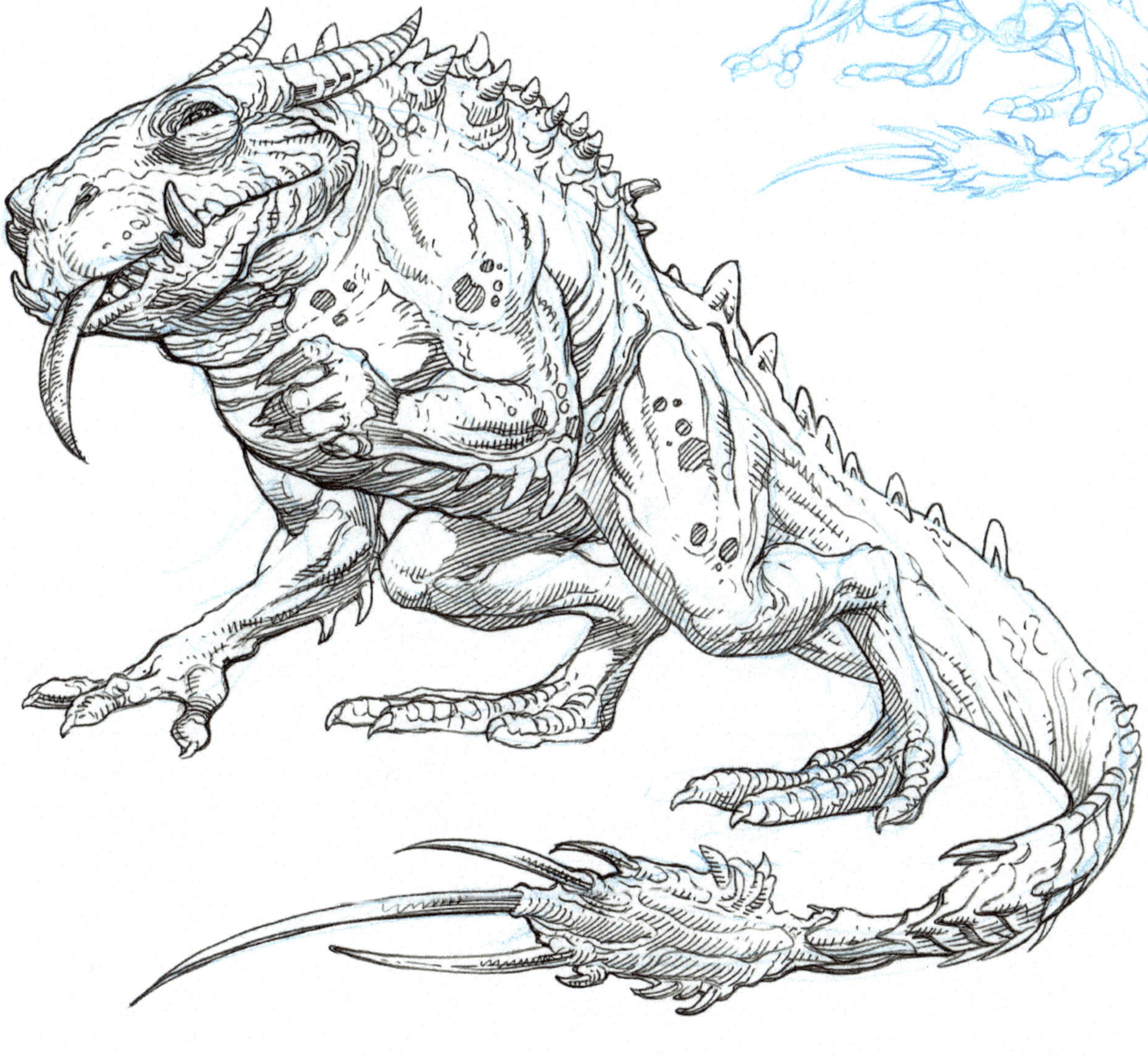

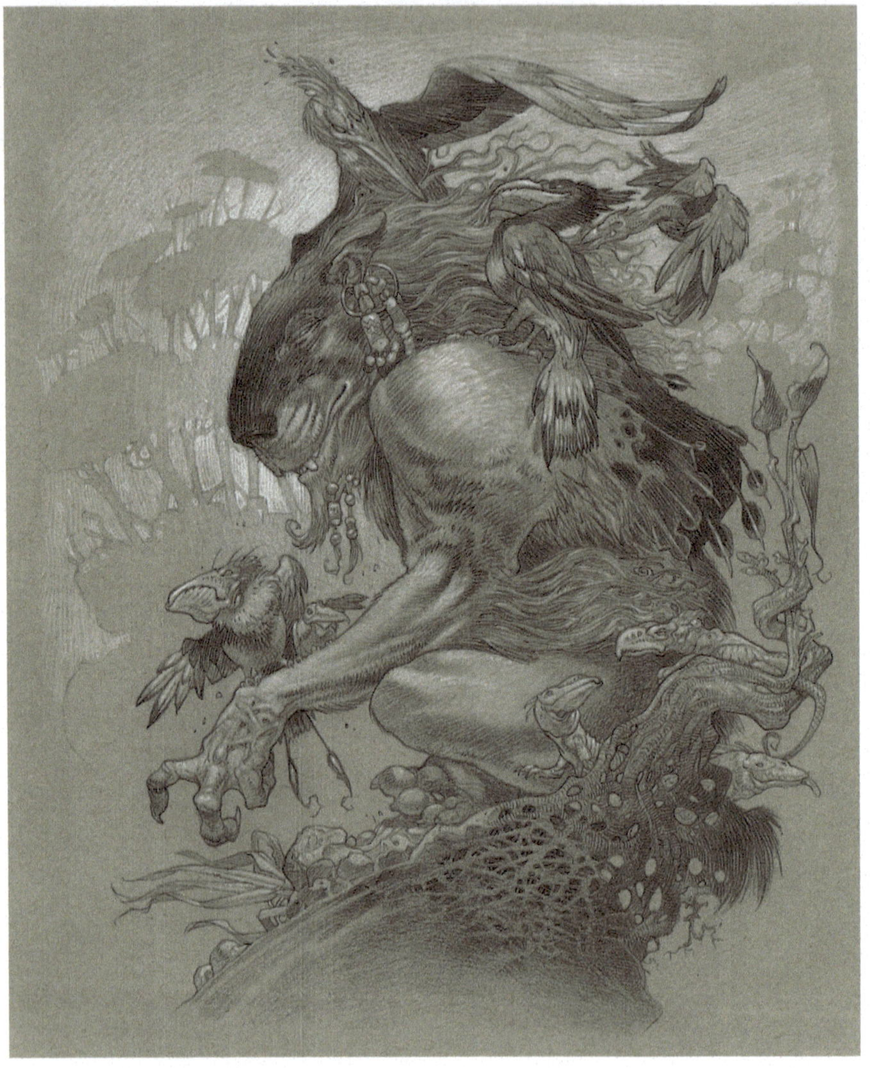

There are so many wonderful things to play with when creating animals: types of hair, scales, camouflage, patterns, and putting them into situations they might not usually be part of.

How do they groom as a social act or get directions from a mouse riding a raven? What are the reactions of a sick dinosaur? Or if your ink takes on a life of its own, what you can bring to life is endless!

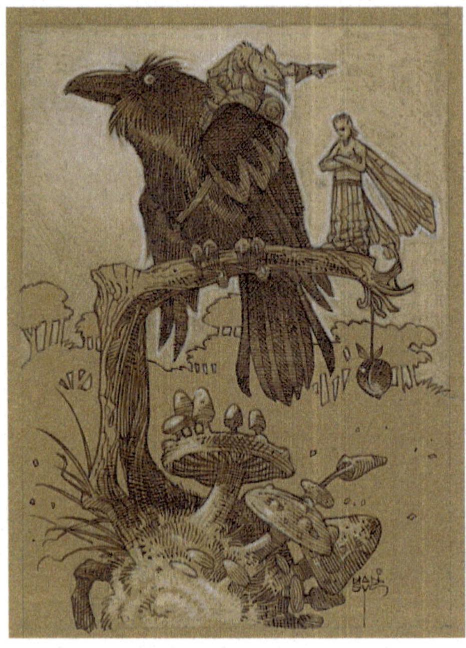

"Grooming" is drawn on toned paper with black and white pencils.

"Directions" is done with brown ink and tan and white pencils.

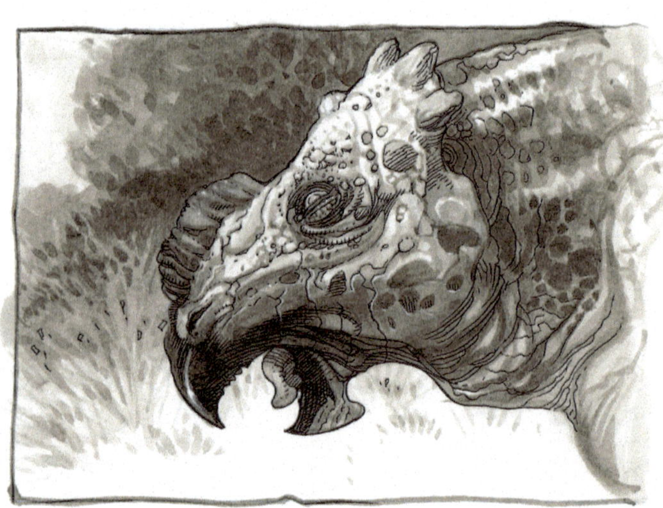

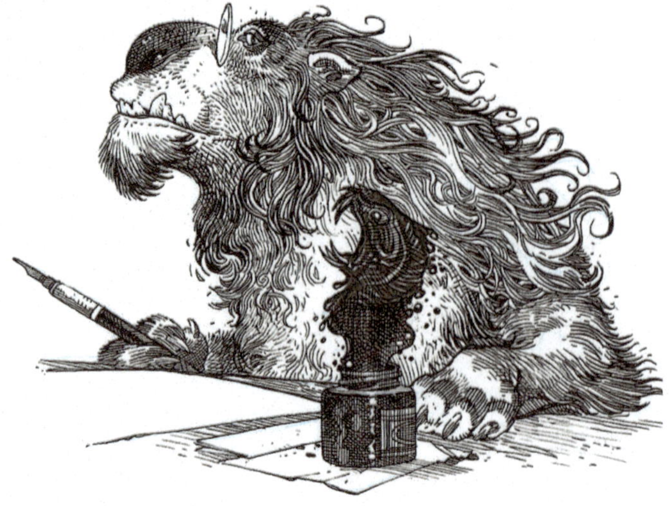

"The Cough" is ink wash on hot press watercolor paper.

"The Daemon" is drawn with black ink with a crow quill nib on bristol board.

When you are creating a character, what can you do to make it unique?

**1. The Warrior Bear:** I drew two types of eyes (one blind), streaks of white hair, and a moustache. The hair on its muzzle is short and gets longer and flowing as we move away from the face. The clothing is very low tech, with plate armor, a leather belt, a sword with a large grip guard for its giant pawlike hands, and a canteen. All these articles are aged and worn. Finally, a companion was added. I used a brown pencil to try and give the art an older feel.

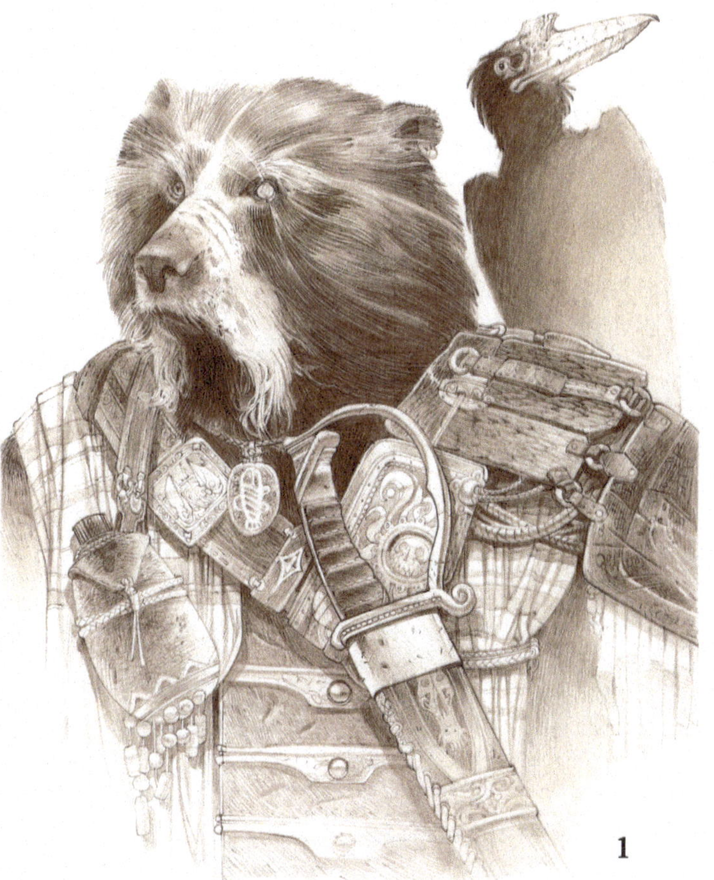

1

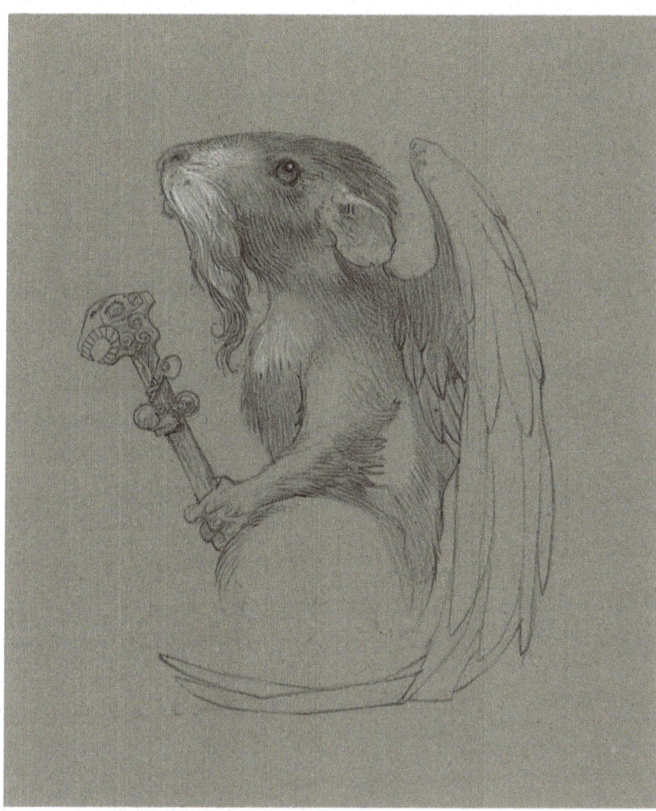

2

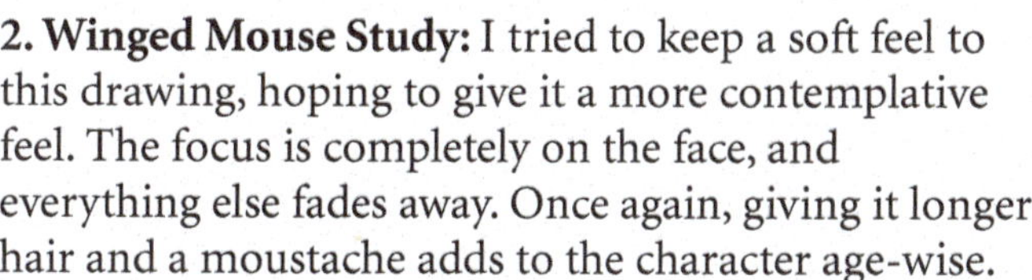

**2. Winged Mouse Study:** I tried to keep a soft feel to this drawing, hoping to give it a more contemplative feel. The focus is completely on the face, and everything else fades away. Once again, giving it longer hair and a moustache adds to the character age-wise.

**3. Are we defined by our smile?** Here the focus is on the teeth, so this character really is defined by its smile. It is an omnivore, in which you have the canines for grabbing and tearing, small fangs in the sides of the mouth to hold food, and molars to grind food. The bristles and feelers on the chin and backup tentacles add another level of adaptation for the environment it comes from.

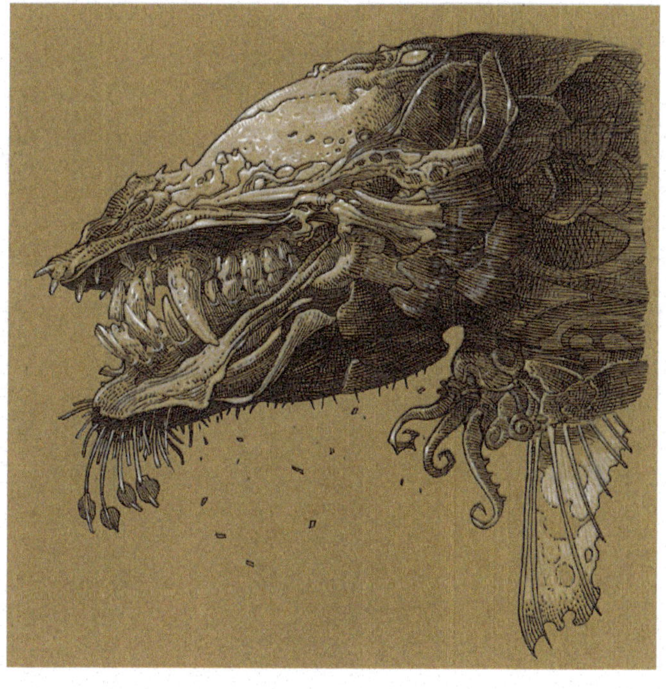

3

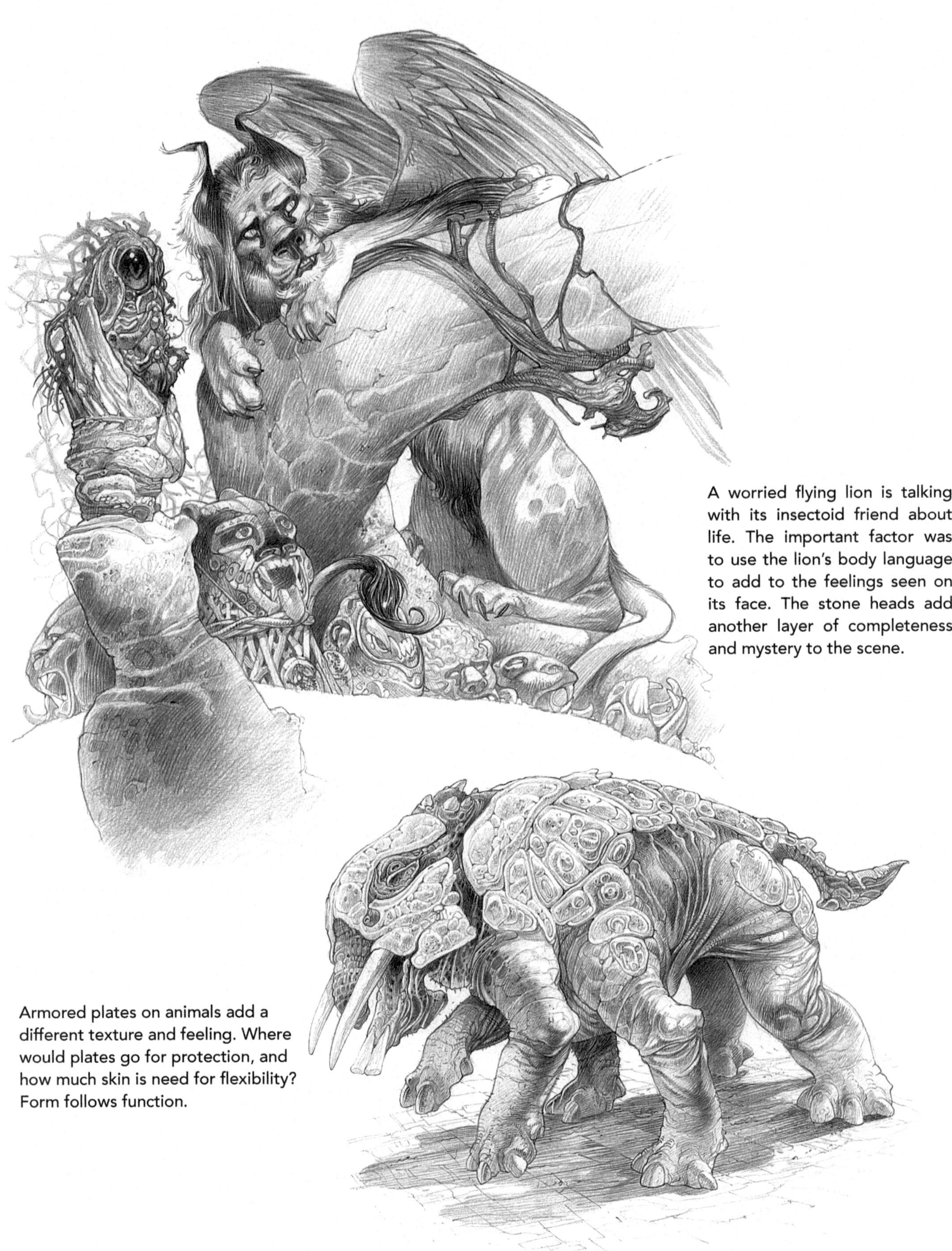

A worried flying lion is talking with its insectoid friend about life. The important factor was to use the lion's body language to add to the feelings seen on its face. The stone heads add another layer of completeness and mystery to the scene.

Armored plates on animals add a different texture and feeling. Where would plates go for protection, and how much skin is need for flexibility? Form follows function.

For both of these drawings, I used Verithin black pencils on Borden & Riley #234 paper.

Kats (known by most people as "cats") have some of the most telling and strange body language. My dog is funny enough, but the kats are just so far advanced in putting you off, ignoring what are you looking at, and displaying total indifference . . . unless you have food.

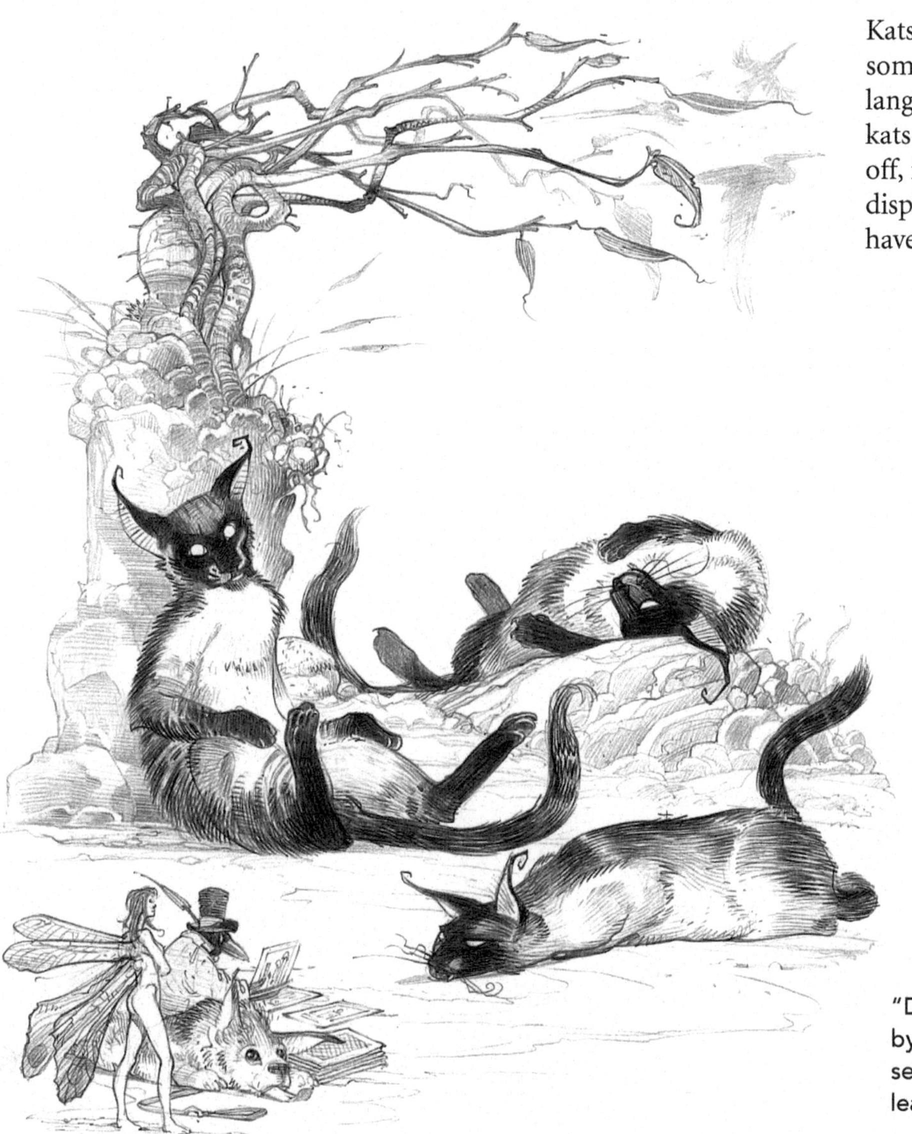

"Dealing With It": having your cards read by a raven in a top hat with a corgi. You can see the friends are not interested, and the lead kat is not happy.

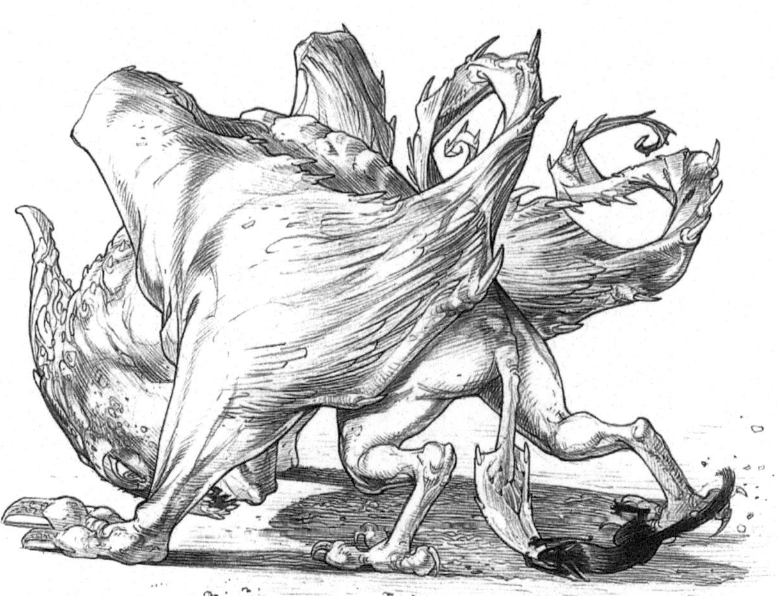

The kats I've owned have shown no fear.

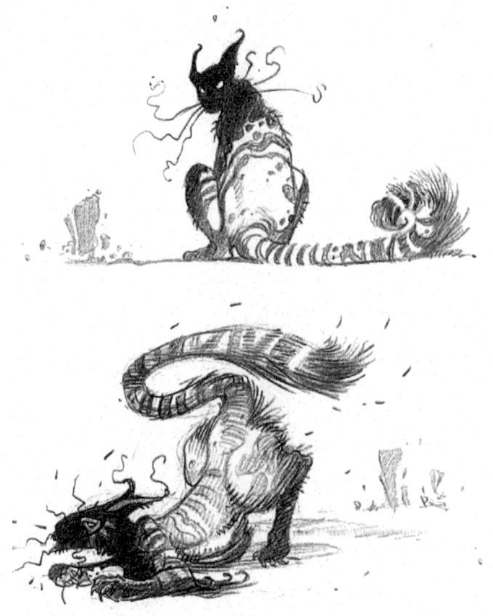

The sketchbook drawings are ways I play with patterns and body posture.

Different mediums give a wide range of results and moods. They also allow you to think of a variety of ways to depict things.

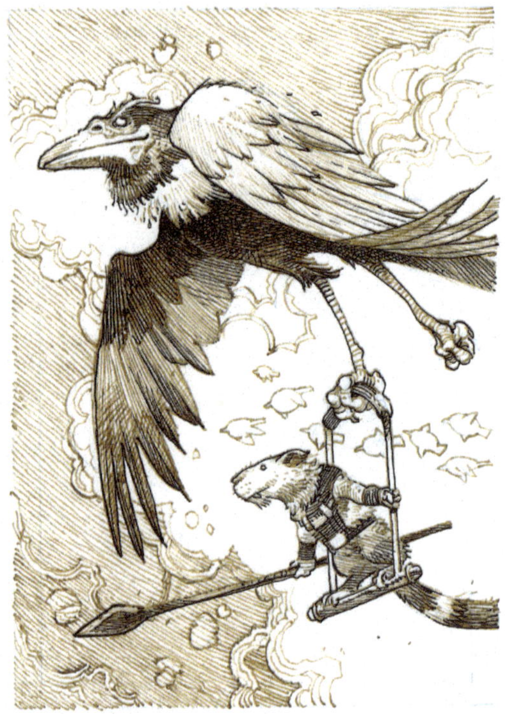

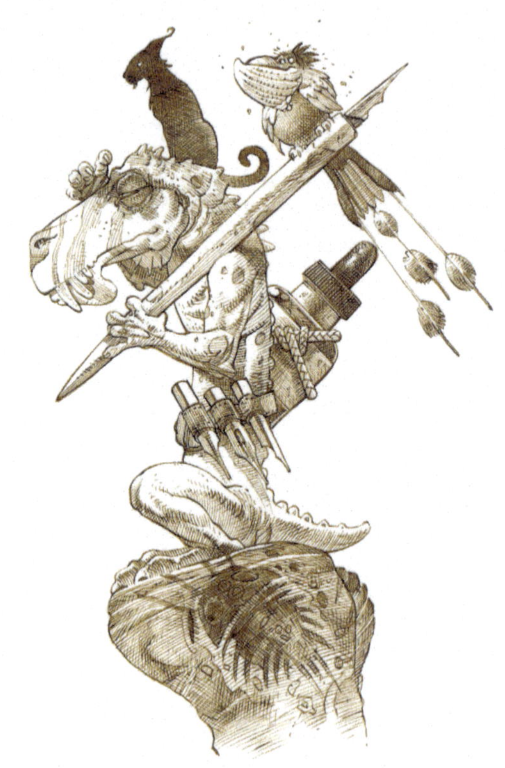

Mixing brown and black inks can allow you to pick out focal points in black and contrast them against the softer brown.

Brown ink will never have the weight of black ink, but the crosshatch can be worked up in many more levels and you can keep a soft feel to the image.

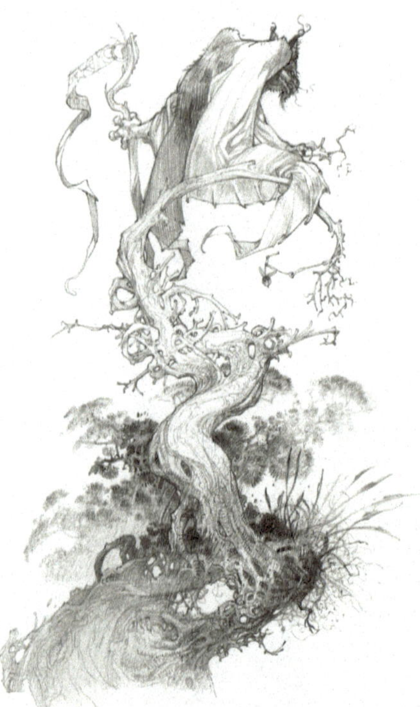

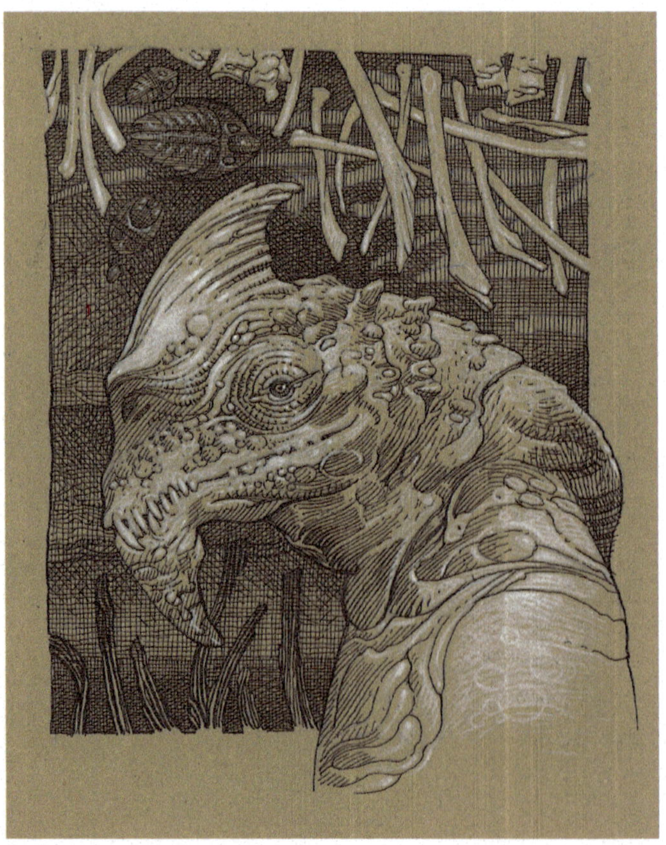

Pencil is still one of the great tonal tools. The range of value is incredible, and the contrast from line to value can be used against each other to create rich surfaces.

A toned ground allows you to draw in the darks and work up the lights. Using whites to move your eye around is a way to play with your image. The contrast from ink to pencil becomes another level to layering.

# HOW DO YOU BRING THE STORY TO A PAGE?

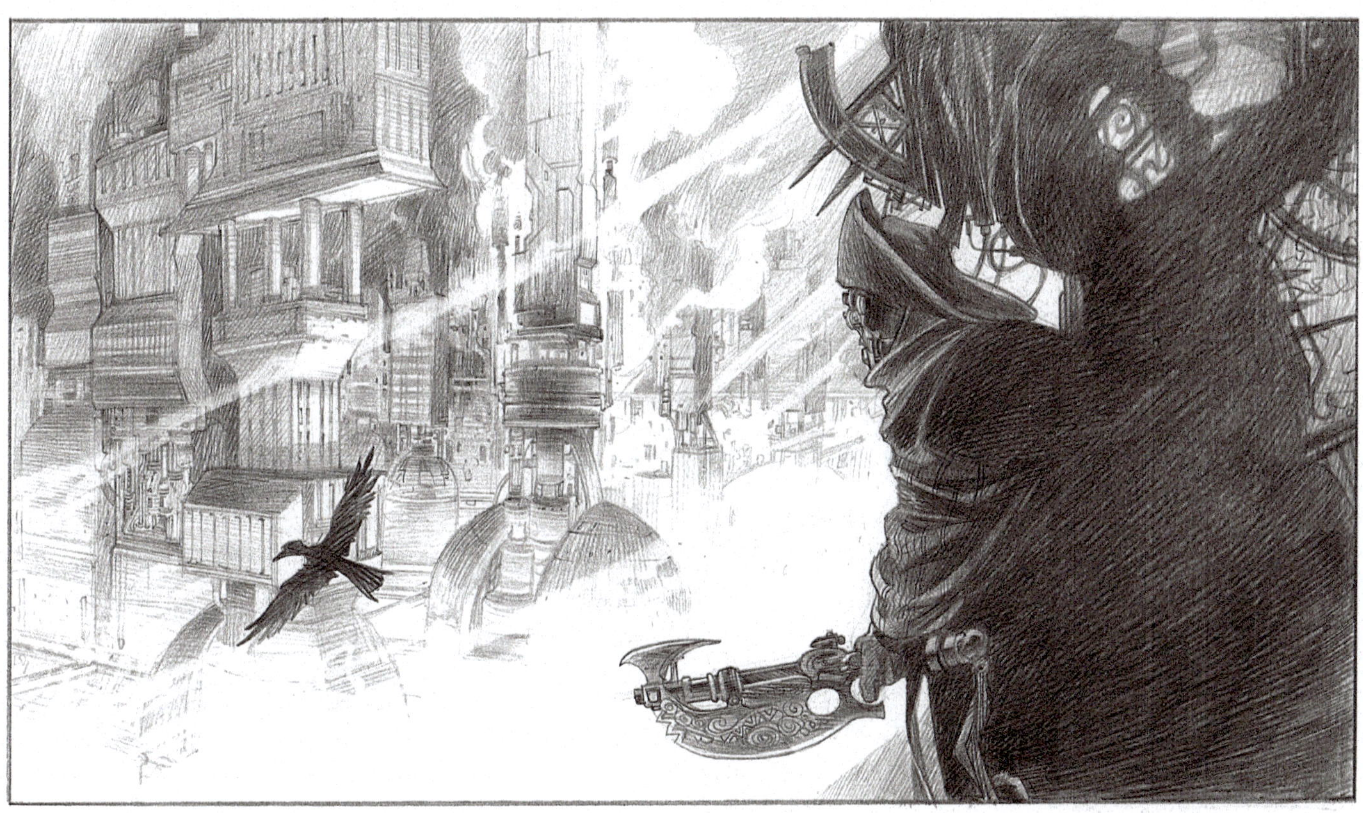

The journeyman and his scout come upon a misty city.

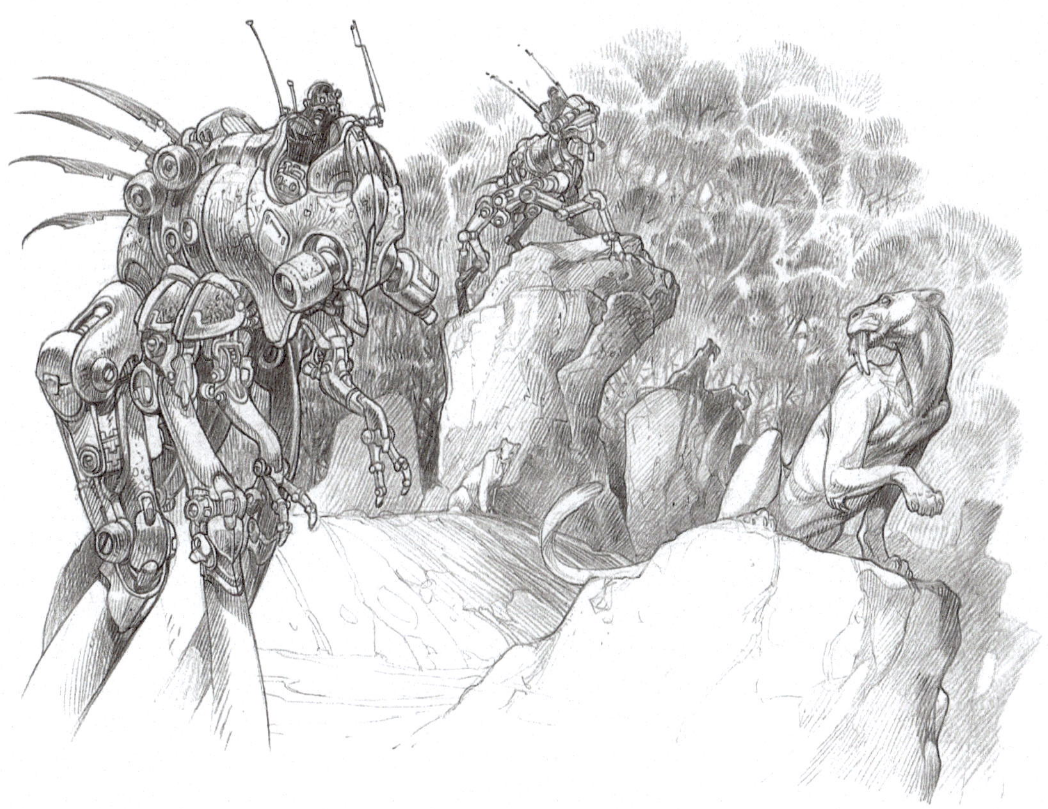

The kat scout is helping robot walkers to a destination.

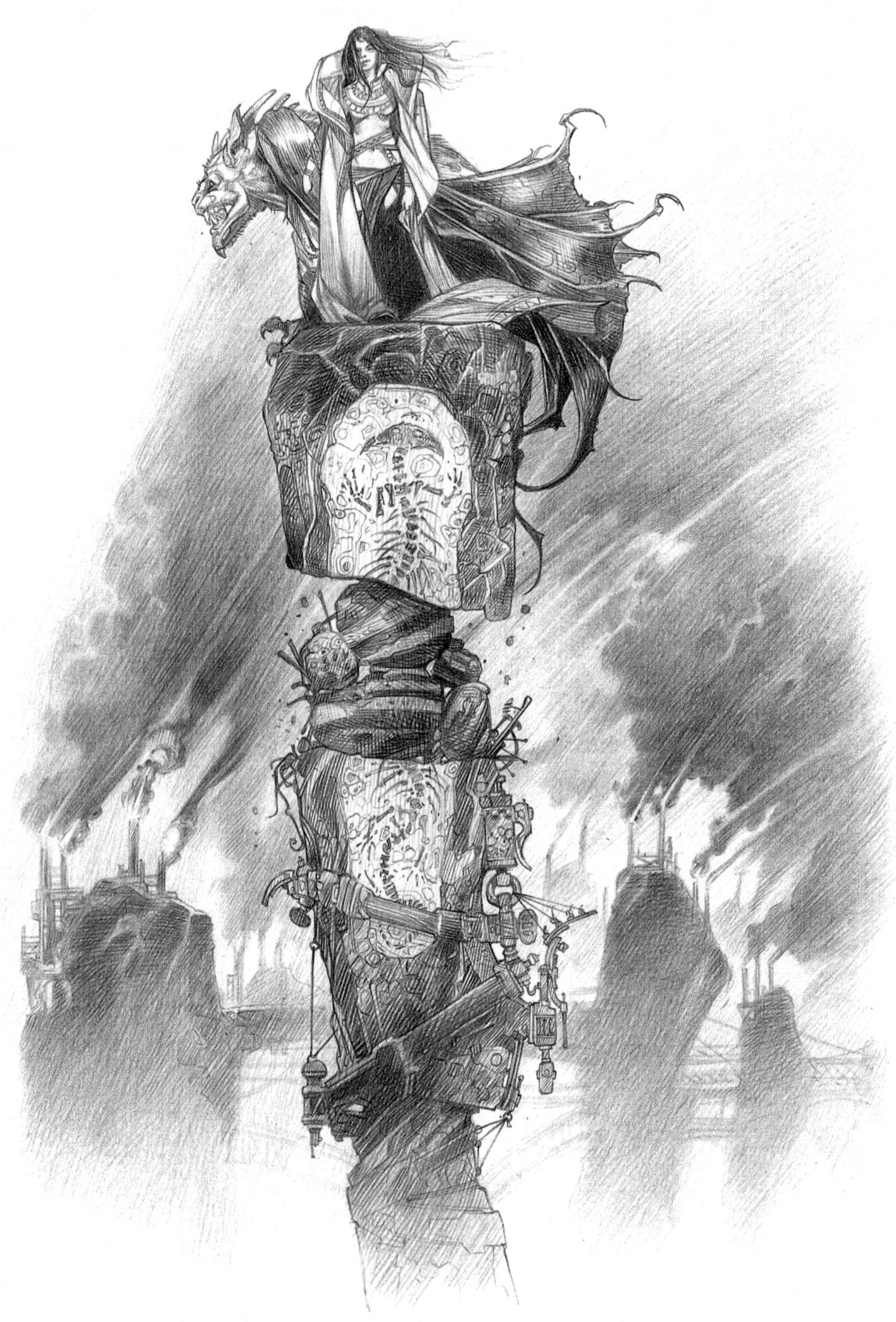

Create a mystery. This rock totem has been put together, balanced, braced, and decorated. So what does it mean? Who can visit and why? At this point, only the bat and woman know.

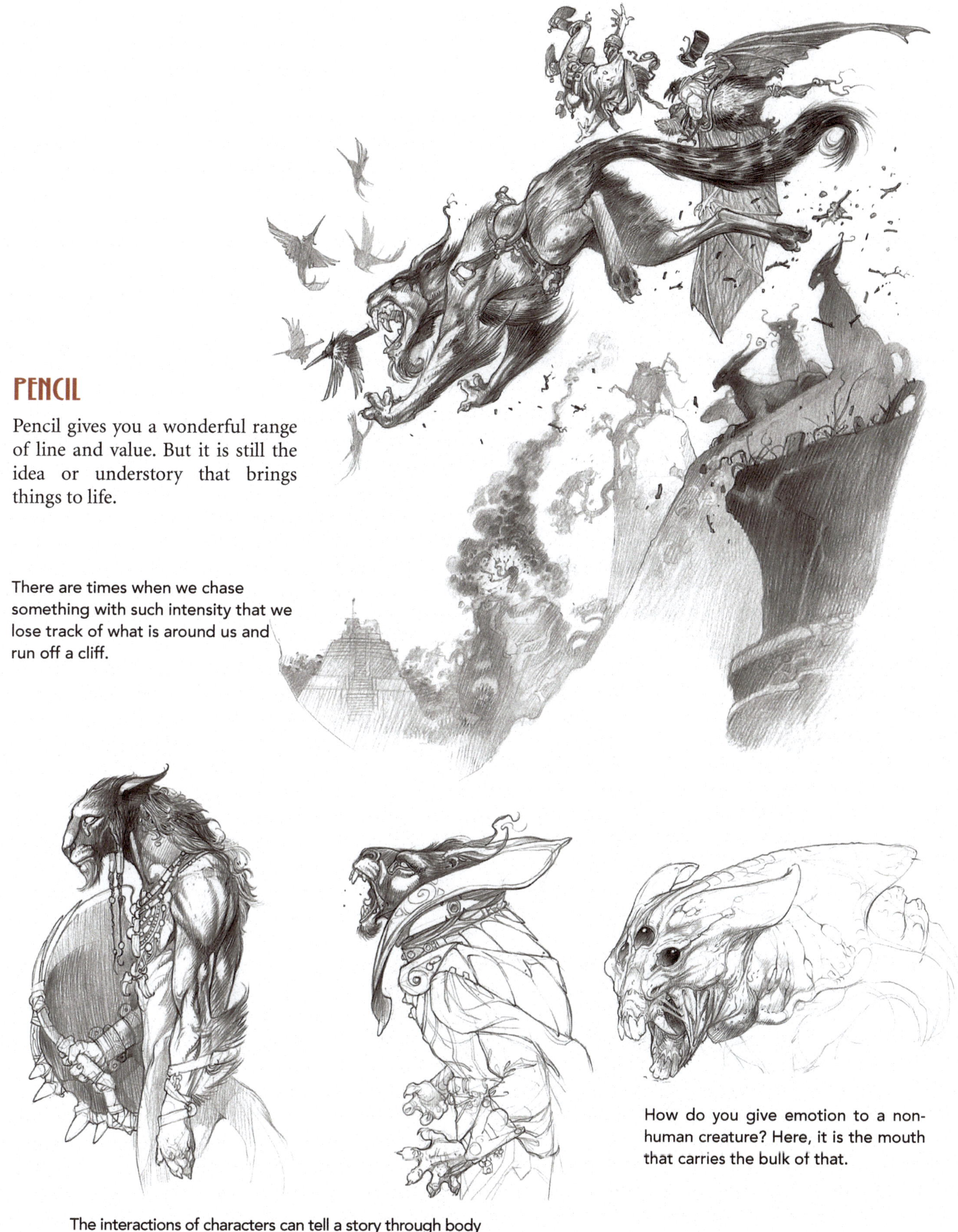

## PENCIL

Pencil gives you a wonderful range of line and value. But it is still the idea or understory that brings things to life.

There are times when we chase something with such intensity that we lose track of what is around us and run off a cliff.

The interactions of characters can tell a story through body language, expression, placement, and composition.

How do you give emotion to a non-human creature? Here, it is the mouth that carries the bulk of that.

One thing I have learned that really helps me to create is to think in different ways. Instead of just drawing a character, I give it a stage. Draw a prop and ask yourself, "What would the character do?" Create the space and put the character in there.

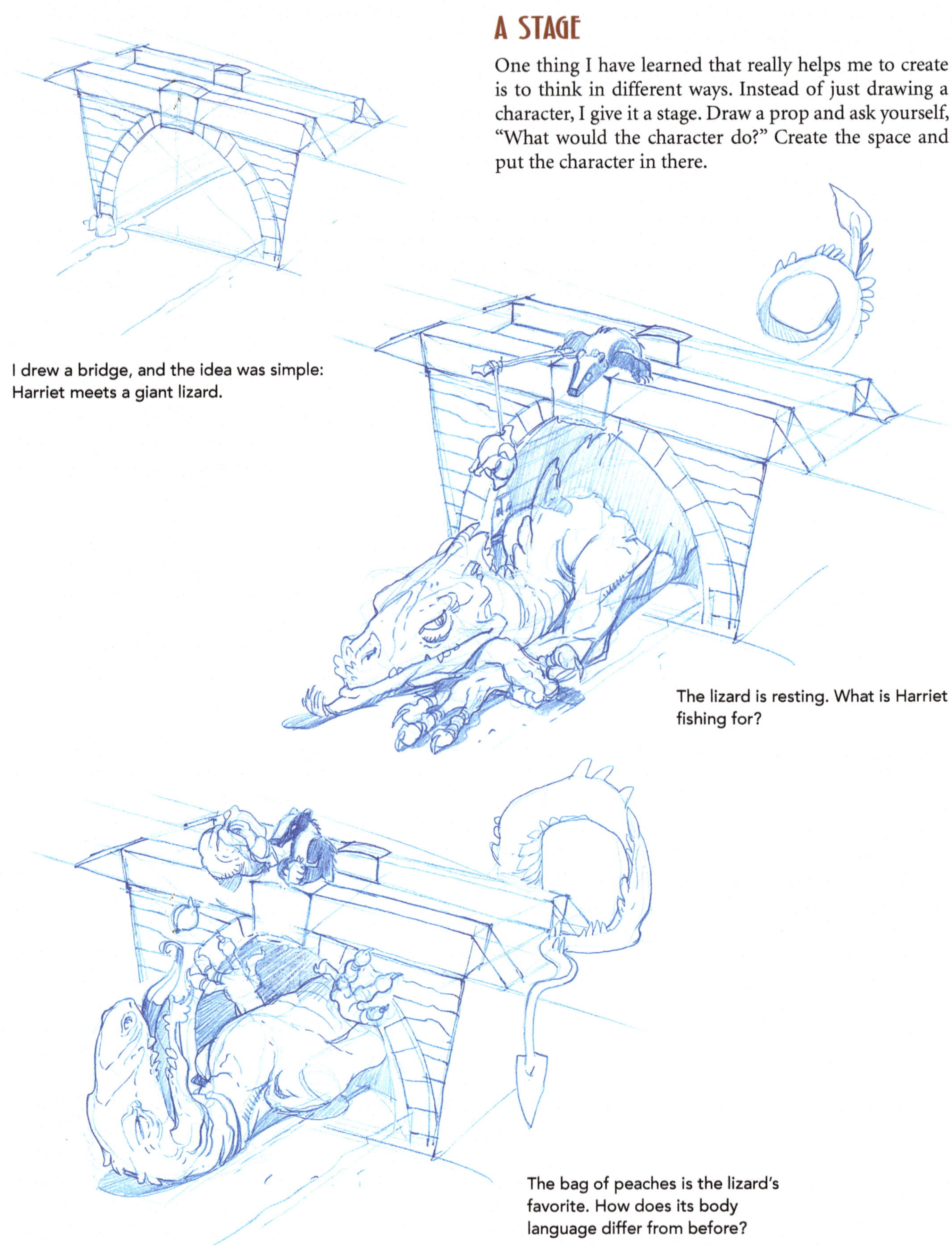

I drew a bridge, and the idea was simple: Harriet meets a giant lizard.

The lizard is resting. What is Harriet fishing for?

The bag of peaches is the lizard's favorite. How does its body language differ from before?

# THE FINAL

I felt the idea of a playful lizard wrapping around would be a lot of fun. Also, watching my kat play added to the development of this drawing. I wanted Harriet to be nose-to-nose with her friend. I wanted the bridge to be subtly twisting from the lizard's weight, and the tail becomes a design element to bring you back to their face-to-face. Finally, you need a strange plant to add to the environment to complete the story.

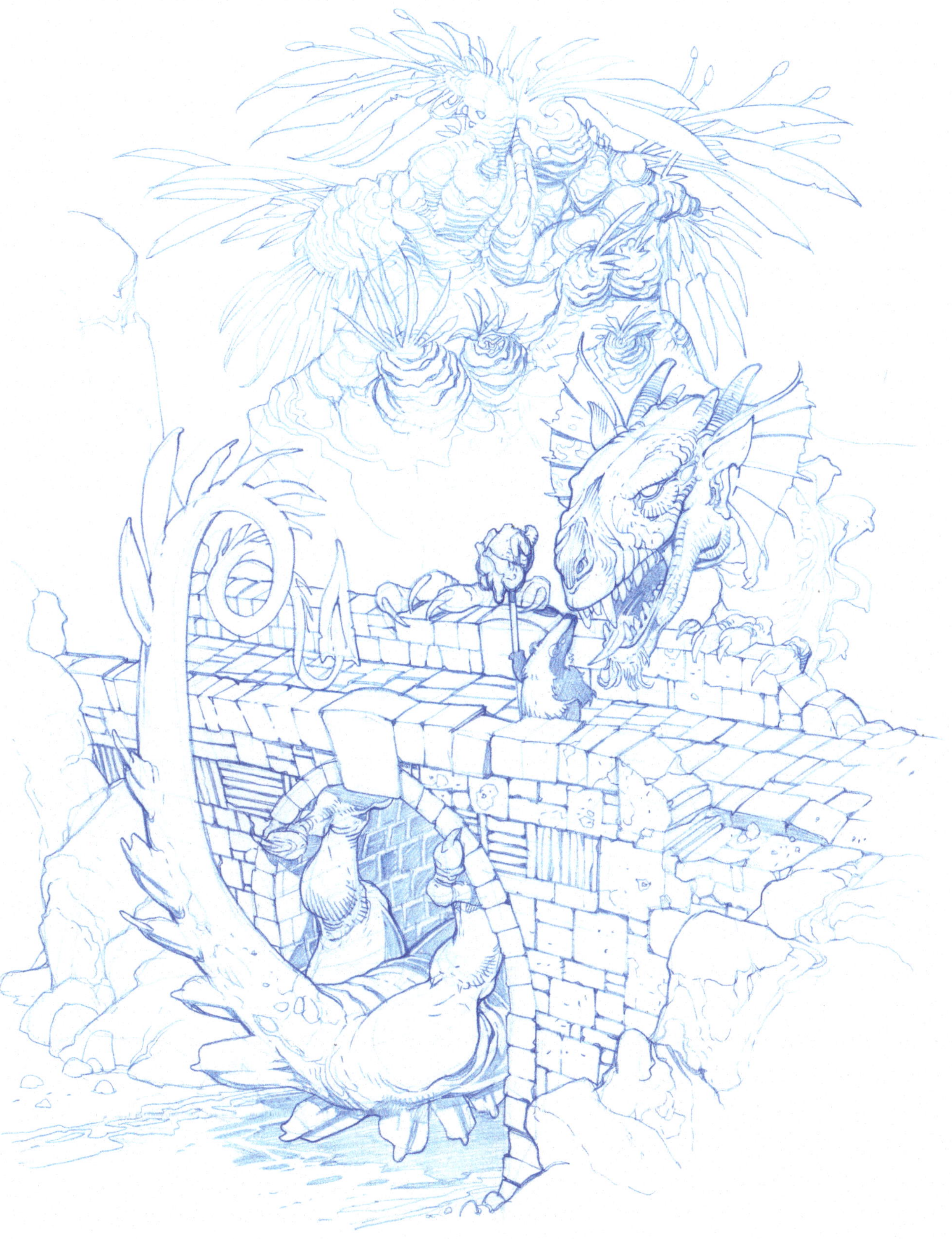

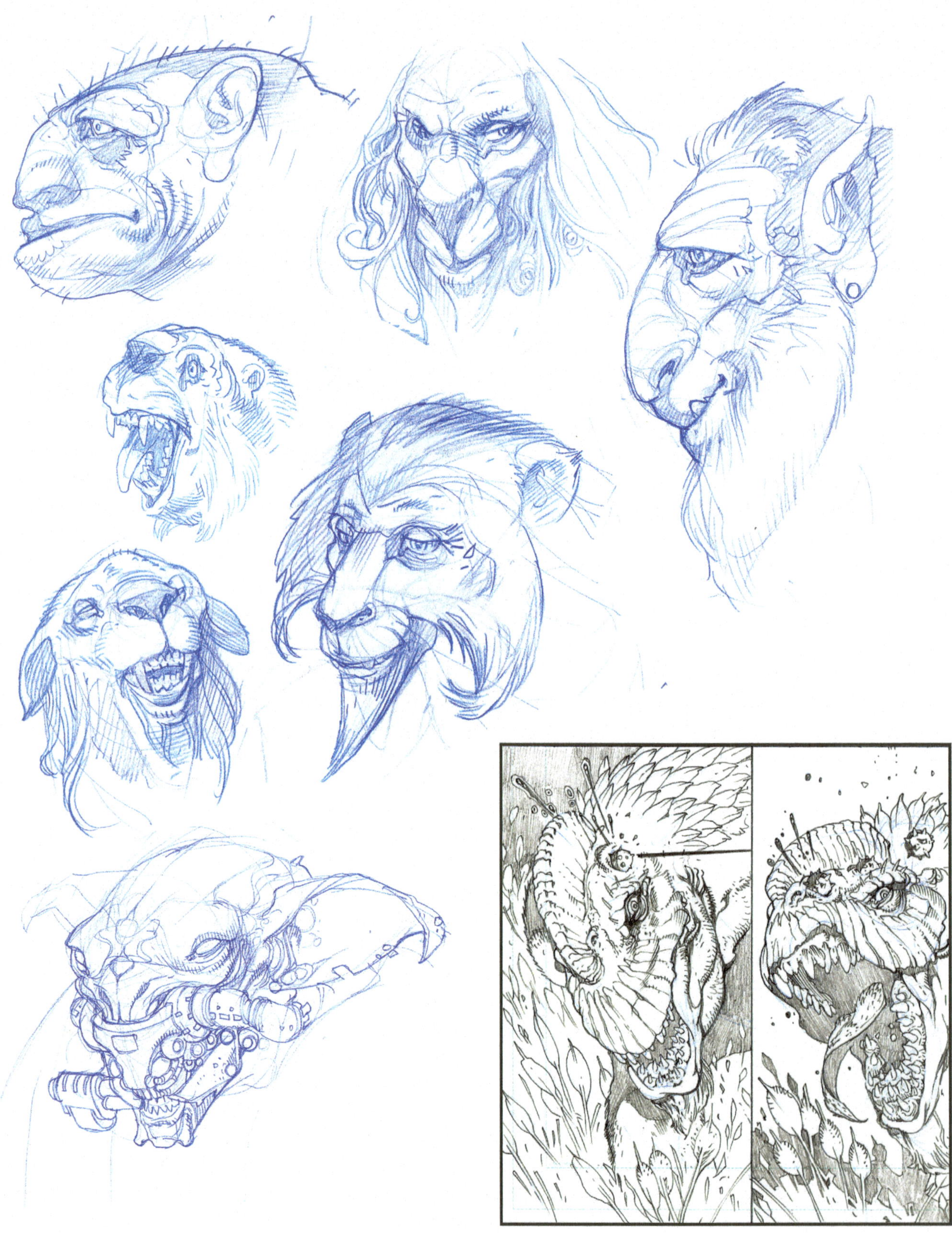

Expressions can become keys to a character. Eyes, mouth, nose, and ears are just a few elements to work with. Can you bring worry into a character? Just by themselves, the eyes can tell a whole story. What is the difference between a wounded stare and an evil side glance? A small smile can bring a happy feeling. Laughter changes the whole look of the face. Masks can hide certain things, but bring out the eyes. Finally, how do you show the reaction of a beast being tormented by a series of blows from spiked balls?

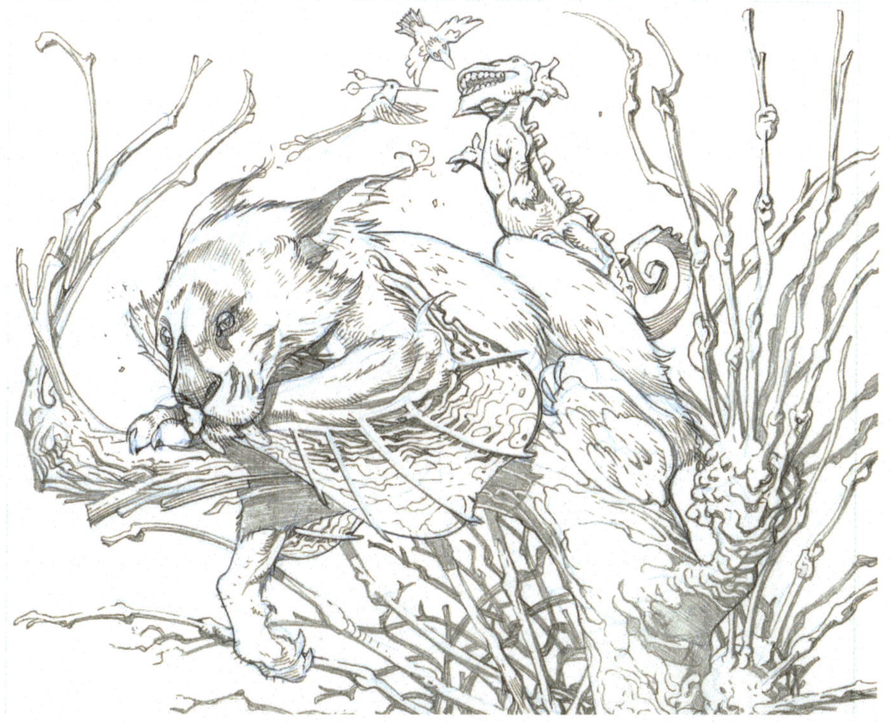

Looking at the pencil drawing, the line and weight of it create the lights and darks. Line can create texture: the hair on the kat, the bark on the tree, the smoothness to the kat's wing, the texture for the small lizard, and the feathers on the birds. The focus is on the face of the kat creature and then on the lizard.

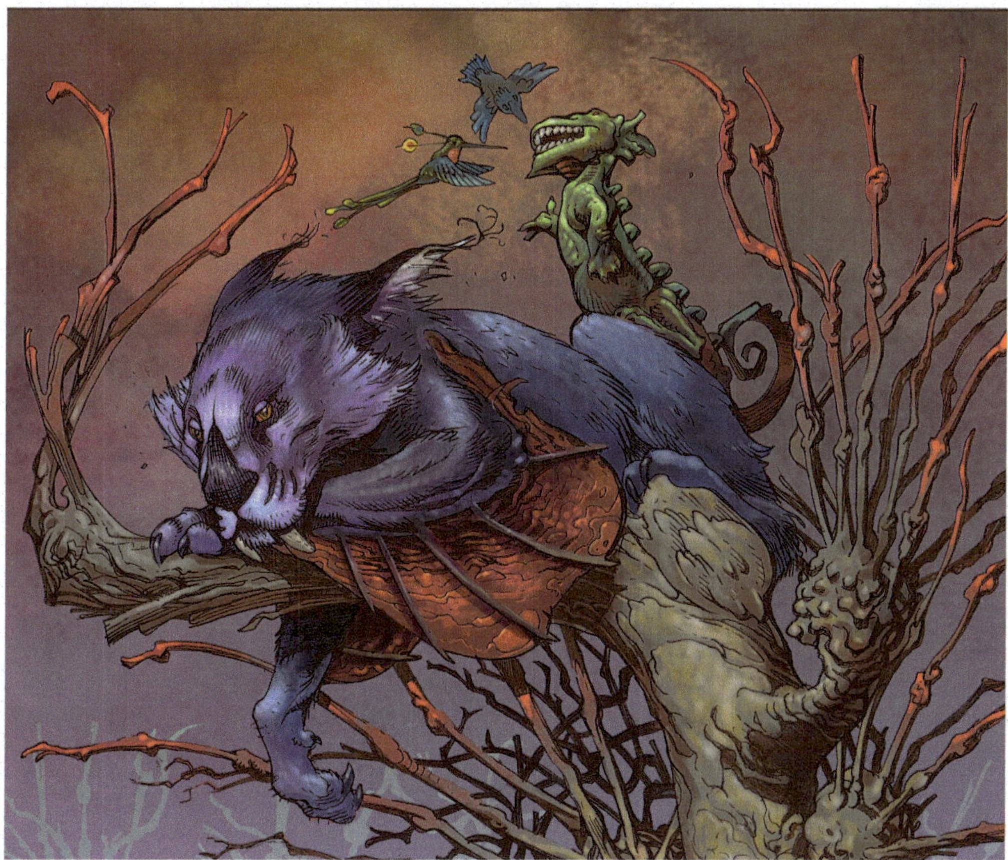

Color can change and create a different feel to a piece of artwork. The background and tree are close in value and chroma; the winged kat is darker in value with a lighter face; and the brightest and purest colors are on the chatting lizard and its background area. So your eye moves to those bright areas and the intensity of their colors. The kat becomes a secondary focal point and is a little subtler.

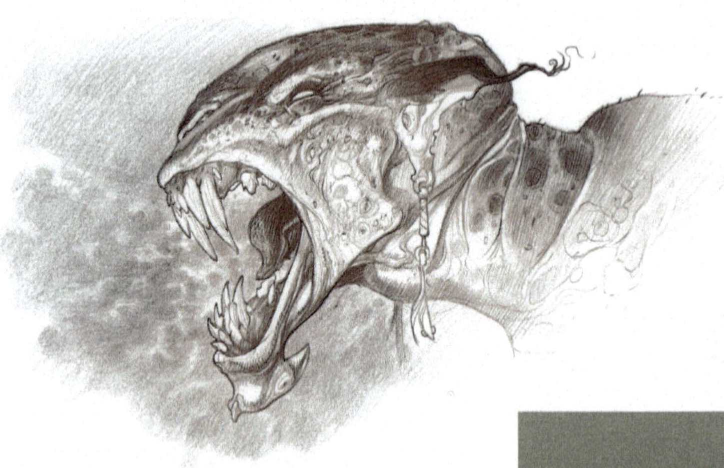

## WORKING WITH A VALUE-RENDERED DRAWING

A finished value rendering can be colored. You can work with a variety of mediums: watercolor, thin washes of acrylic paint that will be repelled by the waxiness of Prismacolor pencils, and Photoshop. Here, I used Photoshop and created a line layer that I changed into a dark-brown line. Then I created a toned paper background and added transparent colors under and over the line work.

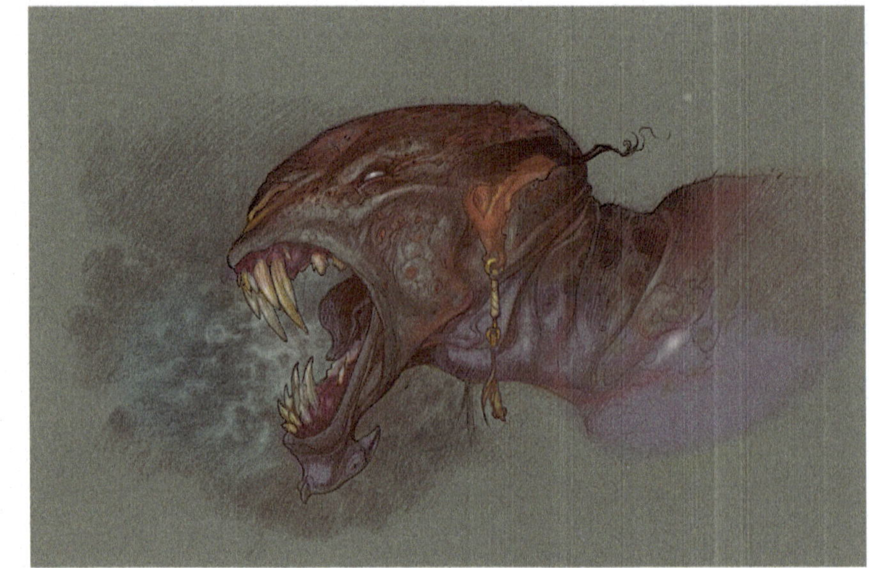

## FIGURE/GROUND REVERSAL

This is a design element used by the old masters, which takes the background and goes from a darker to lighter value and reverses the figure by going from light to dark, or vice versa. Let's apply that to this ink drawing. The main horned creature goes from light to dark, with the accent on the face and little reflected light accents in the dark. The background is darker behind its head, which brings out the face. Your eyes will always be drawn to the lightest light and darkest dark, so the face equals light and the background equals dark, which is the most contrast. Even though the birds are about the same value, the ones on the horns appear brighter because of the dark background. The birds in the lower section appear darker because of the lighter background.

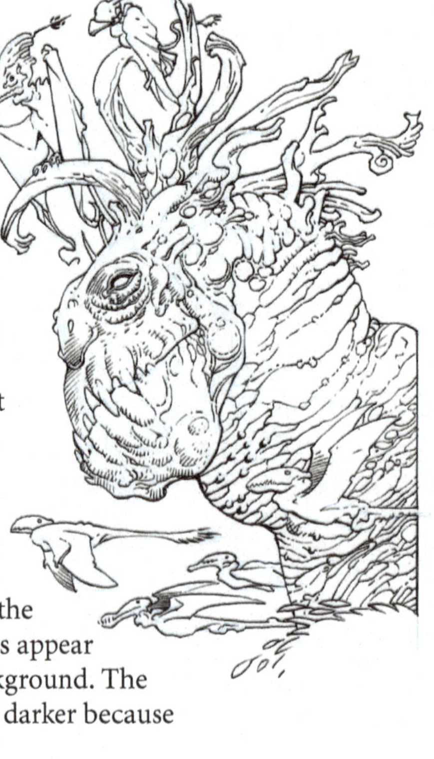

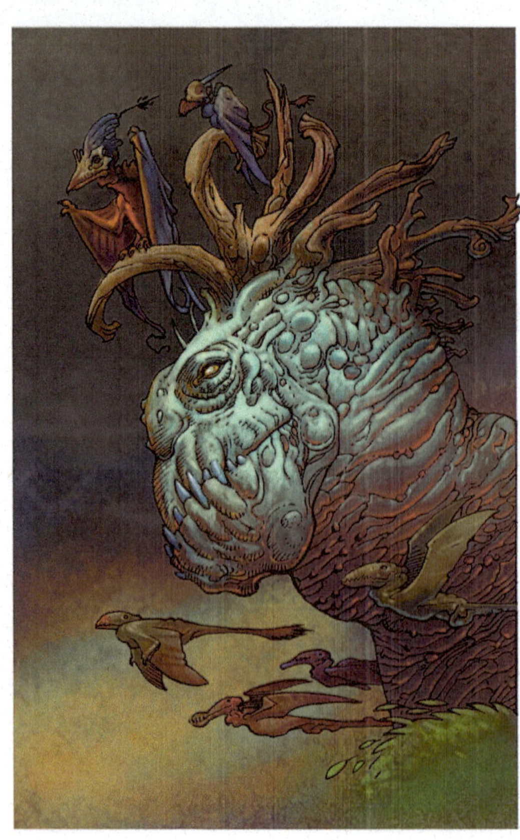

# 5
# BIRDS

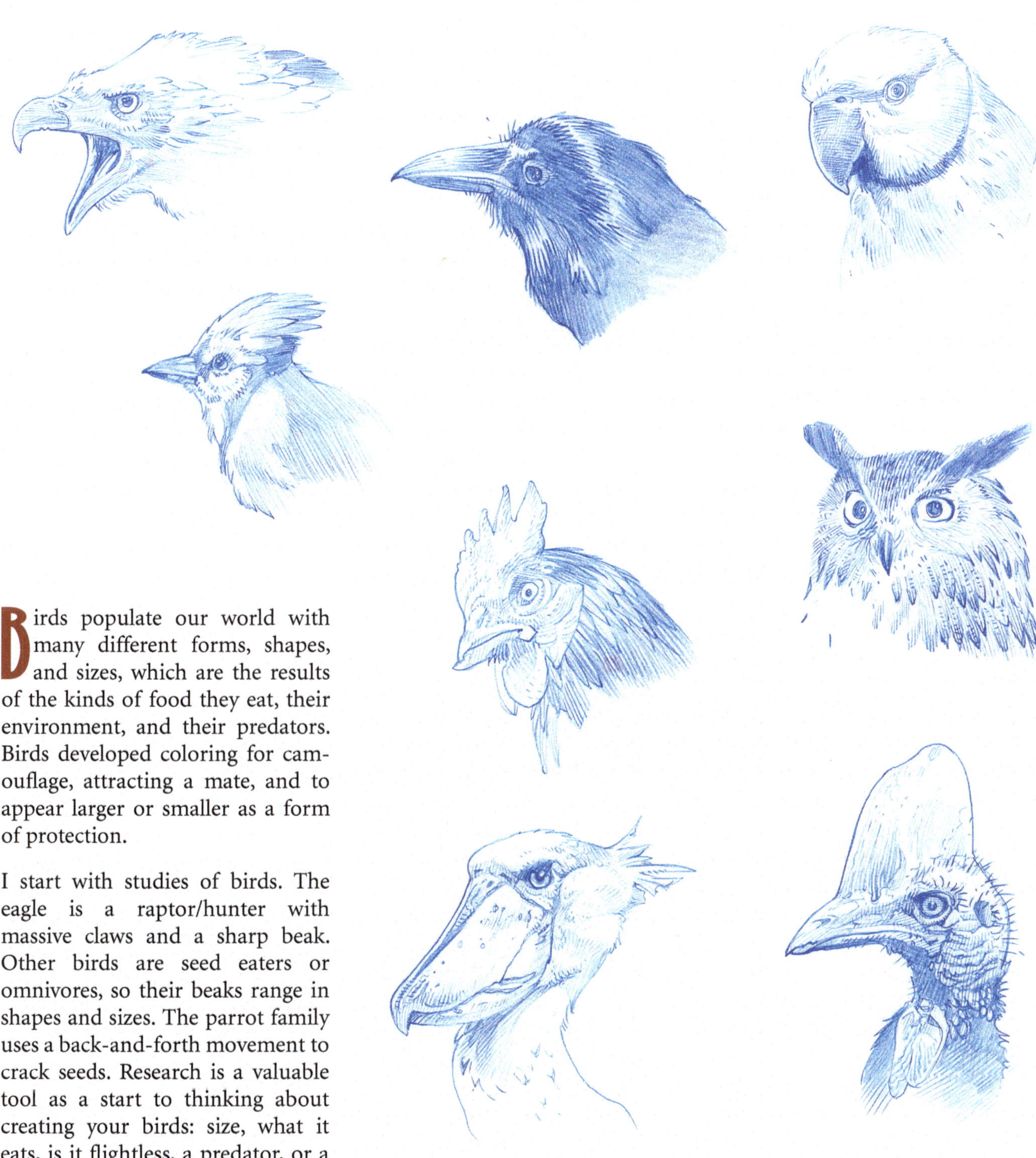



irds populate our world with many different forms, shapes, and sizes, which are the results of the kinds of food they eat, their environment, and their predators. Birds developed coloring for camouflage, attracting a mate, and to appear larger or smaller as a form of protection.

I start with studies of birds. The eagle is a raptor/hunter with massive claws and a sharp beak. Other birds are seed eaters or omnivores, so their beaks range in shapes and sizes. The parrot family uses a back-and-forth movement to crack seeds. Research is a valuable tool as a start to thinking about creating your birds: size, what it eats, is it flightless, a predator, or a simple seed eater.

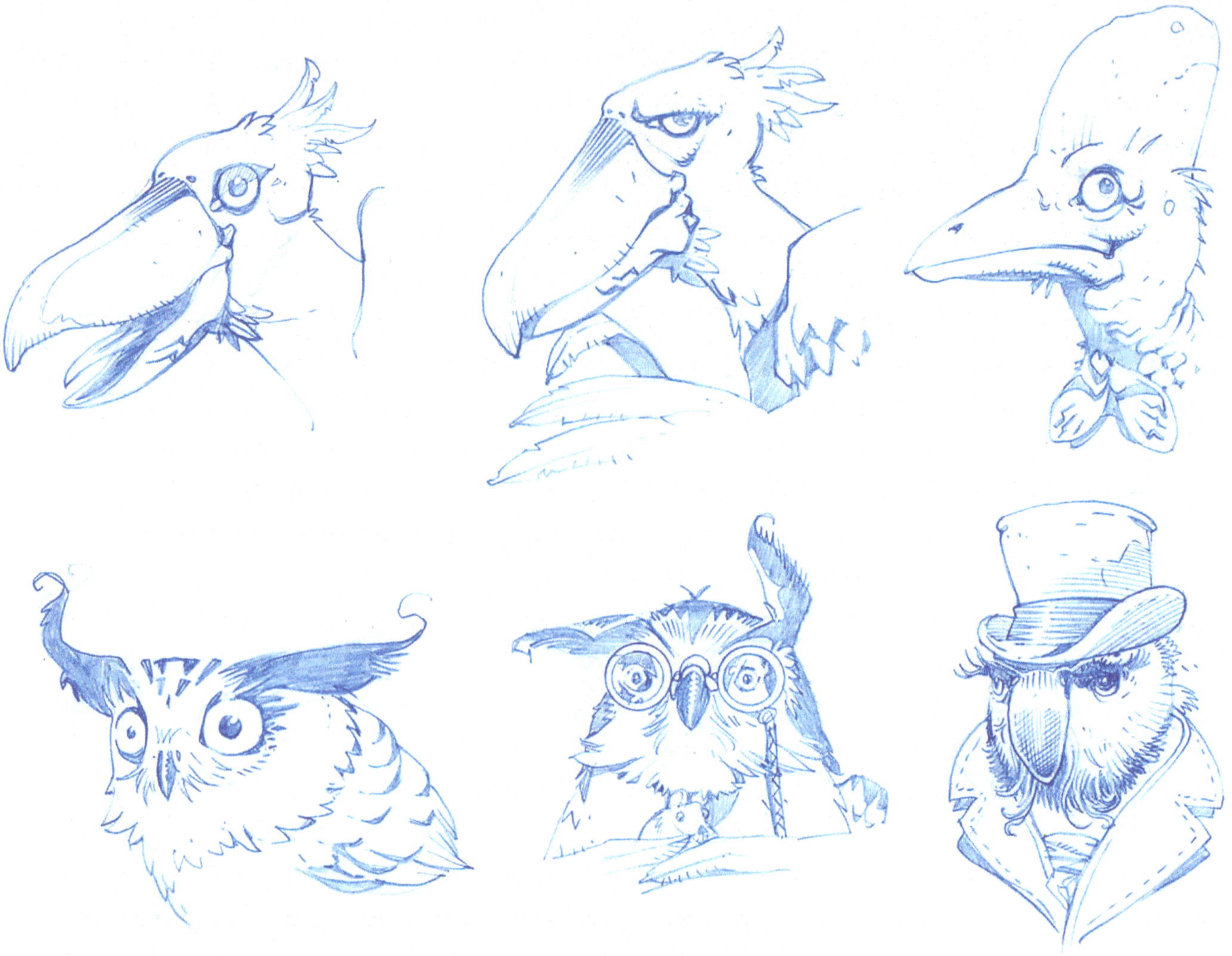

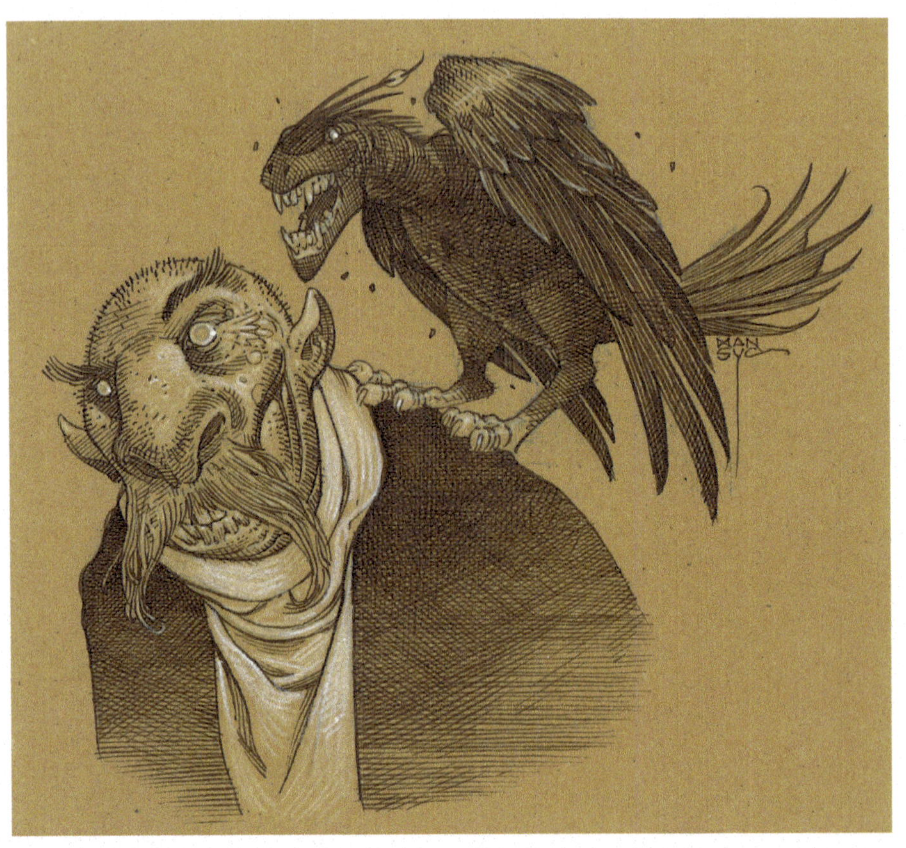

Humor can be another element to the characters. How can you, just with a simpler line, give these birds a whole new look? Here, I simplified the form and pushed the line work to bring out the lights and darks. The element I like to play with the most is eye size. It can be enlarged or shrunk for dramatic effect. It can make a cartoon character even more believable.

And even if you render in a realistic manner, eyes and teeth can be elements to create focal points and expressions in the creatures. Birds with teeth always give me a fright!

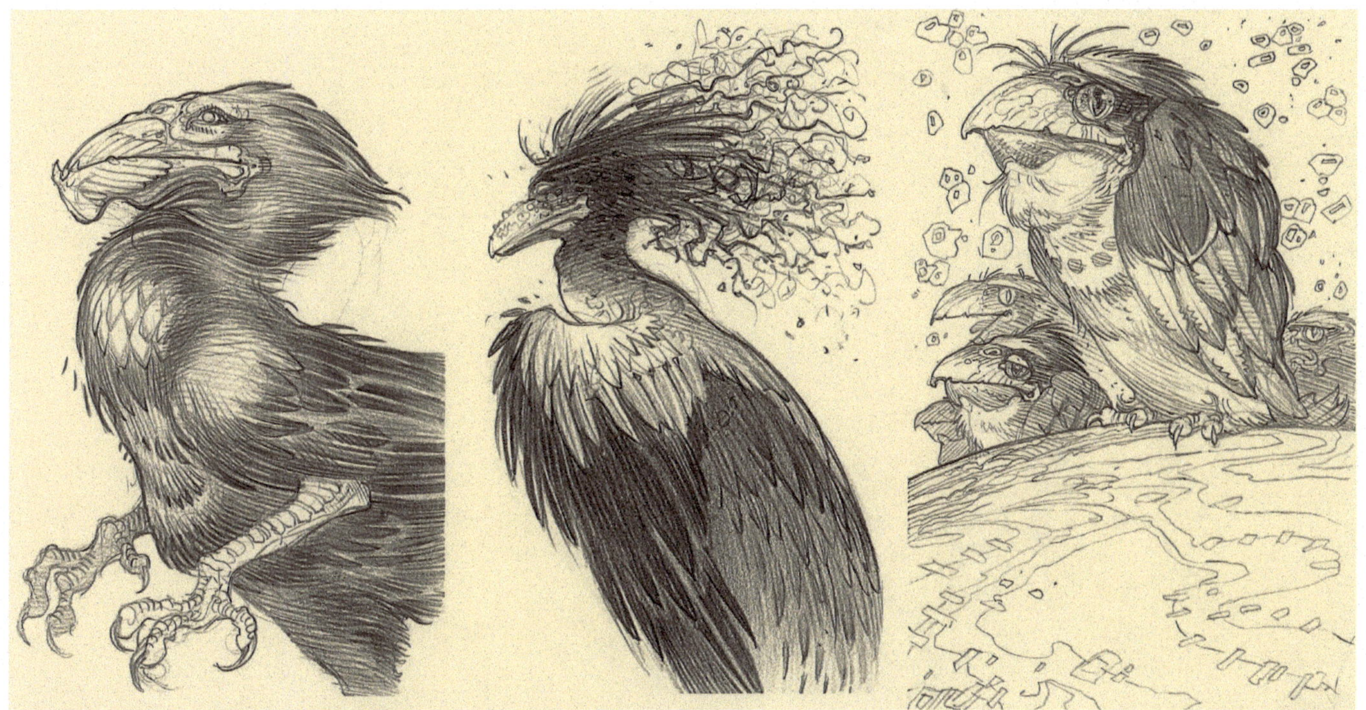

The Moleskine sketchbook is something I carry with me. When I am sitting and waiting, I doodle in it and try out ideas for types of feathers, eyes, claws, etc.

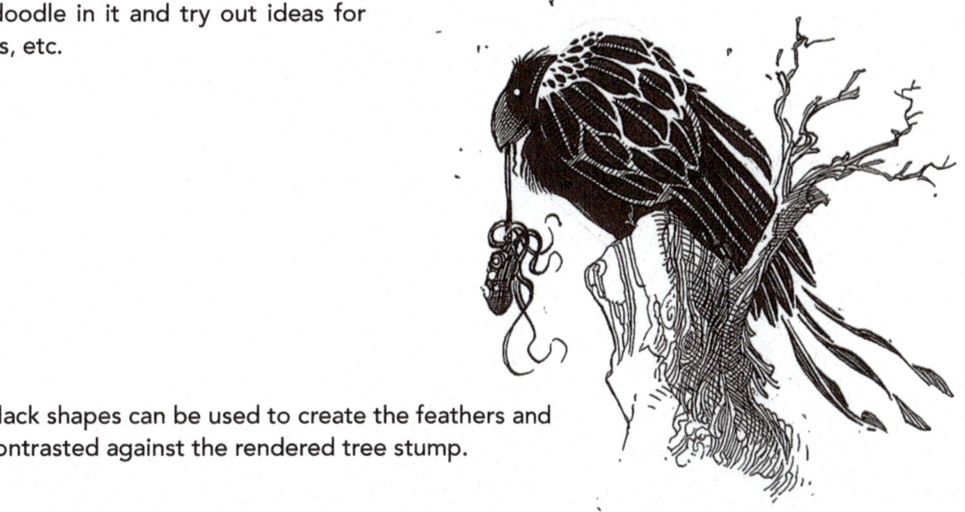

Black shapes can be used to create the feathers and contrasted against the rendered tree stump.

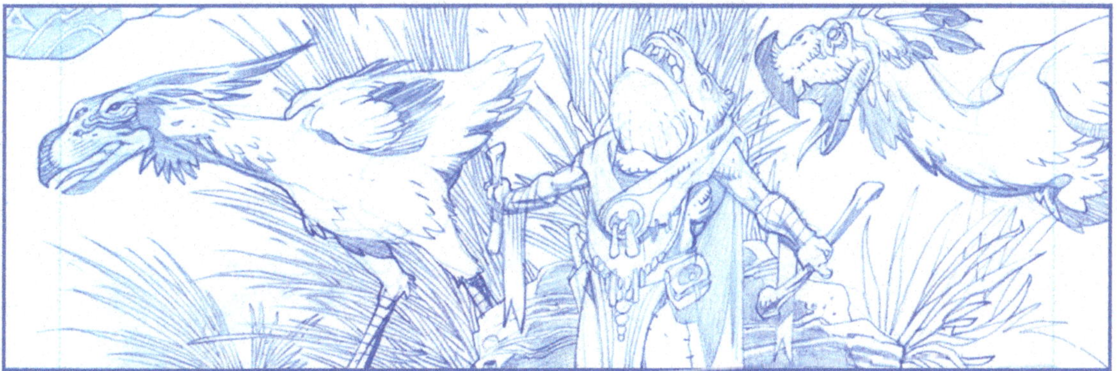

When I pencil comic pages, I try to contrast elements against each other. So here, the grass becomes a background element and the large flightless birds have strong patterns and less defined lines to make them stand out.

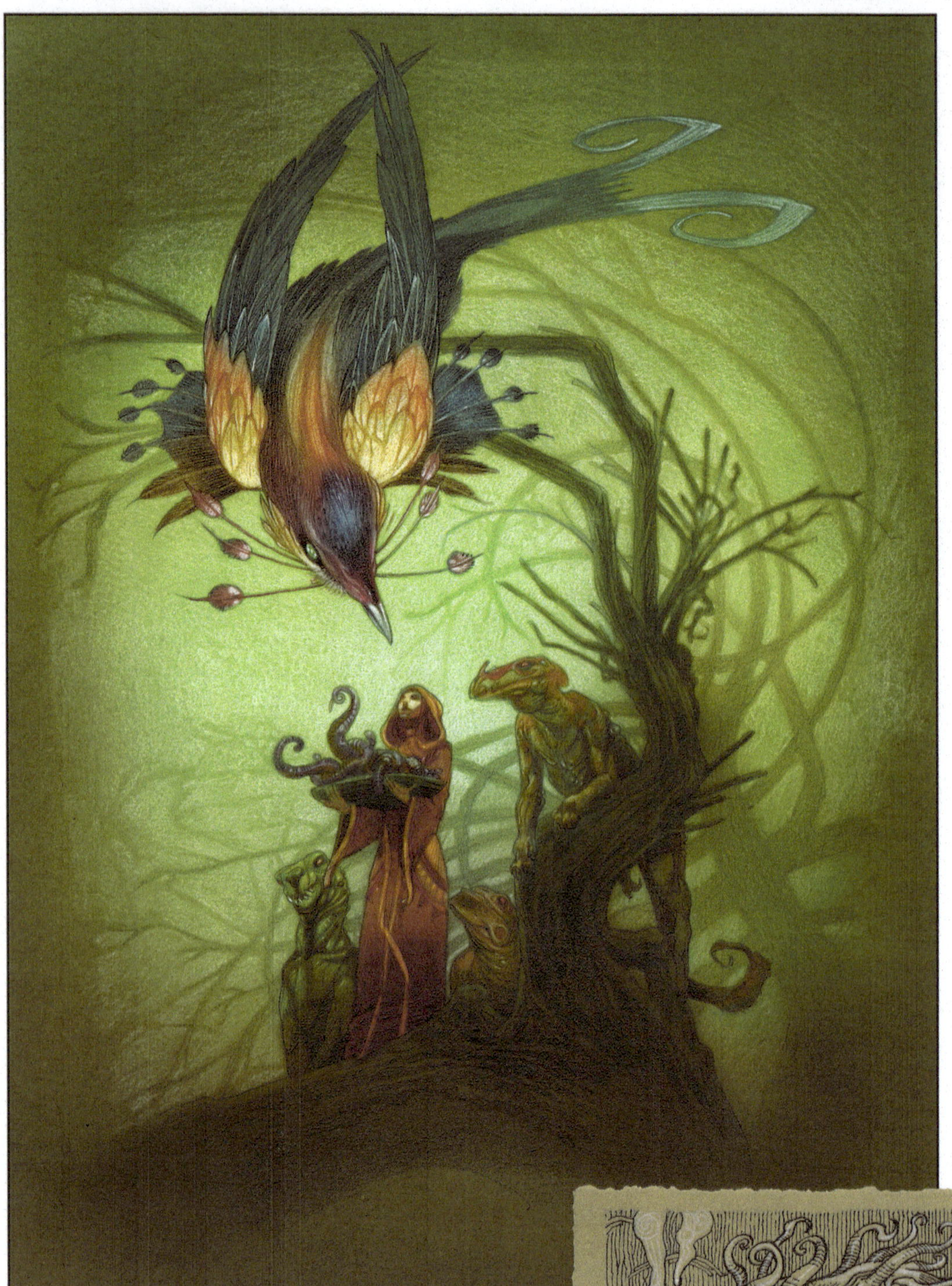

Here are two finished illustrations. The color one is called "The Gift." We all have protocols when we meet. Birds use their plumage for warning, introduction, aggression, attraction, and playful expressions.

The ink drawing is a Lovecraft bird: a mix of bird, fish, octopus, skin wings and, of course, some nice drool.

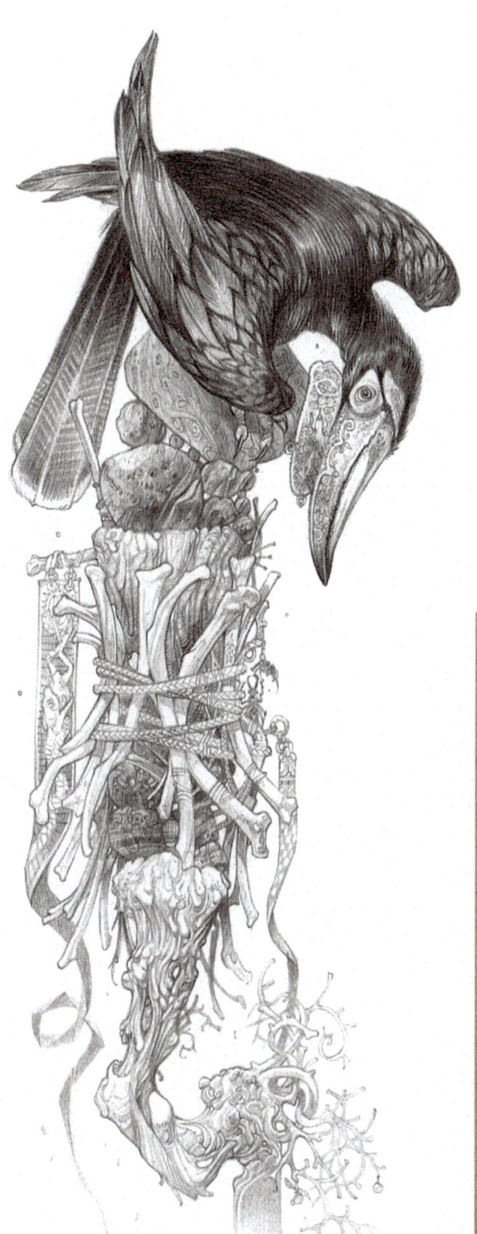

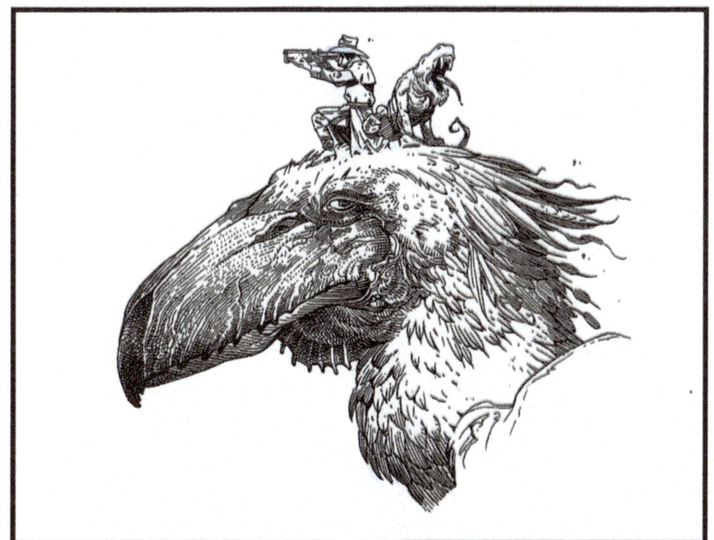

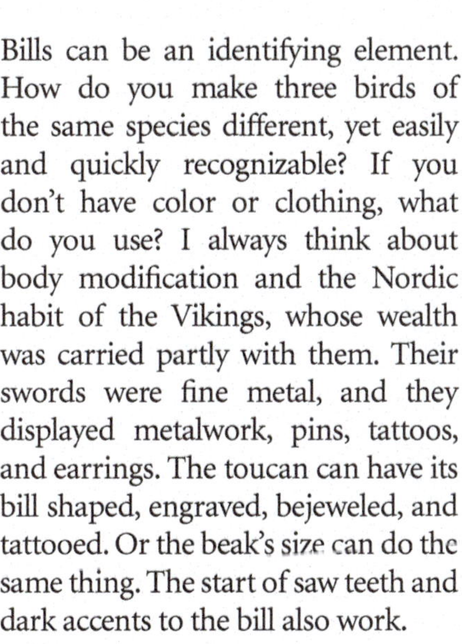

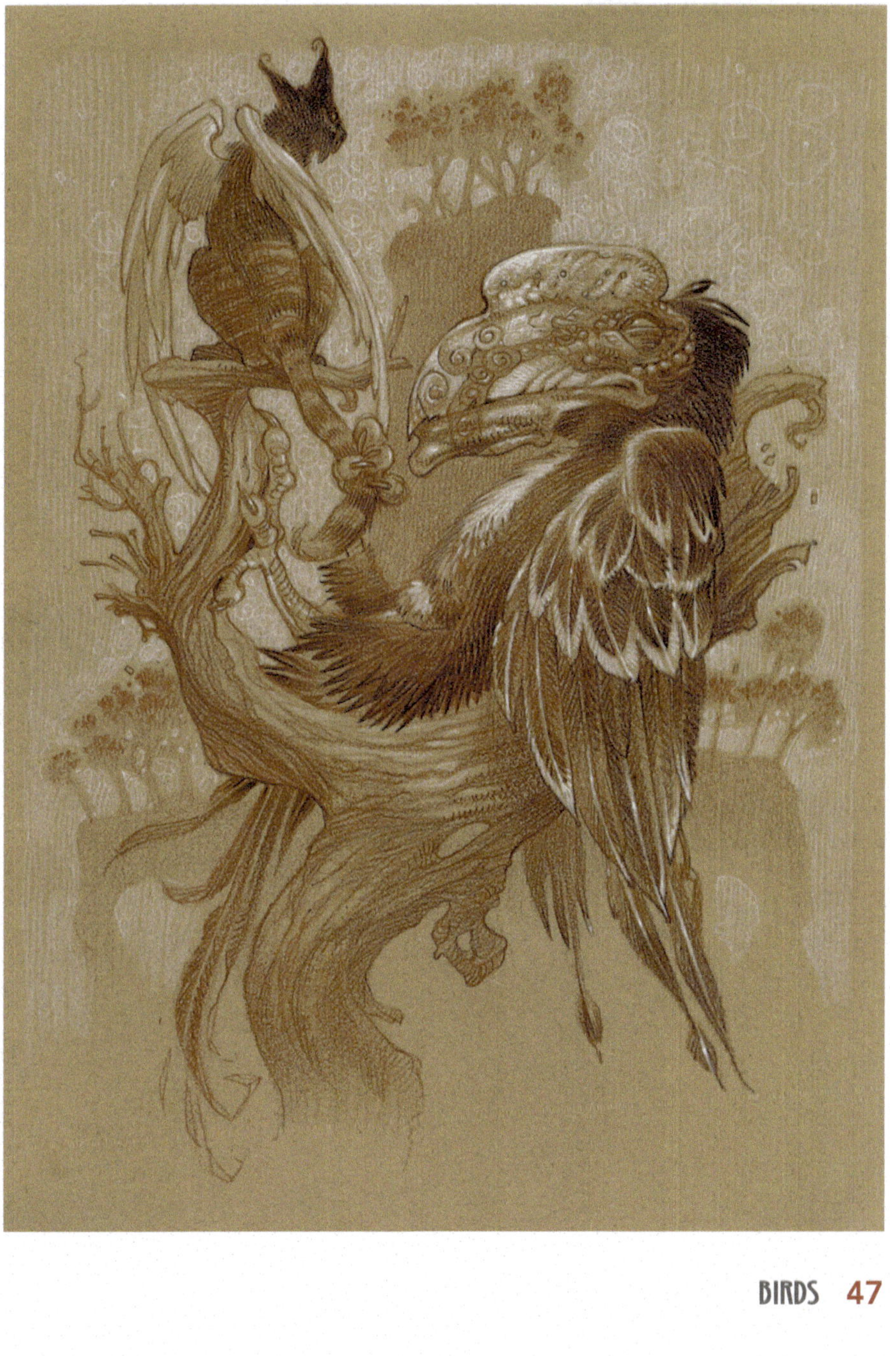

Bills can be an identifying element. How do you make three birds of the same species different, yet easily and quickly recognizable? If you don't have color or clothing, what do you use? I always think about body modification and the Nordic habit of the Vikings, whose wealth was carried partly with them. Their swords were fine metal, and they displayed metalwork, pins, tattoos, and earrings. The toucan can have its bill shaped, engraved, bejeweled, and tattooed. Or the beak's size can do the same thing. The start of saw teeth and dark accents to the bill also work.

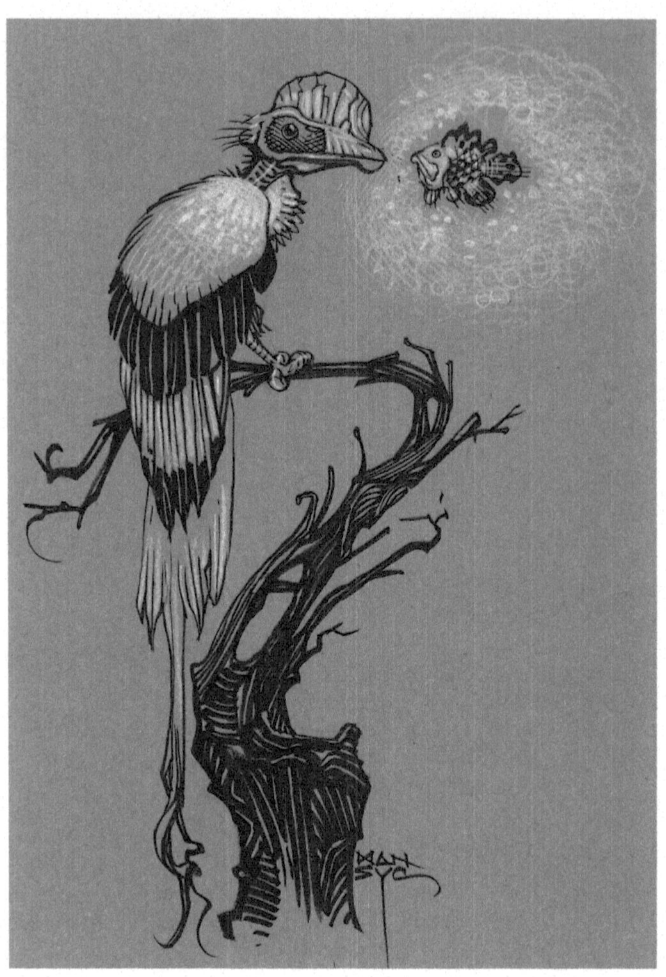

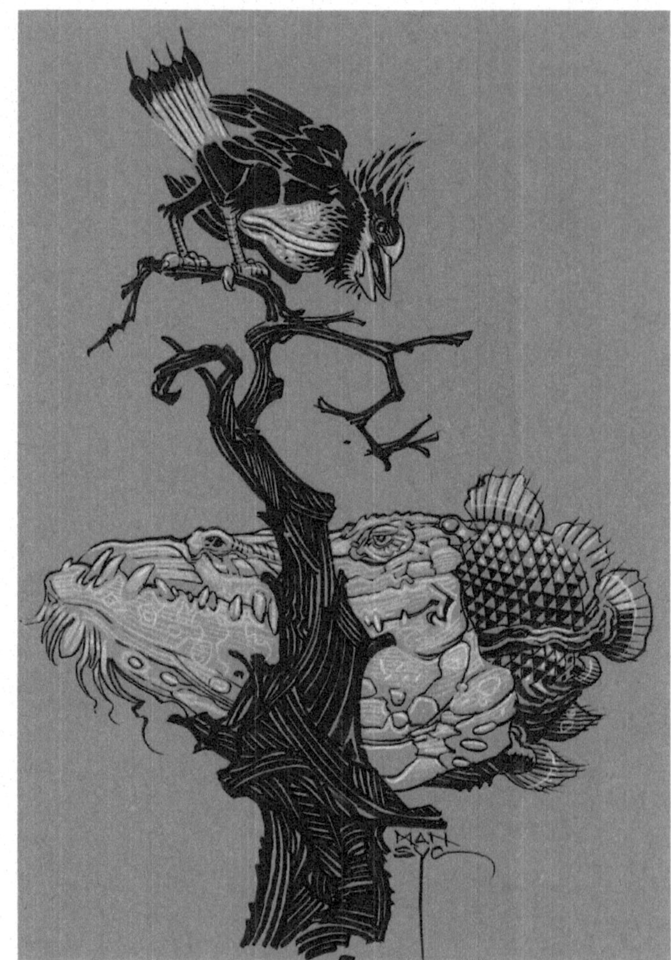

Different tools give you different types of marks and strokes. The brush is one of the most flexible tools in terms of the range you can achieve. When I work with a brush, I can render but also push the line and its weight to fluid widths. It can be used to bring different surfaces into play and make you understate the form for a dark line or stroke. Working with a nib pen or technical pen, I tend to render the daylights out of the surfaces. With a brush, I can pull back and suggest the form more and use blacks.

Gray paper allows you to work up and down from a medium ground. You get to draw in your lights and darks. This is the way I feel most comfortable working.

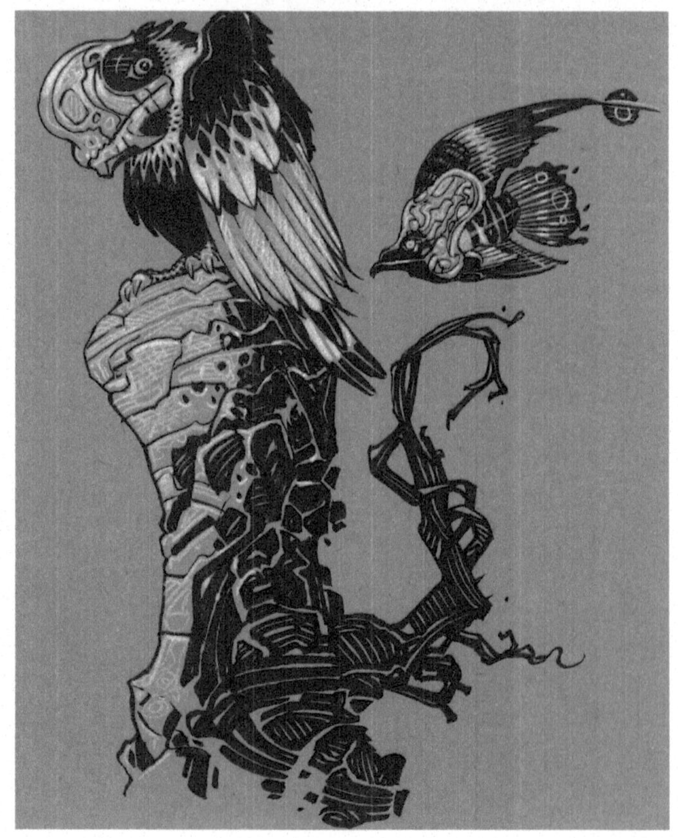

1. Here, I tried to push the large bird-thing—complete with an engraved beak, folded leathery wings, and overtly relaxed seated position—being approached by a couple of slugs. There is a tension created by the soft, small, wet creatures versus the hard-beaked, scaly one.

2. Watercolor is a medium that can range from opaque to transparent. You can work with soft layers and build up to your darks. You have to leave your whites and build around them. This is another way of thinking about how you create your art. So, for me, there is the idea and a medium. Each medium has its strong and weak points, and it is a nice challenge to see what that medium can give you.

3. Pencil is one of my favorite tools. I love to render, blend, and work with line variations and textures. I hope the pencil work captures the energy of the chase.

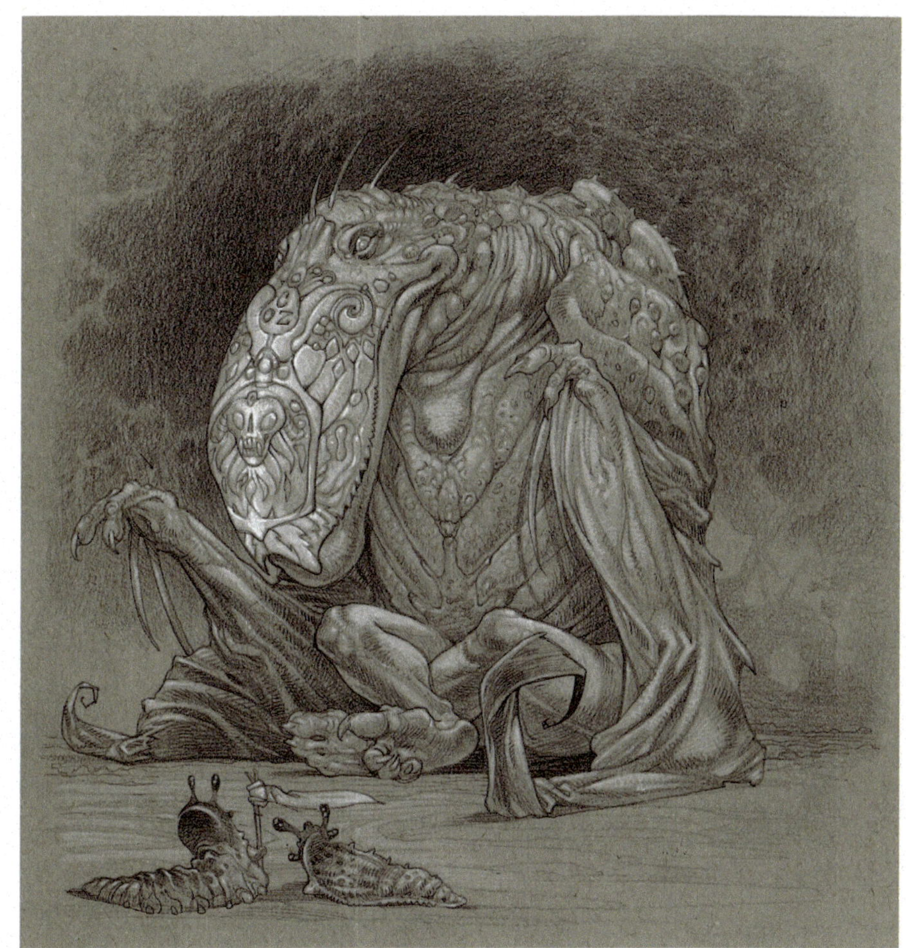

1

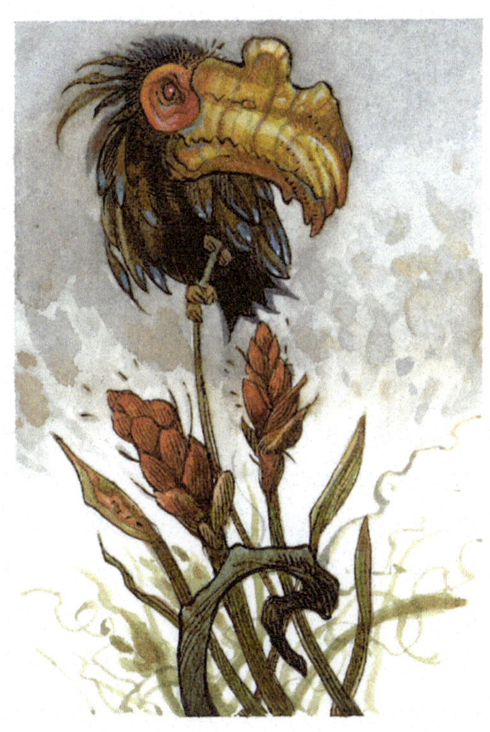

2

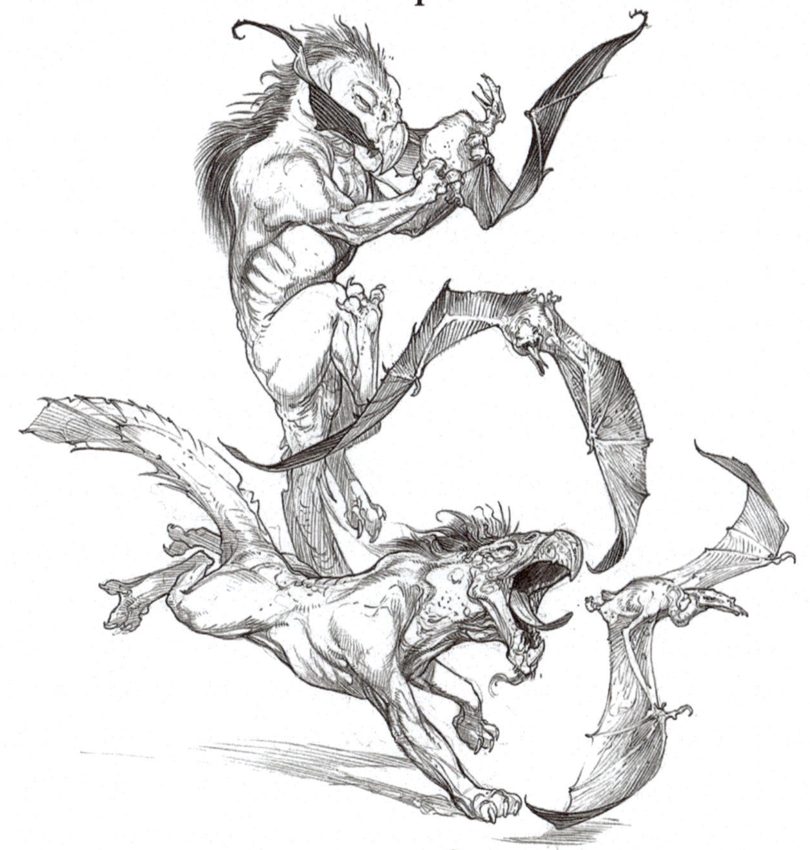

3

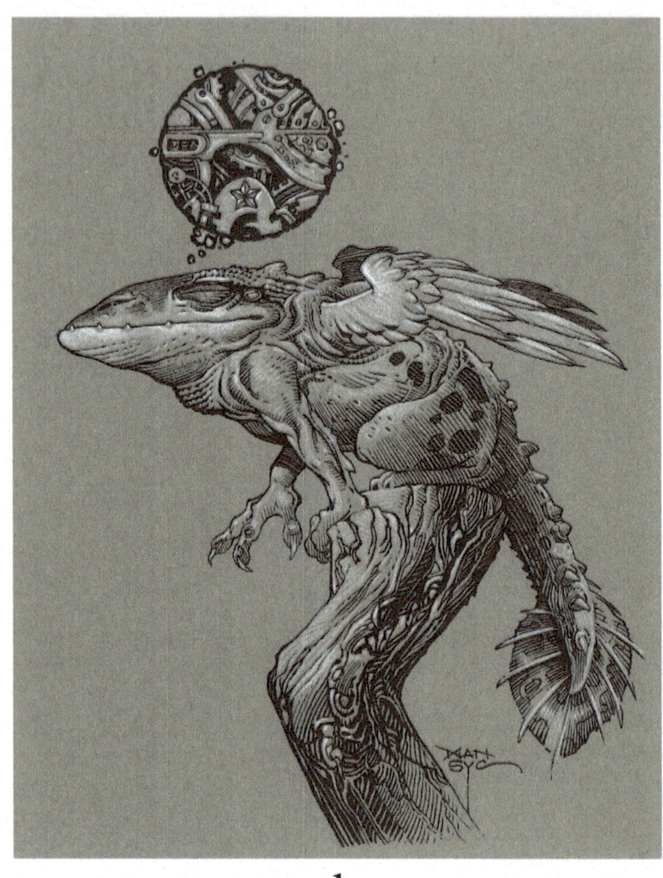

1

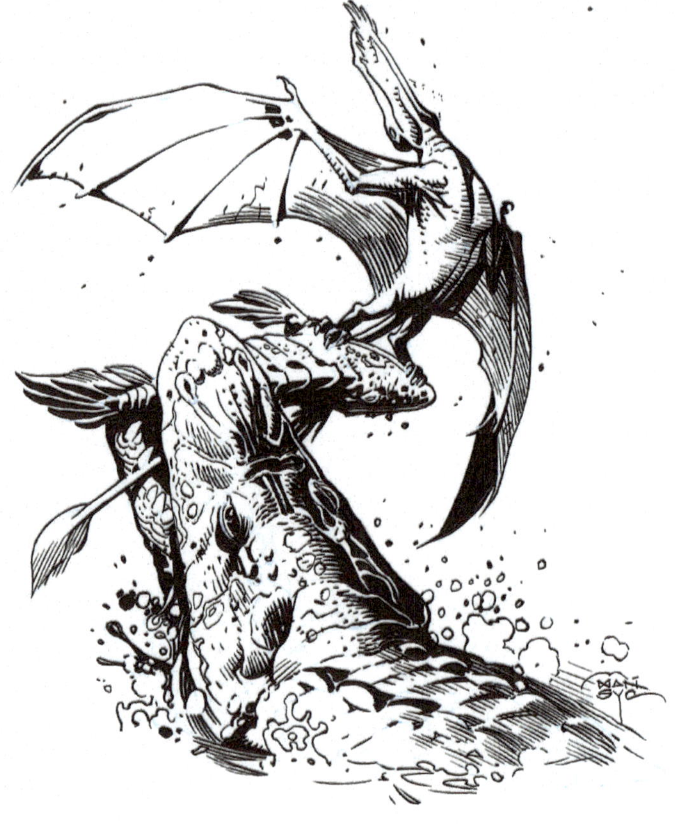

2

## "A THOUGHT"

1. What does a winged lizard think about? Possibly it has come up with a six-star perpetual motion machine. But it doesn't have the communication skills to share that information with us. The drawing is on gray paper with ink, brush, and white pencil.

2. Fighting for food is something that you constantly see in nature. A painting instructor of mine once said, "When you look out at sunset and the lake is calm, the light is beautiful, you have to remember that one inch below that surface *everything is fighting for its life!*" So I used a more graphic ink style and tried to push the energy of this large food robber.

3. Nesting and food are two variables to life: where you build your home and what it is you need to live. Now, are these two different animals? Do they share a symbiotic lifestyle? Or is one just wishing it, too, could have a meal of a nice furry rodent? Once again, the pencil gives a softer range and feel of tones and line weight.

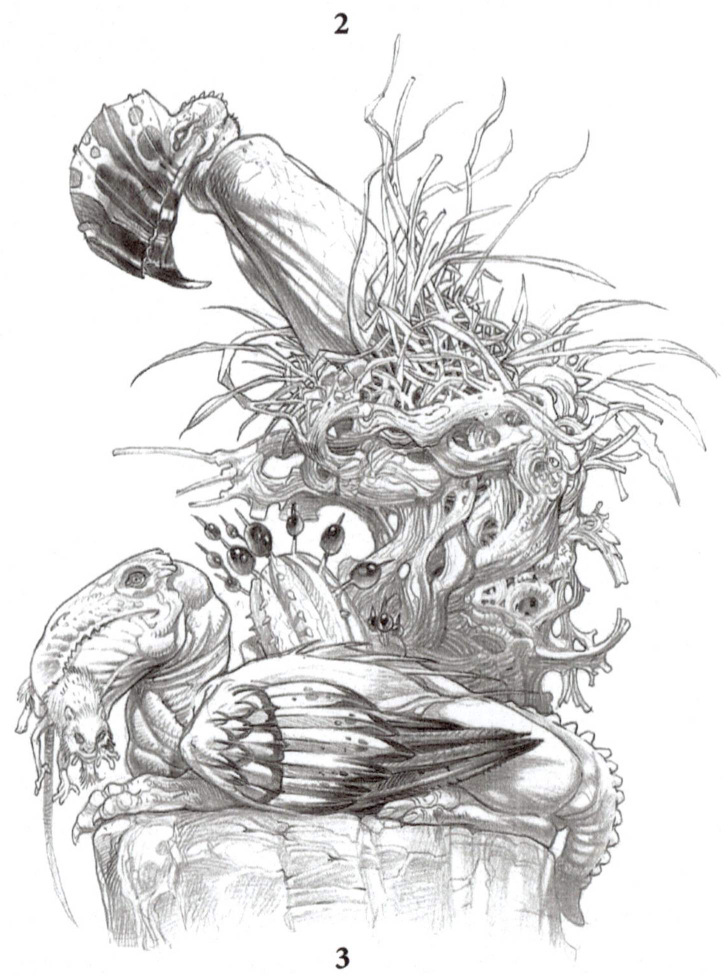

3

# 6

# FISH

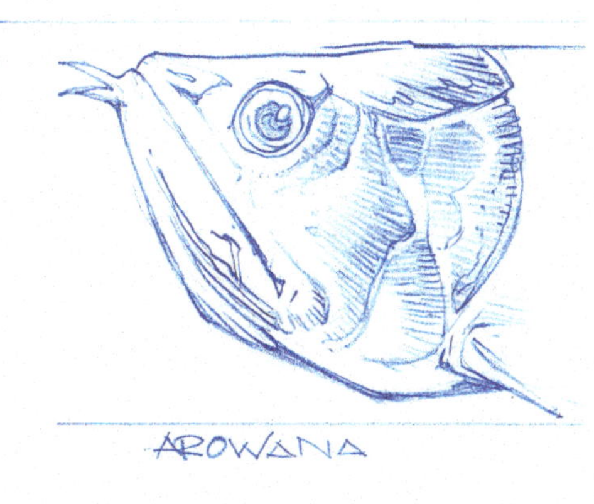

AROWANA

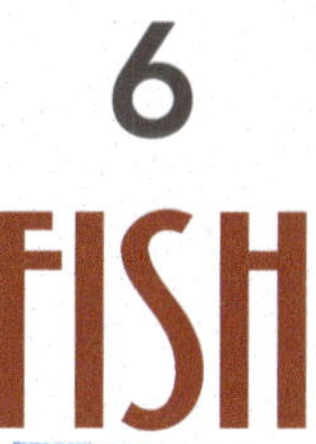

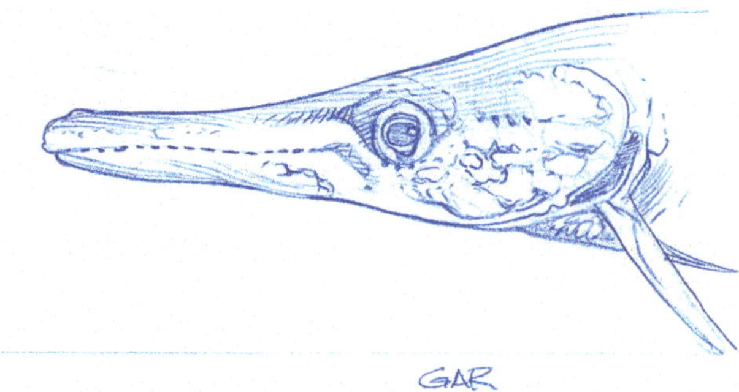

GAR

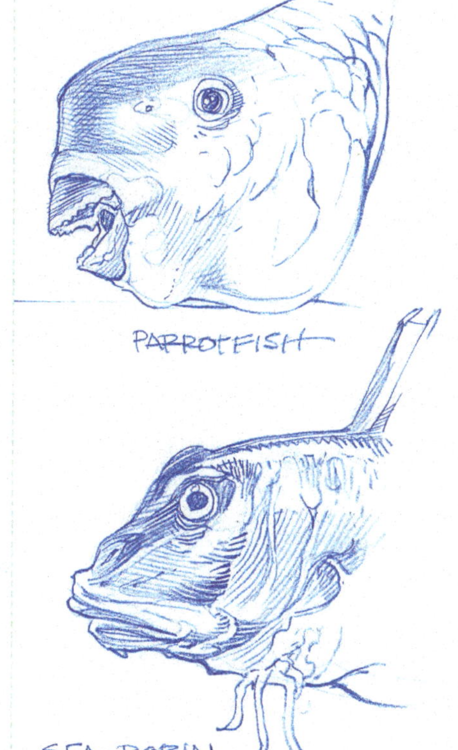

PARROTFISH

SEA ROBIN

GOBLIN SHARK

TANG

GROUPER

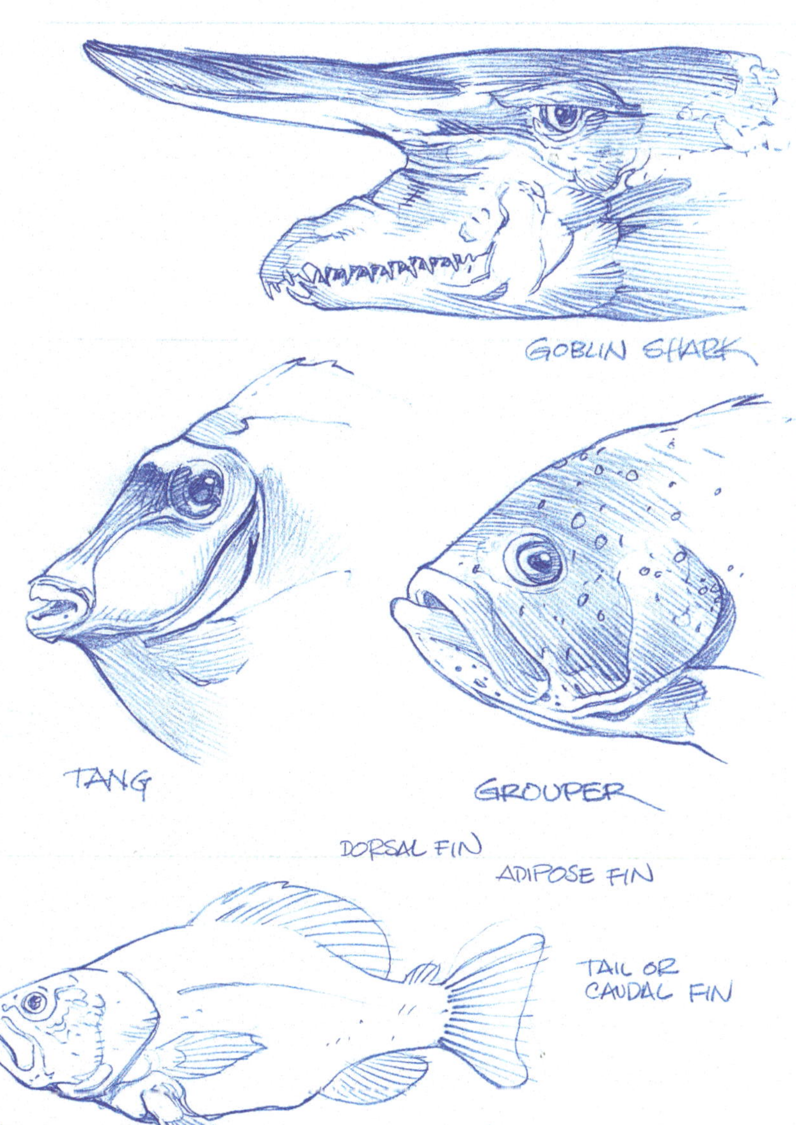


Fish can be a lot of things: food, pets, symbols of fertility, or bringers of knowledge. It is all in how you look at them and what they do and how you will want to use them in your world.

It is important to do research, so let us start with simple information.

Here are drawings of some real fish, showing the diversity found in this species. Also, the diagram labels the different types of fins.

Let's talk about how form follows function and set up a series of questions to help us create the look for these creatures.

1. *Who?* Fish.

2. *Where?* Lake, river, ocean, deep sea, creek, etc.

3. *What?* What does it do? What is it like? Predator? Prey? Beautiful? Ugly? Etc.

4. *When?* A time frame, future, past, prehistoric, etc.

5. *Why?* Why are they here? Food source, farming and the money they make, something to advance the story. . . .

6. *How?* How are they important? How are they transported, or what are they used for?

This gives me a set of building blocks for telling a story with fish.

When I think of all the types of fish you can find, from pet stores to the food market, it is an amazing collection of species, sizes, colors, and varieties that make up this part of the animal kingdom. You can always add more qualities, such as family, male or female, offspring, how they are raised, and growth cycles.

Now you don't always have to do all this backstory, but it can give a very believable character to your fish.

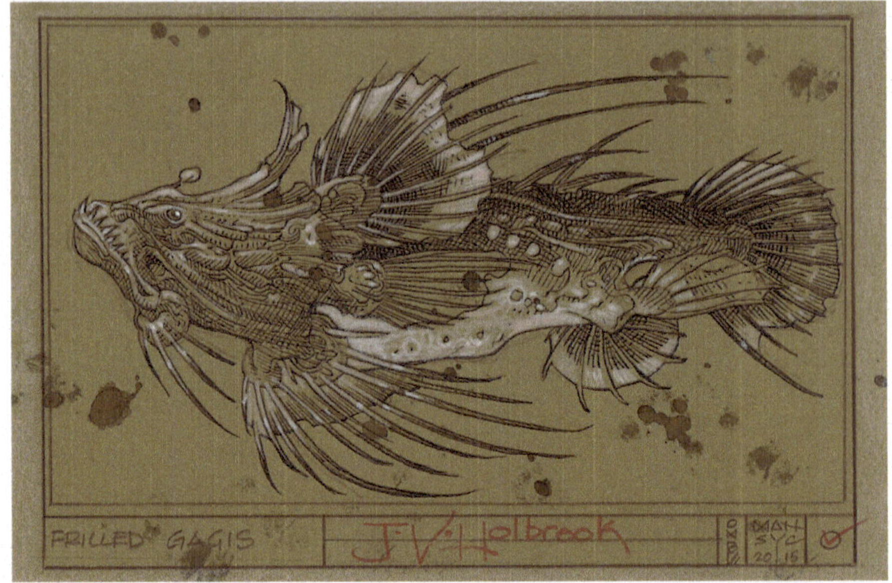

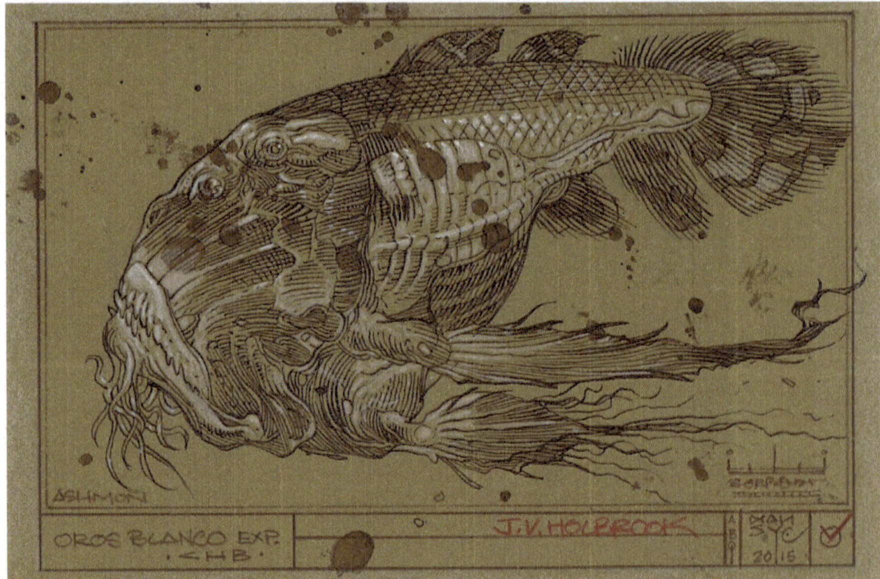

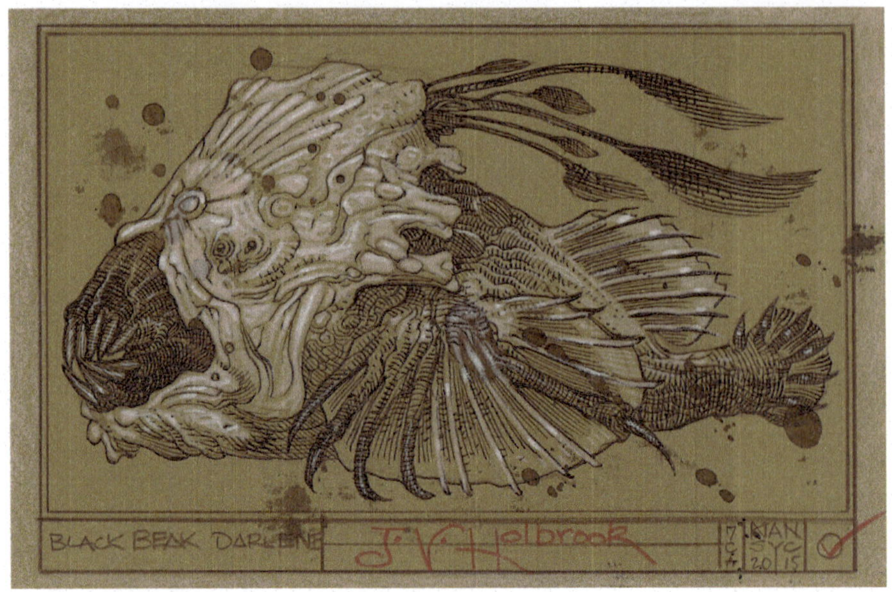

The next step is building our fish.

1. Start with a gesture line to indicate the movement of the head and body.

2. Rough shapes and forms: head, body, tail, and fins.

3. Clarify your shapes.

4. Now a contour line to start to define the form and to develop the surfaces and textures.

5. More finished contour (using line), the start of surface description, and line weight to indicate the light source.

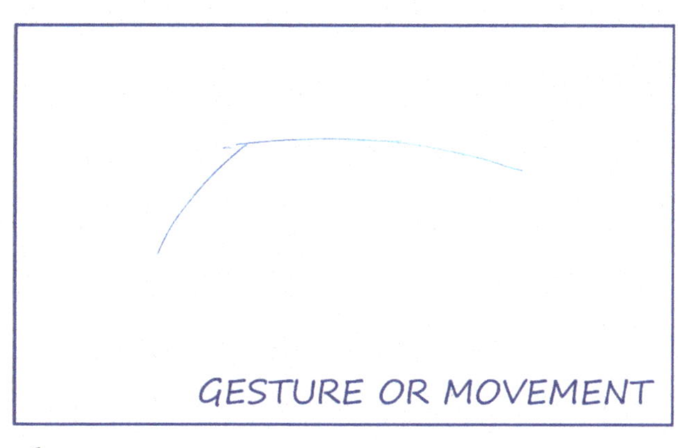


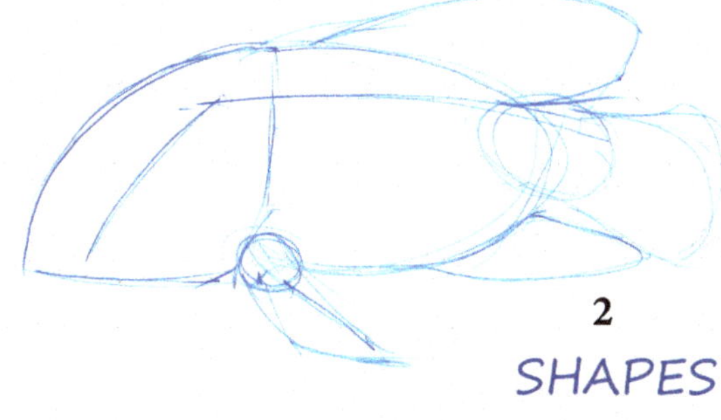


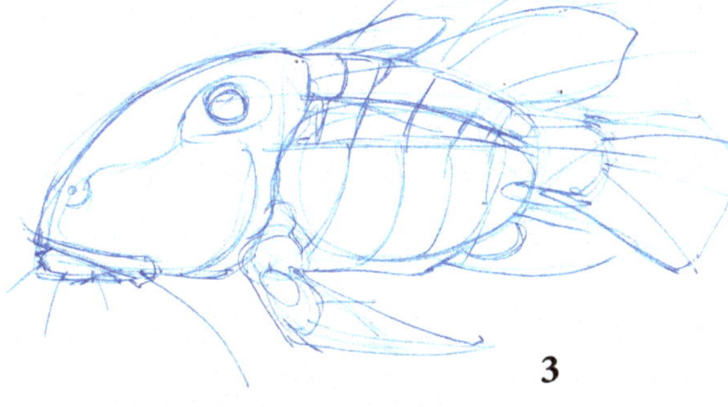


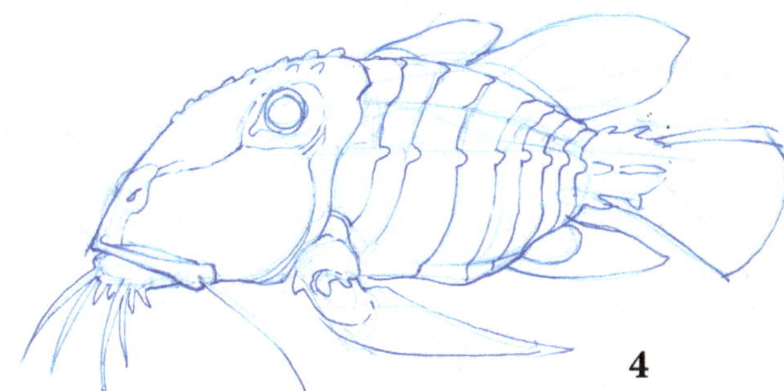


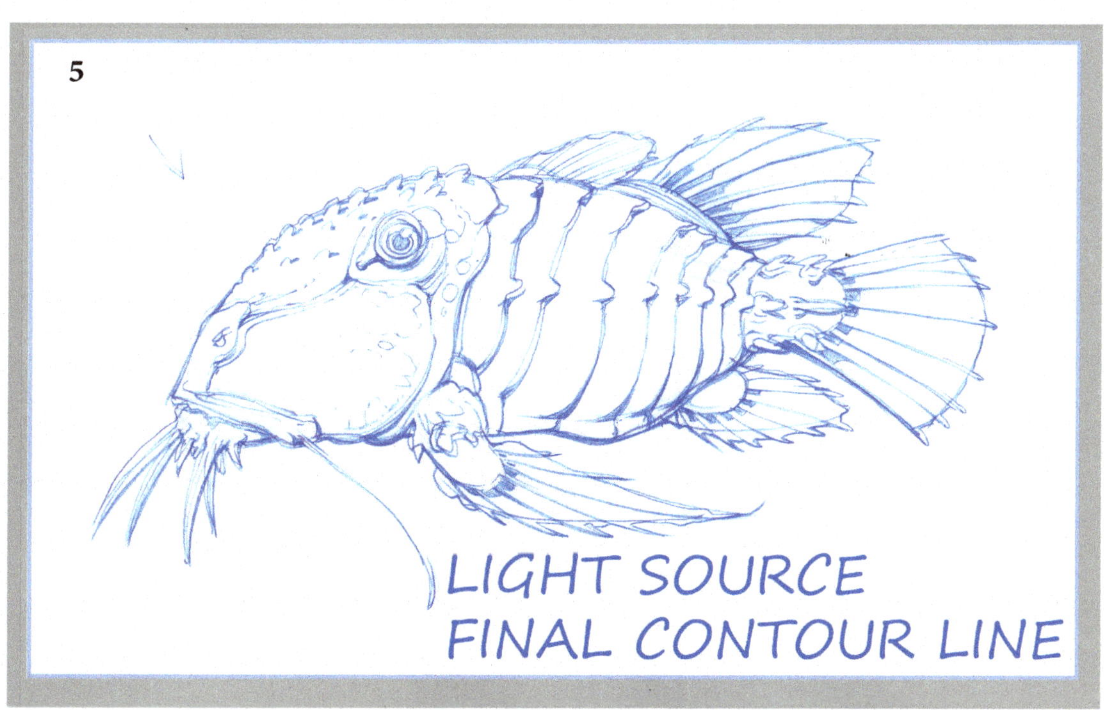

# DRAWING TOOLS

The drawing tools you use will create a certain look.

First, the nib pen has a line that can stay constant. If you push down, it creates variations to the line. It will become thicker with more pressure.

**Drawing 1** is the contour line and form lines to start the fish's development. Here is where I start to develop the light source, which is in the upper left-hand corner. So the lines get darker toward the right.

**Drawing 2** is the first volumetric line drawing. The body is lighter, and some of the fins are darker with patterns. When the lines move away from the light, they get darker and thicker.

**Drawing 3** is pushing the darker values more with crosshatch and creates a different look for our fish.

**Drawing 4** is a contour line with a brush. A brush is a very fluid tool, and your line work takes on a different feel. A thick bold line and adding large black areas are much easier to do with a brush. Each tool has its strengths on how you can finish a drawing. Some artists mix mediums: brush, technical pen, and nib pens.

**Drawing 5** is another variation in brush to push a different look and feel.

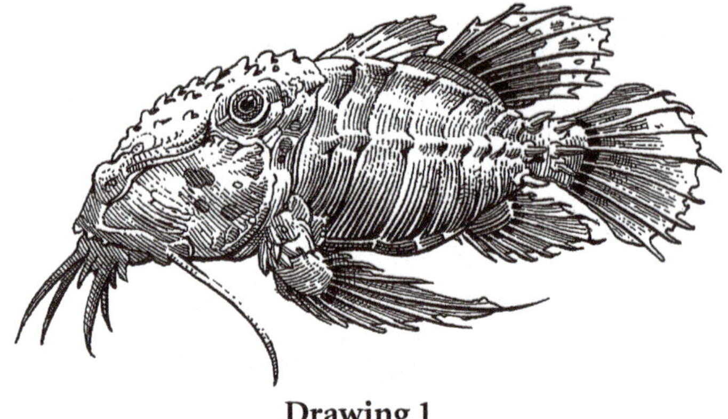

**Drawing 1**

**Drawing 2**

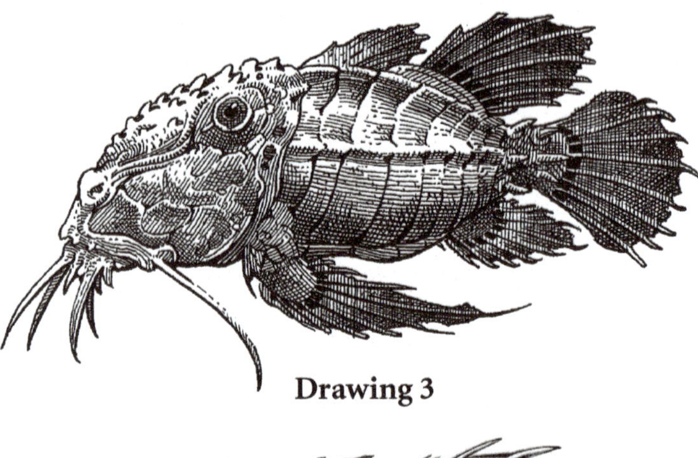

**Drawing 3**

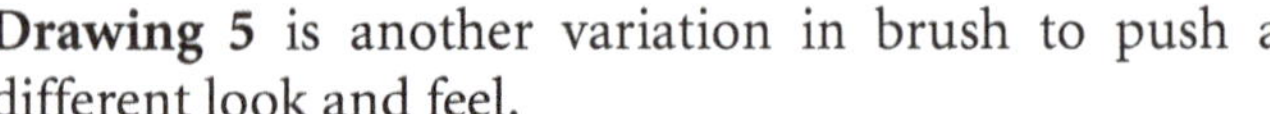

**Drawing 4**

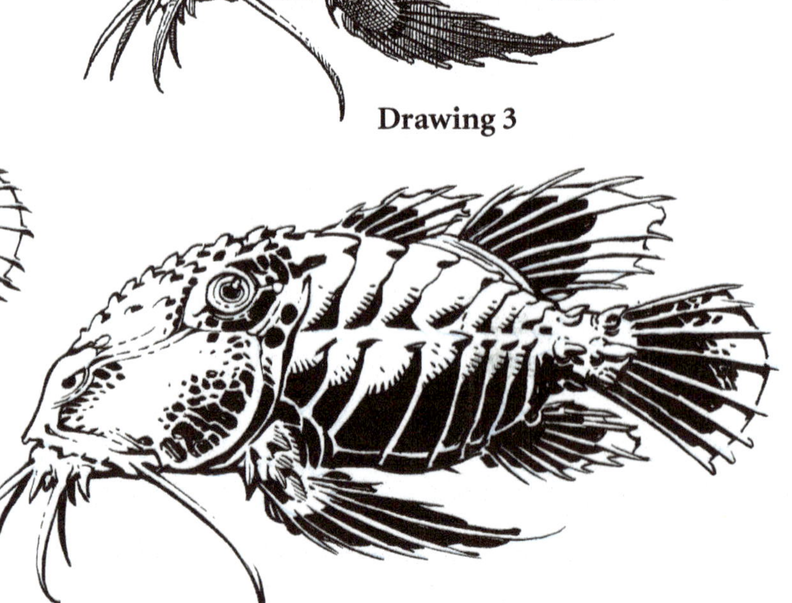

**Drawing 5**

# GRAY SCALE

I come from a background of making art for many different formats, and gray scale is a way to look at your overall value system and keep it in check. This value study can be used as a start for your underpainting by converting this to a brown (or whatever color you want). It helps you to keep track of your lights and darks and to balance your values for reproduction.

Sometimes you don't get to do a finish in color. So a gray scale can be a nice way to flesh out the surfaces and textures in your drawing.

**Drawing 1** was to do a fish with a lighter face and temper into dark.

**Drawing 2** was the opposite, with a darker face and lighter body.

**Drawing 3** added some stripes and patterns.

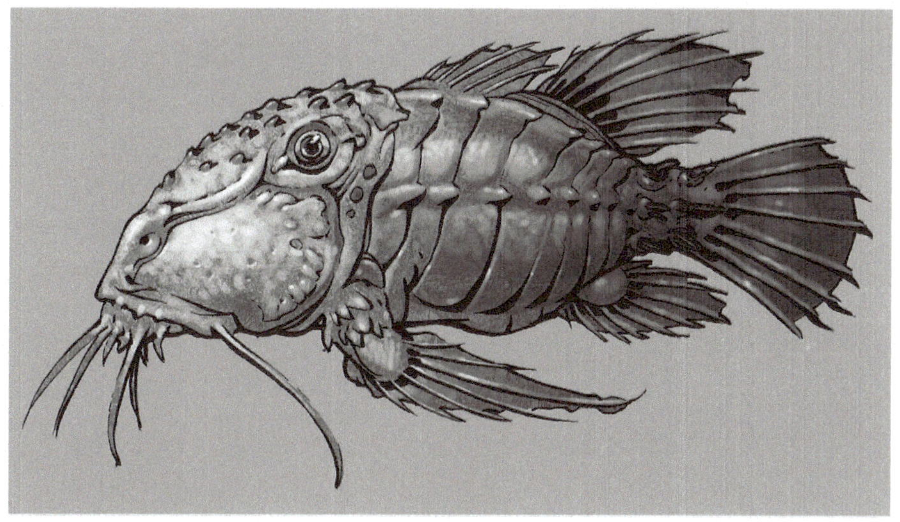

**Drawing 1**

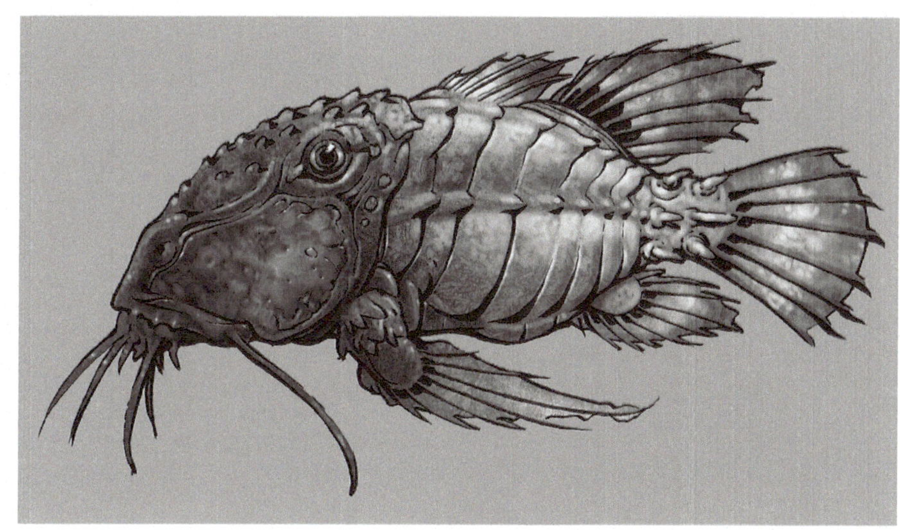

**Drawing 2**

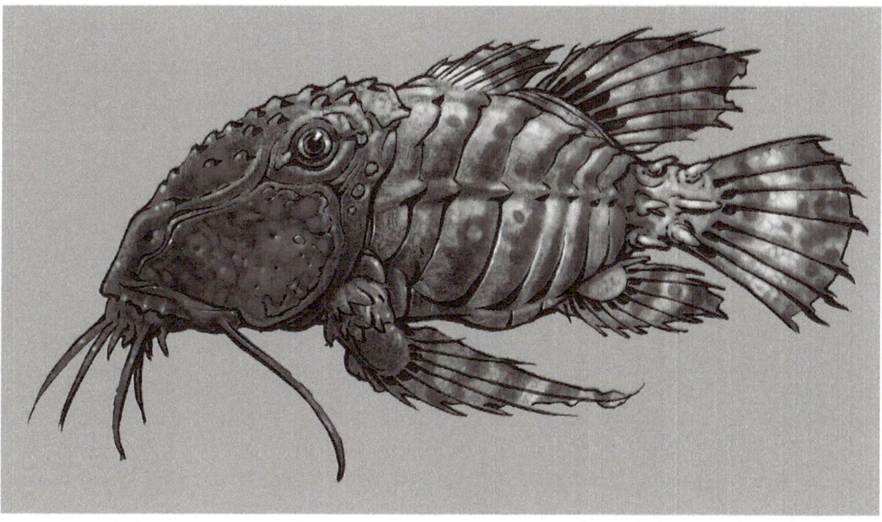

**Drawing 3**

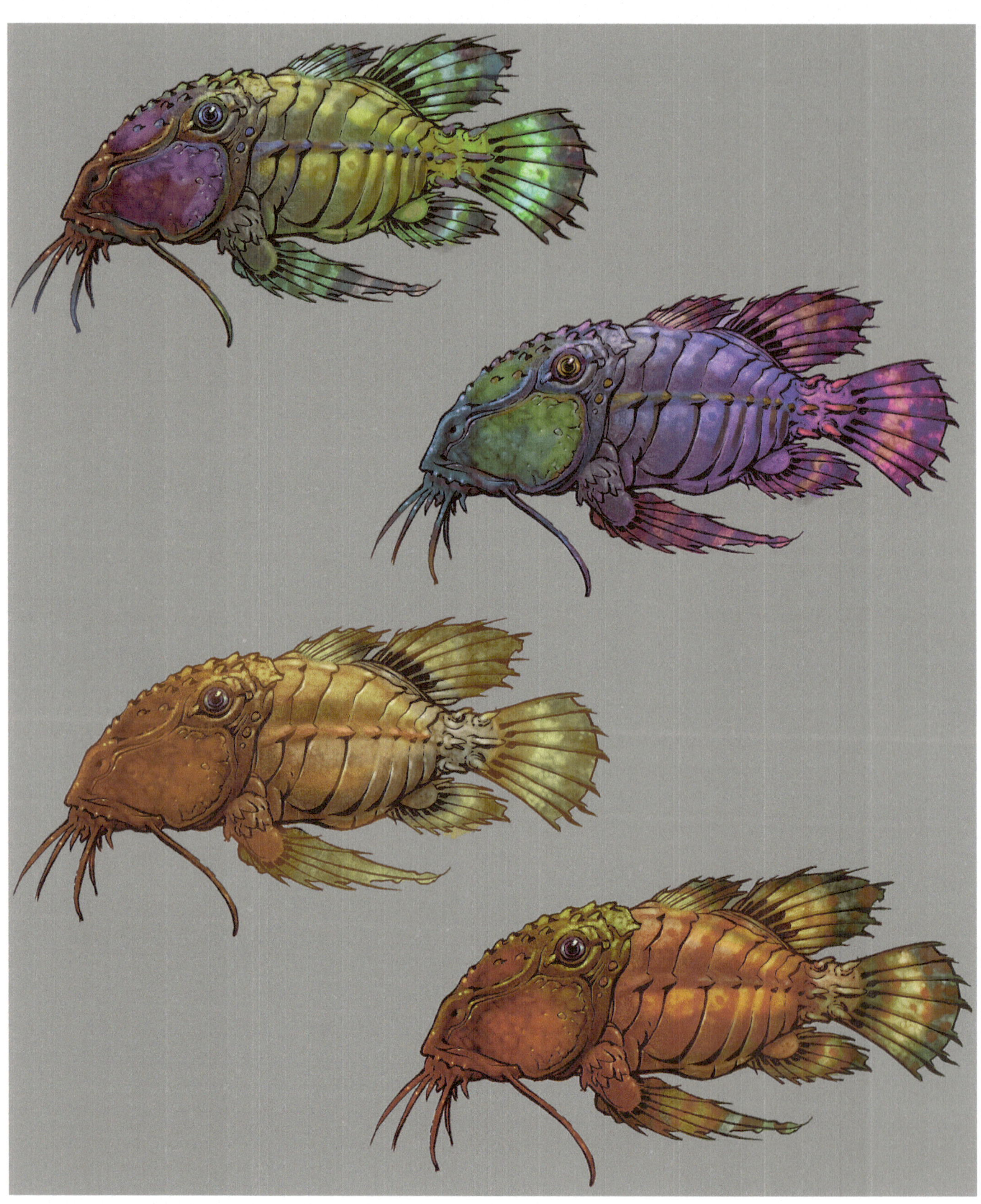

Color can be used to create all sorts of looks for your fish. The fish that live in the coral reefs are brightly colored and have many different patterns and camouflage. Fish in rivers and lakes have various types of designs, and they can range from colorful to neutral. Sometimes the female will be colorless so as not to draw attention. The male may have strong patterns to attract the female.

Ink has always been a favorite medium of mine. It offers such a rich line and expressiveness for line variation, and with crosshatch or washes, you can achieve a different type of softness. Ink also gives you dense darks, which is one of its qualities.

Here are some inked fish.

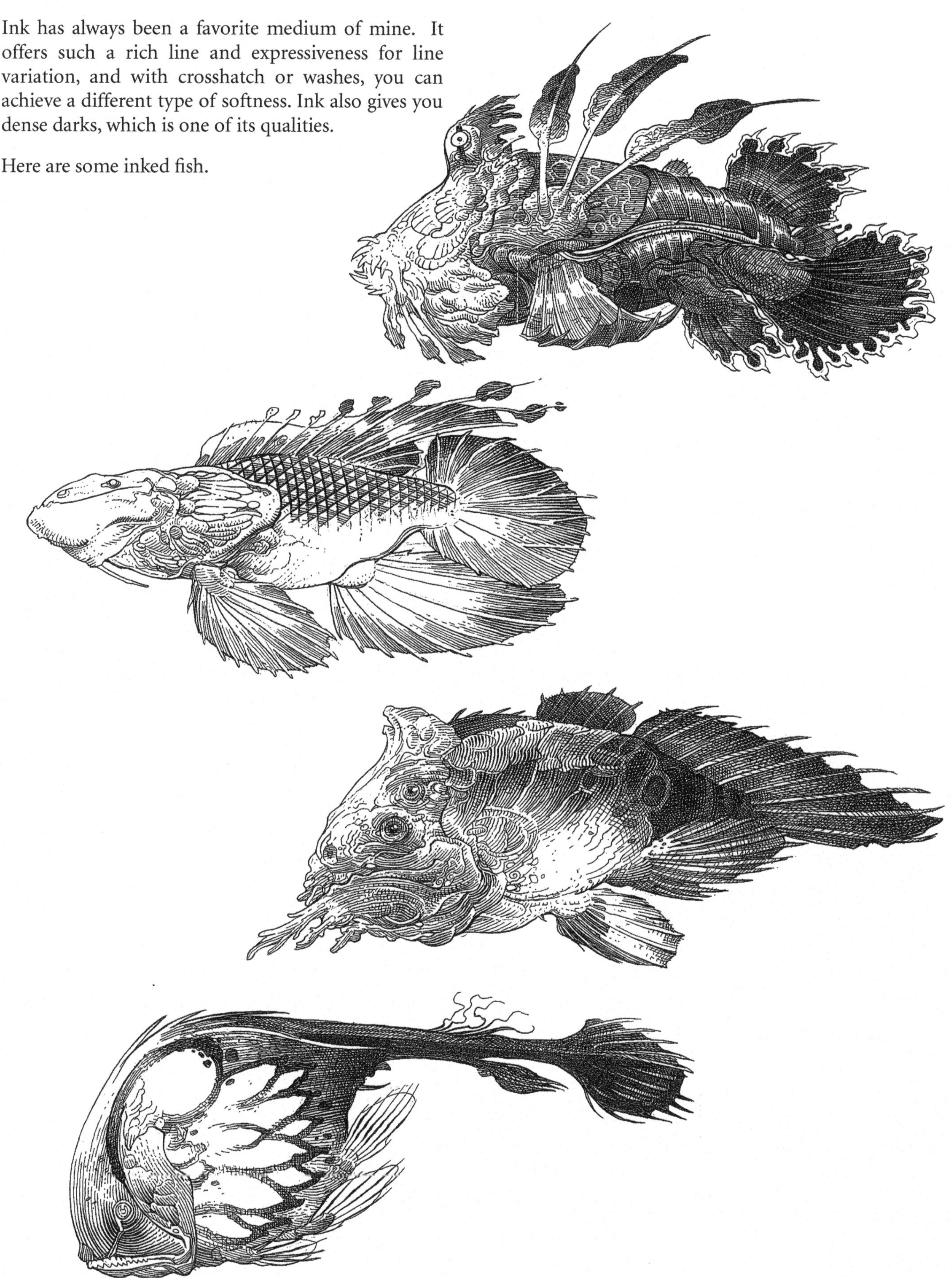

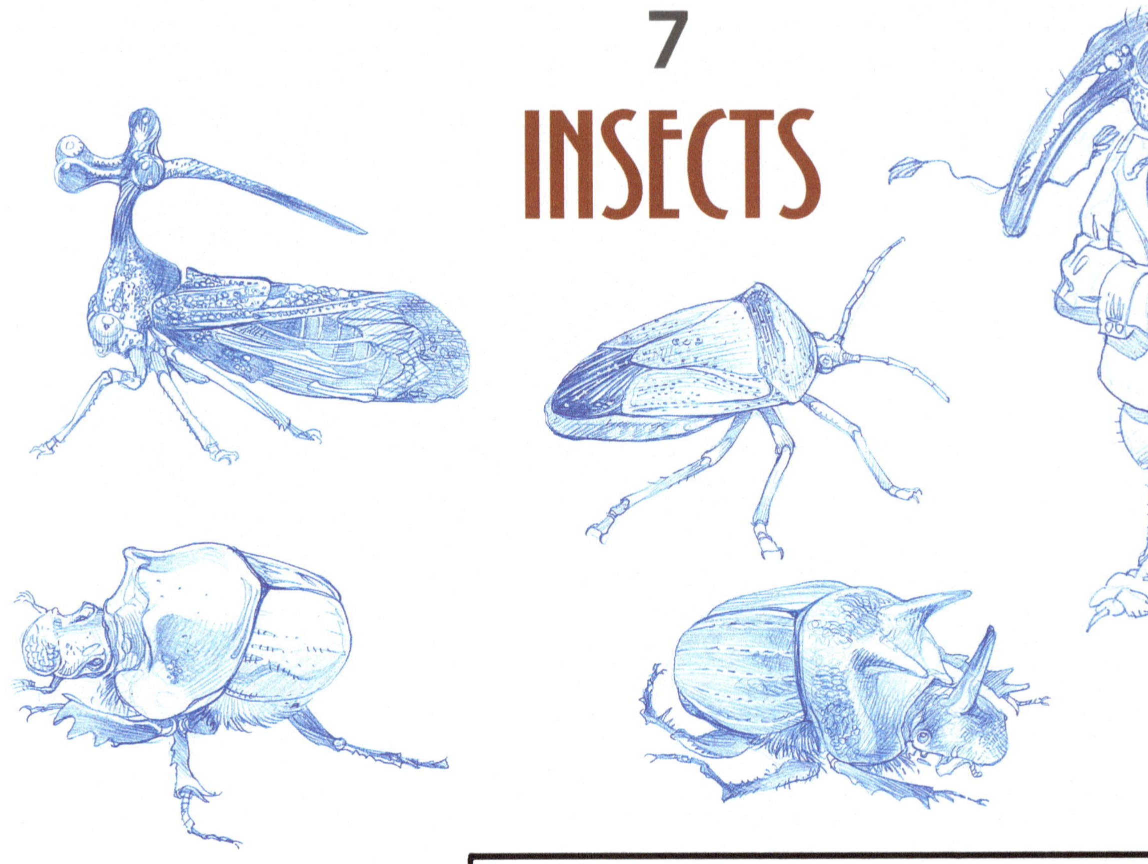

# 7
# INSECTS

Arthropods wear their skeletons on the outside. Human skeletons are covered with muscle and tissue, the armored knights of the world. There are so many different types of insects, and they are the most numerous creatures on planet Earth. They represent 80 percent of the world's species! Insects have been represented in many myths and folktales.

The three parts of an arthropod are the head; the thorax, where the legs and wings originate; and the abdomen, which carries most of the organs.

Their legs work on a similar principle as humans', with the femur, tibia, and tarsus. (Femur, tibia, tarsals, metatarsals, and phalanges are on human legs and feet.) Here, you can see some of the functional variations for running, jumping, catching prey, and digging.

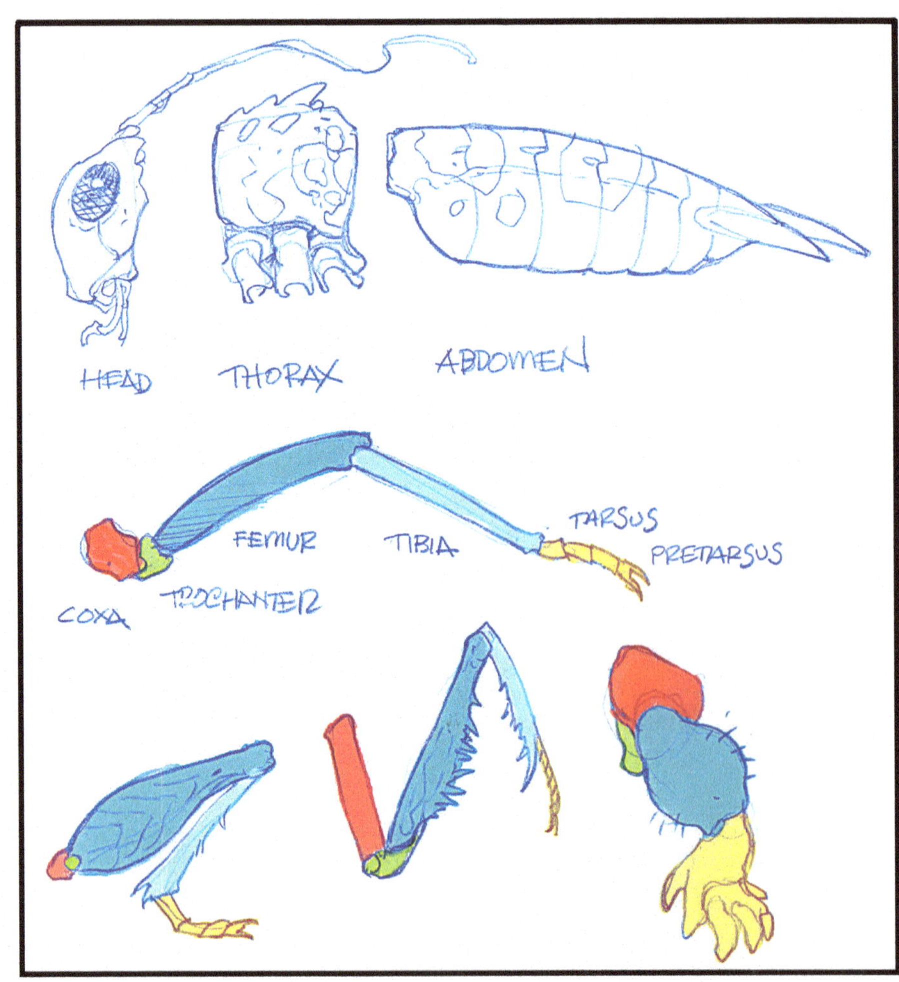

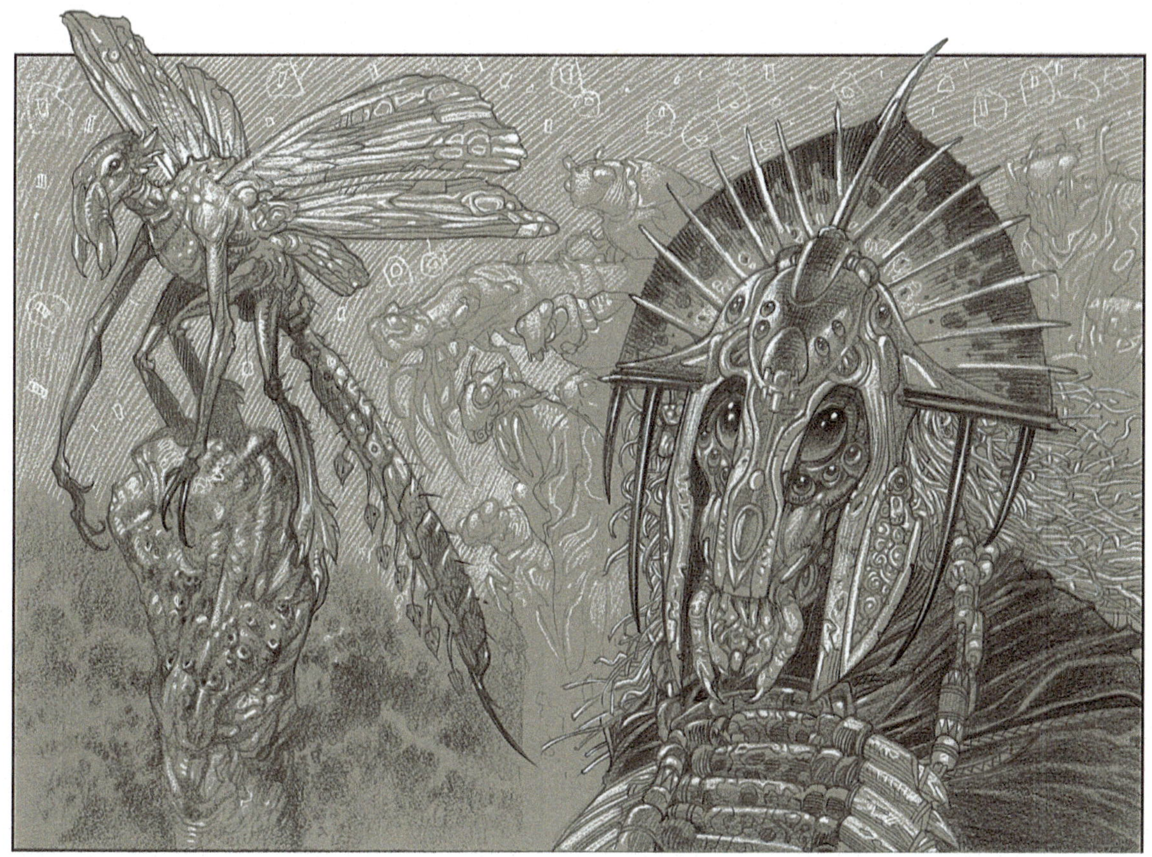

The toned drawing is of an insect god and its messenger from a story set in the *Thunder Hunters* world.

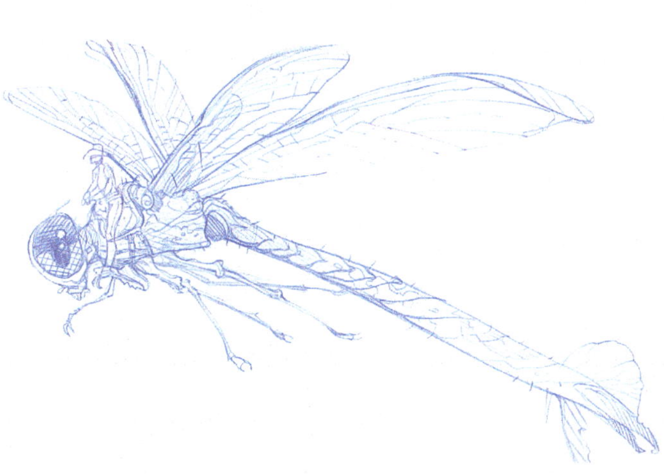

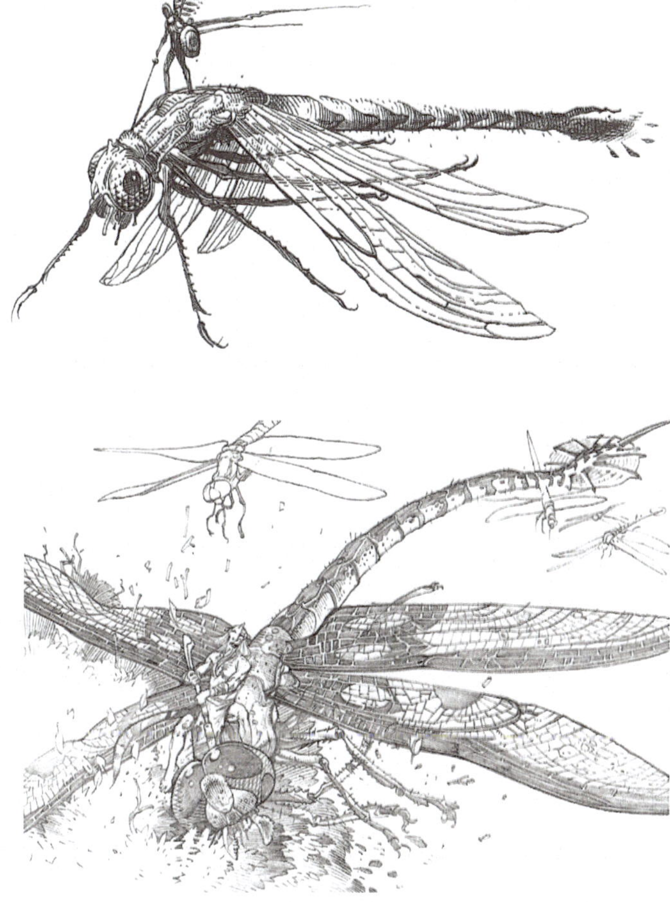

Dragonflies always have been of interest to me. Here in Texas, there are dragonflies of many different types and colors, and watching them in the garden is amazing. Here are some different dragonfly riders.

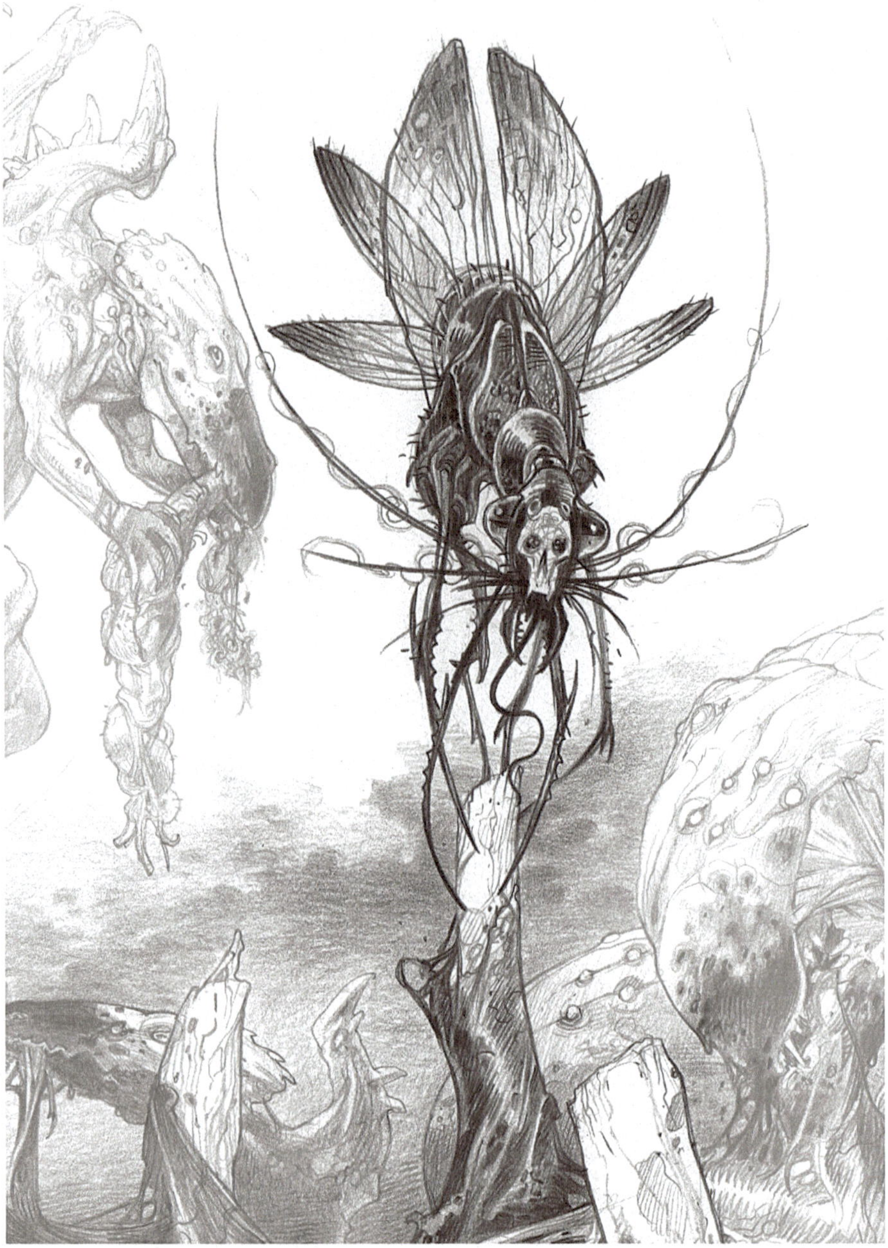

Carrion beetles help recycle organisms in the chain of life, so I did a death-face beetle among other carrion eaters starting the cycle.

Grasshoppers and locusts come in a range of body shapes and sizes. They are harbingers of good and evil, depending on when and how they come. The plague of locusts that eats all the crops is not welcome. But as a food source, they can be cooked in various manners and consumed.

The look that I worked with on the grasshopper was more of an old woodcut, using cross-contour lines to wrap the form. And because it is old, it has some type of branch growth.

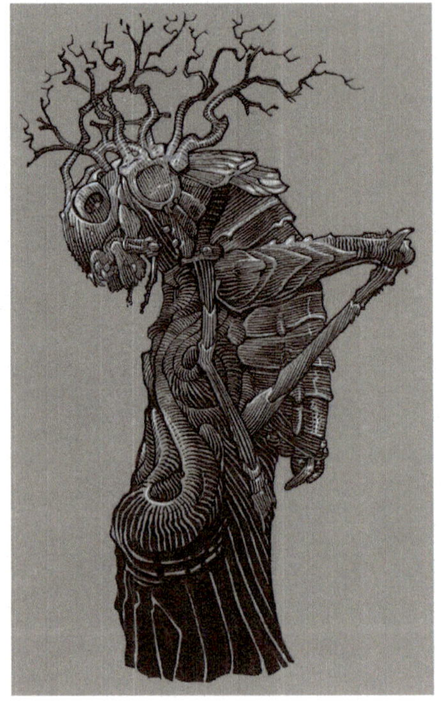

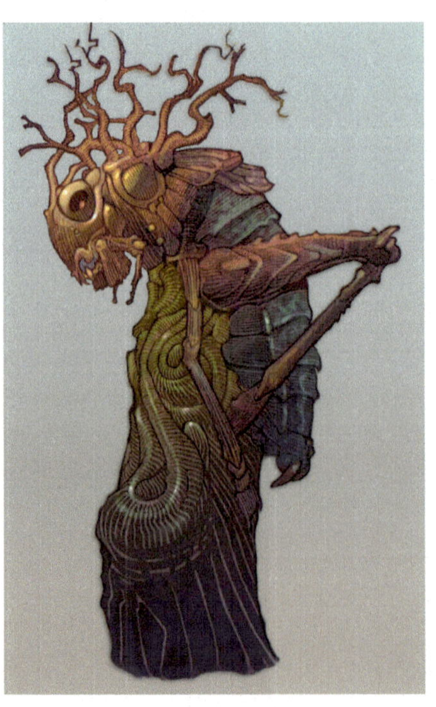

Let's twist the rules and add more legs, a small abdomen, teeth, and a complex shell with withered wings. The greatest thing is you can do this! It's your world to push down any path. Those paths can be as far from reality as you want. The one rule that I do try to follow, though, is to make it feel believable. With that said, your creation should have a form, volume, and function to be a life figure. Push the rules as far as you want. It can be nothing but a mouth with teeth. Can you make it work? This is the question you should ask yourself.

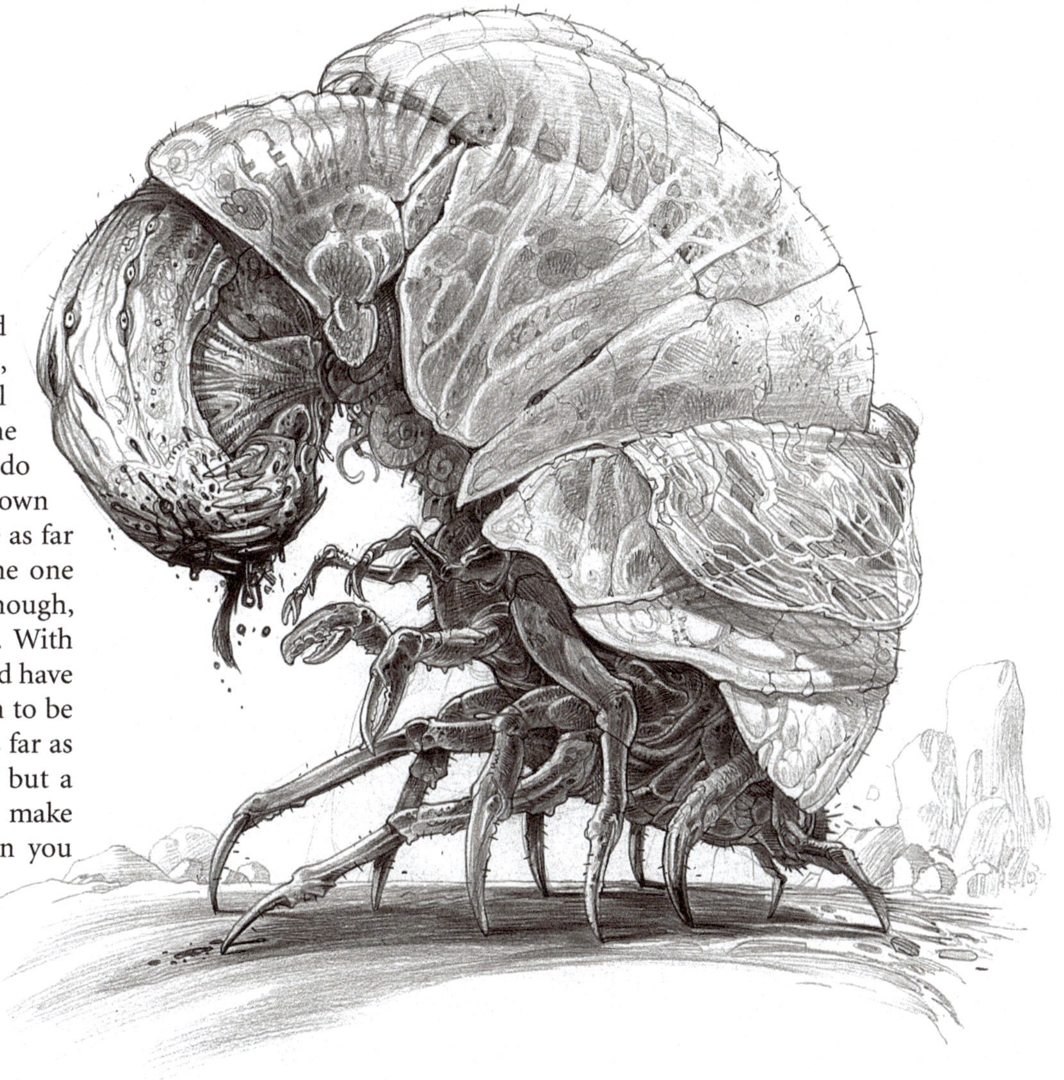

## DOING STUDIES

I was working on a story that had sand fleas. Here are some of the variations in line.

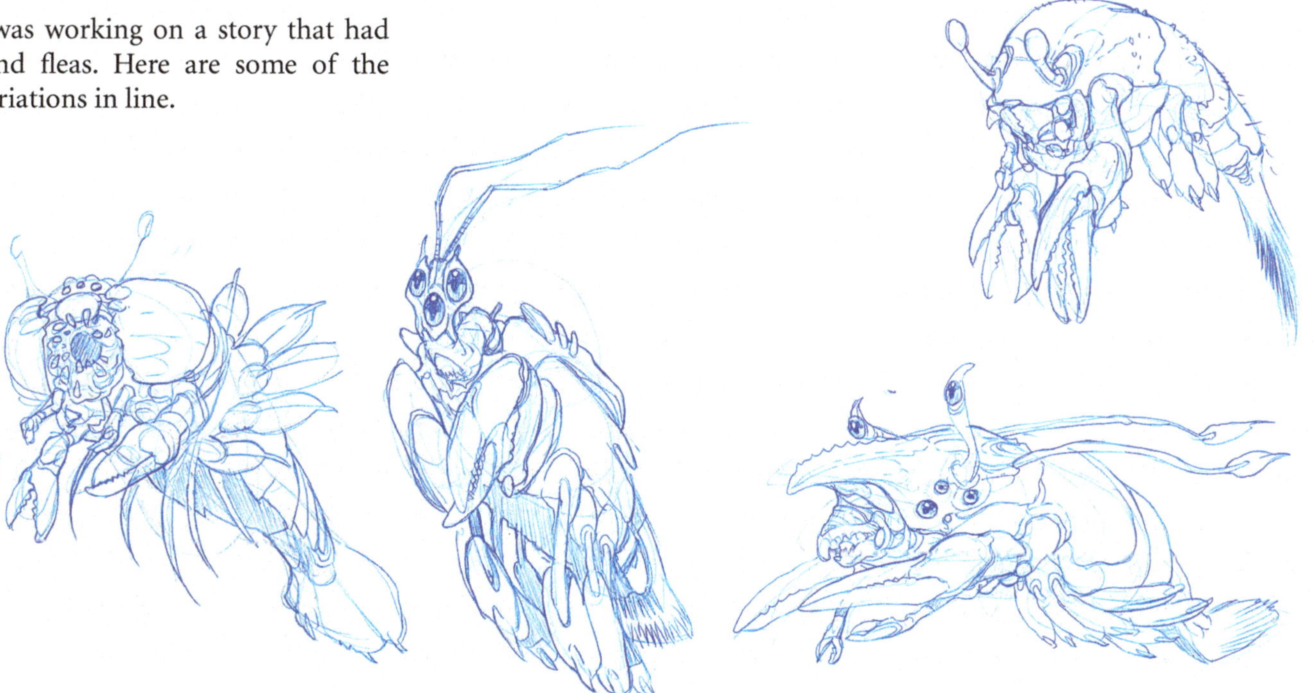

I once watched an ant colony start its new growth pattern and send out its winged queens. This led me to two thoughts: One, was it a heavily armored queen or could it be one of the royal guards? Two, what would a flying Venus flytrap creature that hunts down these flying morsels look like?

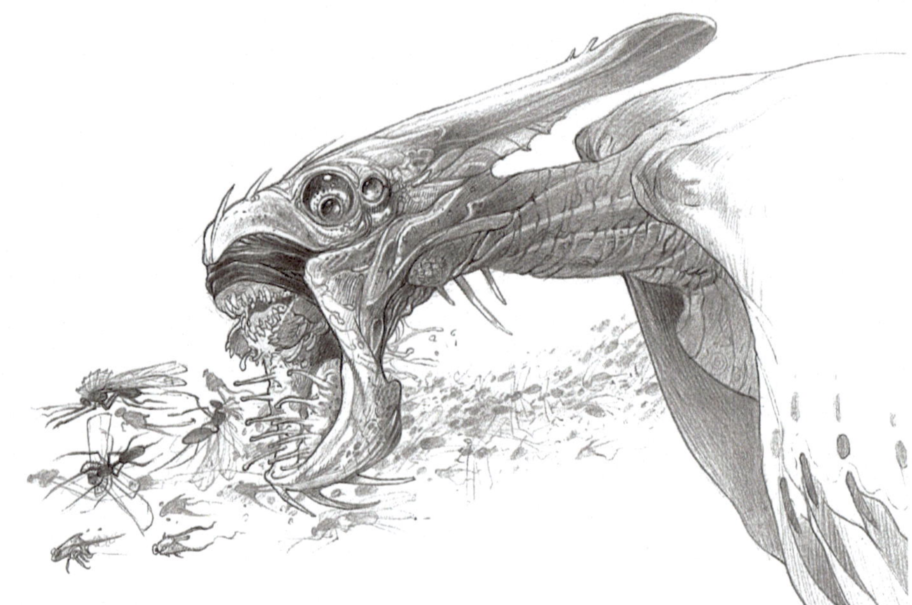

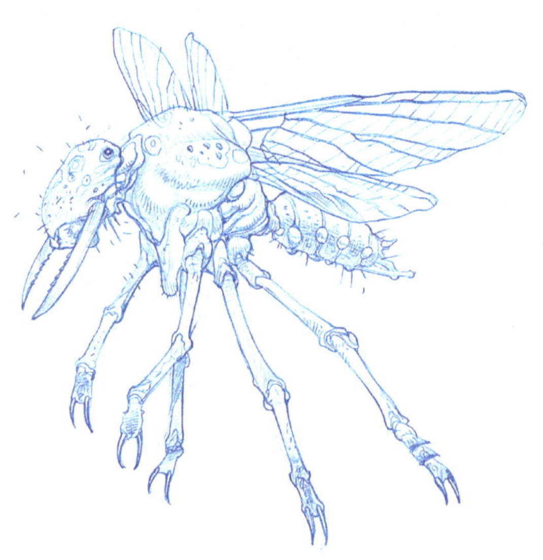

## "THE CROSSING"

The pencils of the page with the sand fleas. They are active little creatures jumping and leaping. But the more important questions are "What do they eat?" and "Do you want to walk across their sand?"

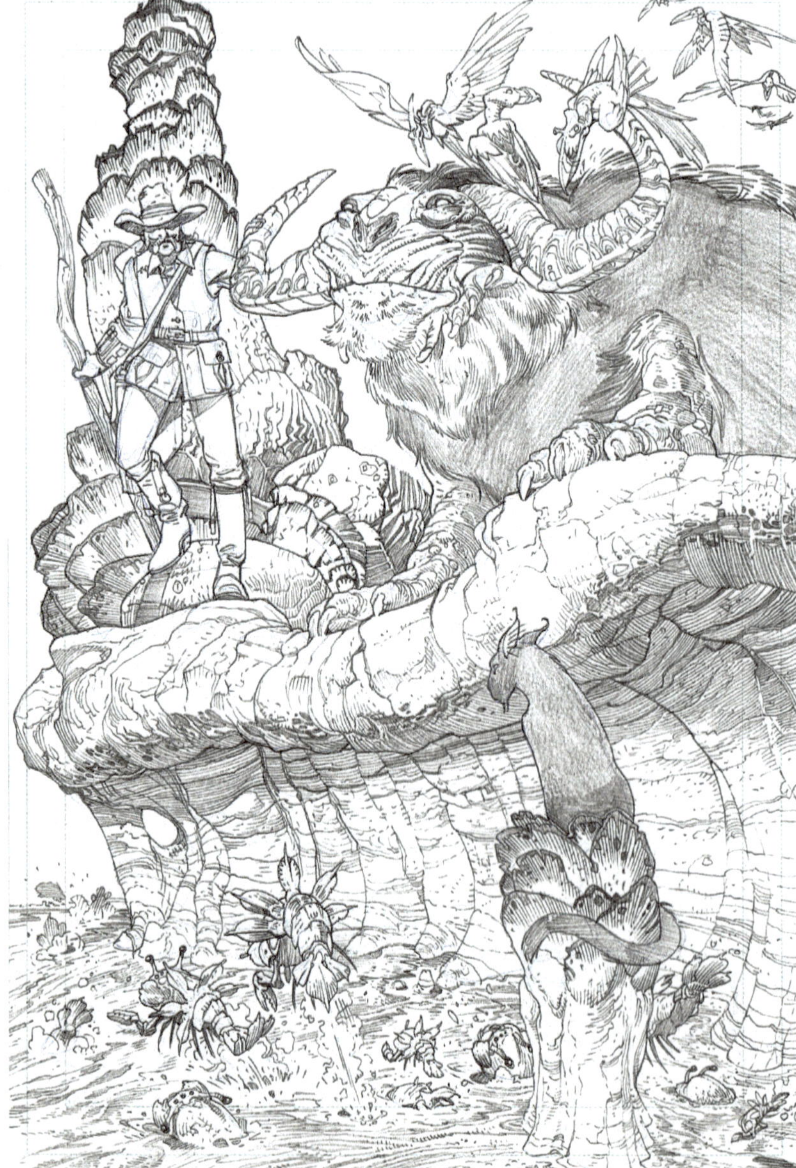

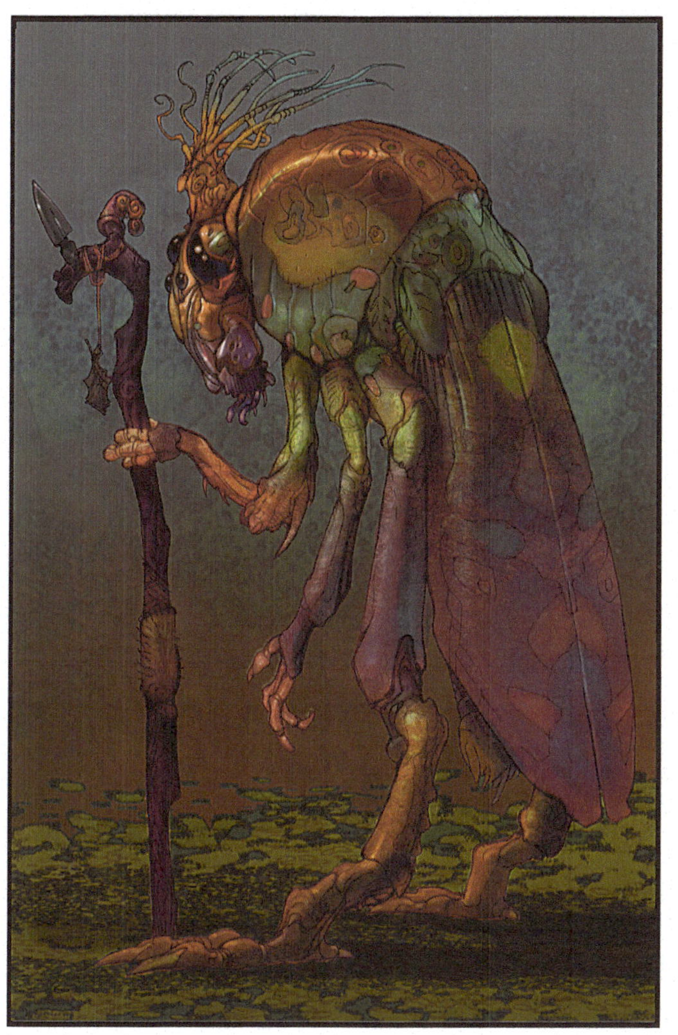

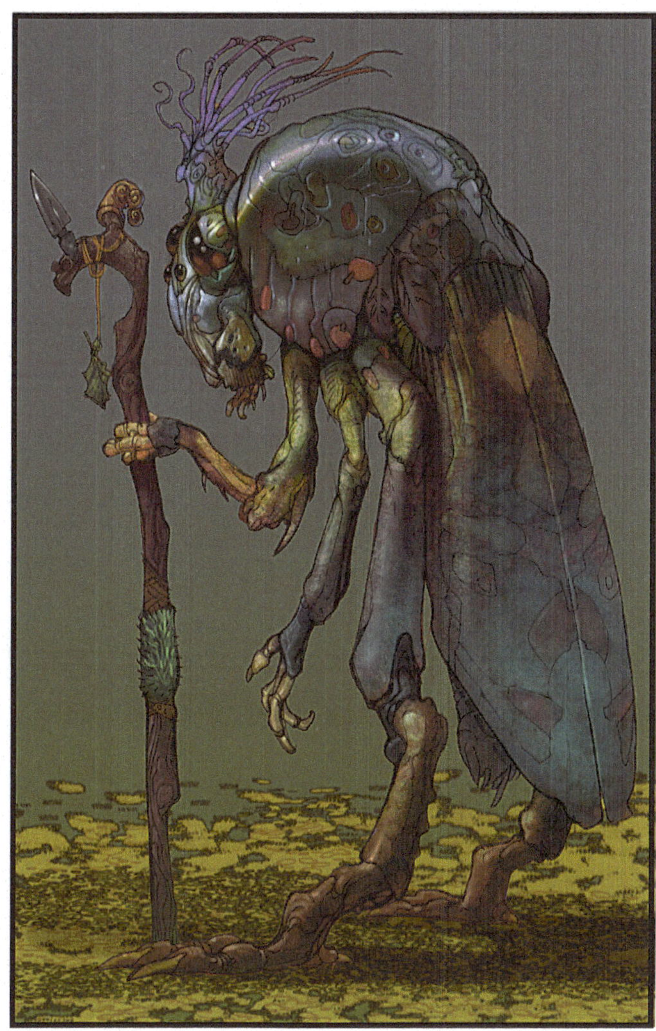

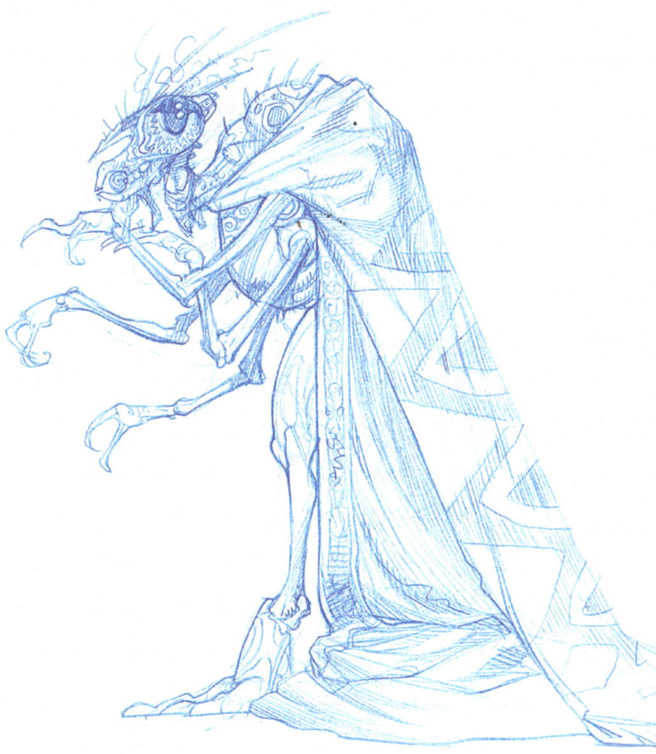

If you put four of the same species of beetle on your desk, at first glance, they all seem the same. It's not until you observe them for a spell that you are able to tell them apart. The easiest thing to do is use color or body adornment. So here we have the red and blue insect shamans. In a video game, you could use the same model and assign different skins to it.

One thing that I try to do with my creatures is give them body language. How do they stand? What are their hands doing? Types of clothing? What personal objects do they carry? Body decoration?

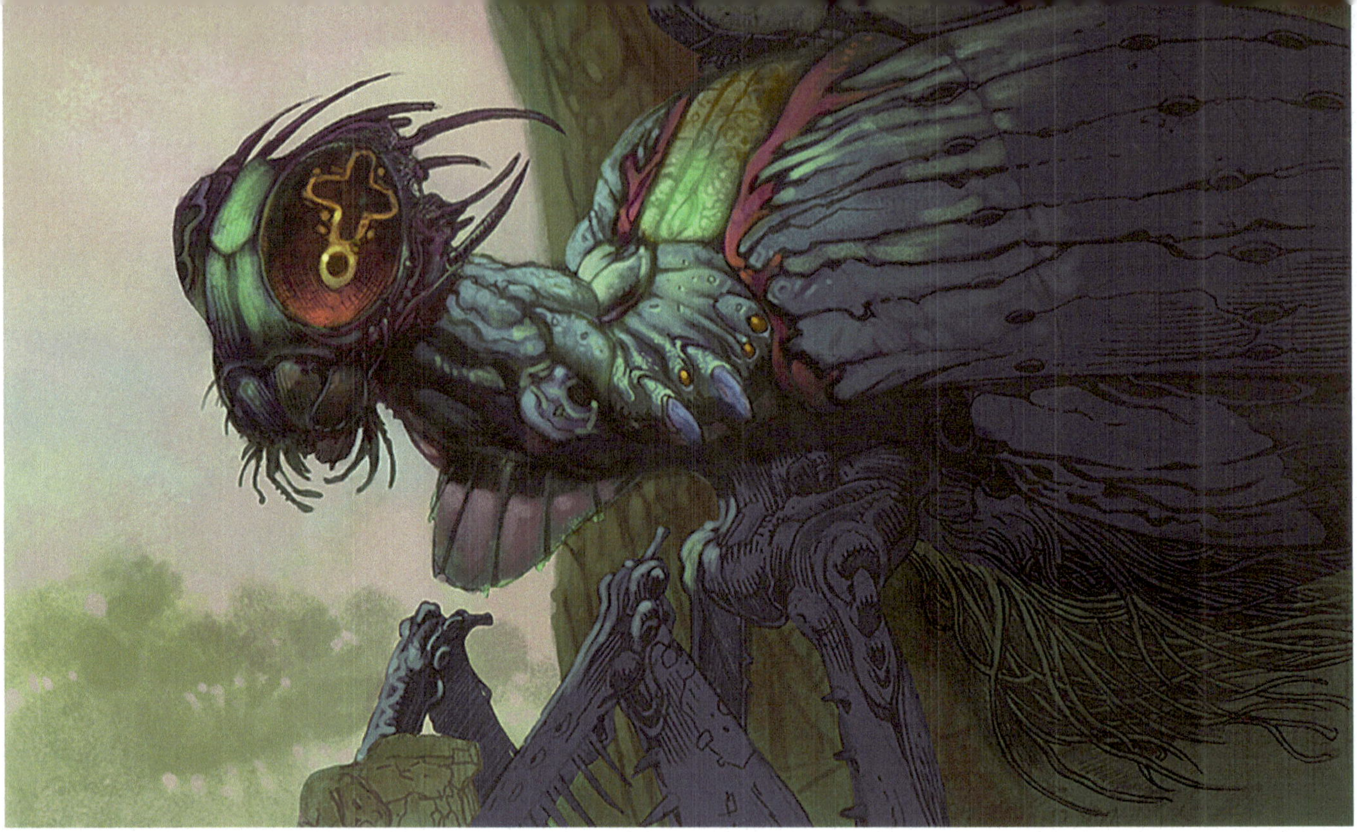

Iteration becomes something you think of and do very quickly on the computer. You can work from gray scale to color, layer soft tones, change colors quickly for your roughs, and then polish and finish.

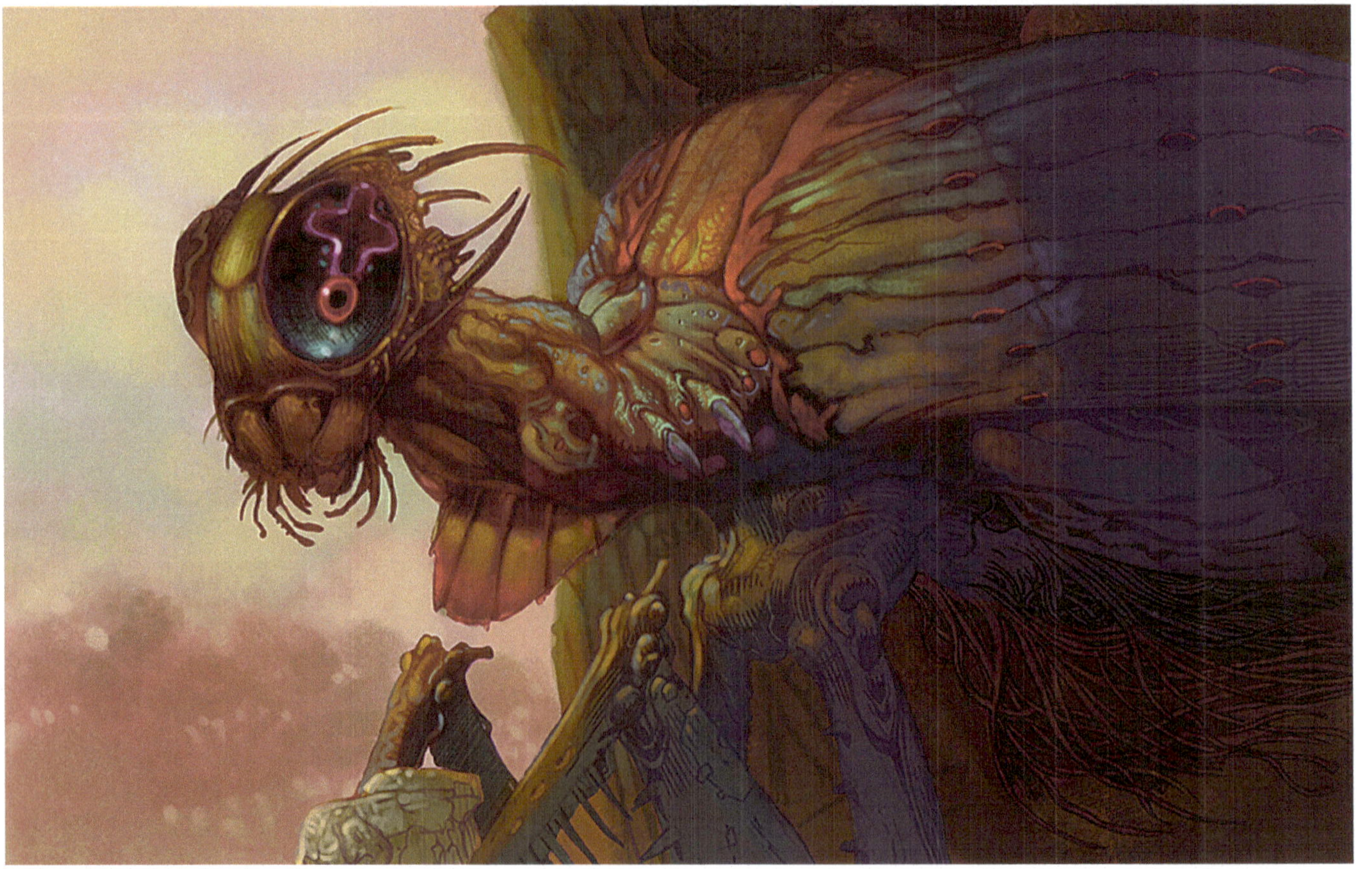

It is nice because you can take chances and see what mixing does. I can take a gray scale, turn it into a brown (or whatever color you want) underpainting, and then keep building.

# 8
# SURVIVAL



The Hunter-Gatherer has different ways of surviving. The food that we eat or that eats us can be an element to create all kinds of levels in a world. There can be more than just a large stein of fermented brew and a turkey leg. How do the characters hunt? What do they hunt? How does that fit into the society as we will come to know it? Everyone has a favorite dish that no one else in the family will eat. And the opposite is true: where everyone fights for that special dish. There is all the food we have at our celebrations, from weddings to holidays.

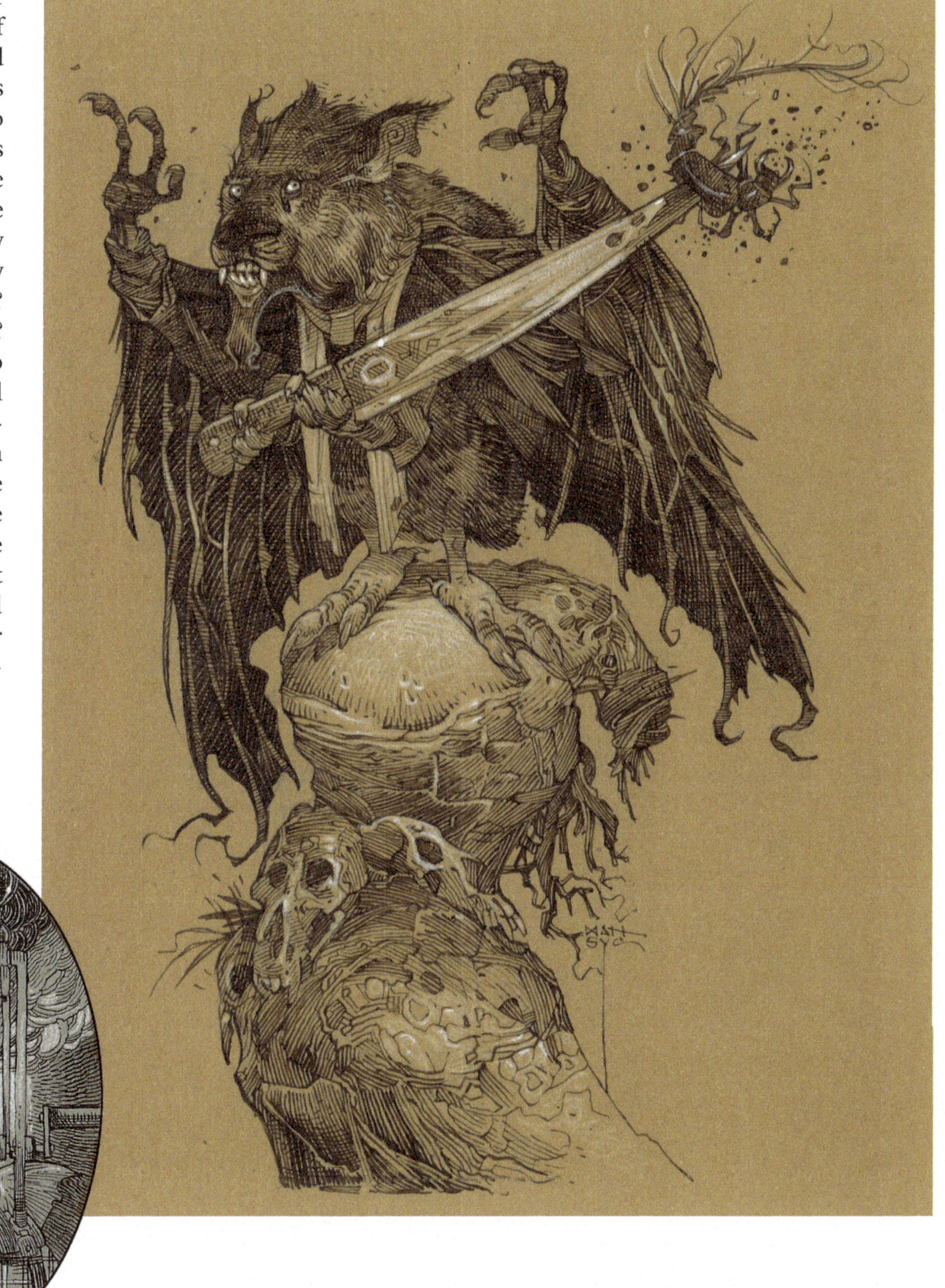

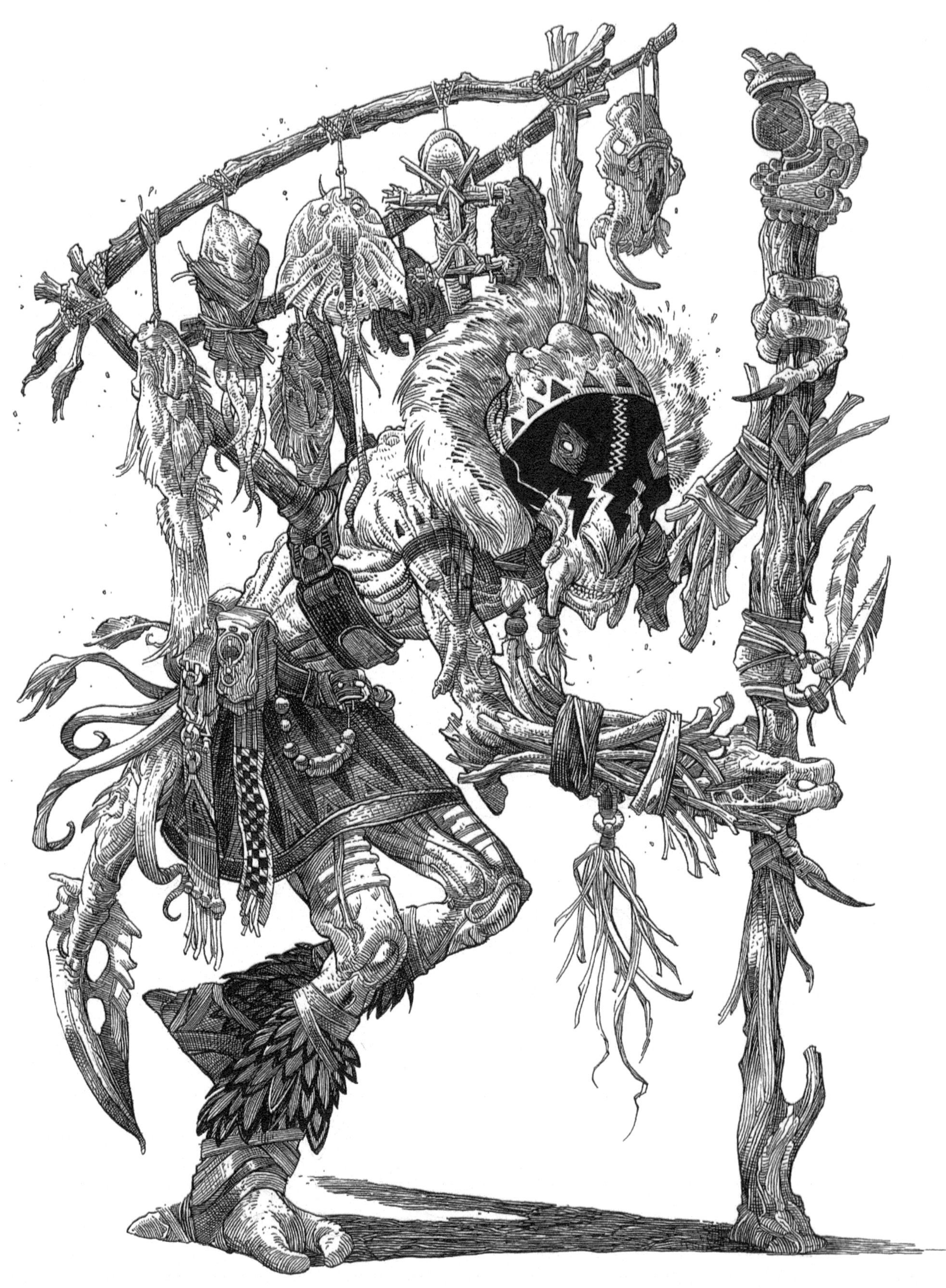

How do you bring your catch to market? Are these elements in the cure for what ails you? The start of magical potions? What will the shaman bring, and how do you ingest it? There is more mystery about food that you can bring to your world.

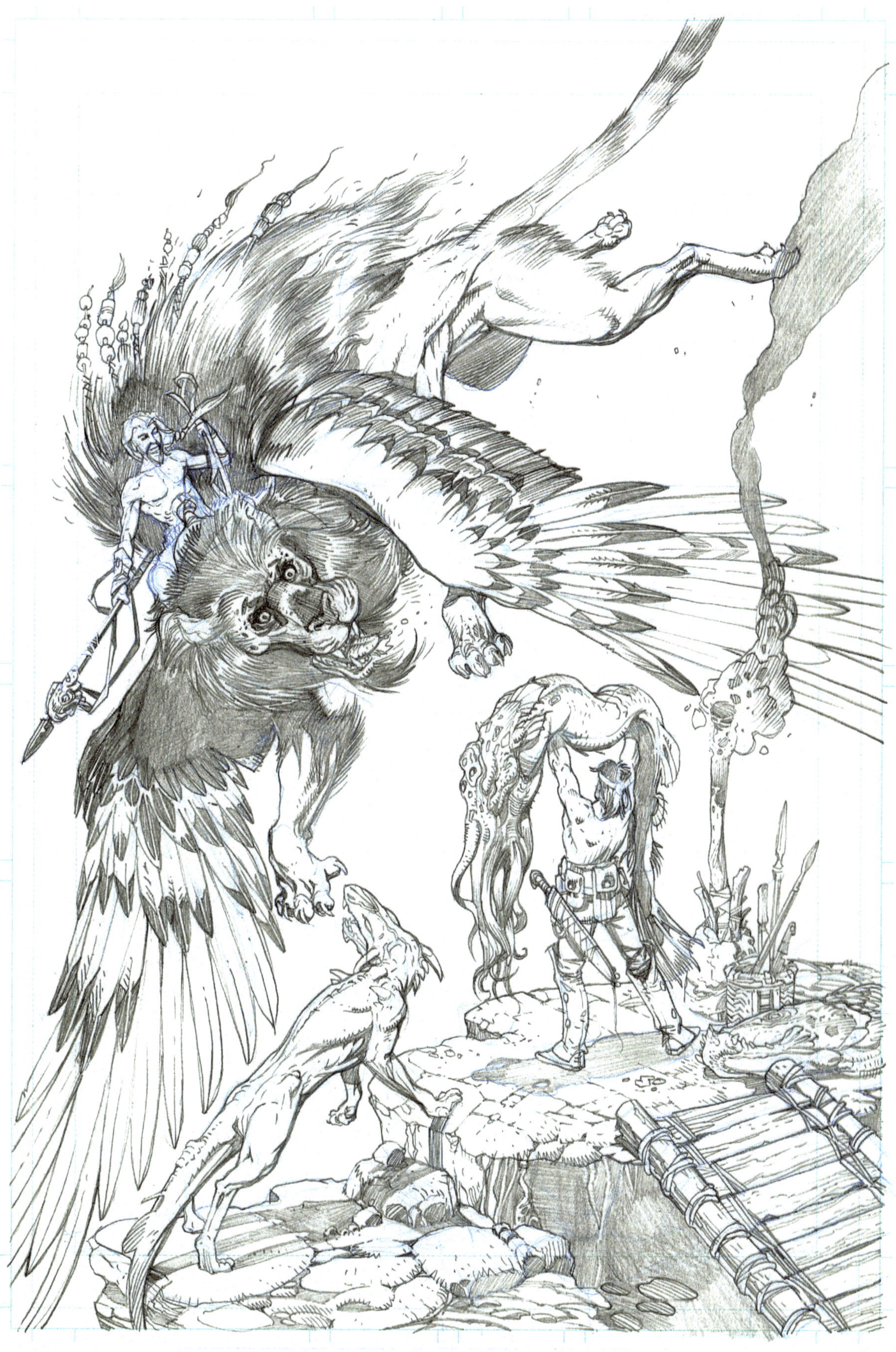

You can use food for exchange, trade, or barter. Think of all the fishmongers, meat peddlers, pastry shops, and bakeries. This is a small selection of what can be in your world.

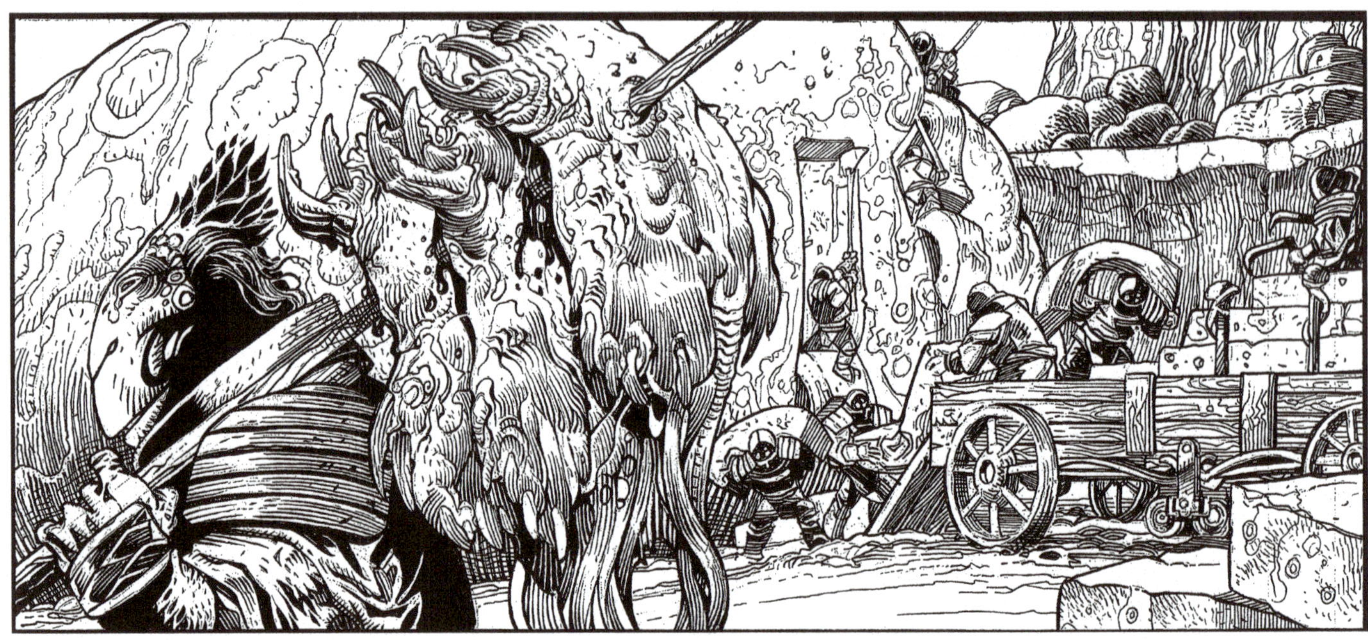

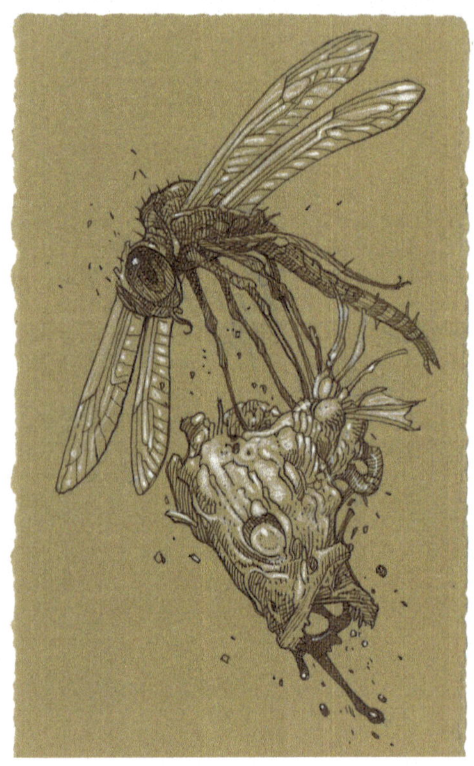

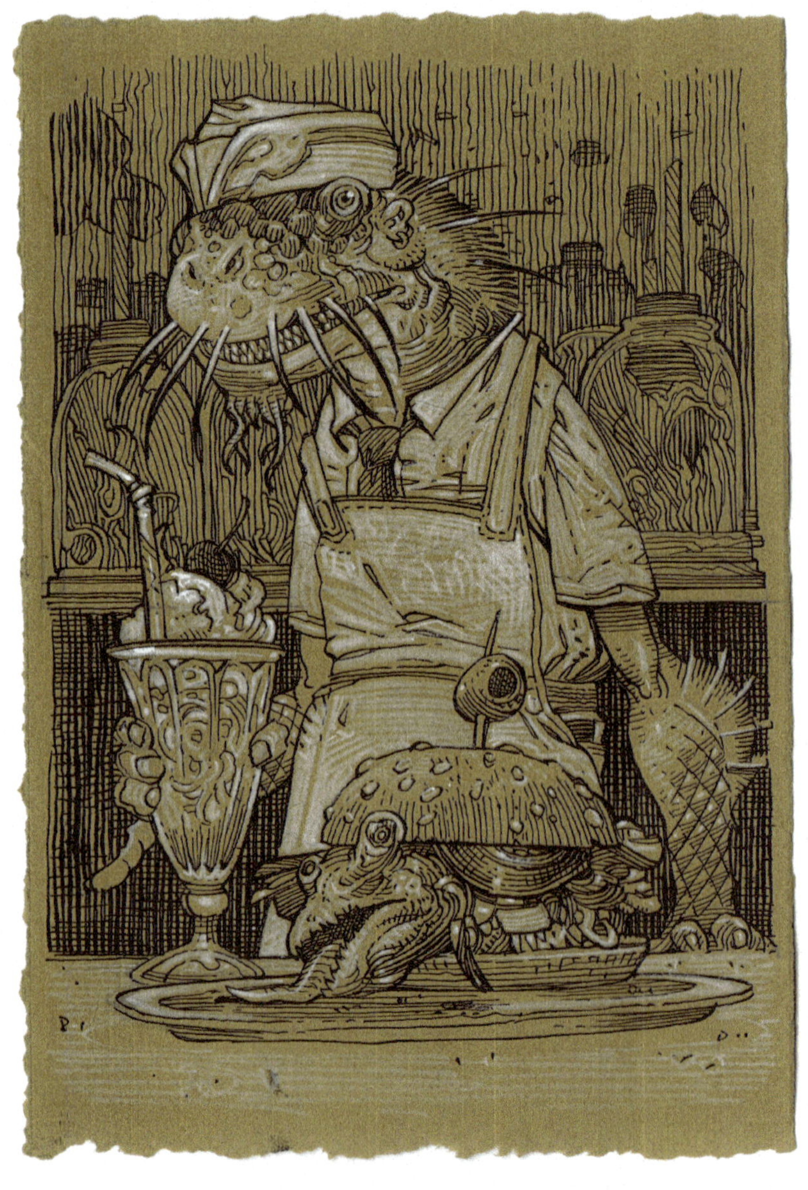

The top ink drawing is of the Giant Jellyfish hunters. You can see the huge jellyfish slabbed in the background. One of the hunters is carrying the speared parasites that live on and in the creature. Do we eat everything of what we hunt?

The second drawing shows that everything must eat, even the insects.

Third, a soda jerk in the world of Innsmouth, because we all have our favorite eatery!

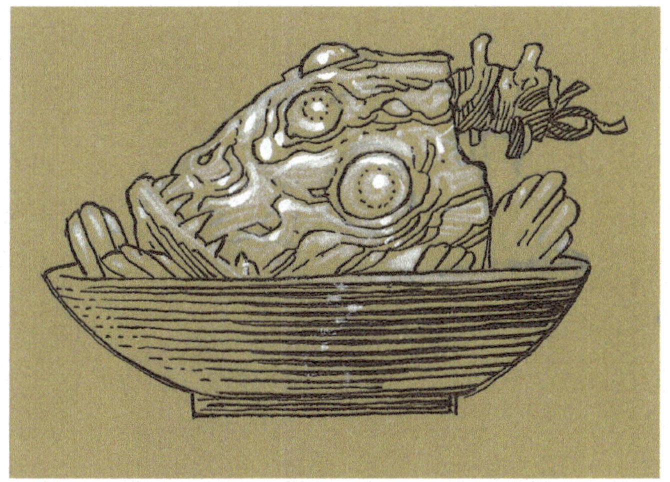

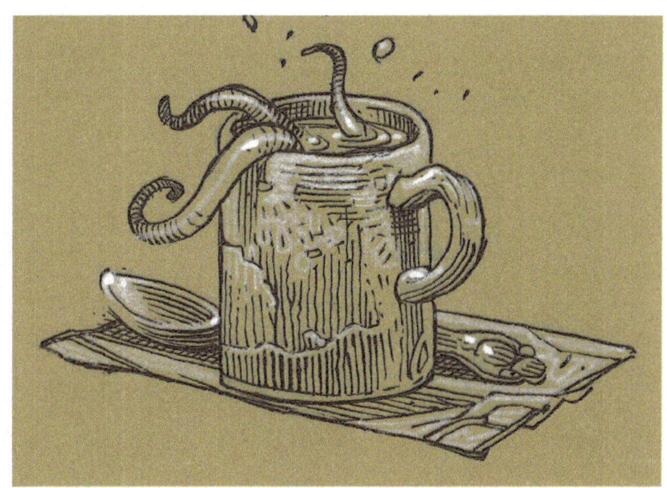

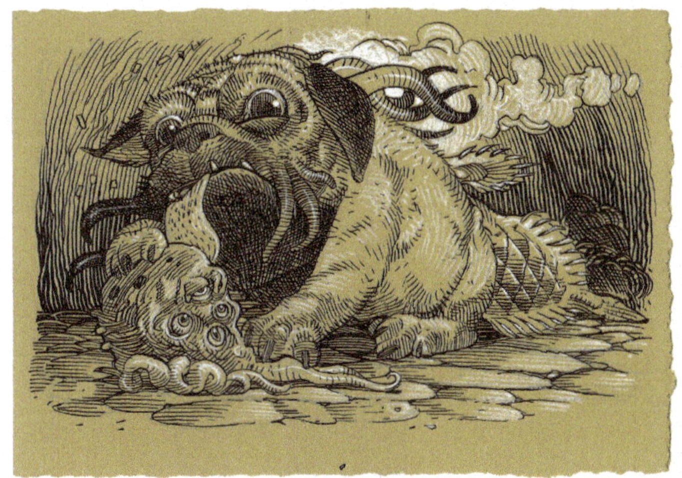

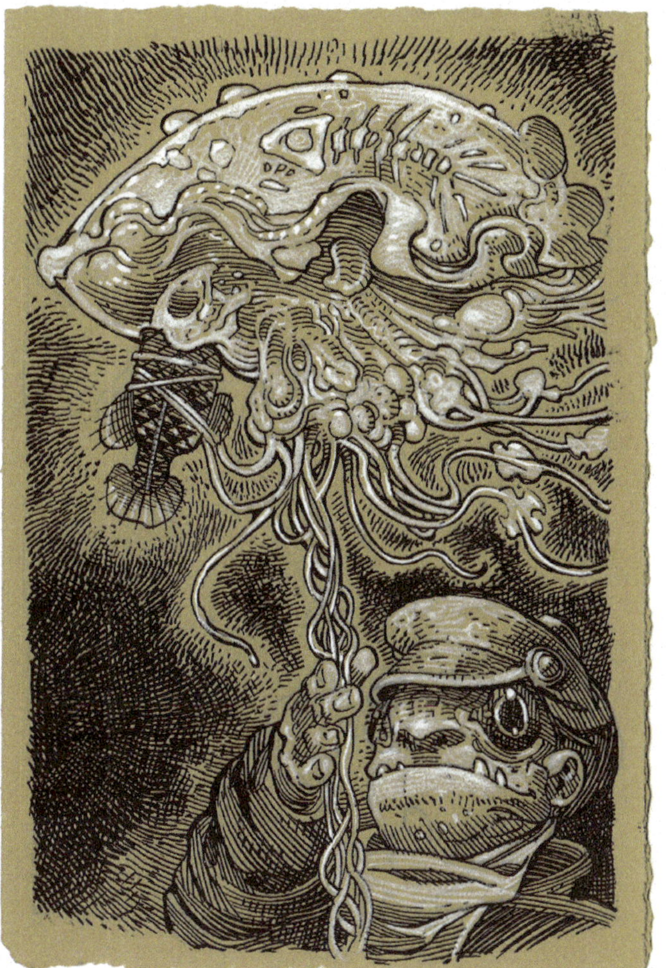

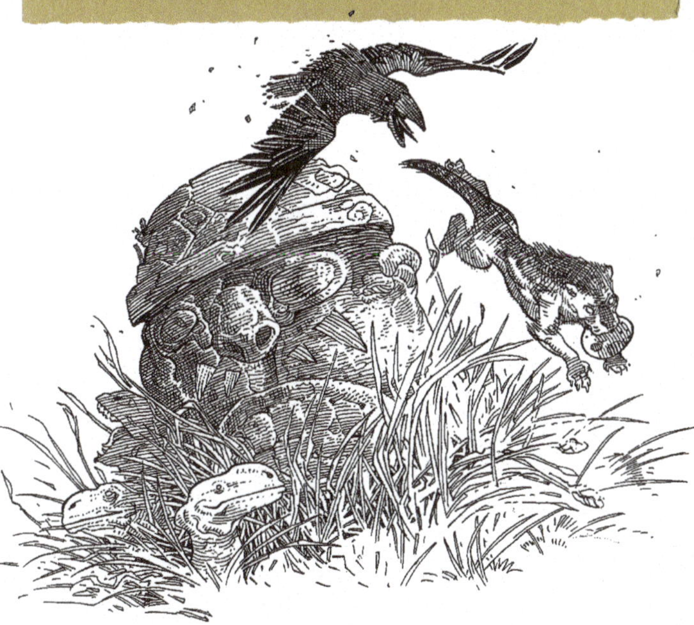

Sometimes it's the little things that can get you thinking. It's the appetizer at your favorite restaurant, your morning drink, a snack for your pet, or the feeding of your beloved jellyfish. Then there are those who work a little harder to bring in the food. All these can be detailed elements that bring life to your world.

This is how I add color to a drawing when I want to keep the pencil line as an integral part of the finished piece. This can be done in several ways. First, in Photoshop, change the pencil layer to Overlay mode and paint beneath it. I prefer to separate the line out and have it on a layer by itself. As I paint, I have the line visible and work on the color layer below.

Step one: I paint the underneath color, using a two-value start to the flats (light side and dark side). Then, using the Dodge tool, I lighten up the noodles. You can see here the flats and the flats with line.

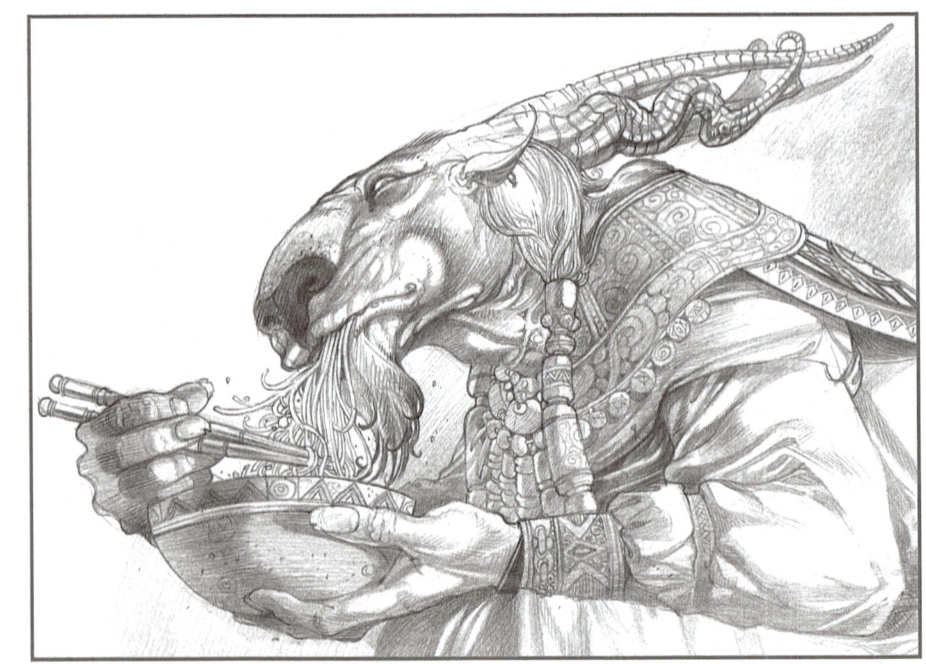

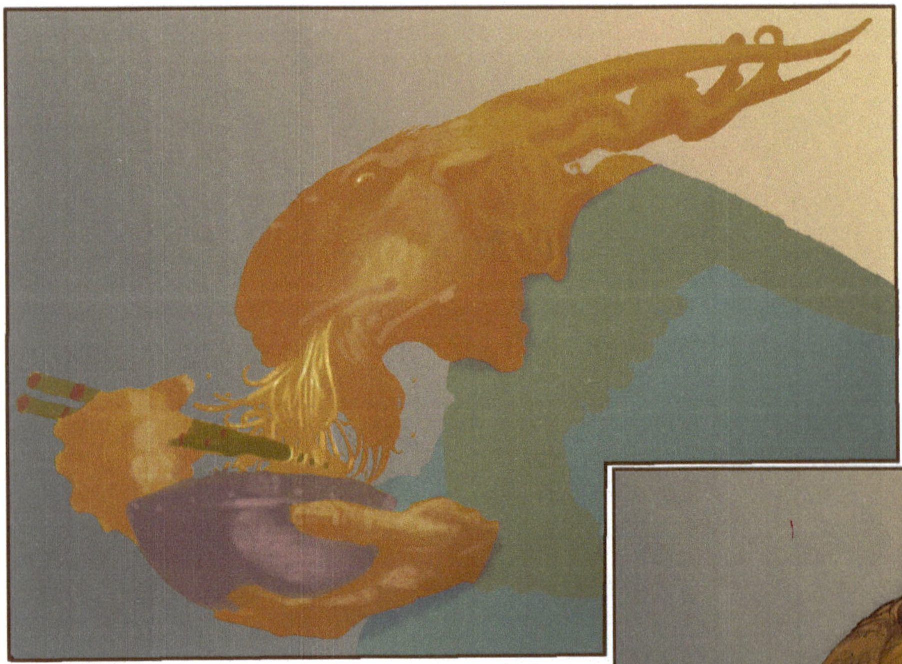

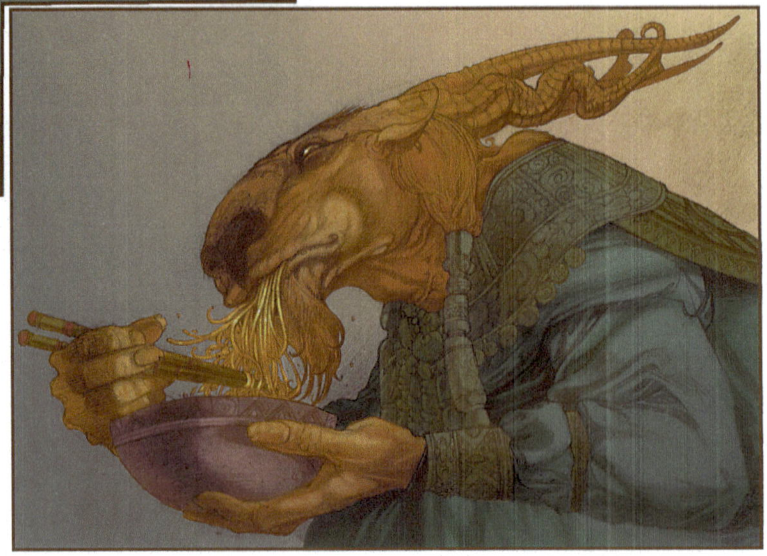

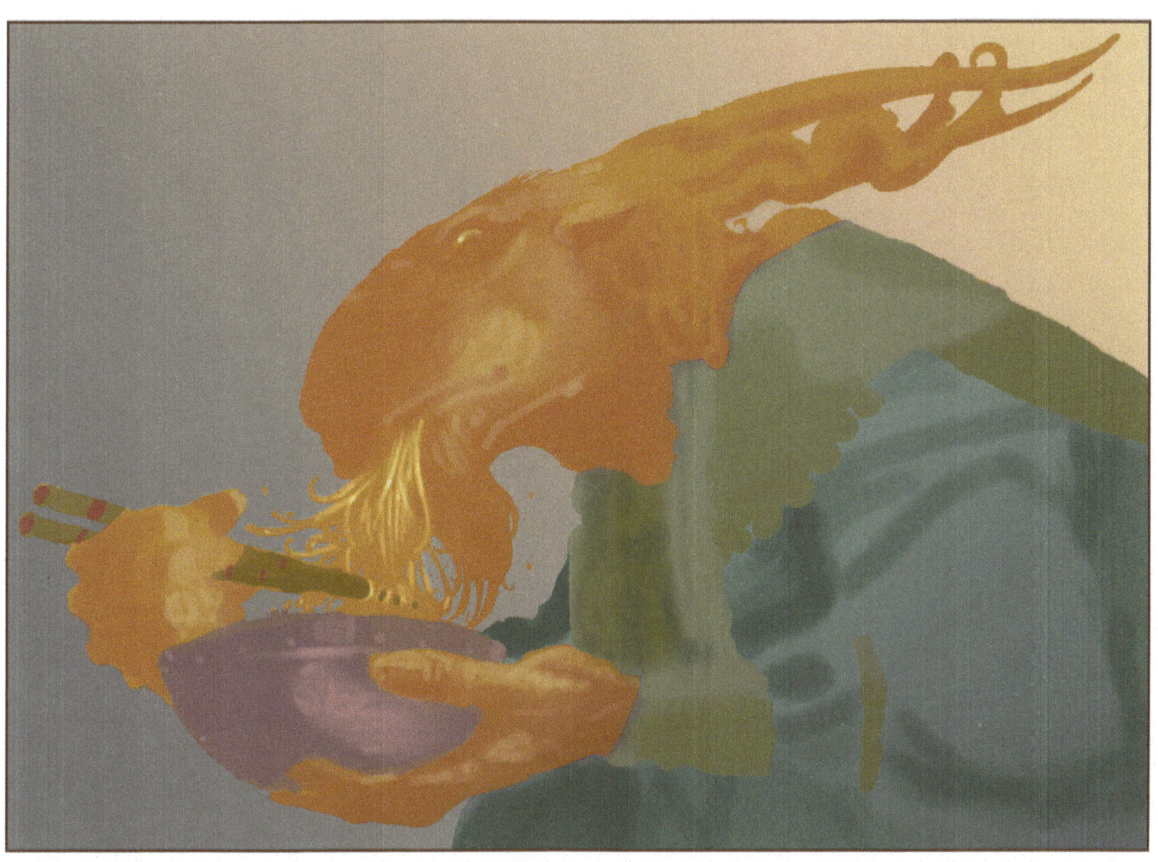

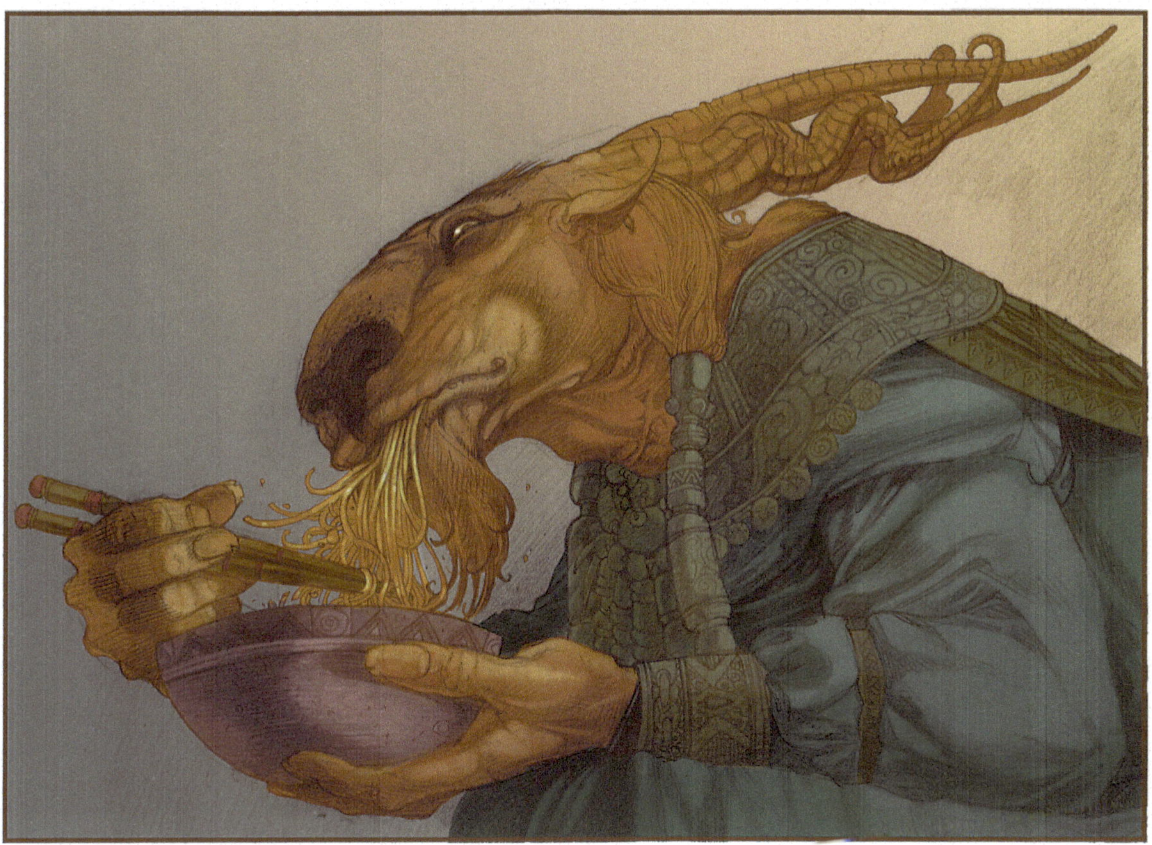

More work on the flats to add to the values. I try to put in the lightest light and darkest dark and then work the values in between.

Here is the final color flat and the completed drawing. When I work this way, I have only two layers in Photoshop: the color flat and the line. At a game company, you have to keep everything in a strict working order. You can't have a thousand layers because you work on other people's files. The rule of thumb is "Keep it simple." I do make channels for a lot of the individual elements, and channels add less to your file size than layers.

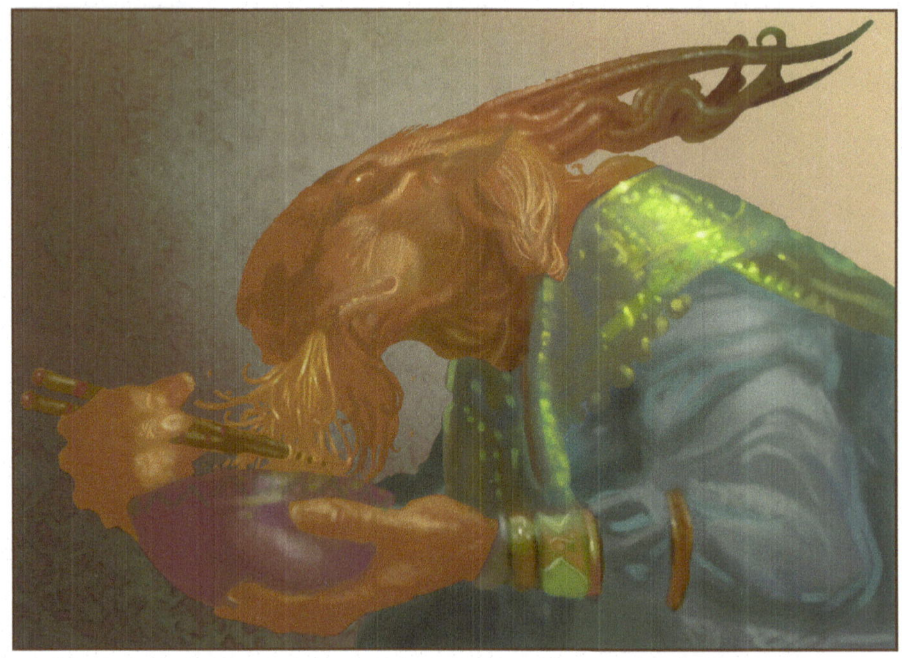

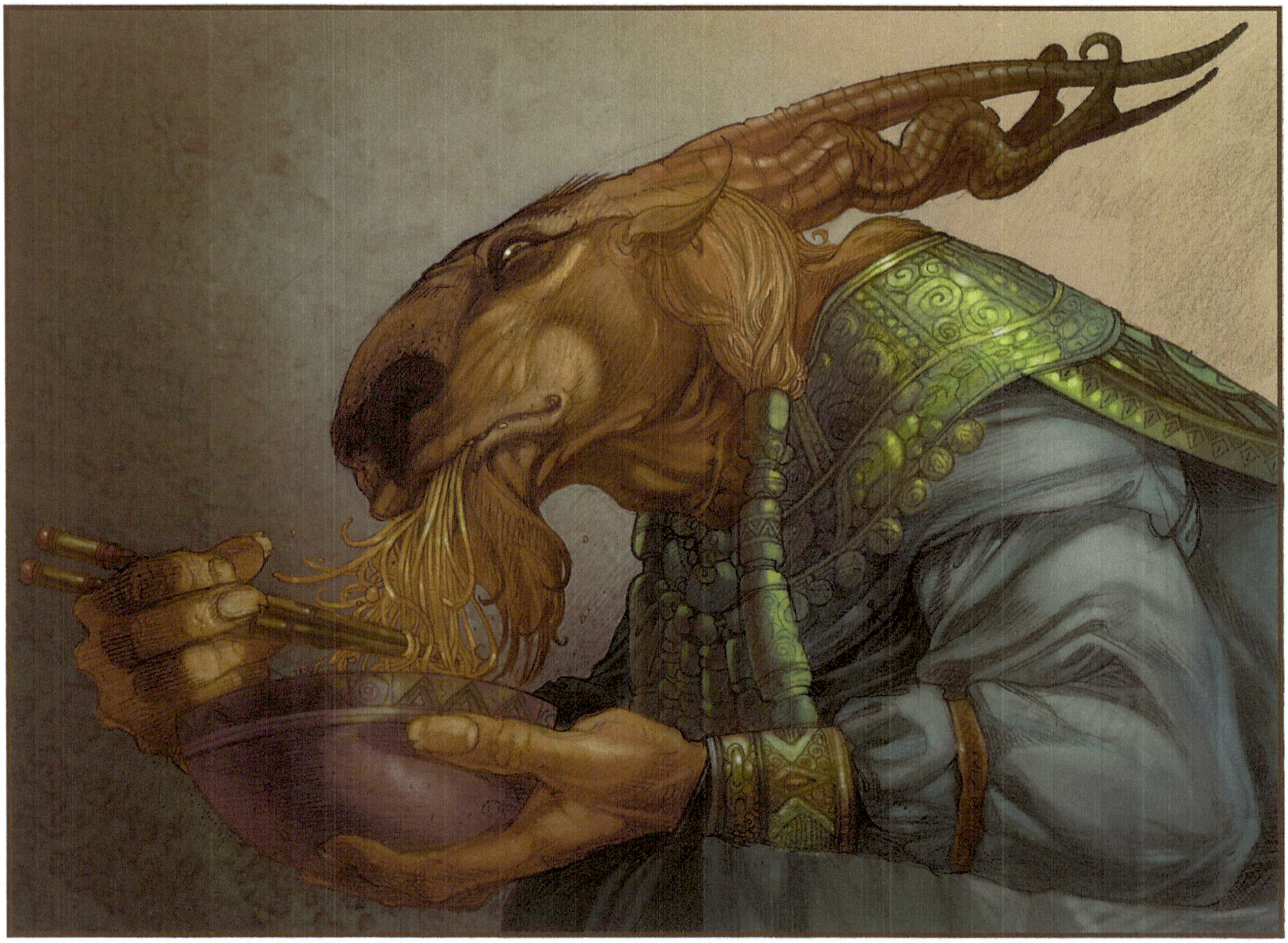

# WARFARE

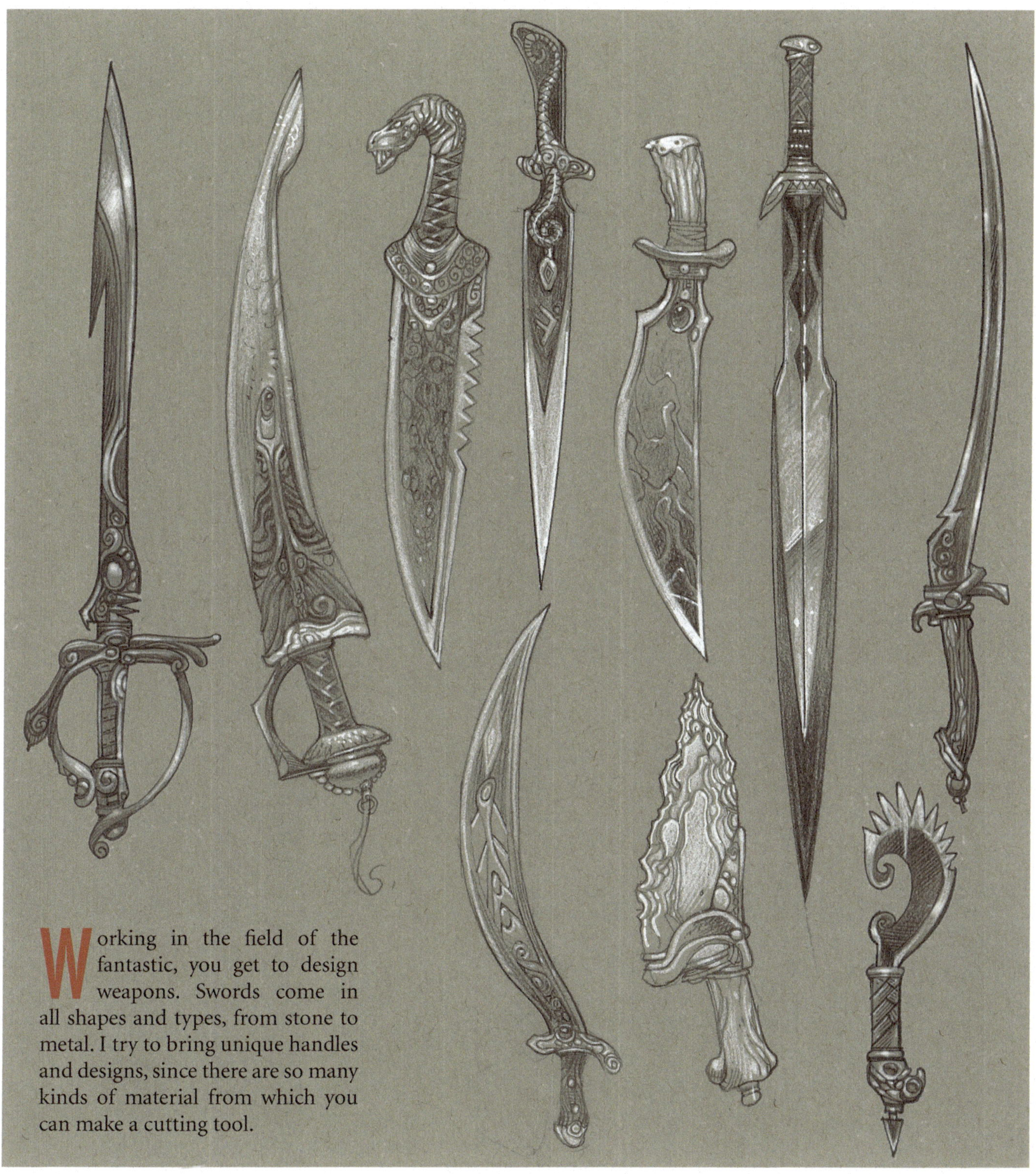

**W**orking in the field of the fantastic, you get to design weapons. Swords come in all shapes and types, from stone to metal. I try to bring unique handles and designs, since there are so many kinds of material from which you can make a cutting tool.

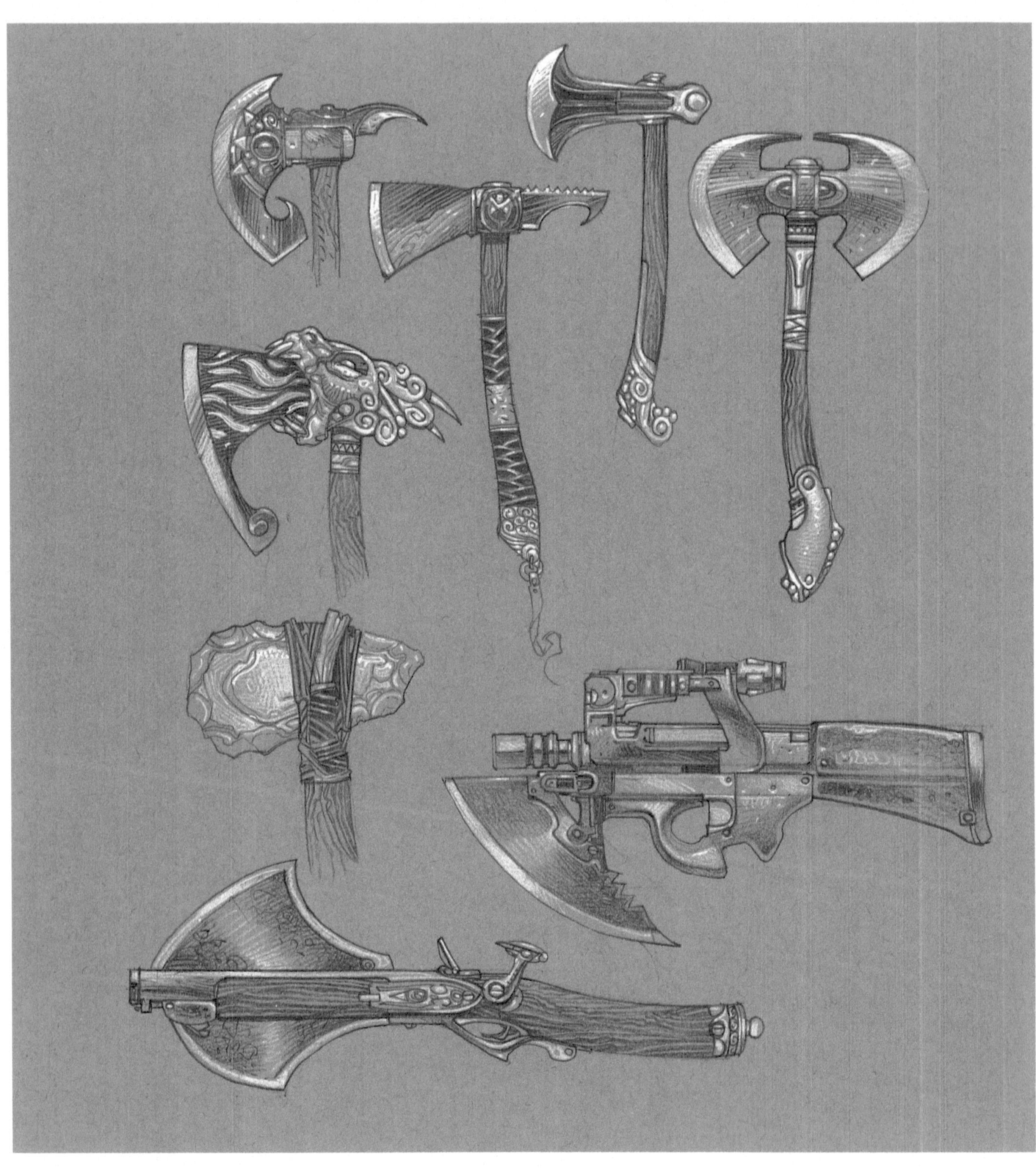

The same thing can hold true for axes. What type? Throwing, ceremonial, working, battle, or a simple survival stone? The ax was added to some early black-powder weapons, and who knows? It even can be part of a contemporary assault rifle.

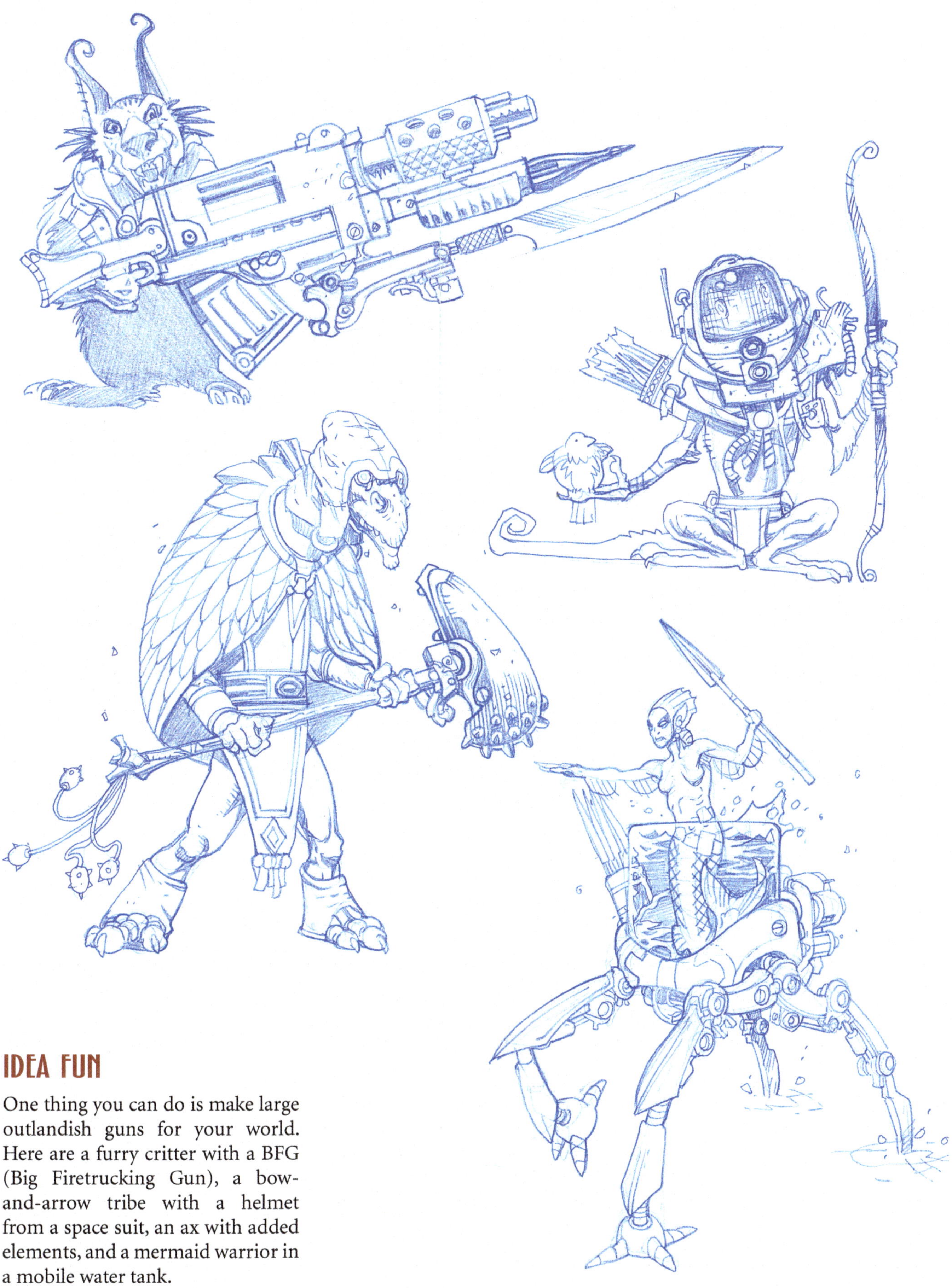

## IDEA FUN

One thing you can do is make large outlandish guns for your world. Here are a furry critter with a BFG (Big Firetrucking Gun), a bow-and-arrow tribe with a helmet from a space suit, an ax with added elements, and a mermaid warrior in a mobile water tank.

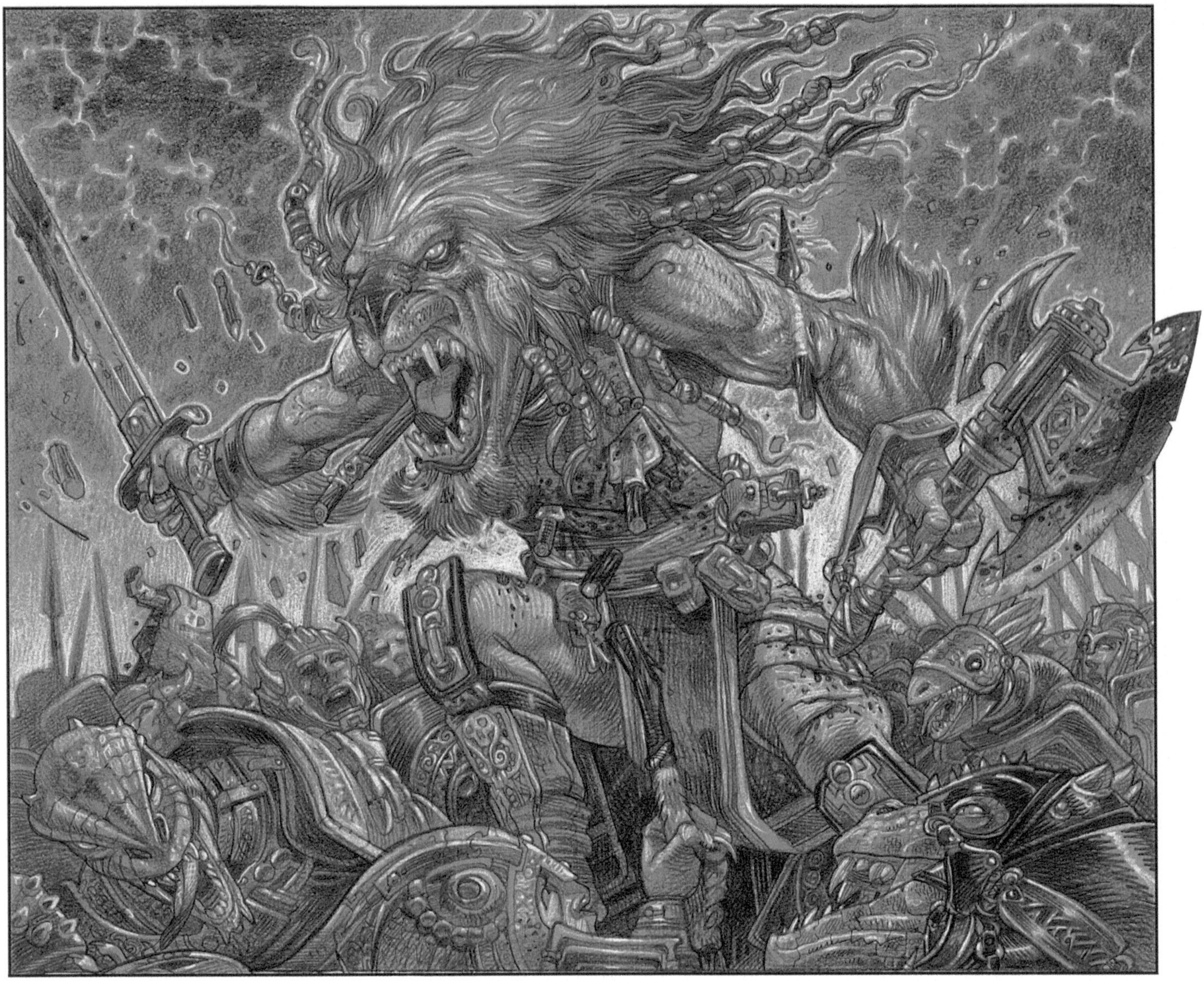

When it comes to putting it all together, each warrior will have favorite weapons. Some armies are made of ragtag groups pulling together and gathering arms from fallen foes.

We also have a tendency to try to make ourselves a little more unique and stand out. This can be everything from coats, armor, hairstyle, belts, boots, etc. I tend to push this more than anything else. I've done military and uniformed characters and prefer the dirty, grubby home-style warrior.

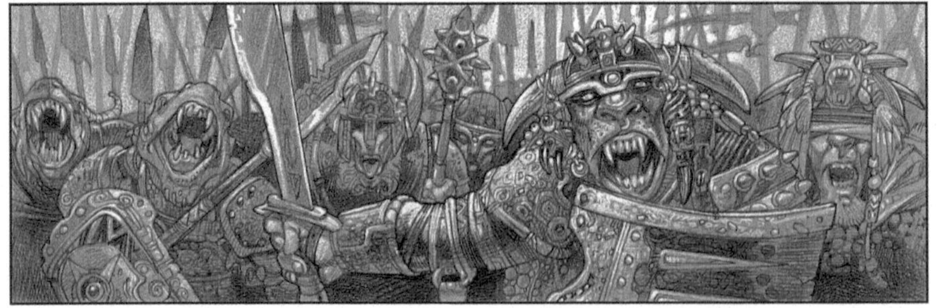

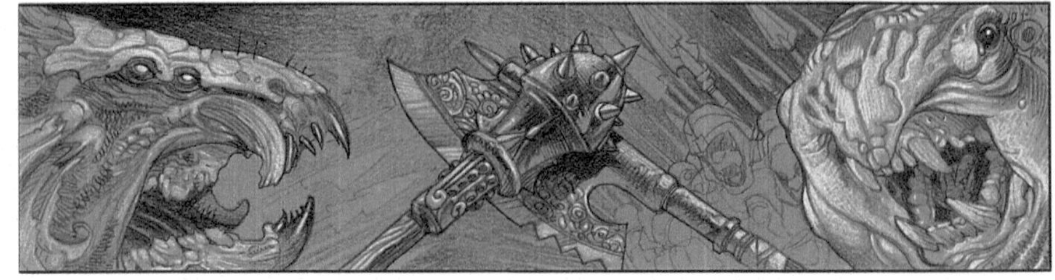

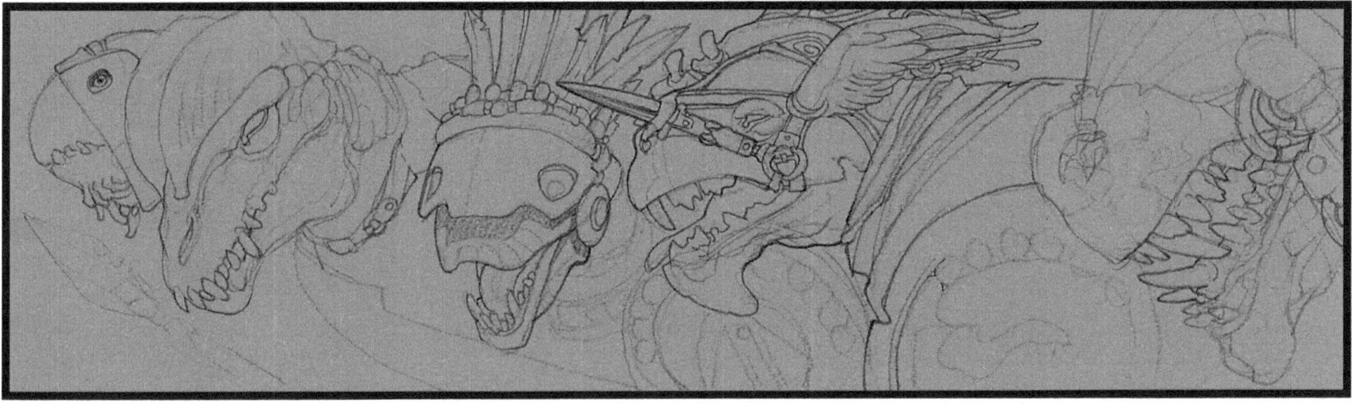

## Step 1

I start to develop the forms of the figures with just line and contour. I get a feel for the lights and darks by the line weight. In other words, I apply more pressure to the pencils and create a heavier, darker line and then lighten that pressure to give it less weight. I try not to create a constant line around the figures, but one in which, with thick and thin sections, I can develop the light direction.

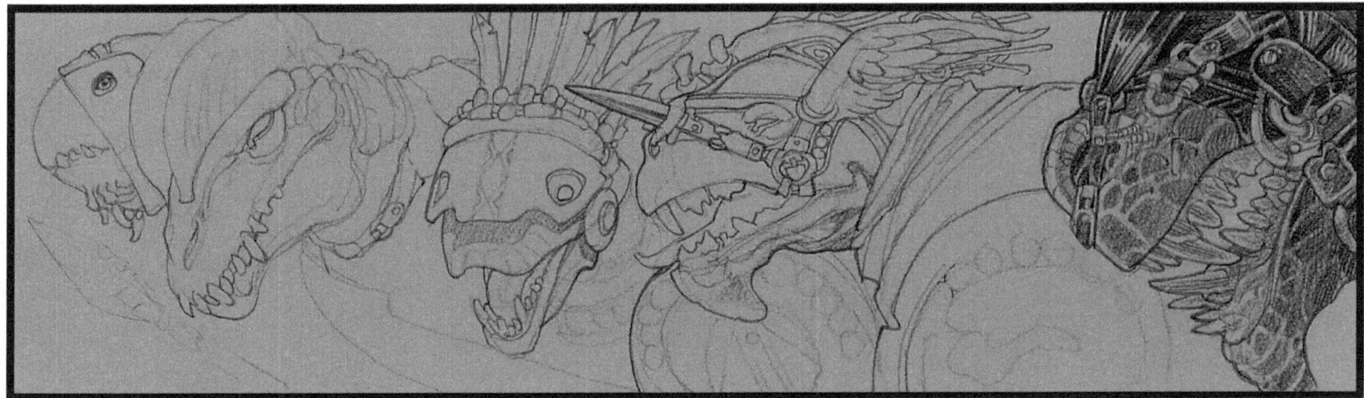

## Step 2

I use three layers to create space: the foreground, which is the closest to the viewer; the middle ground, which is the midlayer of the stage; and the background, which is the last layer. If you think of the picture plane in these three layers, it does not matter how deep your space is. It can easily be broken down into these elements.

The second step to this process is light. I am going to have a dark object in the foreground, my major lights and focal point will be in the middle ground, and the background will be the second darkest area.

Now I'm rendering this as a darker form.

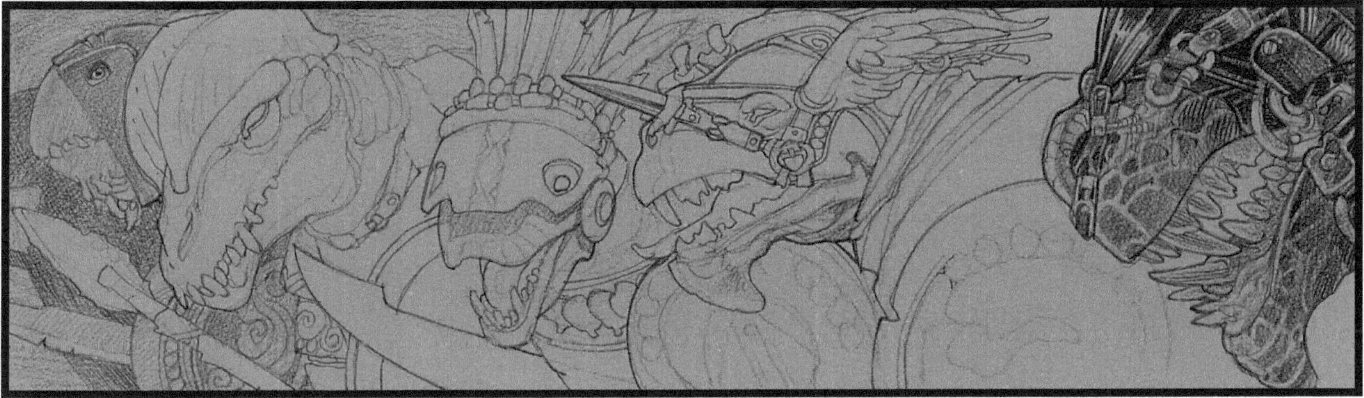

## Step 3

The background is started, and here I try to keep the values closer. To create a softer background, I will restrict the values and keep them close in range.

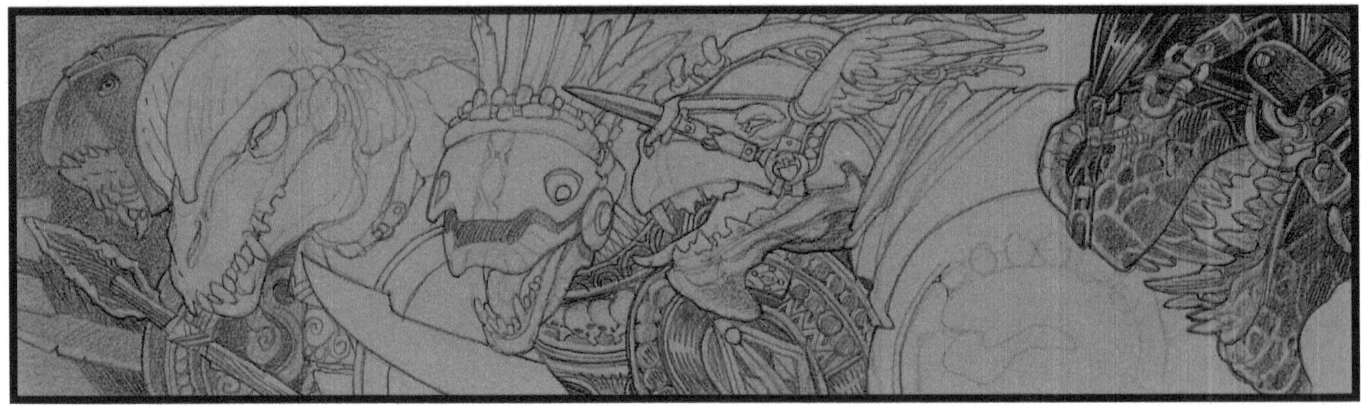

**Step 4**

I'm starting to bring in detail to the middle ground. This is the area I want the viewer to look at first. It will be the focal point of the panel, so it will have the strongest lights, darks, and the most visible detail in the drawing. It also will have the biggest value range.

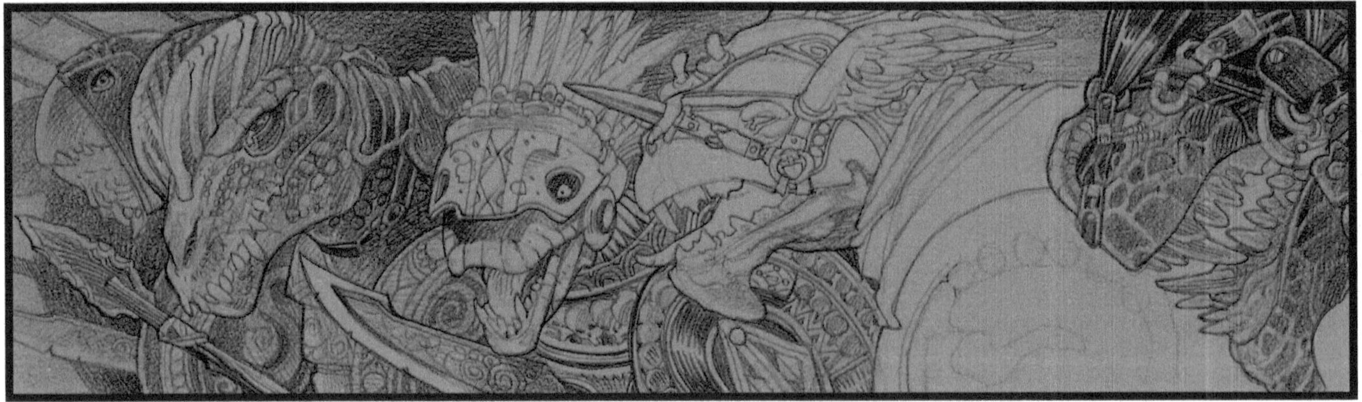

**Step 5**

Working still from the background forward, I try to keep the first two figures softer and darker and then add more detail and surface decoration on the third and fourth figures. The figure on the right is still the darkest.

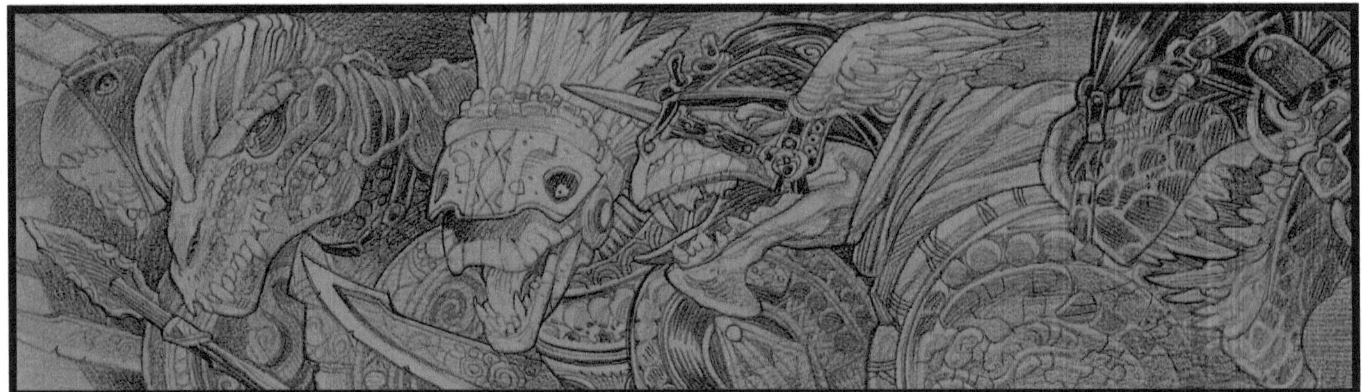

**Step 6**

I've balanced out all the value and line work. Next will be the whites, highlights, and touch-ups to make the foreground, middle ground, and background work together.

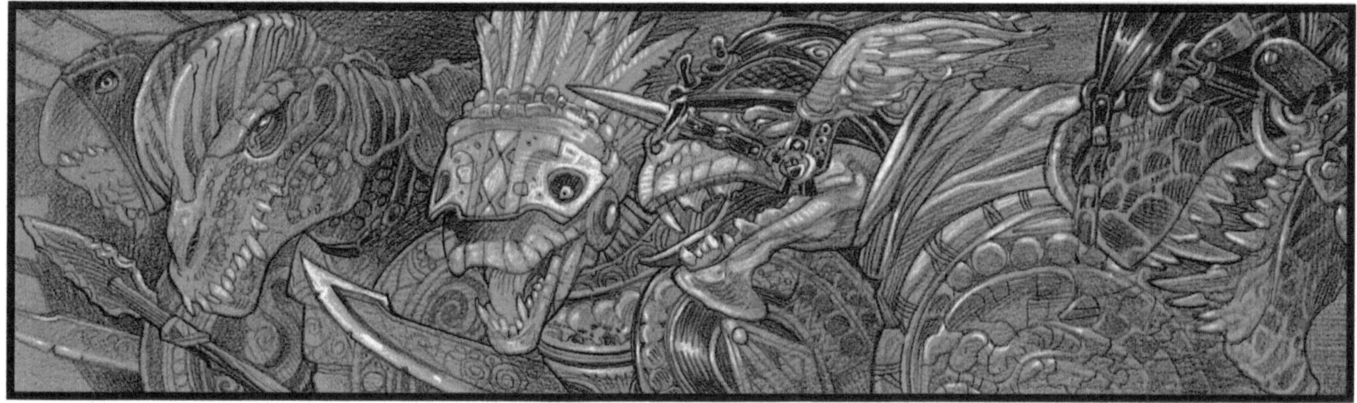

## Step 7

The white pencil is now used to create the highlights (brightest light) and other lighter values. The whites are added and adjustments made to make the space work. I've tried to make you look at the two middle ground figures. They have the brightest lights, darkest darks, and the most visible detail. The foreground and background have closer value and some small highlights, but they are not as bold as the middle ground.

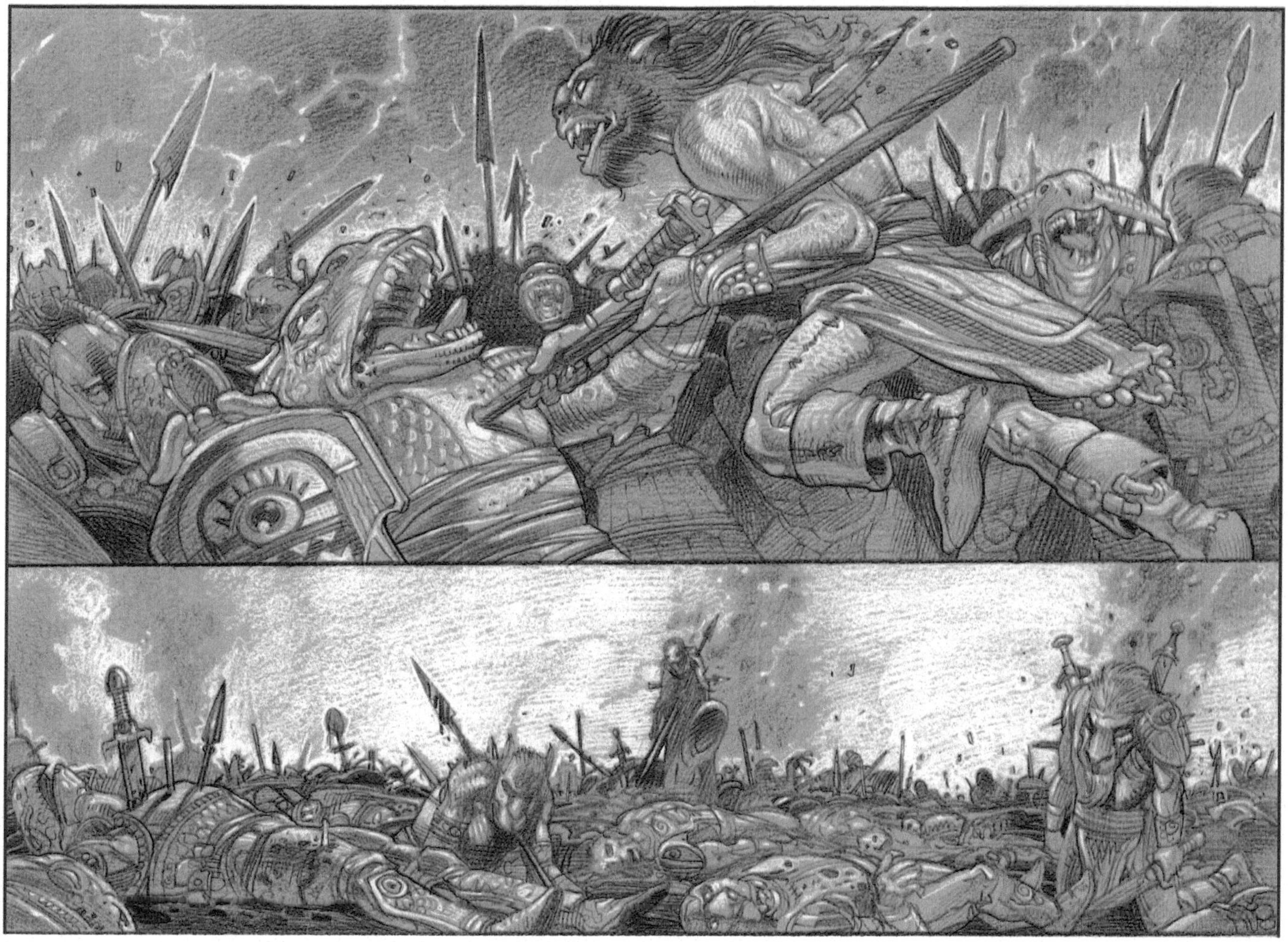

In the top panel, I've made two lighter and more detailed figures to stand out against the darker background. In the lower panel, the sky is bright and all the warriors are in the darker area.

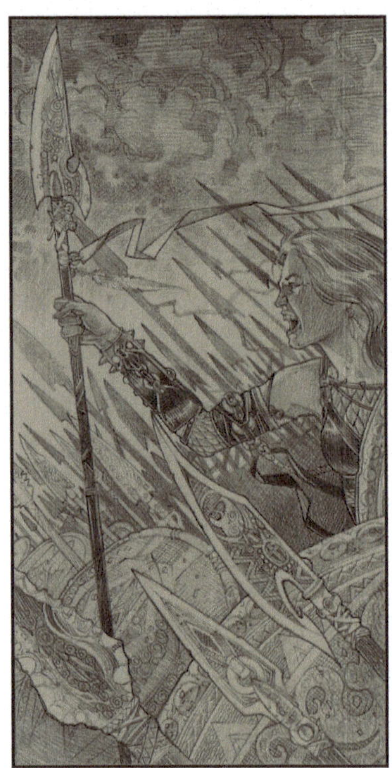

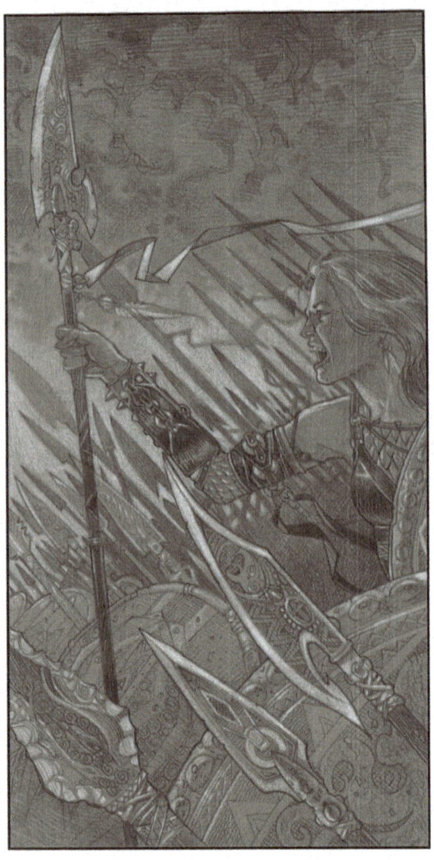

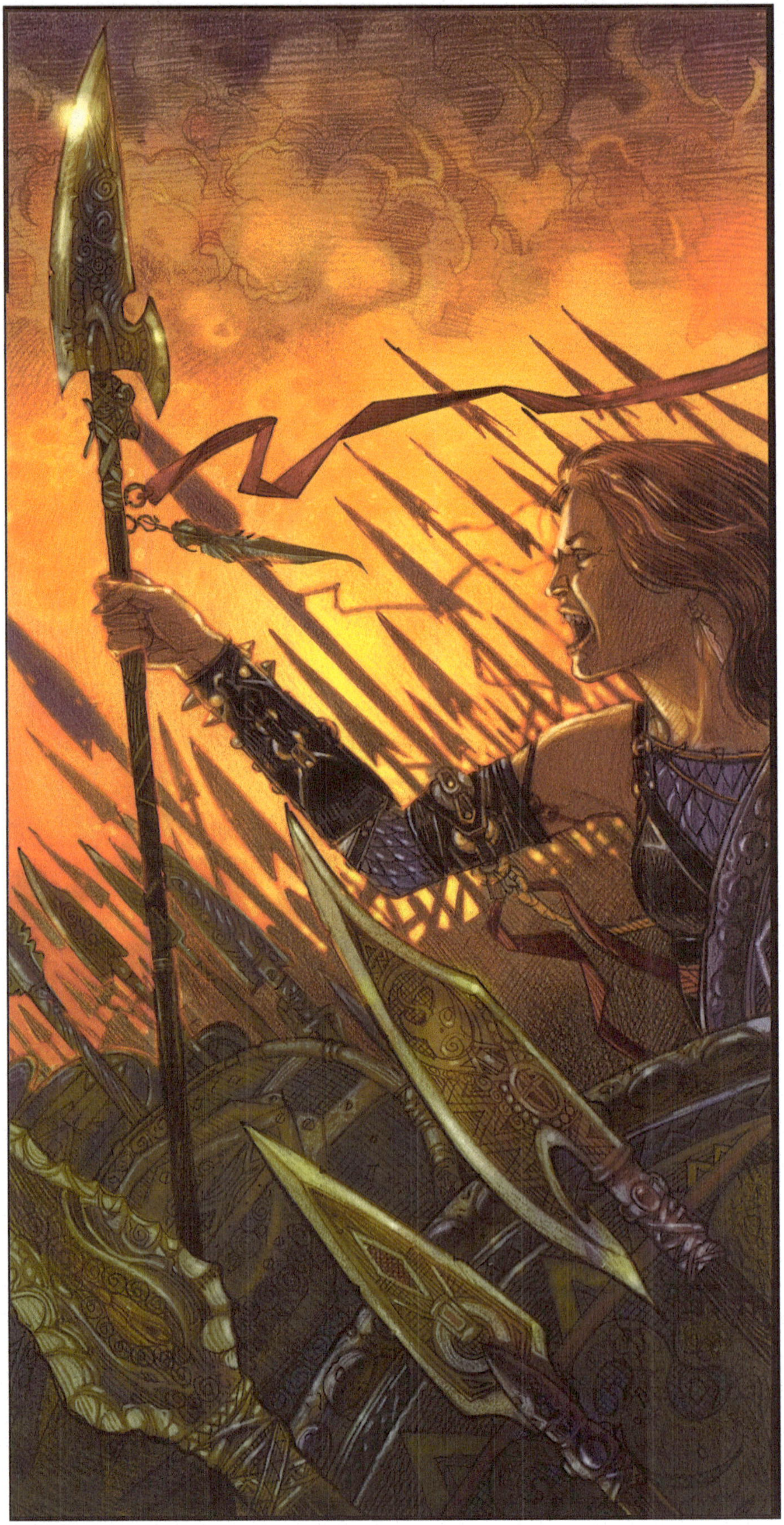

Once again, the gray paper and black pencil, the addition of whites, and in this case the drawing is carried to a finished color piece.

# 10
# SPIRIT

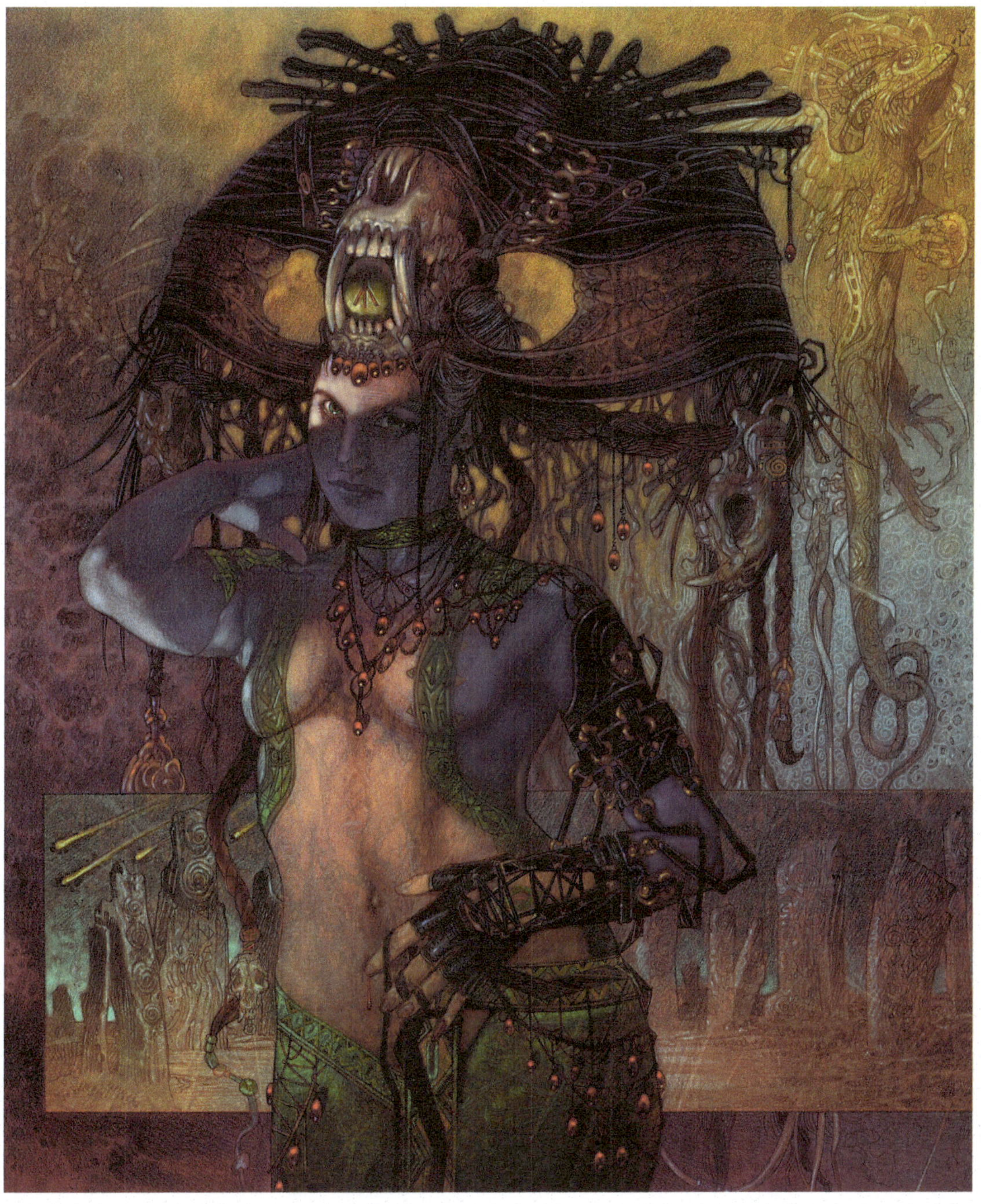

Codes, beliefs, and values form a culture's inner spirit. The relationship to the environment is a huge determination of the civilization. Symbols, acts of social etiquette, and expressions of given laws become part of an interwoven tapestry that defines the society. Leaders can be men, women, and animals. The power of a shaman or medicine man/woman will be defined by the culture.

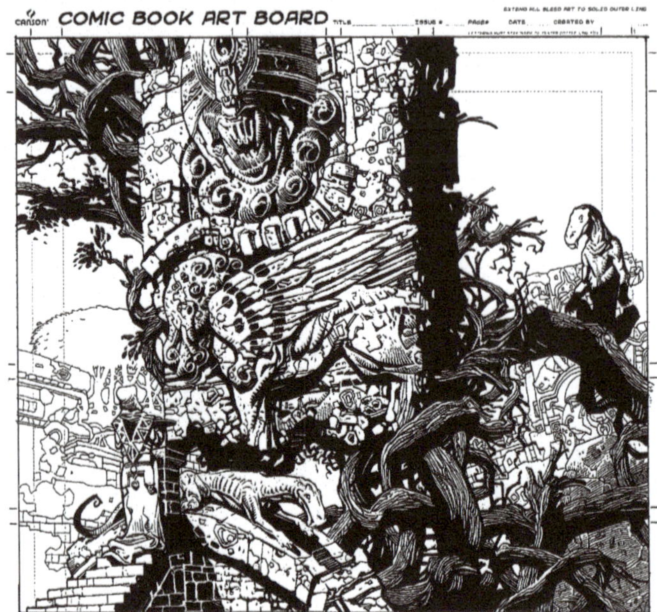

Places of worship can be complex or simple. They can cover all kinds of environments or be in a specific spot. They can be new, old, or respected ruins. For me, nature always plays a big part in this development. The relationship to our environment and its life forms becomes a basis for the survival of a culture.

An old ruin can still have some magic.

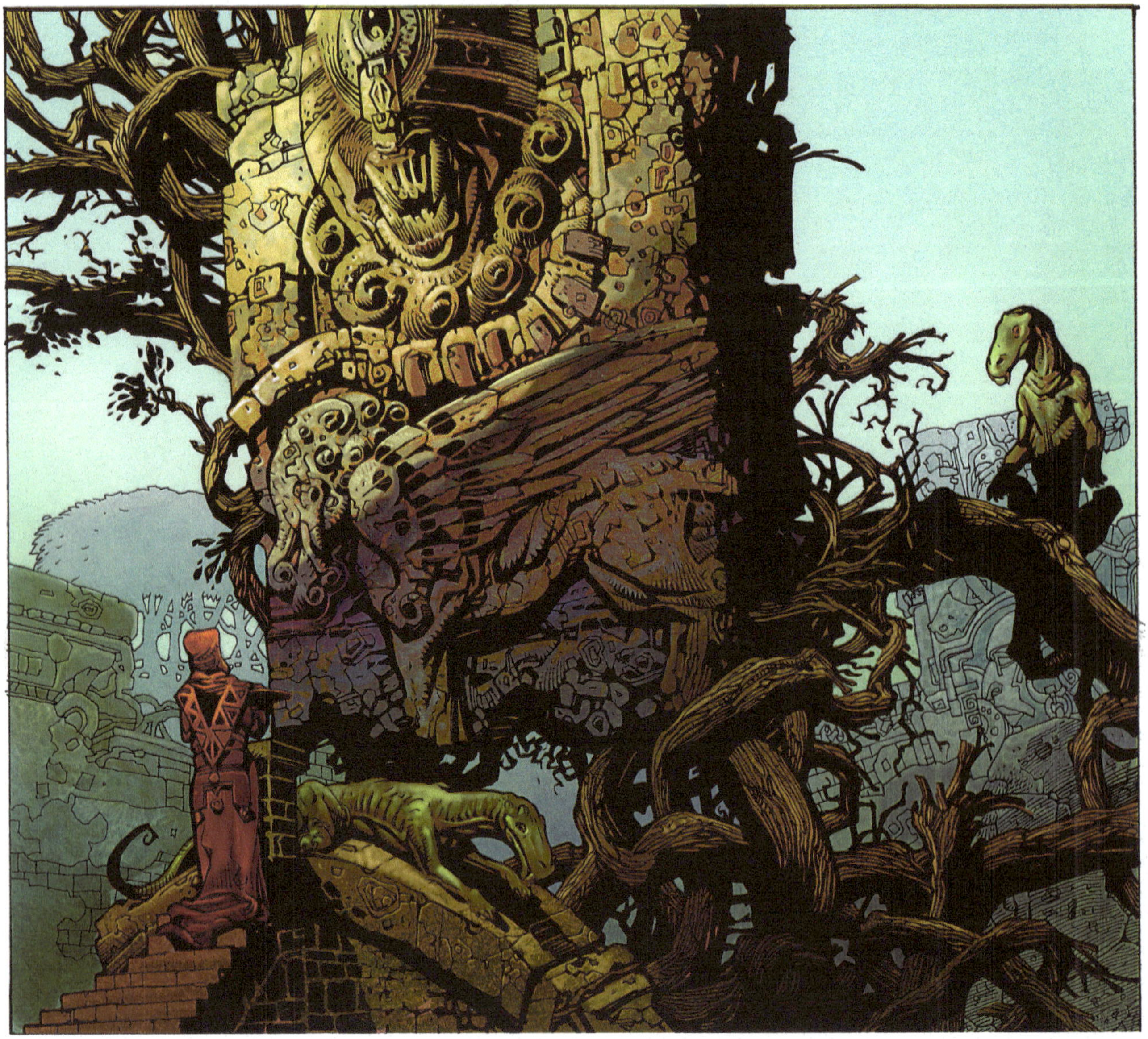

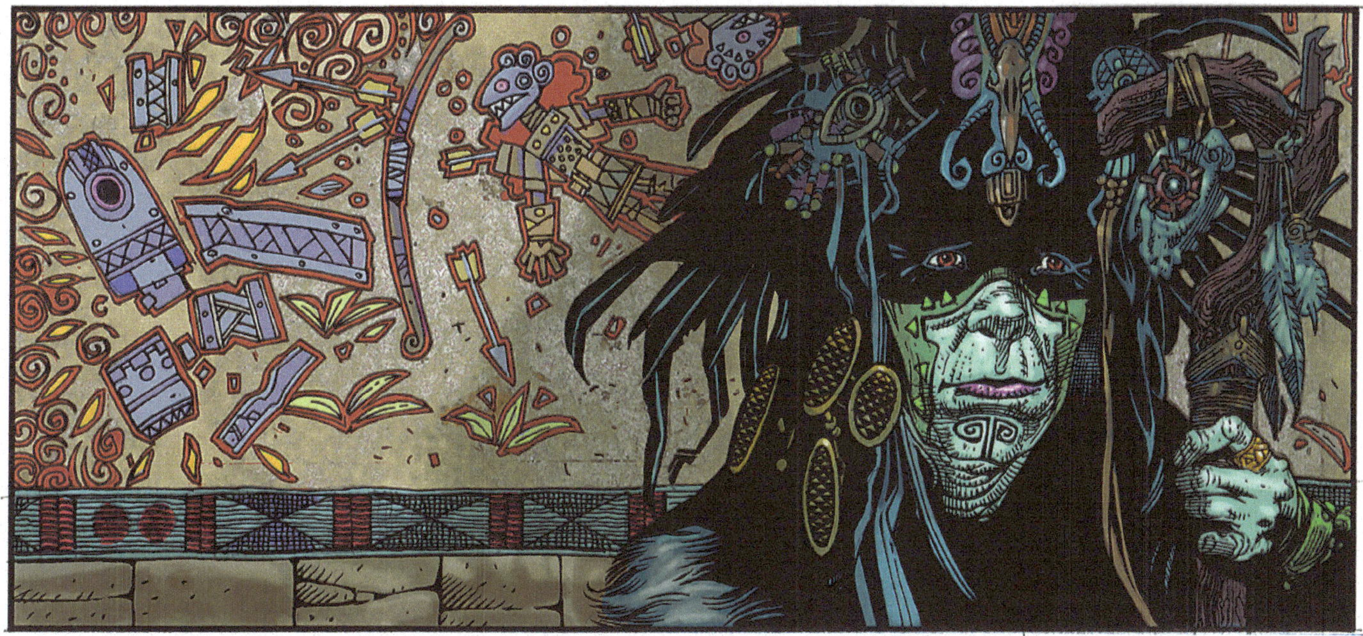

In one story I wrote, the lead priestess is part of a guild that weaves the tapestries of history. They are the keepers of the past, creating and hanging the weavings of time in their monastery.

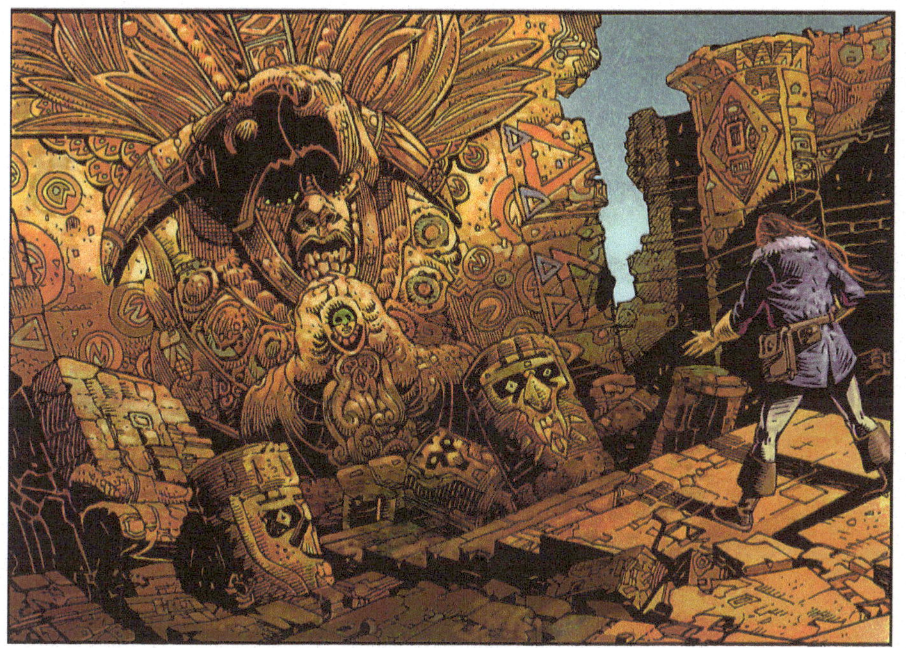

The heroine of this story comes to the ruins of one of the temples as part of her quest.

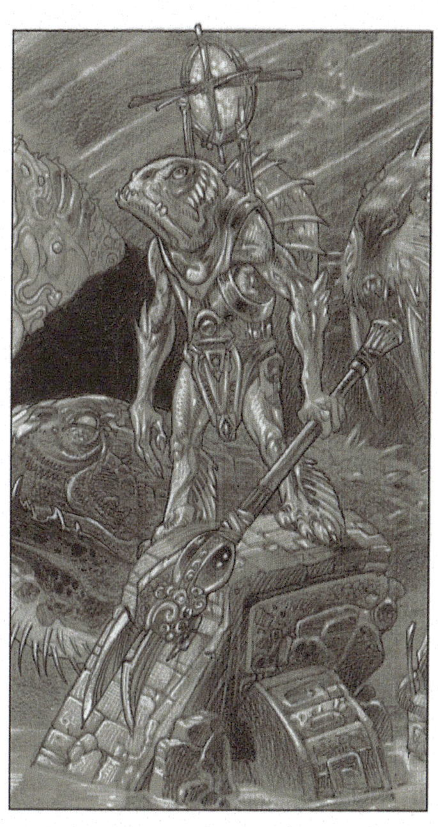

Gods can take many forms. Here is my representation of the God of Water for a story.

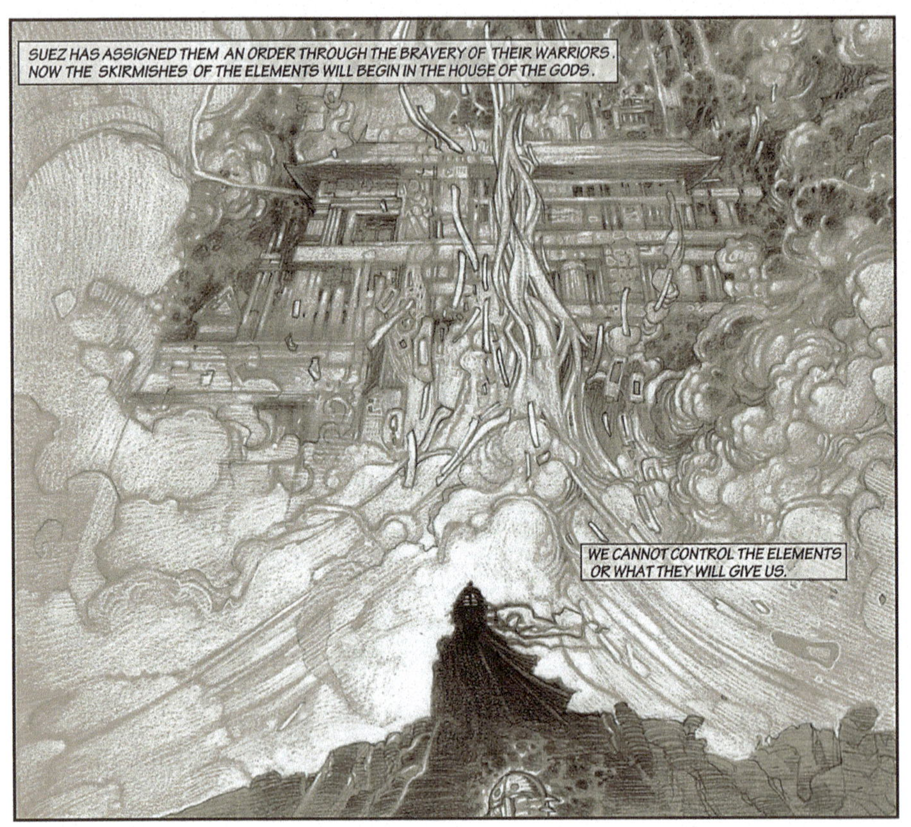


The house of the gods can be anywhere: the sky, underground, all around us. It goes back to how you want to bring these elements into your story.

The same can be said about reclusive sites. The discovery of old structures and the mystery behind them are great food for fodder. Your world can take many turns, from horror to real life.

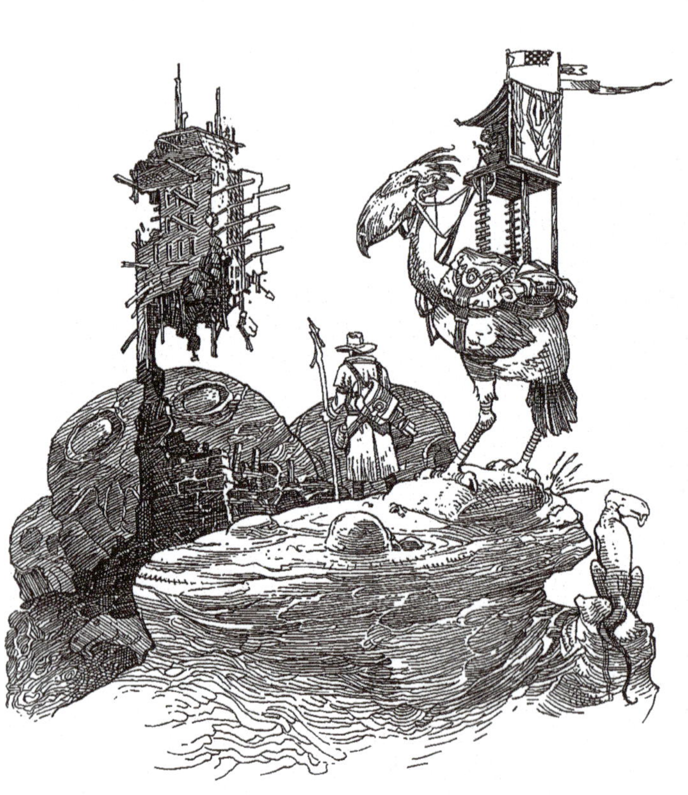

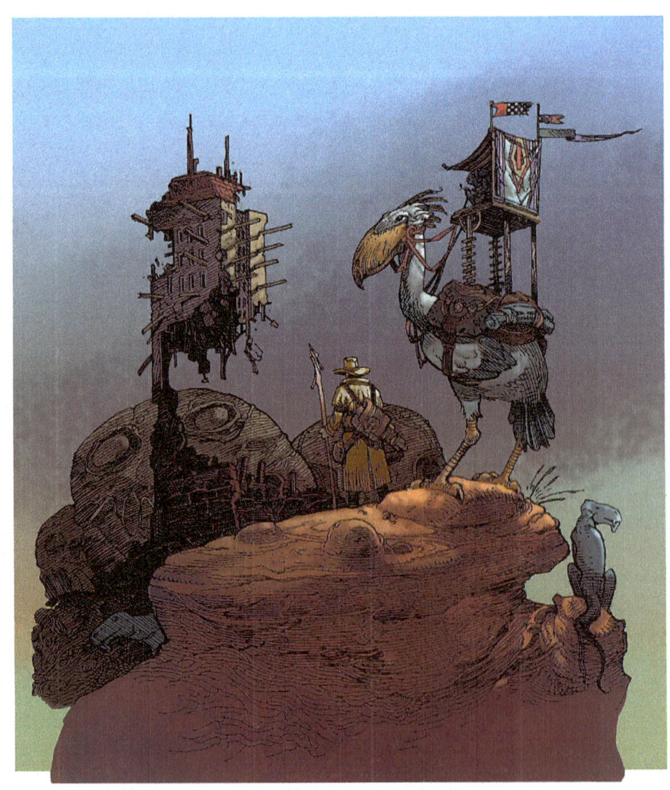

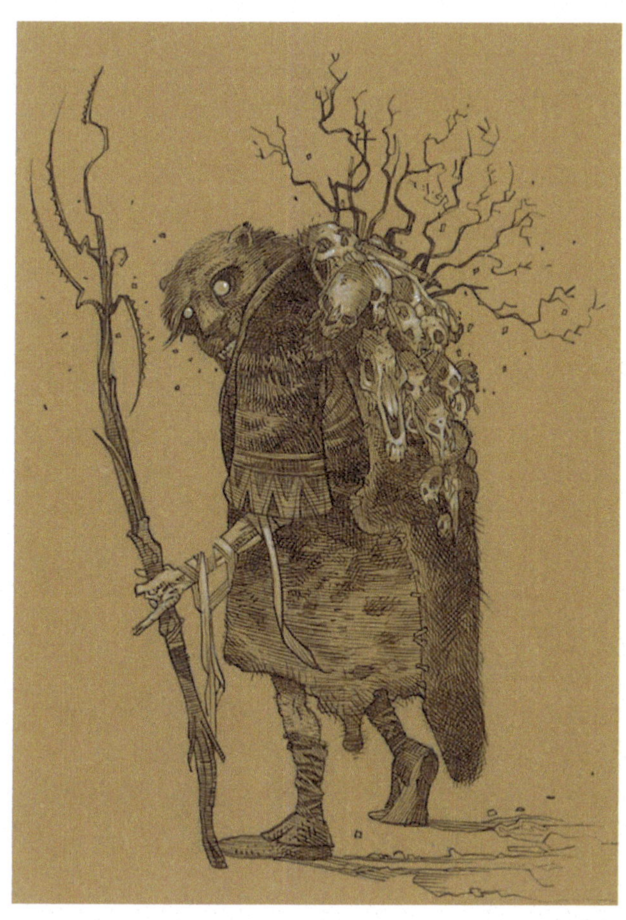

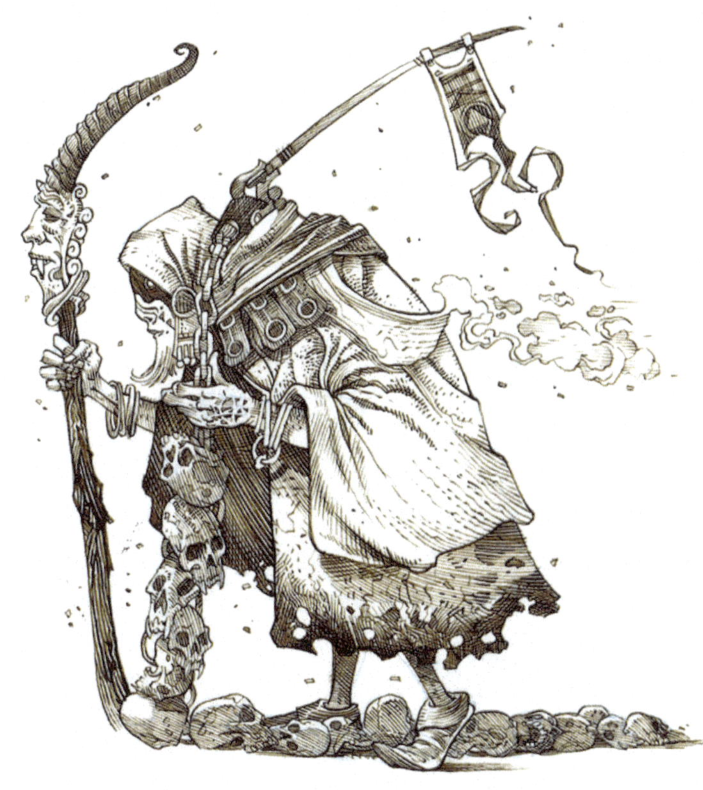

There can be a sense of mystery to these magic men and women: capes, furs, skulls, potion bags, masks, body adornment, tattoos. What is it that will make them understand their abilities even more and bring them closer to the answer? Then they will give some of their power back to the tribe/society when asked or paid. They can have their own agenda: saving the tribe, becoming the rulers, or even taking on the role of new gods.

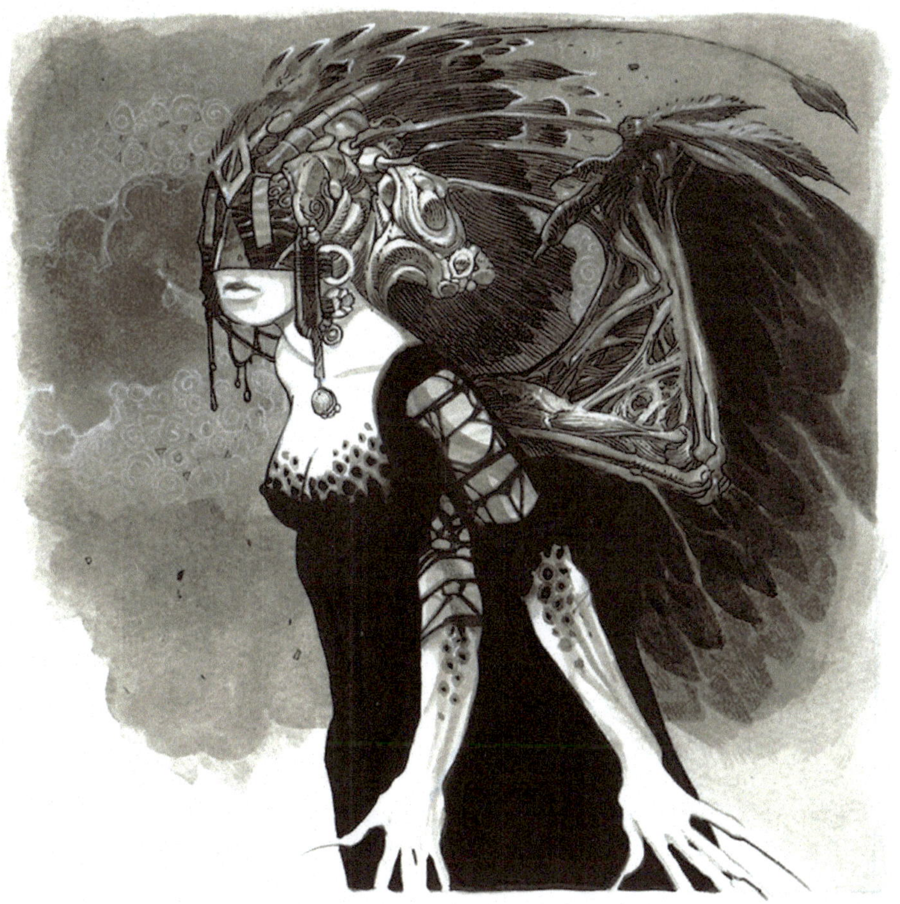

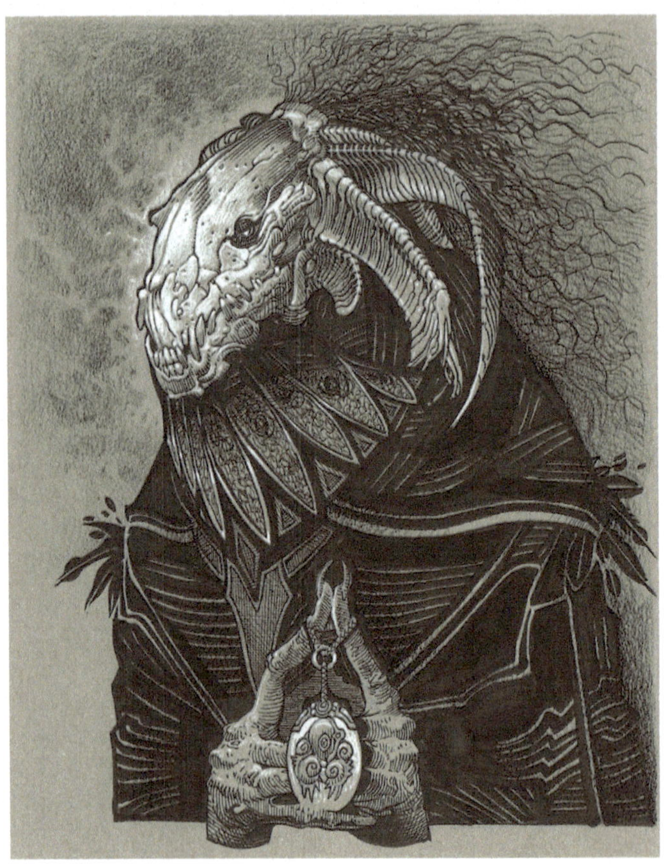

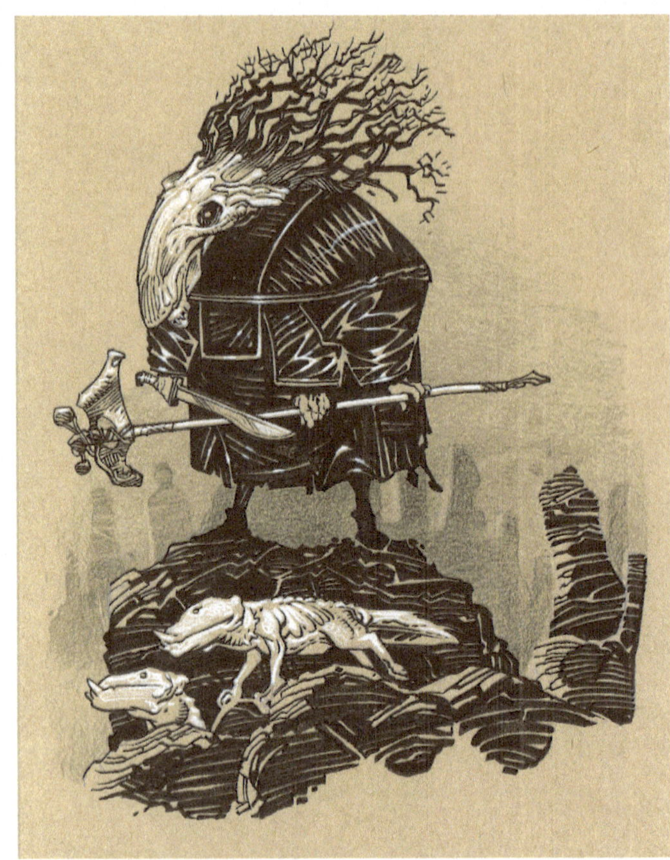

Dealing with spirituality is one of the most complex idioms to work with. There are many levels and thoughts.

Many things have become symbols for belief or icons for groups. If we look at countries' flags, we see the colors used, stars that become more cosmic, symbols for the state, heraldry, animals. . . . We can go on.

Another belief is the symbolism of animals as guardians, spiritual advisers, harbingers of good and evil, and overall attitude. The Egyptians worshipped kats. Kats kept the rat population down. Rats spread disease and ate grain, which was vital to the welfare of the people. Yet in the Middle Ages, kats became linked to witches and warlocks, with their evil stare and silent ways of hunting your soul.

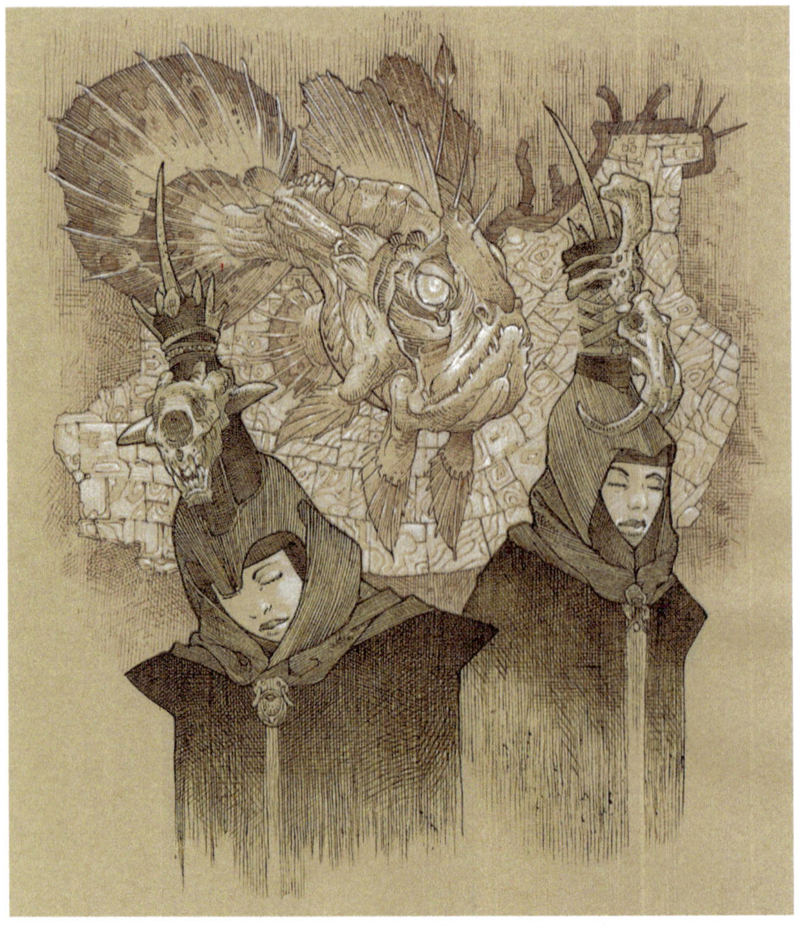

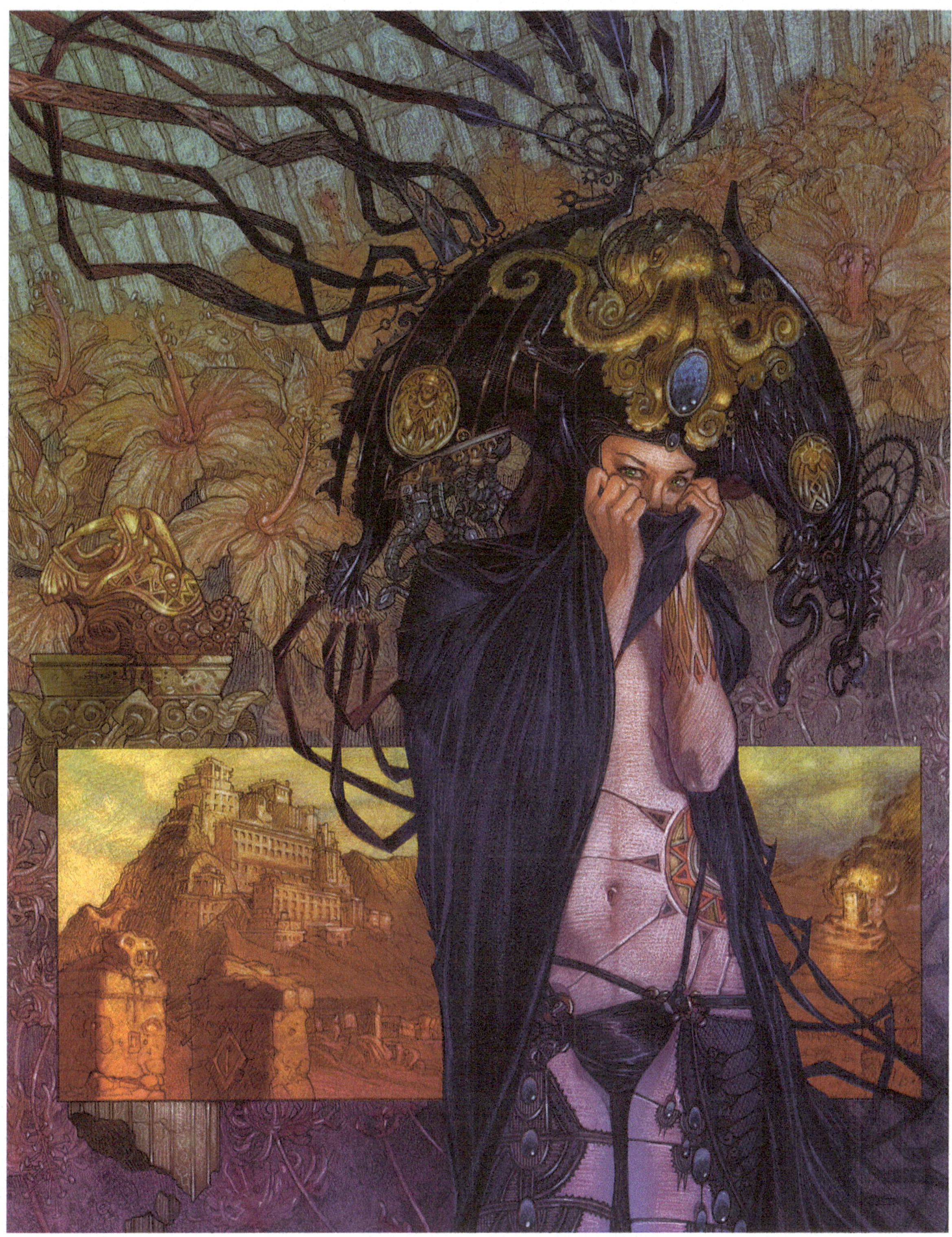

There are certain shapes that are consistent through most cultures: the square, the circle, and the triangle. There are also many icons and symbols that are based on these three shapes. The square becomes a base or structure to build from; the circle comes back to itself; and the triangle has three points, a prime number.

In astrology, each month has its own stone, weaknesses, strengths, number, years, and animals. So there is much more to the question "What is your sign?"

When you create a civilization, ask: What do they believe in? Who are their guiding forces? Where do these beliefs come from? Why do they believe? The answers will give you enough material to help round out your society.

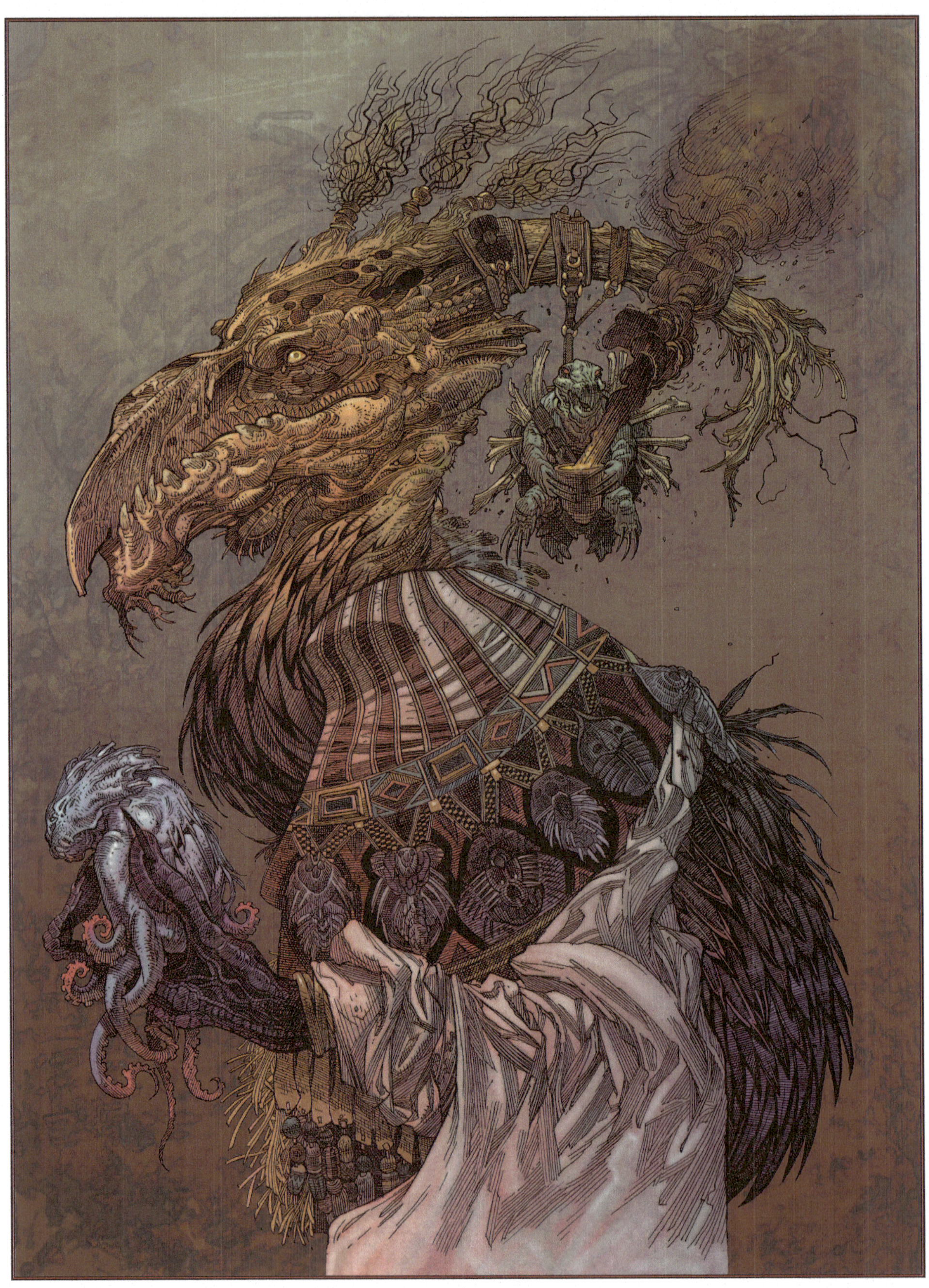

There is a tradition called "smudging." You burn a small hand-held bundle of sage and walk through your house. As the ash falls, it starts to cleanse your home of bad energy. You then sweep up the ash, going backward, to complete the process. This shaman carries a smudge turtle at all times to keep the bad spirits away.

# 11
# WARDROBE

The words that travel through my mind are *Dress for Success*, *Dress Up*, *Dress Down*, *Dress for Your Age*, *Dress for Fashion*, and *Fashion Alert*.

When I create new fashions, there is much to take into account: shirts, coats, footwear, pants, dresses, jackets, and waistcoats. Next are the levels of your groups: from the wealthy to the poor; guards to dress guards; religious leaders to shamans; military to warriors; workers of all shapes and sizes; and anything else you want to bring to life.

Fabric will become a factor. If it is printed, woven, or made from hides, each creates a new type of decoration and workmanship. Woven fabrics can have embedded patterns and symbols, applications of dyes, inks, etc. Other decorations can come in the form of beads, shells, feathers, fur, belts, bags, pouches, buttons, zippers, necklaces, rings, chains, wrist guards, spurs, holsters, knifes, hats, eyeglasses, and so on. It becomes a rather complex series of ideas to bring one character to life, but it is fun!

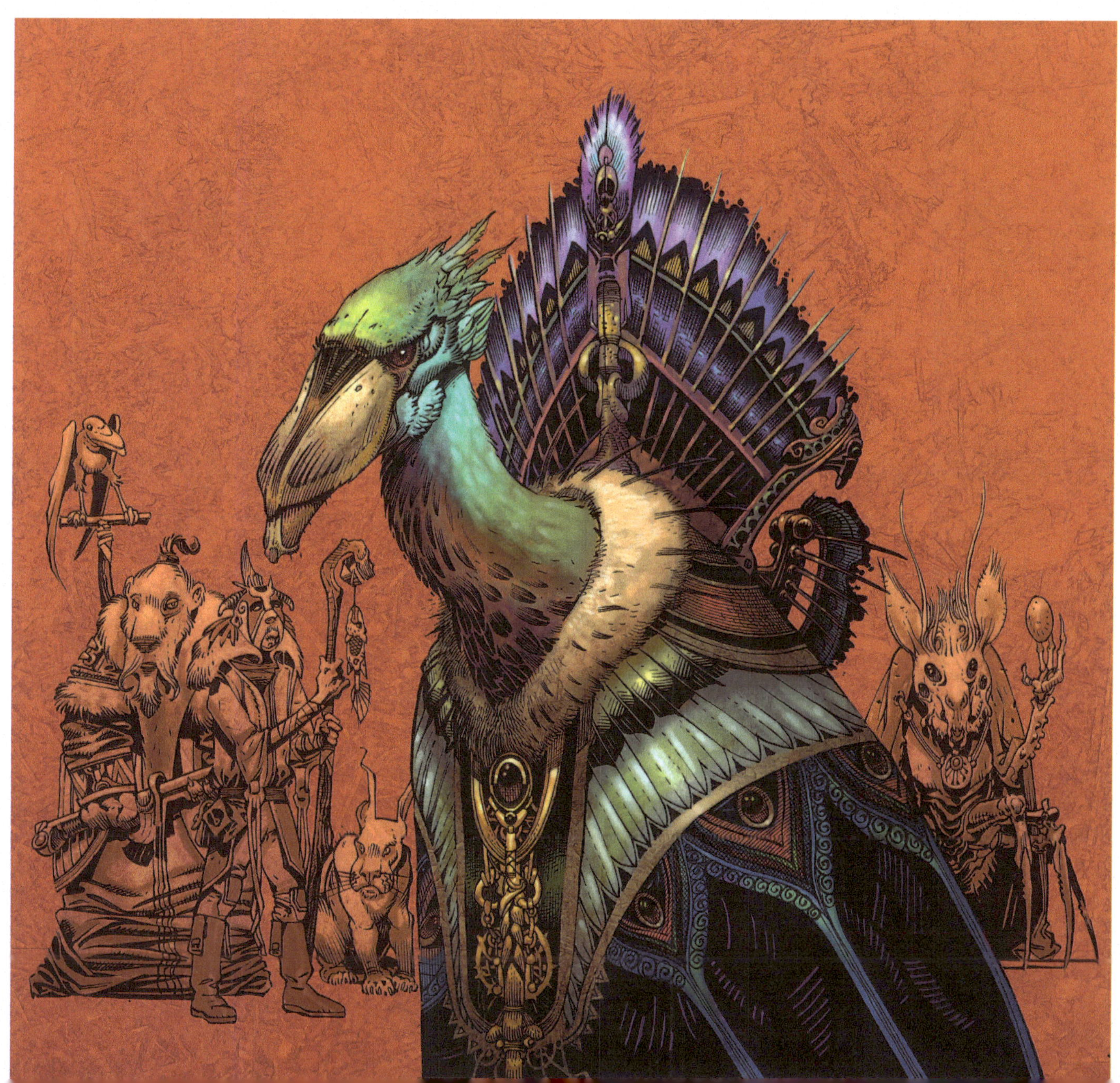

1. Mr. B Raven is decked out in his finest vest and cape to dance with the lovely Ms. P Rabbit.

2. The signal corpsman wears a hat with a decorative strap and medal of valor.

3. The best new hairpiece, braided and beaded locks, and the metal chin beard are the start of this outfit.

4. The librarian's trimmed beard and cloak with magnifying glass.

5. Jonas is wearing his big brother's clothes with the hope of growing more quickly.

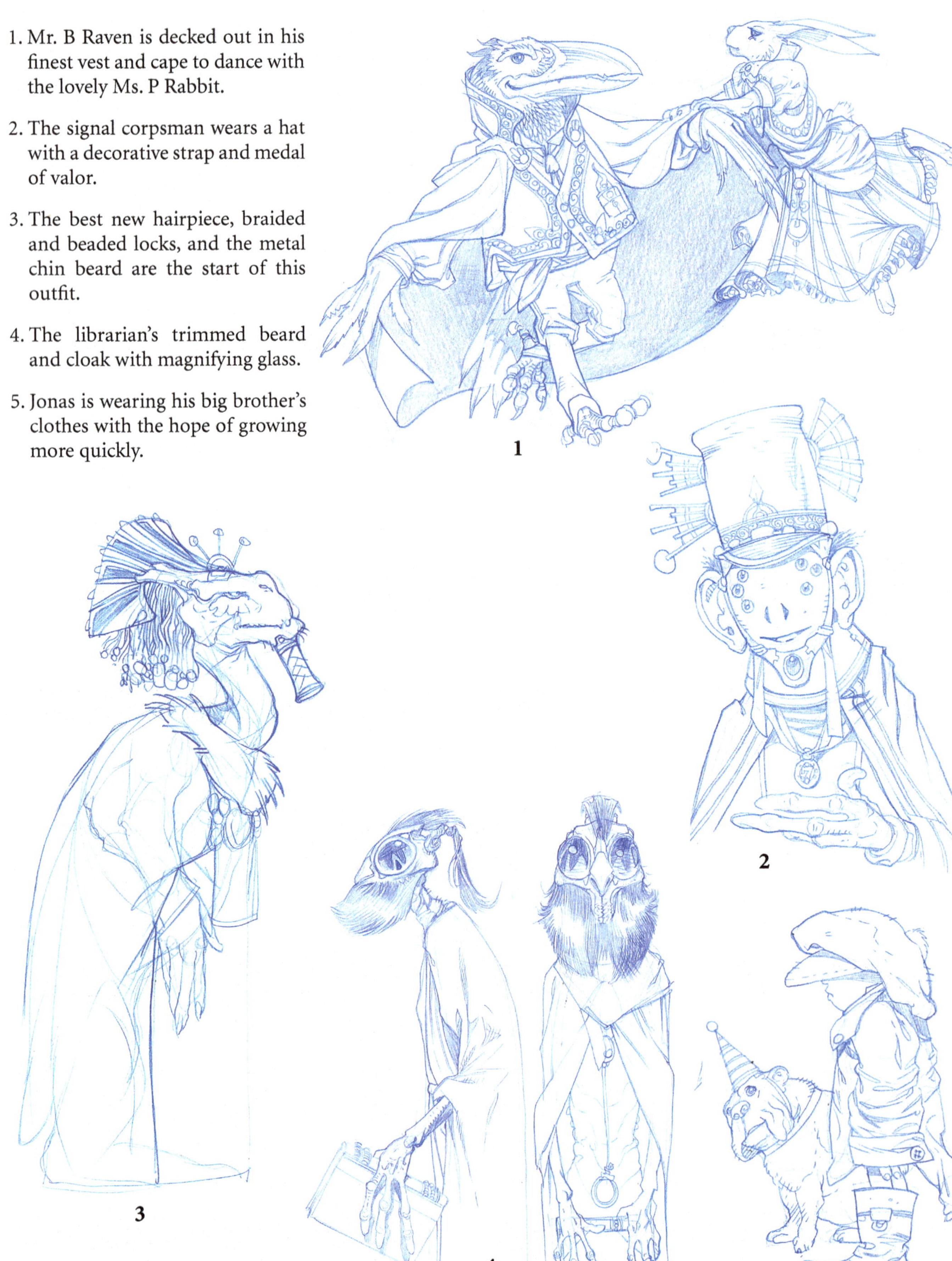

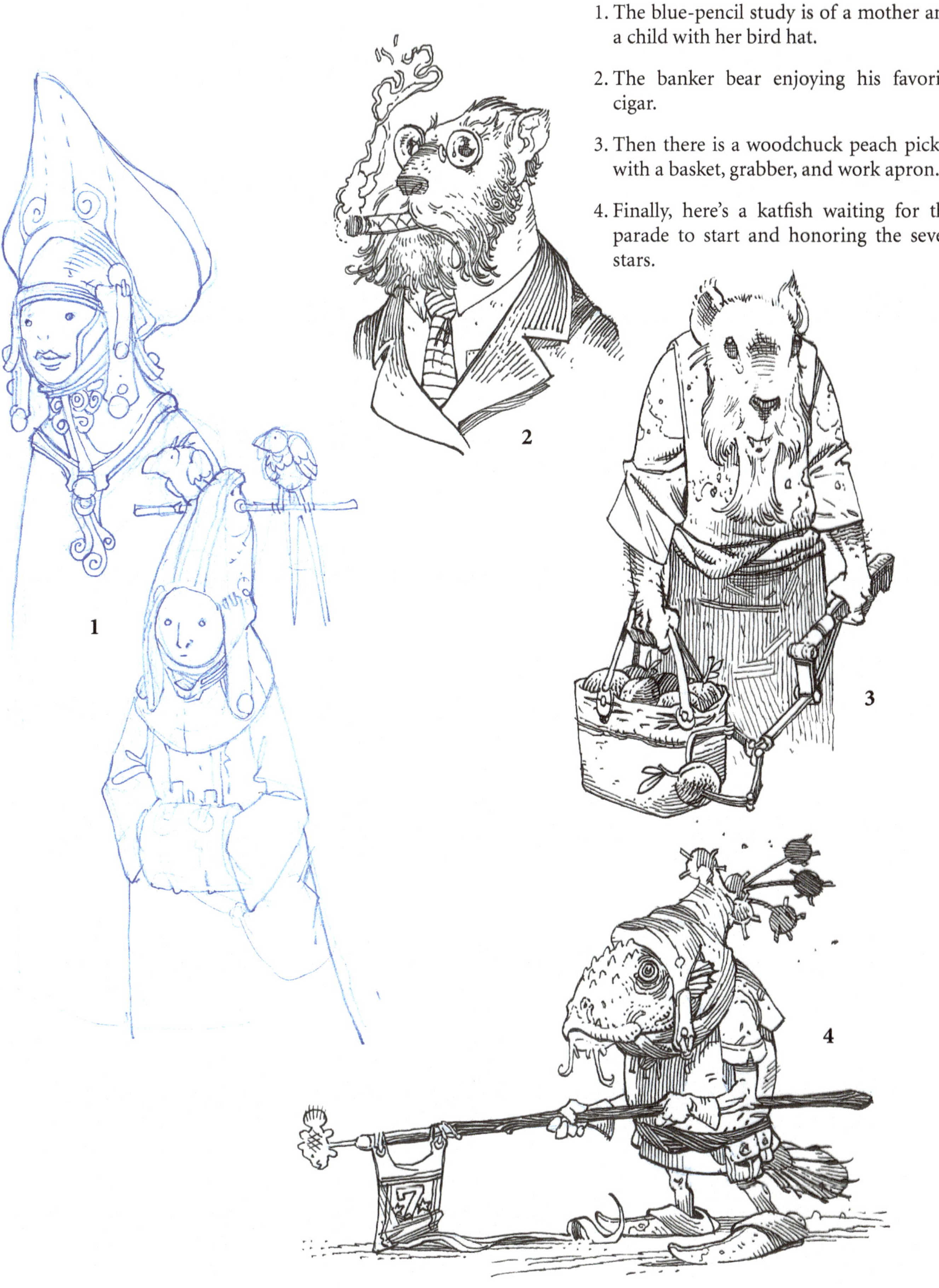

1. The blue-pencil study is of a mother and a child with her bird hat.

2. The banker bear enjoying his favorite cigar.

3. Then there is a woodchuck peach picker with a basket, grabber, and work apron.

4. Finally, here's a katfish waiting for the parade to start and honoring the seven stars.

# HEADDRESSES OR HATS

The sketchbook becomes a wonderfully playful tool. How many different types of headdresses or hats can you come up with? Fish headdress, primitive mountain tribe, sci-fi pilot, Roman rework, steampunk with a dash of humor, fishmonger, zombie. . . .

# CEREMONIAL HEADDRESS

There is so much you can observe and bring into your world of creation. Here are the pencil drawing and the final color work.

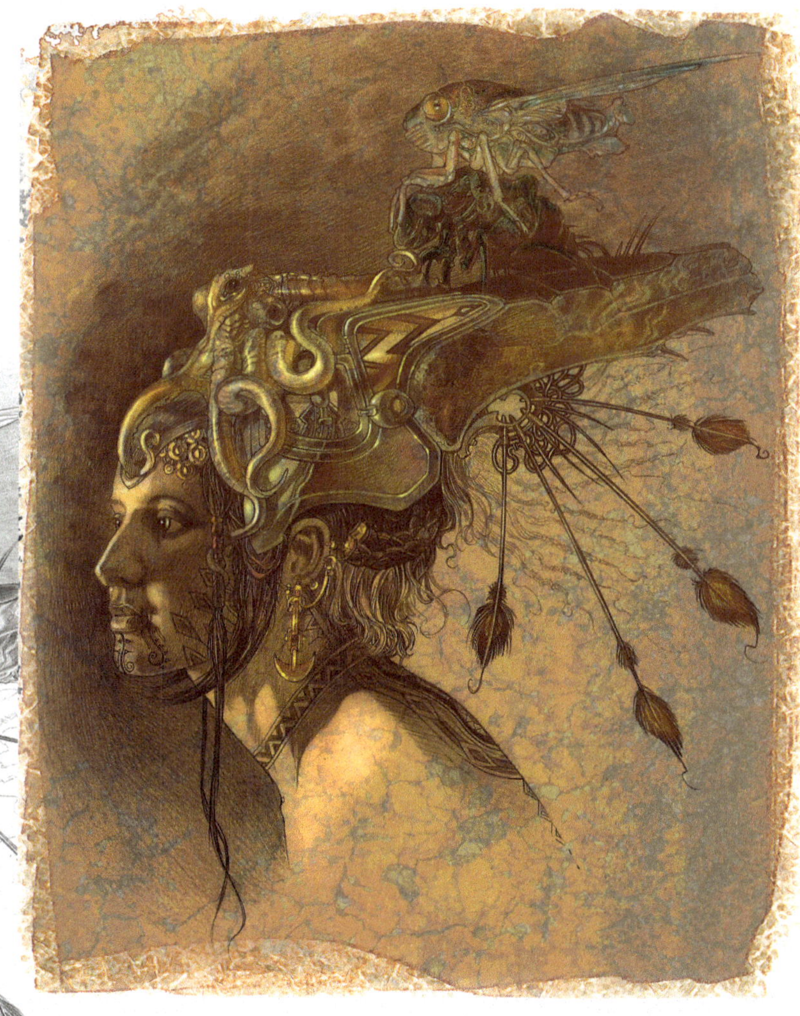

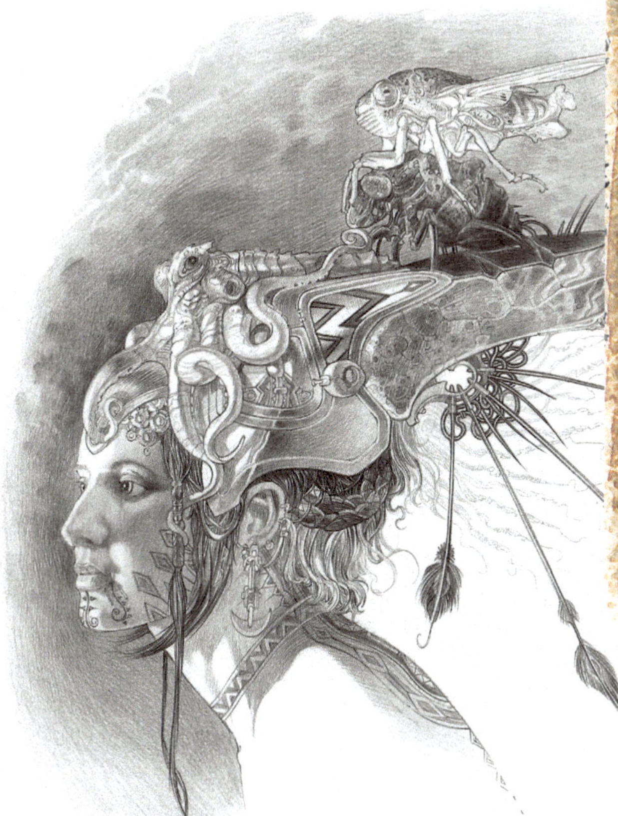

The arrival of the cicadas headdress of the sea queen allows me to play with many things I've observed in nature, along with spiritual facial tattoos.

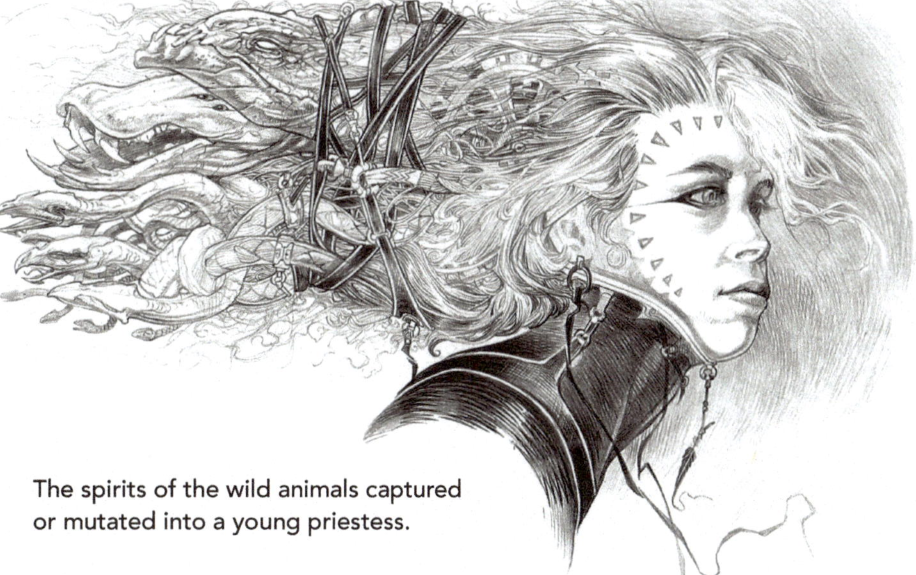

The spirits of the wild animals captured or mutated into a young priestess.

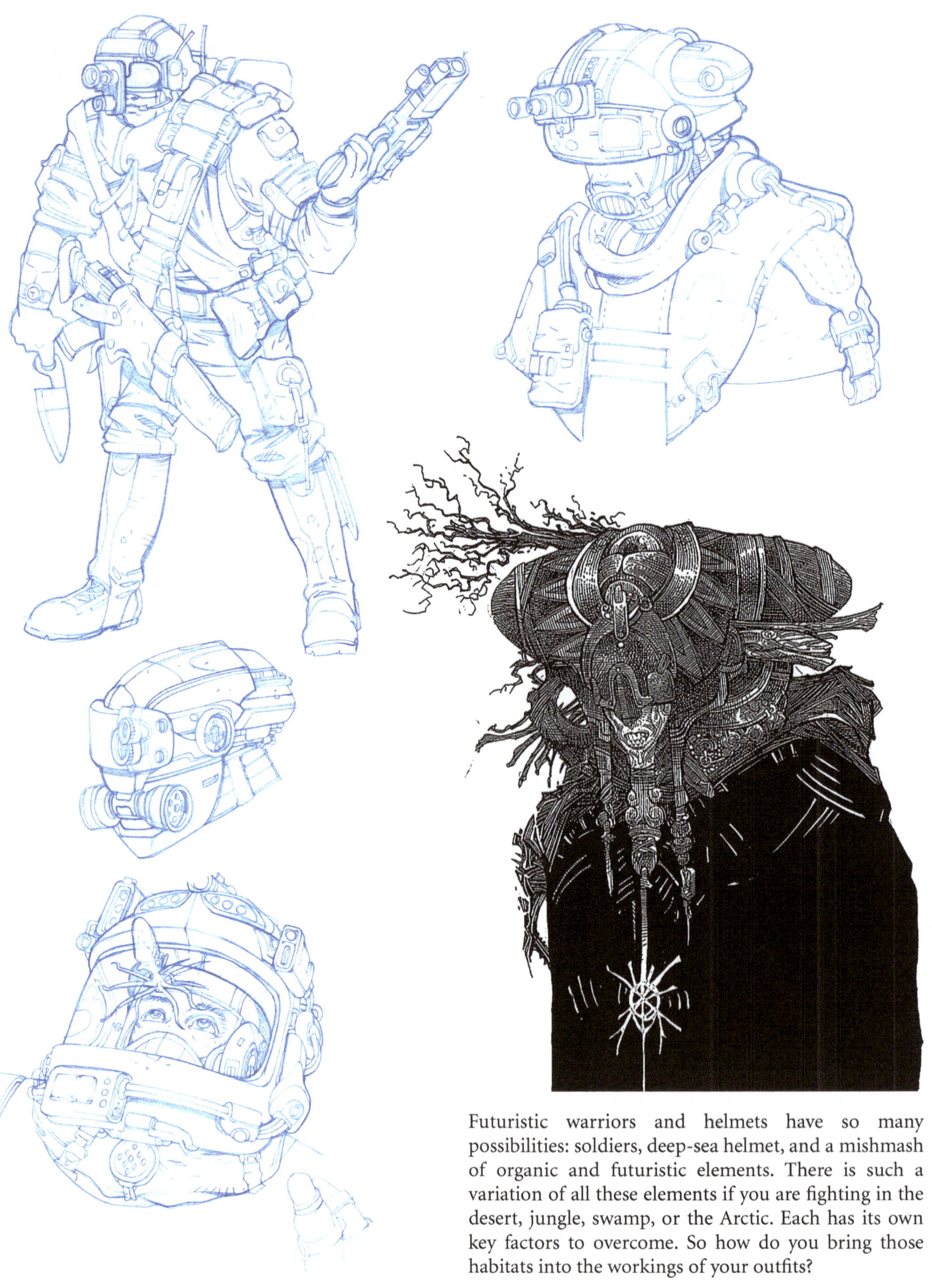

Futuristic warriors and helmets have so many possibilities: soldiers, deep-sea helmet, and a mishmash of organic and futuristic elements. There is such a variation of all these elements if you are fighting in the desert, jungle, swamp, or the Arctic. Each has its own key factors to overcome. So how do you bring those habitats into the workings of your outfits?

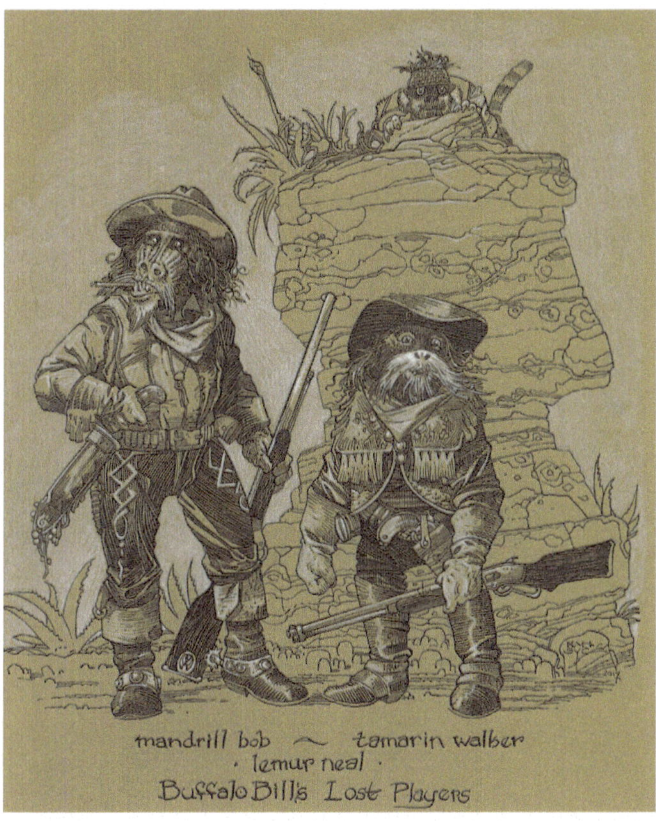



The Old West is also a favorite of mine. So if you add a dash of anthropomorphism and Buffalo Bill's Wild West Show players, who knows what you can come up with?

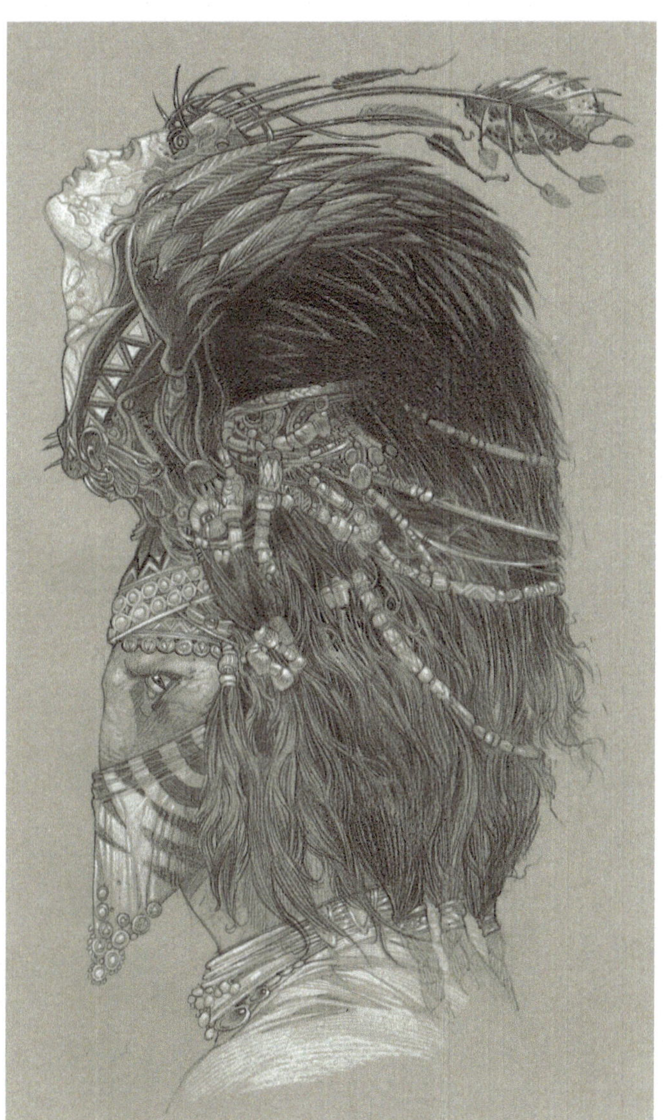

The tall hats of the Queen's Guard and headdresses of African tribes can be used to depict status, and in this case the clan's face is seen.

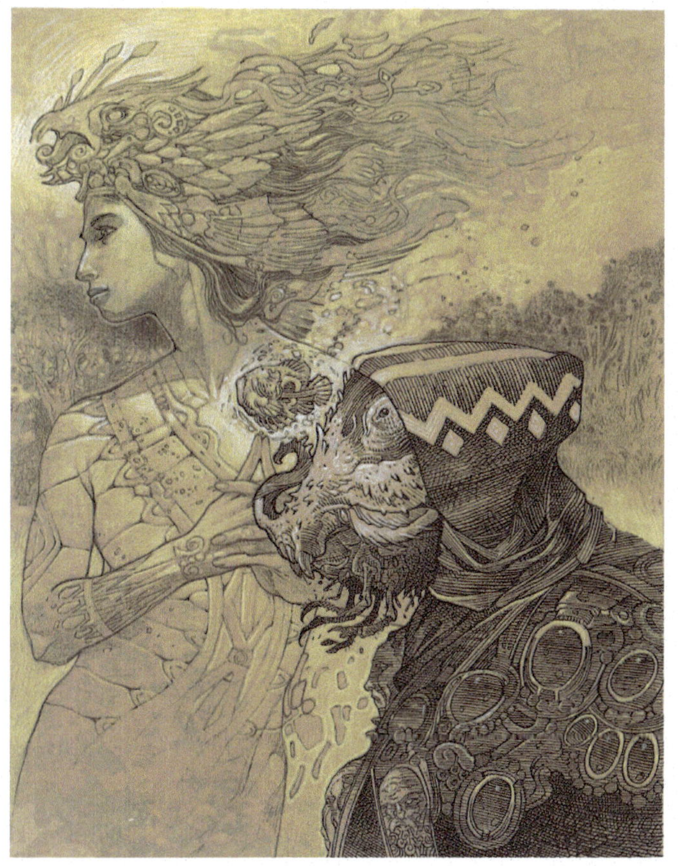

A meeting of two different races was the idea for this drawing. Note the contrast of a headdress and body modification versus the cloak and jeweled shoulder pieces.

In the Vermilion Sands live the Giant Jellyfish hunters.
Here are some of the drawings I did to bring their
hunting garb to the finished product and a finished
panel from the story, complete with the parasites that
live in and on the jellyfish.

Note: Since doing this, I have found out that jellyfish
have no brains. So I can do one of two things in my
world: keep the brain out or give them a brain.

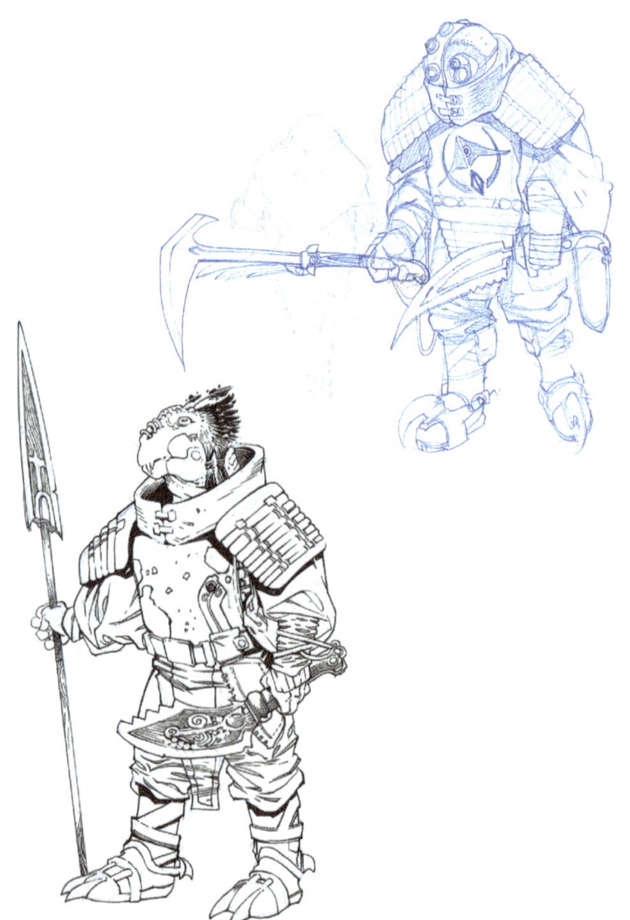

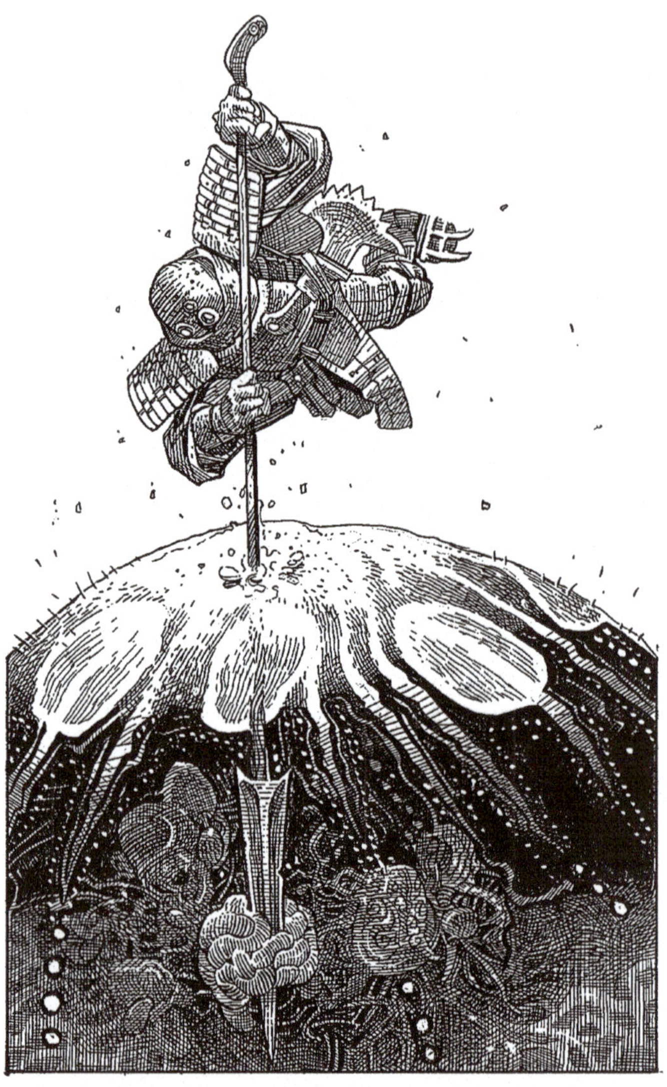

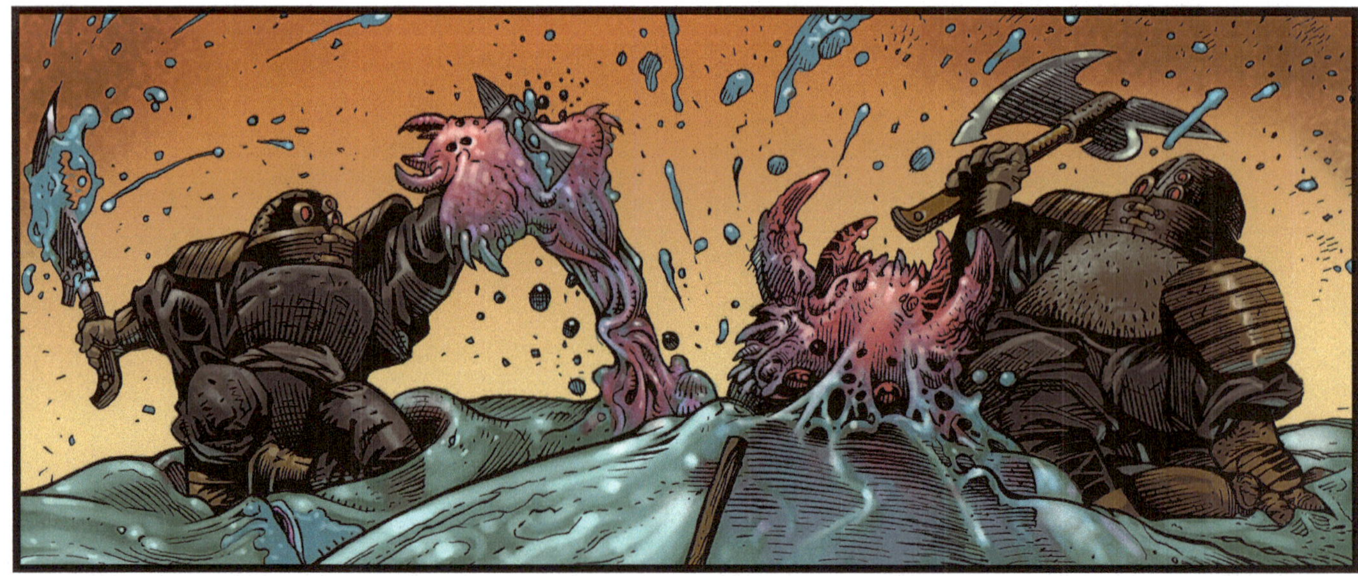

# 12
# ARCHITECTURE



**W**hen designing buildings or lodgings, two of the major factors are how and with what you build. The simplest structural elements are the post and lintel. In the prairies of the United States, the pioneers made sod houses. This is where the term *sod buster* came from. There were not many trees but an abundance of grass, which had deep four- to five-foot roots. These were trimmed into blocks and used as material to build a structure.

A lattice of wood sticks that are woven together shows up all around the world. This can be covered with adobe, mud, and then some mud bricks. This is the basic structure for wickiups and tentlike structures.

In the Southwest, there is a type of rock (shale) that splits in layers. It is cut and stacked to form structures. The amazing thing is the wall is thick, built from two or more layers, and sometimes the stonework is turned to create vertical designs.

The Navajo built with a layering of wood, which was then covered with adobe.

Brick, whether cut or baked, has allowed for a whole new structure. The arch was made by building a frame and cutting stones to fit together. Once the frame was removed, the weight of the stones held the shape.

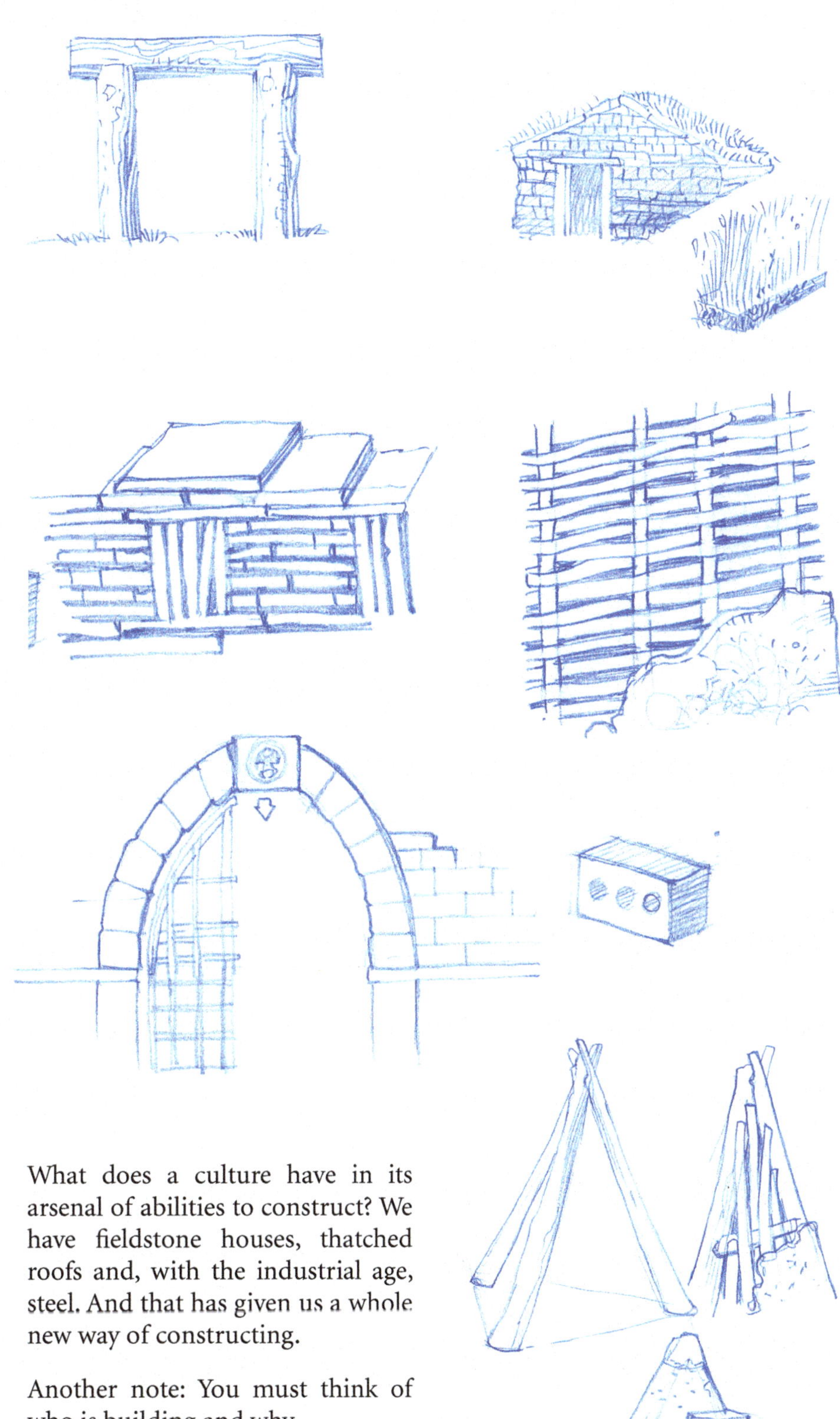

What does a culture have in its arsenal of abilities to construct? We have fieldstone houses, thatched roofs and, with the industrial age, steel. And that has given us a whole new way of constructing.

Another note: You must think of who is building and why.

The sketchbook is an important tool. I use it to try different ideas, from quick sketches to more detailed roughs. It also allows you to use a range of materials, from markers to pencils, and go in any direction you choose. These are studies in different areas and styles of architecture.

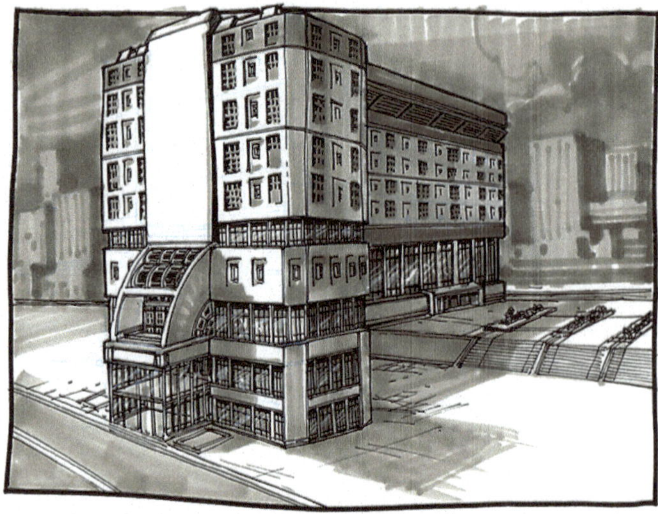

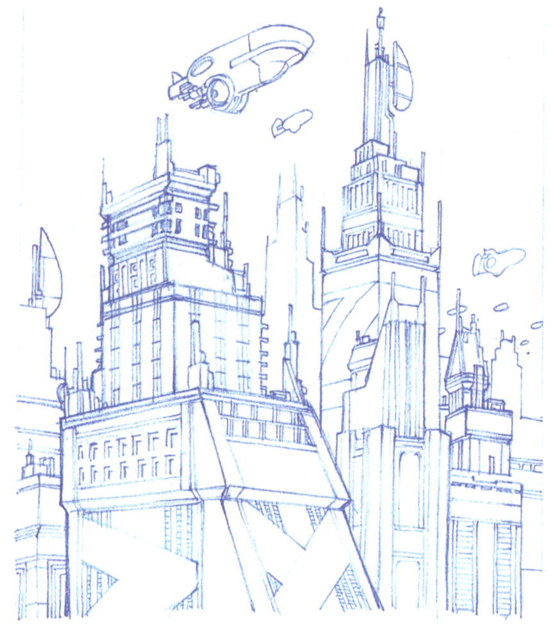

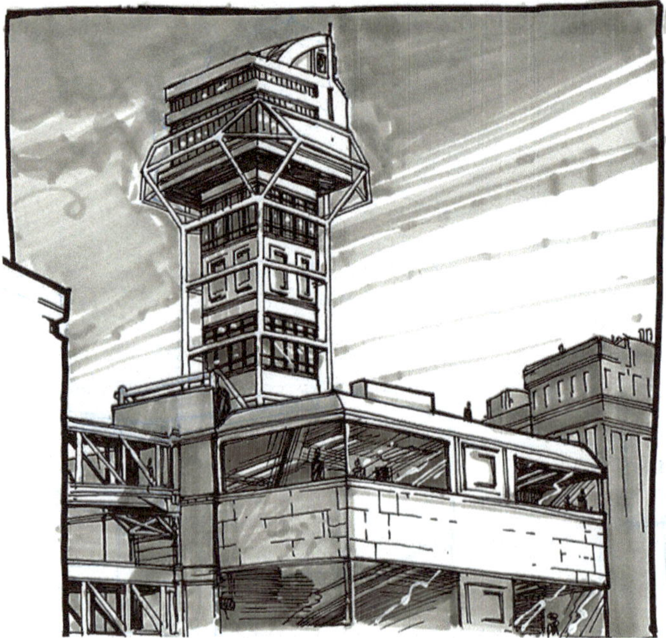

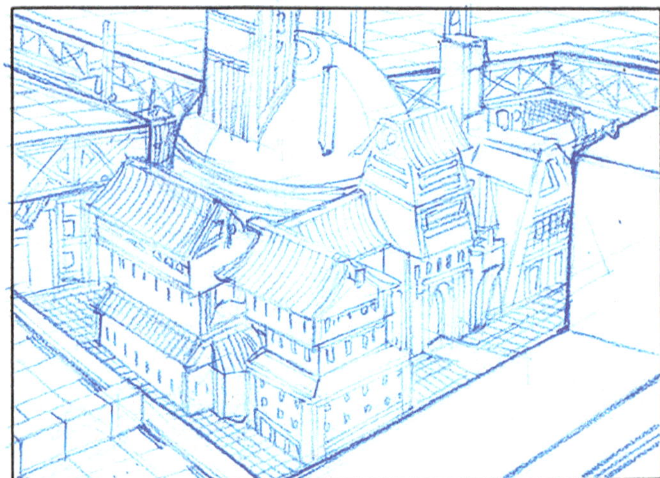

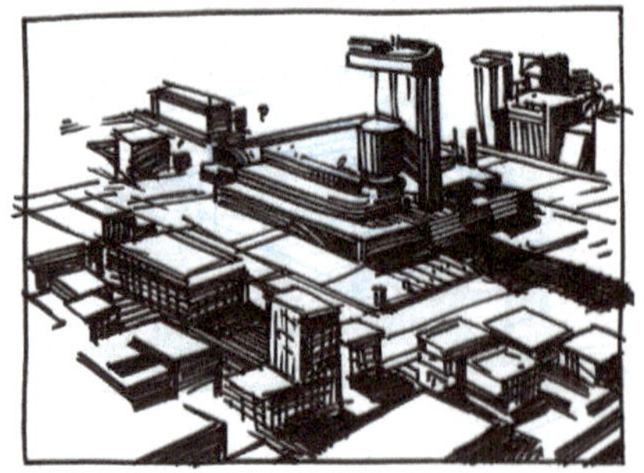

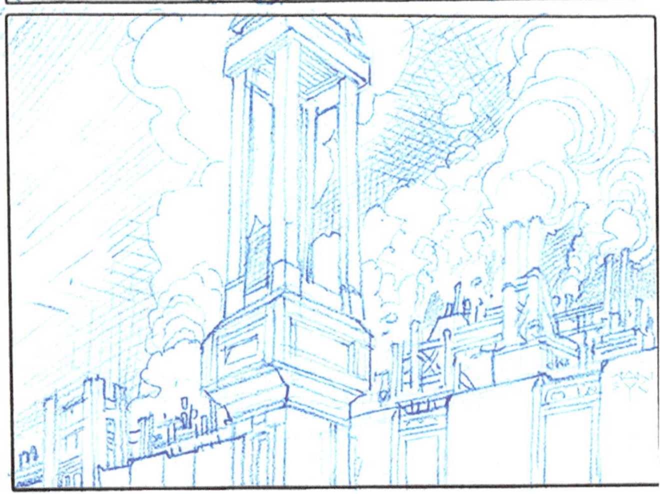

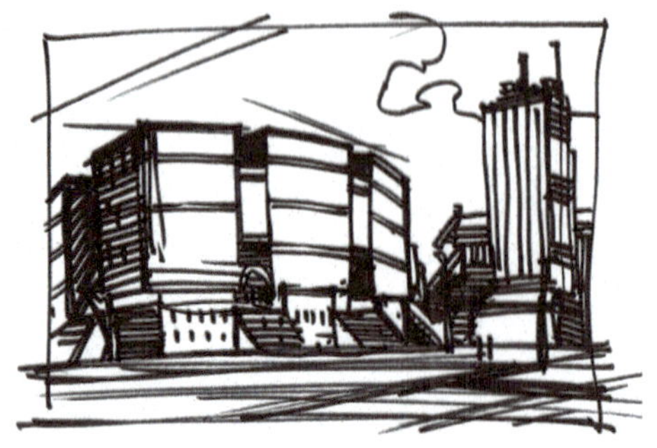

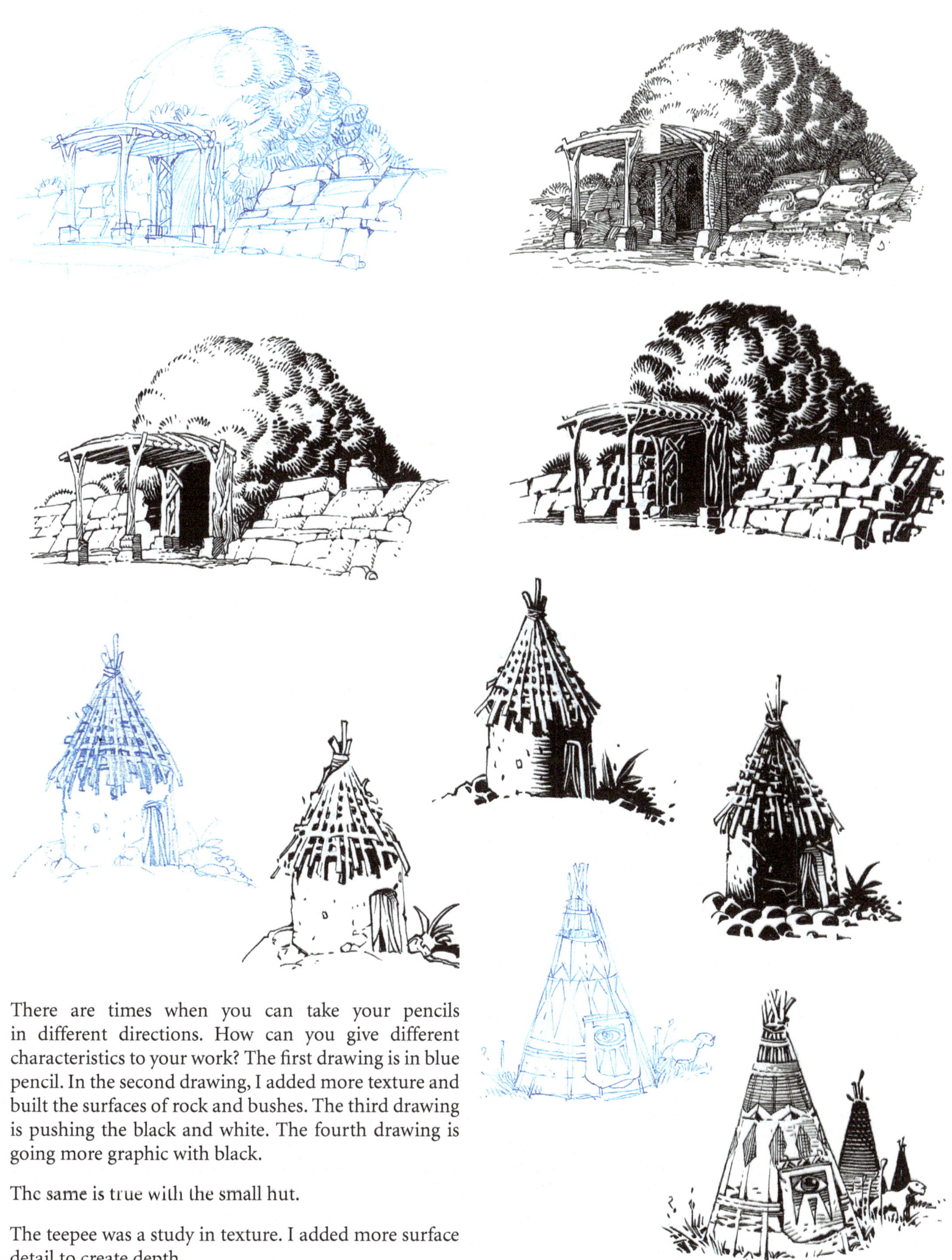

There are times when you can take your pencils in different directions. How can you give different characteristics to your work? The first drawing is in blue pencil. In the second drawing, I added more texture and built the surfaces of rock and bushes. The third drawing is pushing the black and white. The fourth drawing is going more graphic with black.

The same is true with the small hut.

The teepee was a study in texture. I added more surface detail to create depth.

A solution to a drawing can be stretched in different directions. It depends on what you want to achieve in your finished artwork.

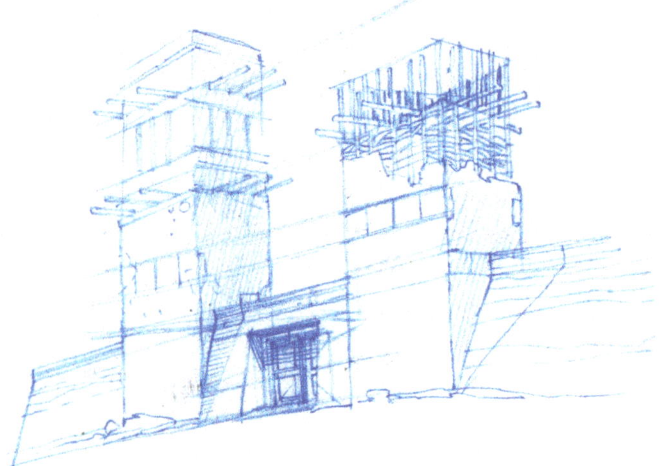

This structure includes a gateway, using the idea of bricks, mud, and letting the wood interior stick out. I construct the forms in blue pencil and then add ink.

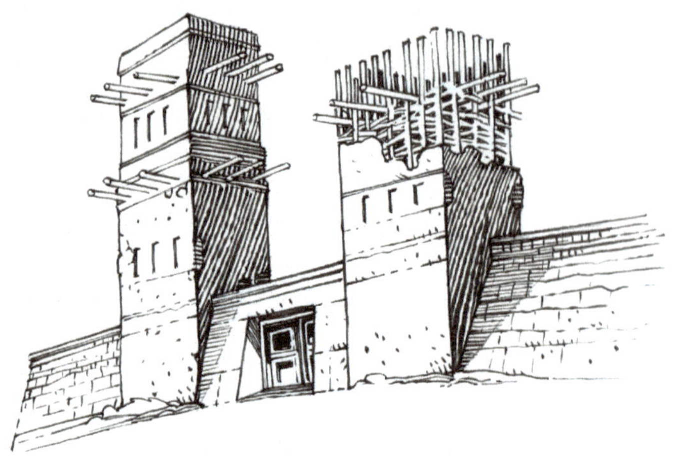

Inking what was penciled.

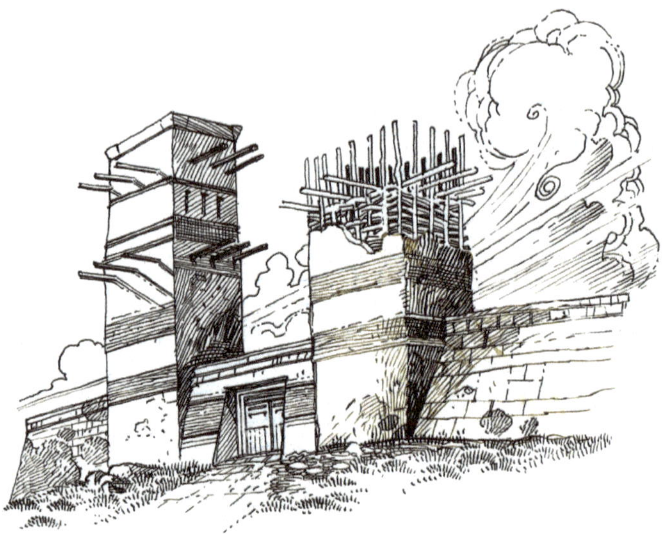

Pushing the drawing further, with more textures, surfaces, clouds, and a ground plan.

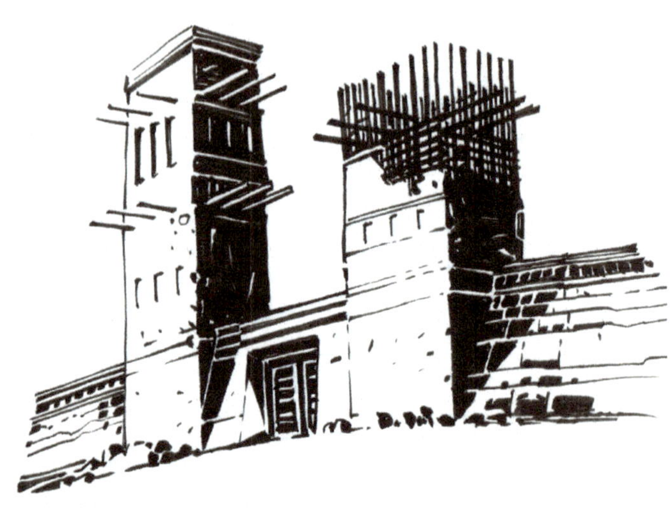

Going for a graphic black and white that just shows the lights and darks.

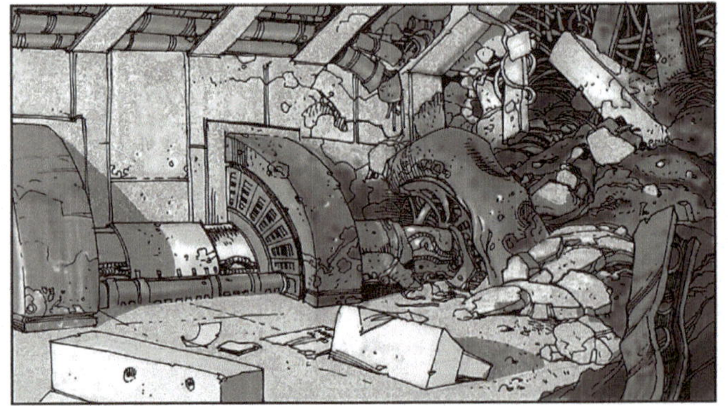

These last two drawings are marker renderings. Here, you have a little more tonal range.

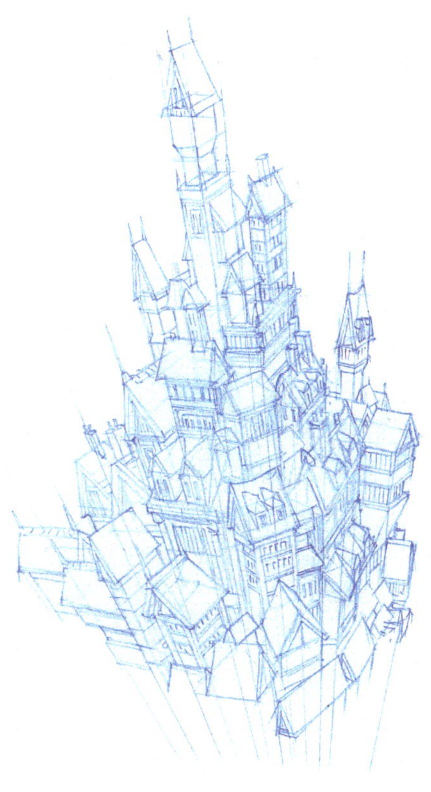

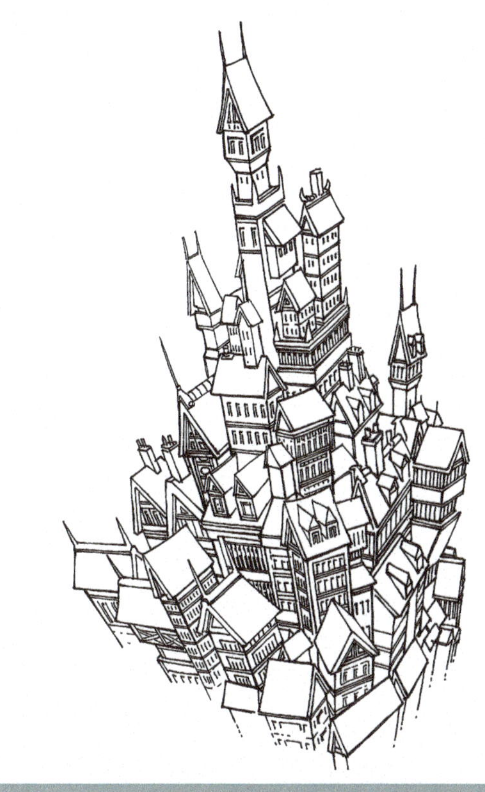

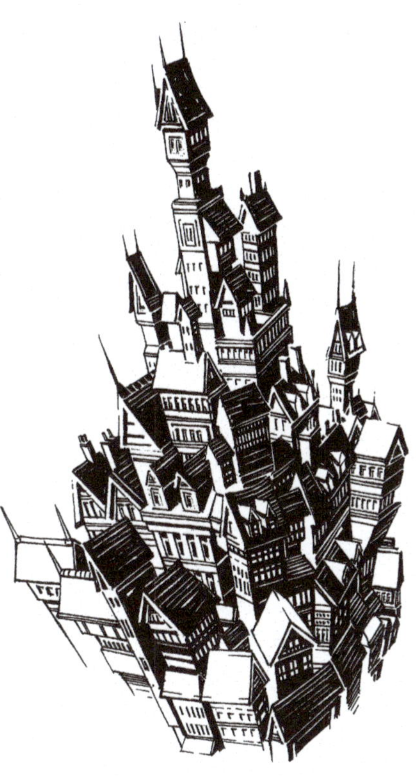

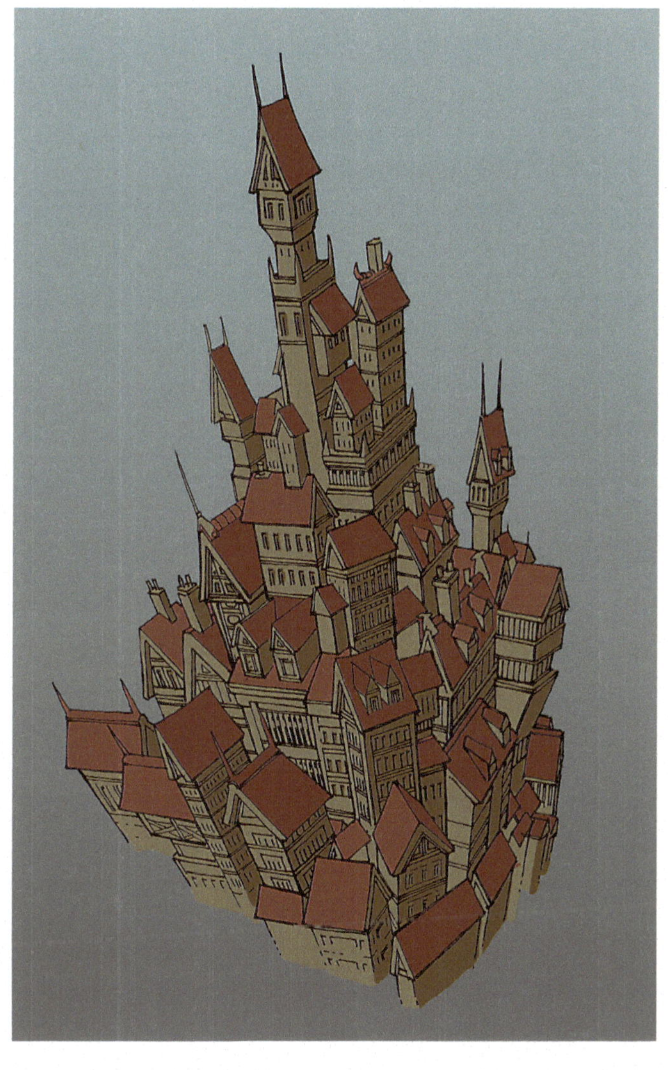

Using three-point perspective, I've created and exaggerated a view of a mountain city. Next, I inked the drawing with a technical pen. Working with it as just an ink comp, I took a light source from the upper left and blocked in the light and dark sides. This became the model start for the colors. The buildings and roofs are two different values.

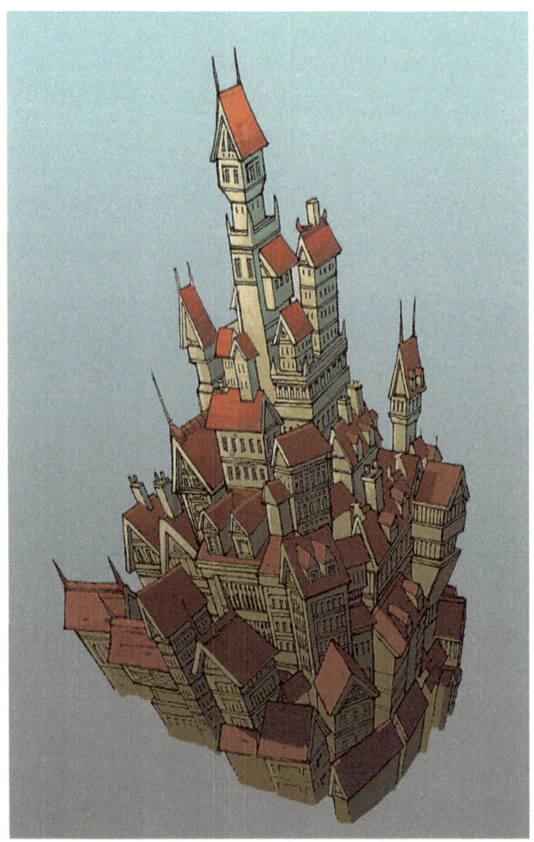

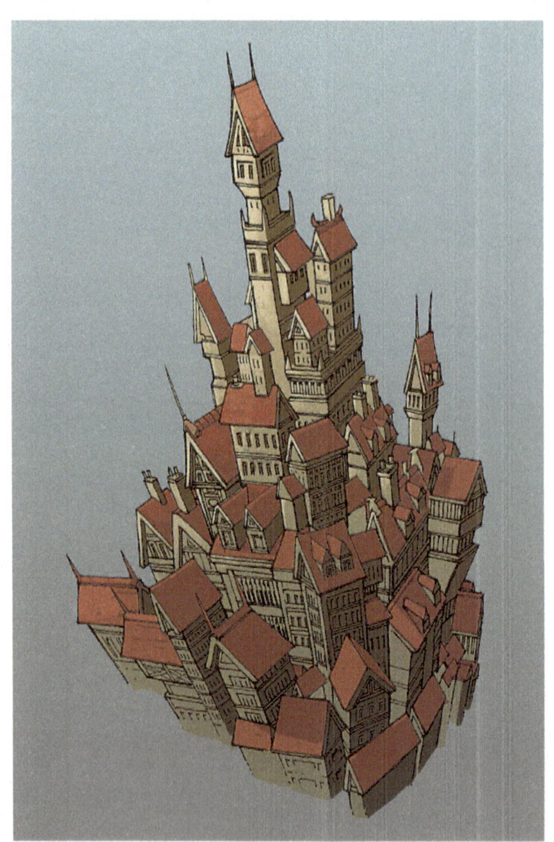

Now, to bring out the highest towers as a focal point, I'm lightening the top roof and light sides of the building, which brings them more toward us, and letting them taper down into darker values. This will create a deeper space than in the earlier drawing.

Let's push the darker values at the base of the building more, so our range of values is even greater.

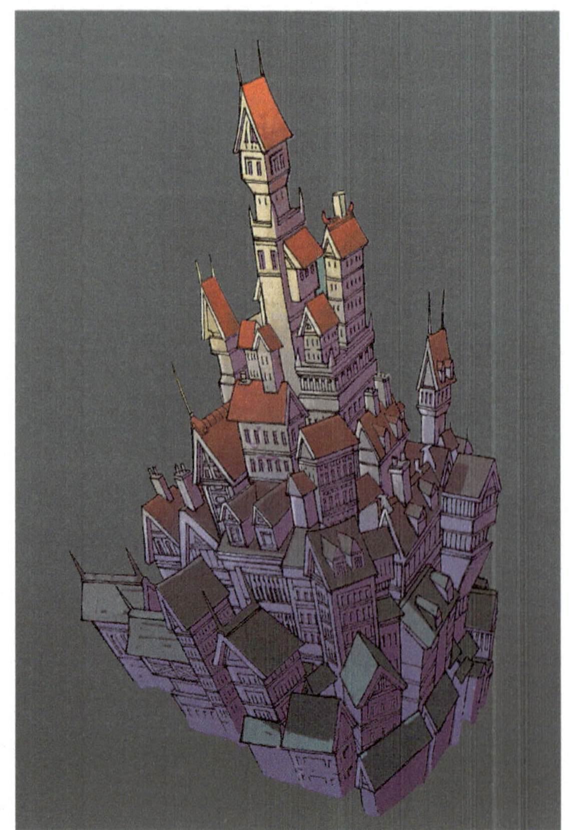

Let's push a sunset feel by keeping the bright pure colors at the top that are being hit by light and bringing in a blue tint to the darks and shadows.

# IDEA: TWO FRIENDS MEET FOR "THE VISIT."

I love to work in different mediums. These are ink washes, and like markers, they give you a greater range of grays. These drawings just wanted to be more fleshed out with tone. I tried to keep the first one a little more playful, with the stylization of the figures, clouds, and birds. The second one, even though humorous, is more representational.

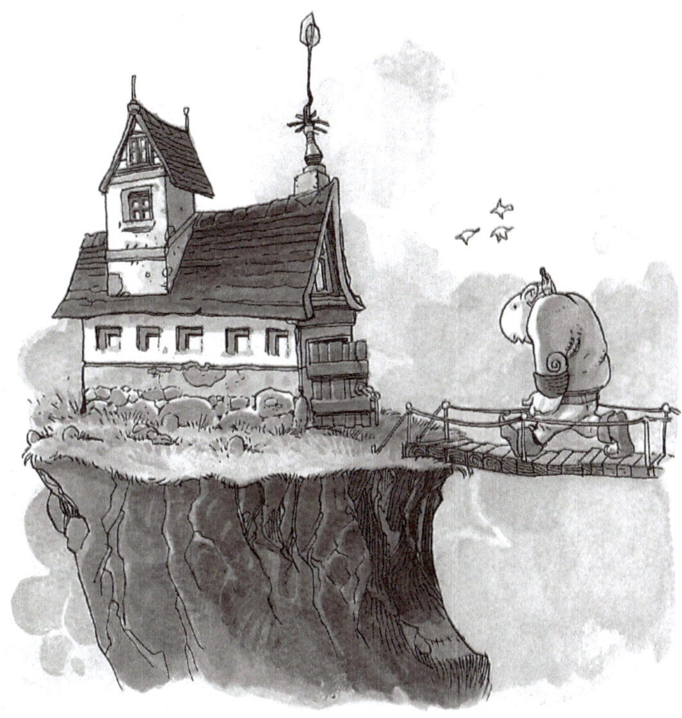

Elwood brings James home after a hard day at school. They tell stories and laugh. But will Elwood be able to come in? And is he the troll walking across the bridge?

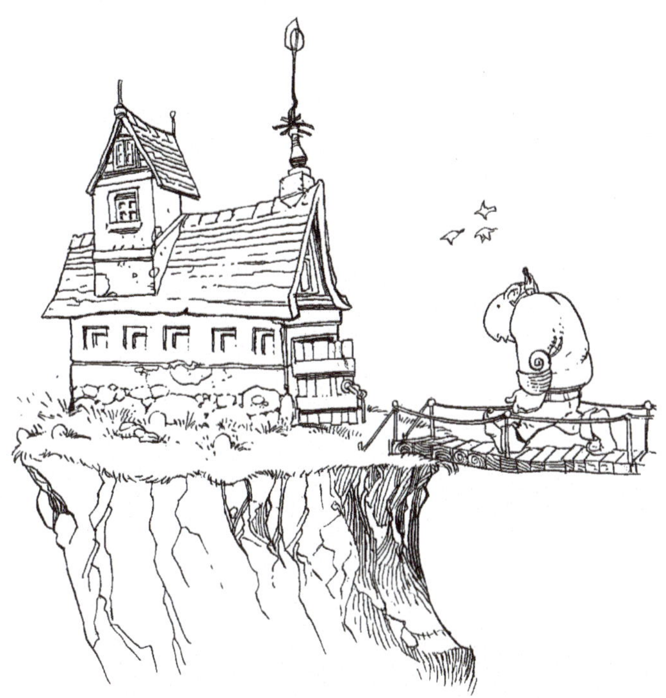

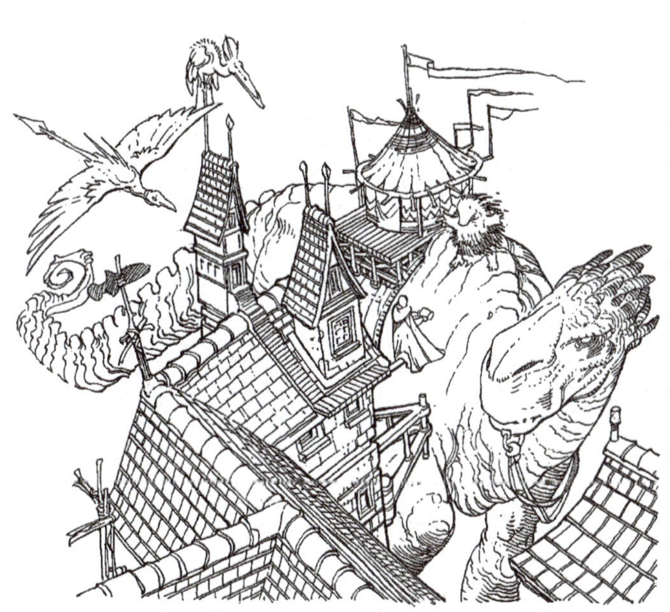

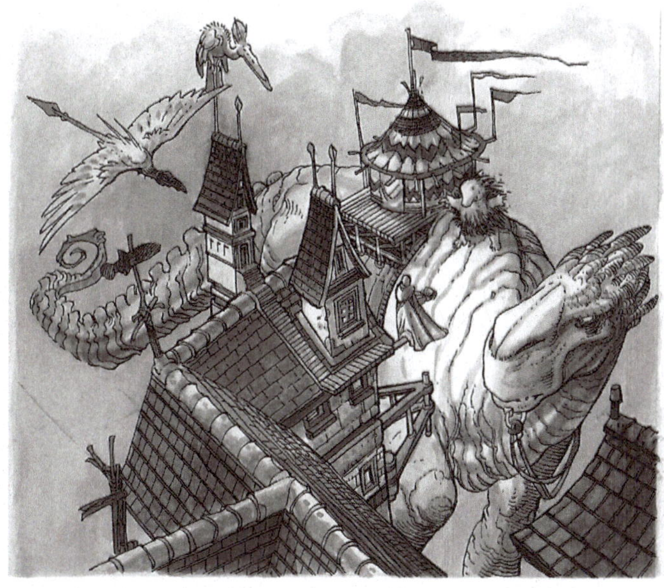

Jaster Hedgehog always rides its lizard in its entire splendor to pick a fruitcake in the castle of Monks of Betowain, who also are known for their fish weather vanes and collection of large ginkgo birds.

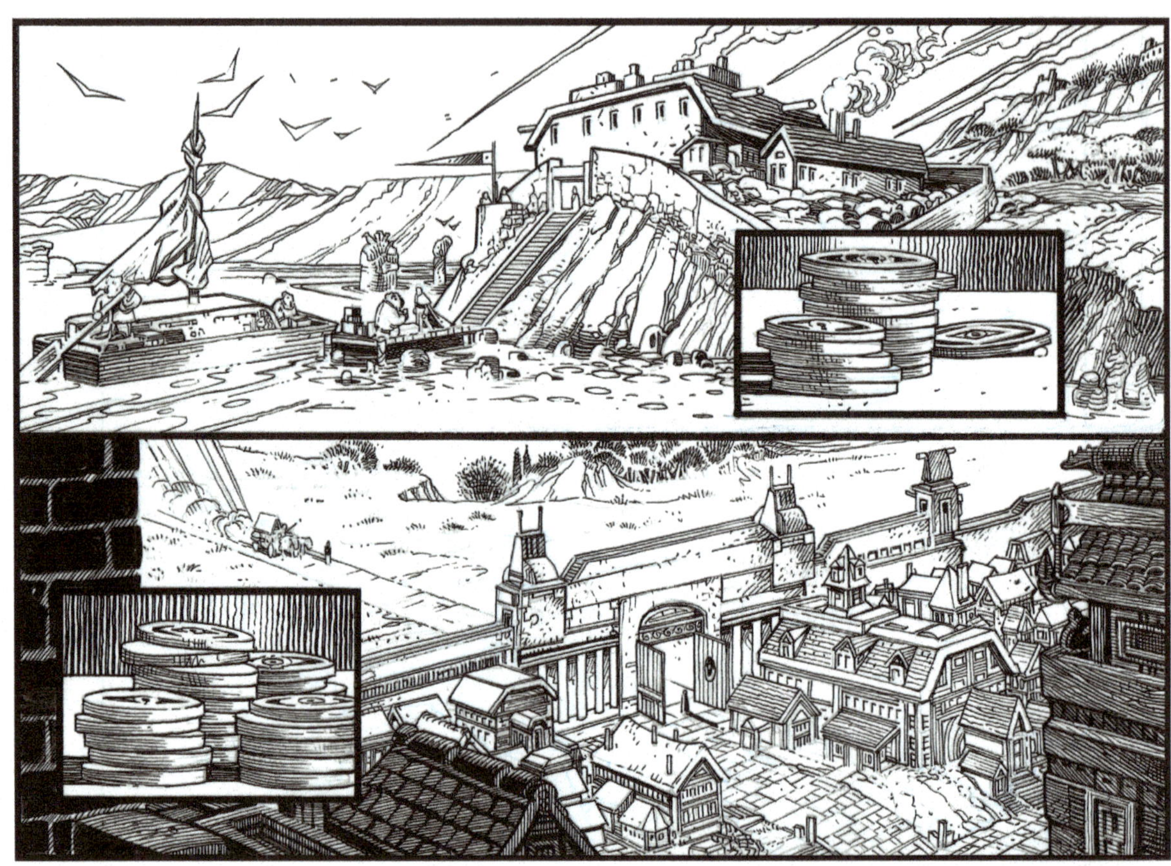

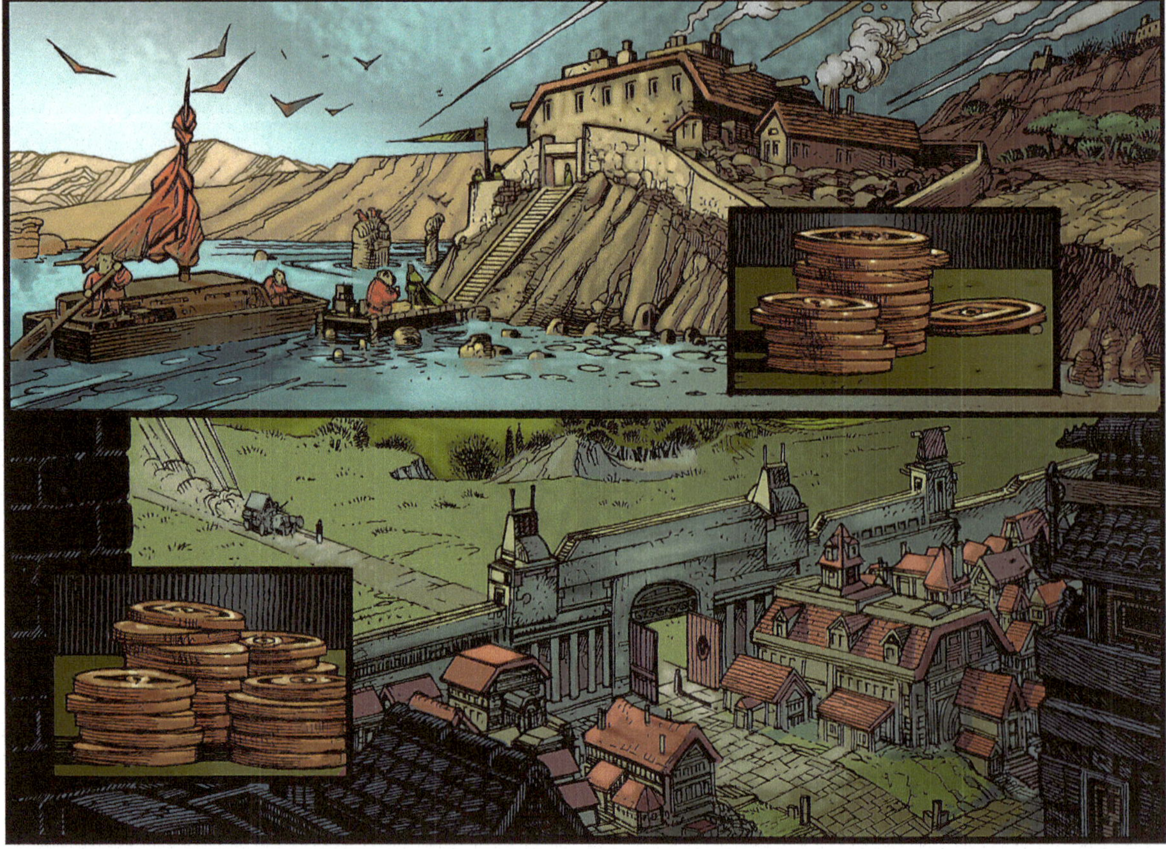

In my comic story *Scent*, we follow the sale of material to make perfume. These panels follow it from the barren coastal city to the inland castle, and as it goes up, so does the price.

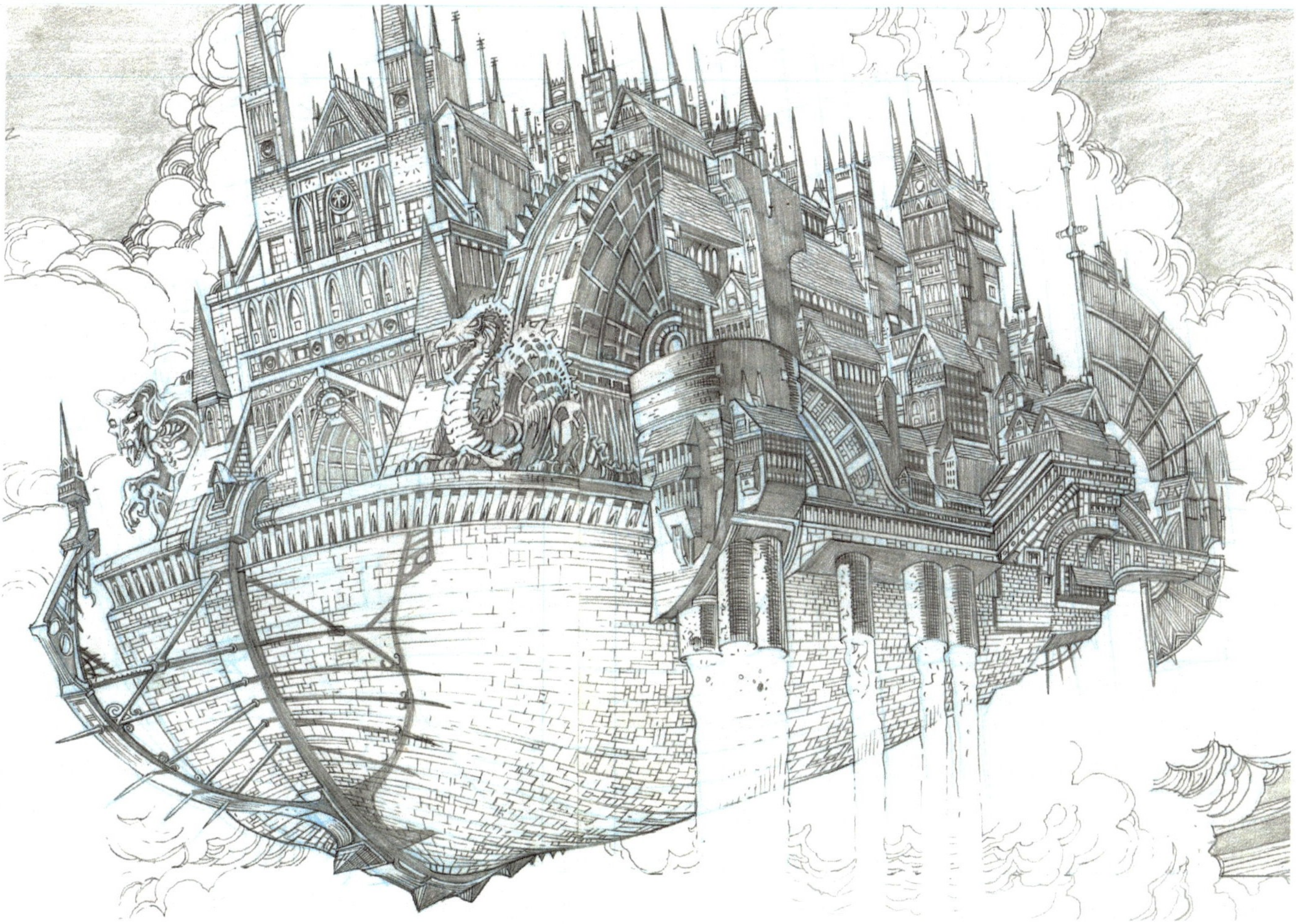

Now what would happen if your technology was based partly in the Gothic era (mid-twelfth century to sixteenth century) and you could build a flying Cathedral City? The Gothic style has spires; your vaulted ceilings come to a point and are ribbed to hold a lot of weight; columns are more slender and decorative elements are quite elaborate.

On the other hand, no matter how far we have come, there is technological ruin and decay. How would metal fray, large elements rust, and machine graveyards be created?

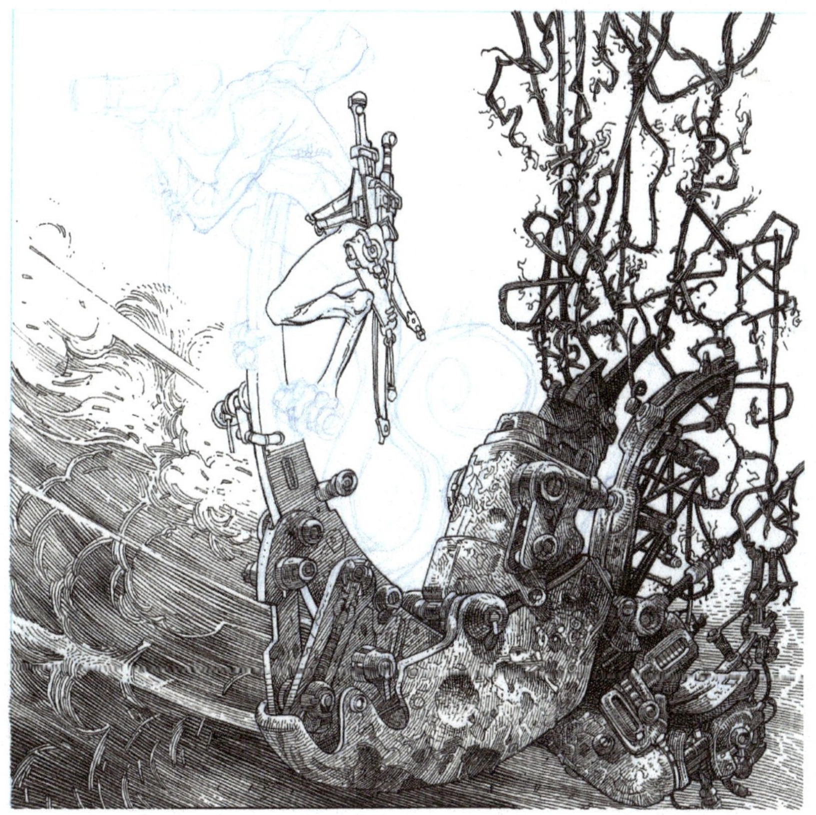

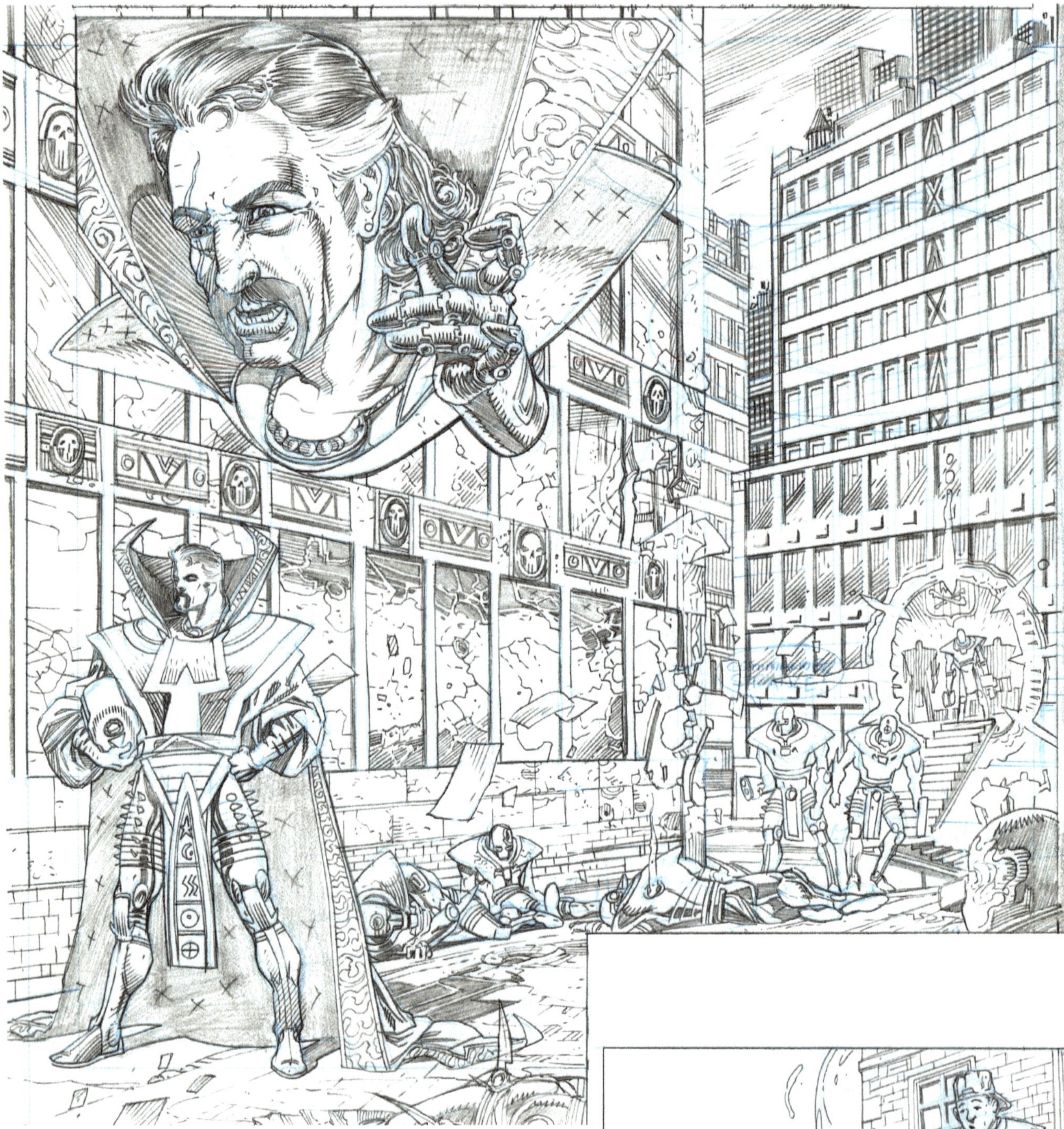

There will be times when you have to draw certain cities and places. What does a downtown area in a huge metropolis look like? New York City is very different from Houston or Chicago. Each area has its own problems. You will have huge contemporary skyscrapers, old brownstones, and turn-of-the-century houses in Manhattan. One the biggest elements that cross over are museums.

In this last panel, kids are playing street hockey. I use inline skates, which help date your time frame.

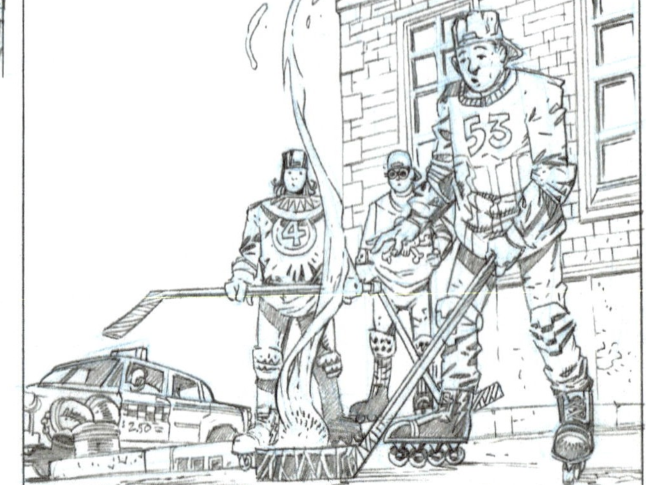

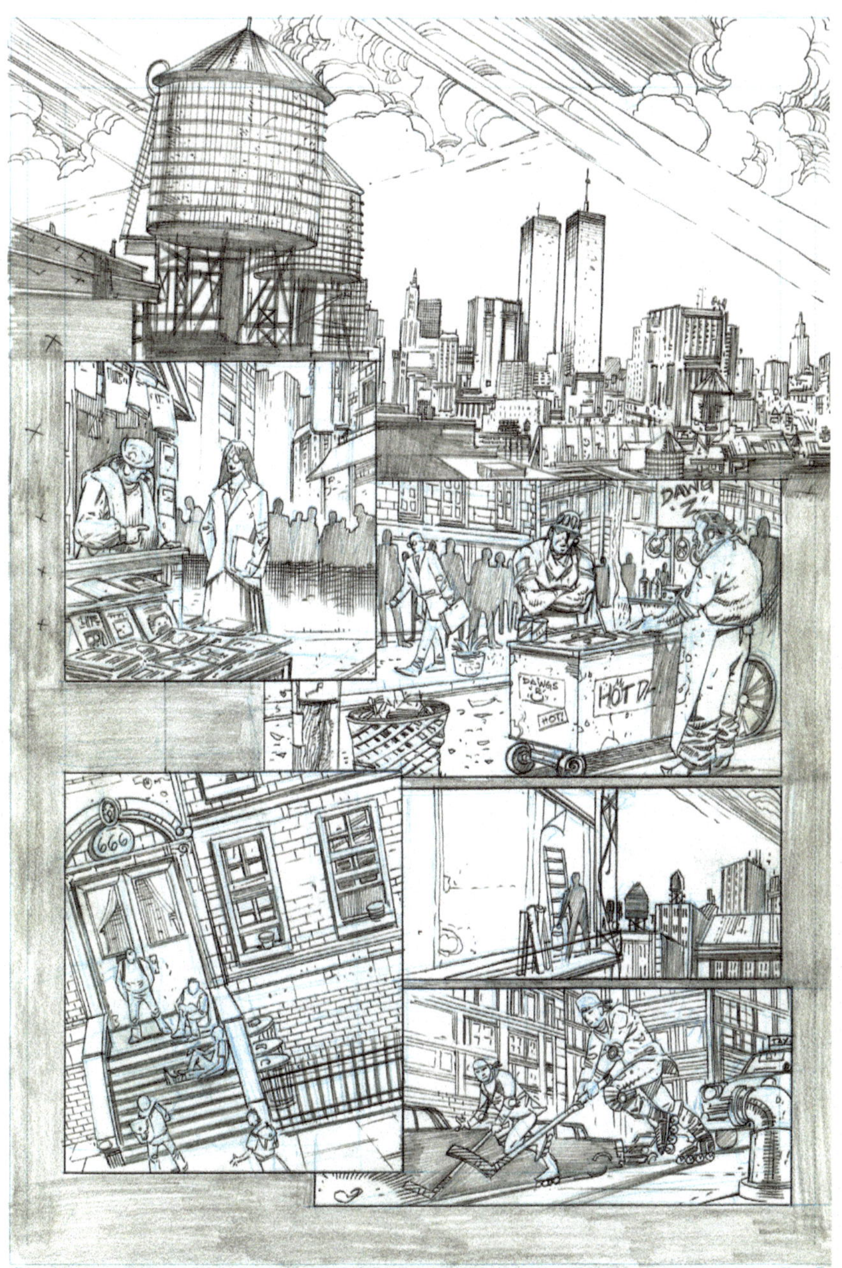

The story in the pencils starts in a large city. Even today, there are water towers on roofs. Where I grew up in North Dakota, we had huge water towers. In New York City and Chicago, there used to be newsstands and food vendors. The food vendors are still around, but you don't see that many newsstands anymore. So this will date the time of your story. Sign painters and large billboards are different now. The computer has changed that marketplace.

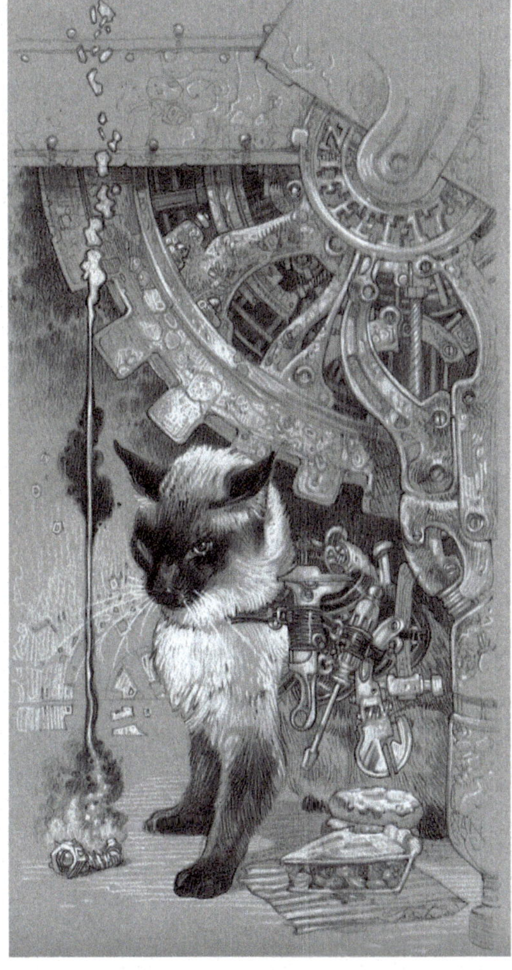

Doing a portrait of my kat, I thought it would be nice to make him a repair animal in some strange machine area, replacing burned-out bearings and bolts. Here, lunch is being interrupted by work on the Ziffel 17.

One of the hard things for me to draw is an airplane. When I did a pinup page for a friend, the series had a lot of planes. My idea was to work on the repair area. Engines must be cleaned and fixed, guns reloaded and replaced, and paint touched up. Our supply list for our work yard: crates of bullets, engine parts, tool chests, ladders, carts, wheel blocks, and papers (so they can add to the motion of a figure flying through). It all adds up to create a believable environment.

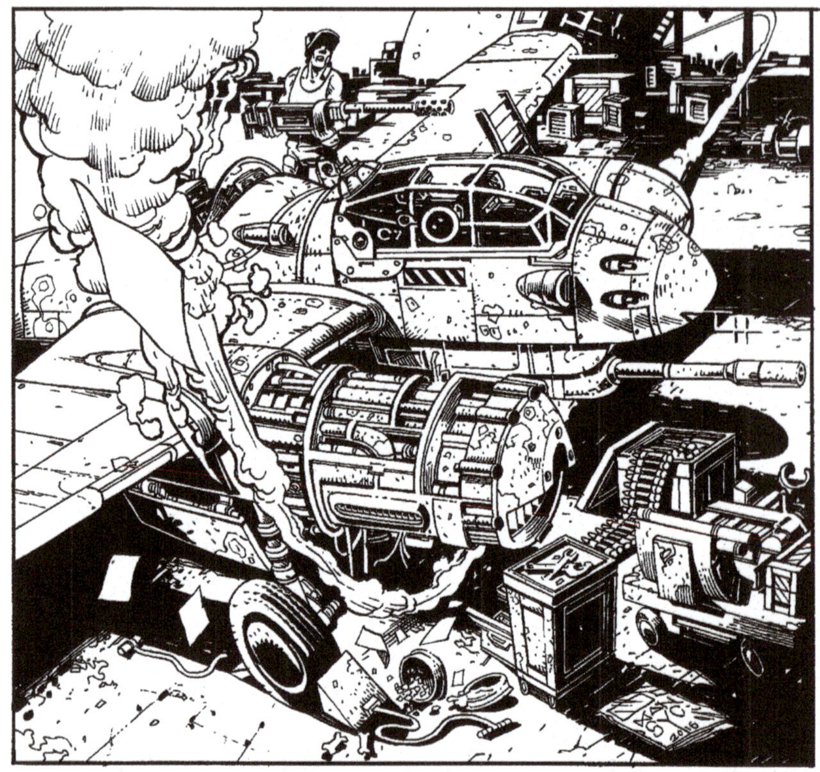

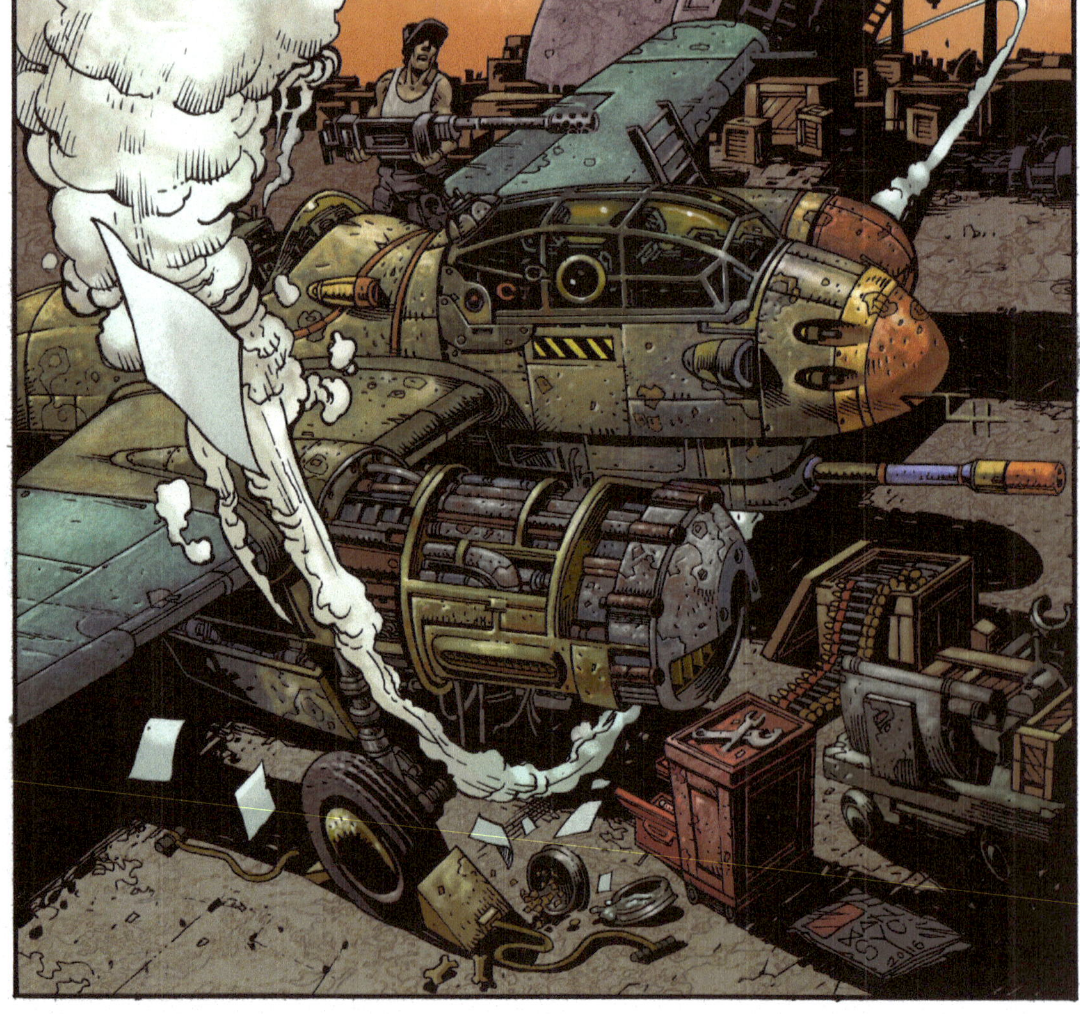

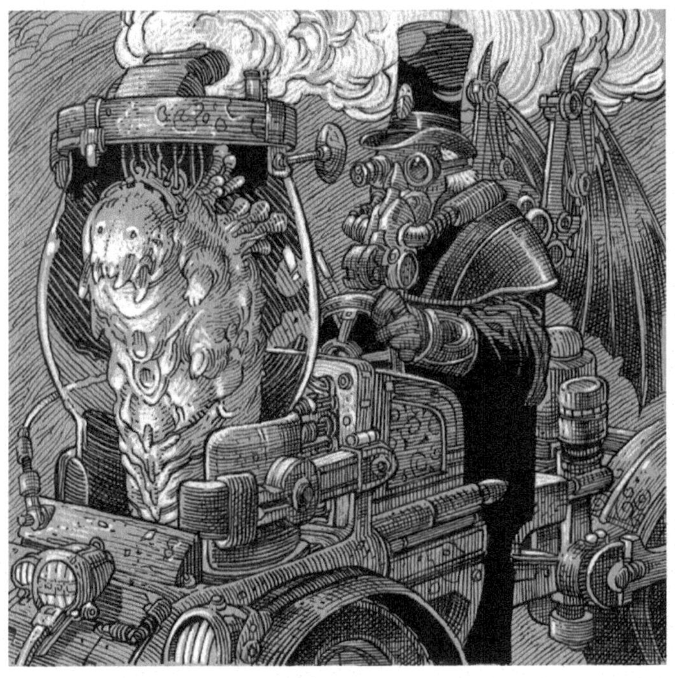

Gertrude travels in the best motor coach and has a well-dressed driver. She is in her protective jar, which is sealed, controlled, and connected to environmental controls.

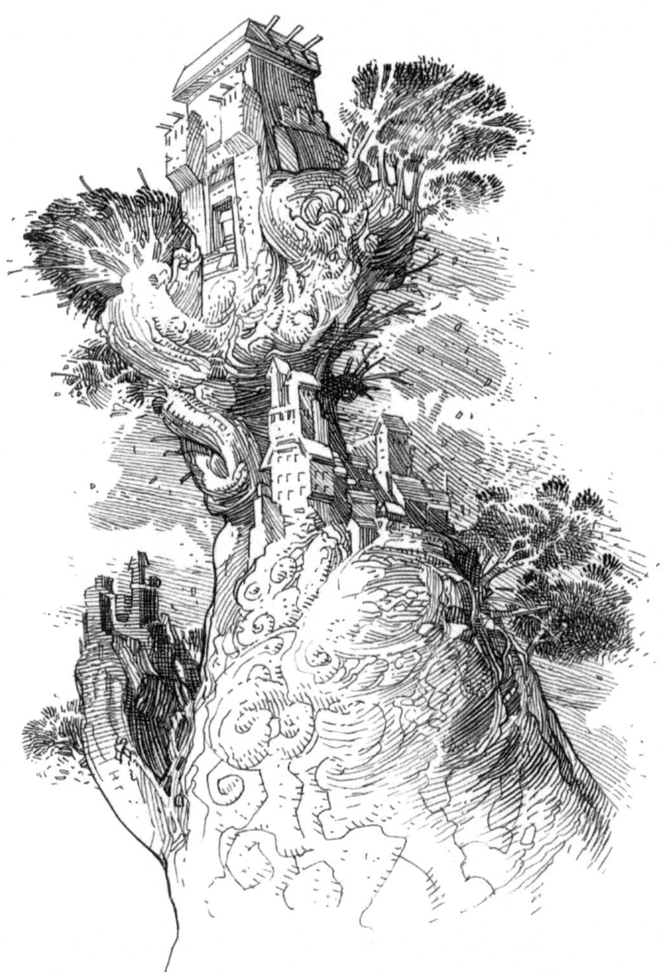

In a habitat that is all tall peaks and ironwood trees, you can build castles in the trees. Your mode of travel could be

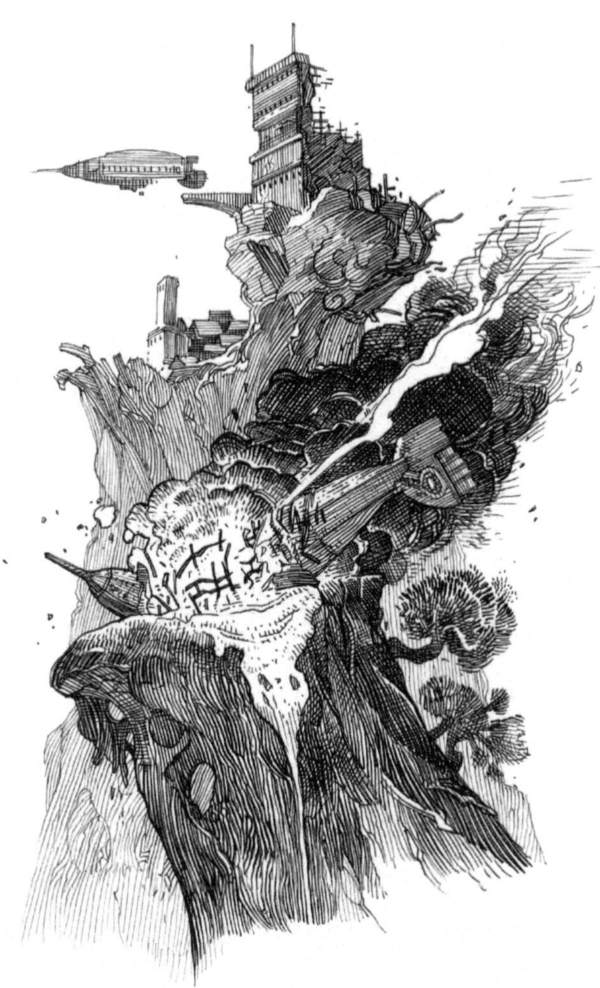

zeppelins and flying machines. Malfunctions here can be dangerous and costly.

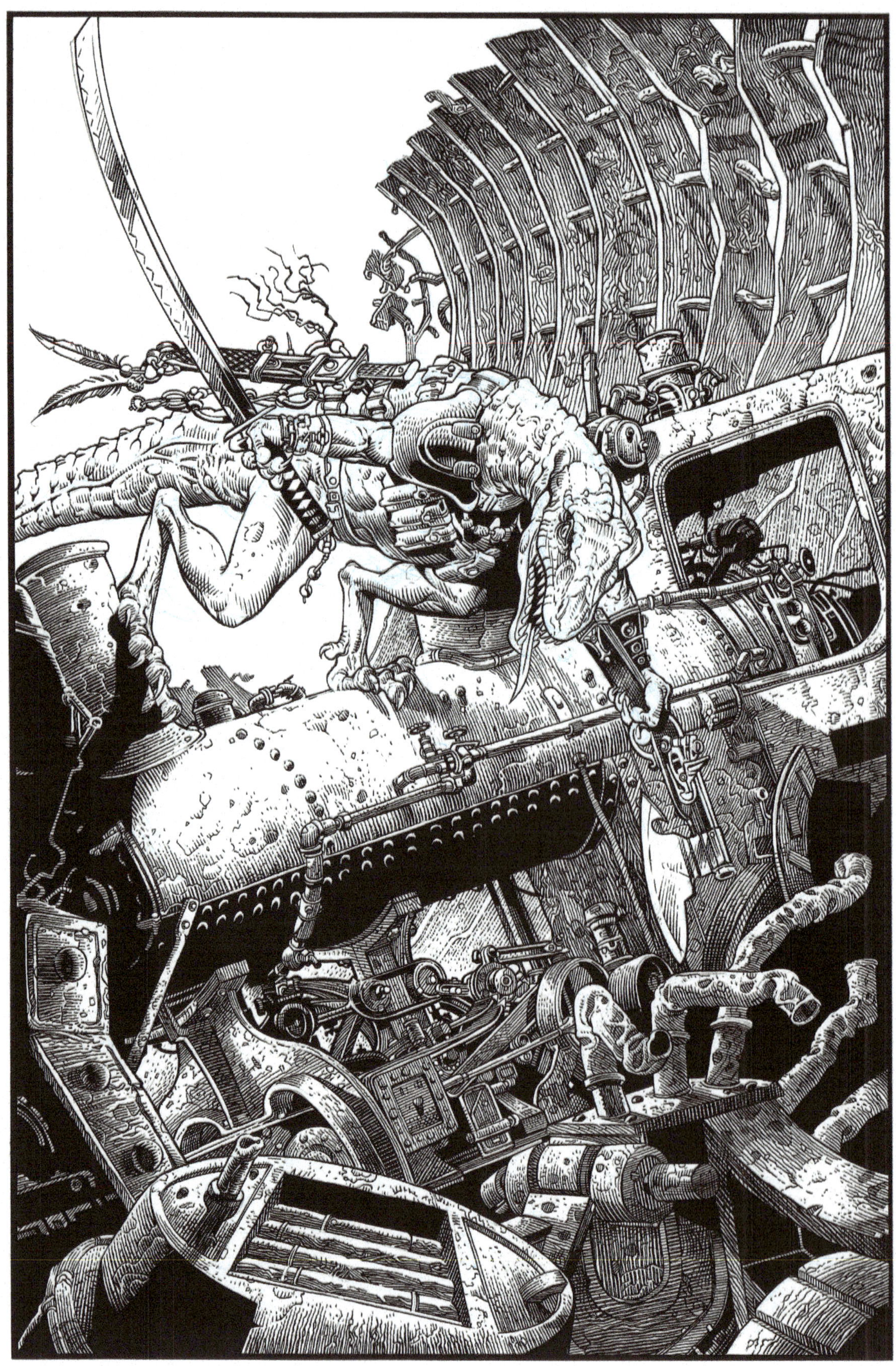

Dinosaurs, samurai swords, flintlocks with ax heads, steam tractors, and dead tech. What is there not to like about this setup to start a drawing and create the beginnings of a new world?

# 14

# TRANSPORTATION

Caravans of giant lizards, flying machines, and bats to ride on—these are but a few ways of getting around in a new world. Transportation can be mechanical or organic, but they both get the trick done. As you build up the habitat and the world, you can easily adapt for each section with a range of vehicles. If you have a person riding a six-legged horse that is talking to a frog creature driving a tank, you already have set up interesting parallels that can add to your story.

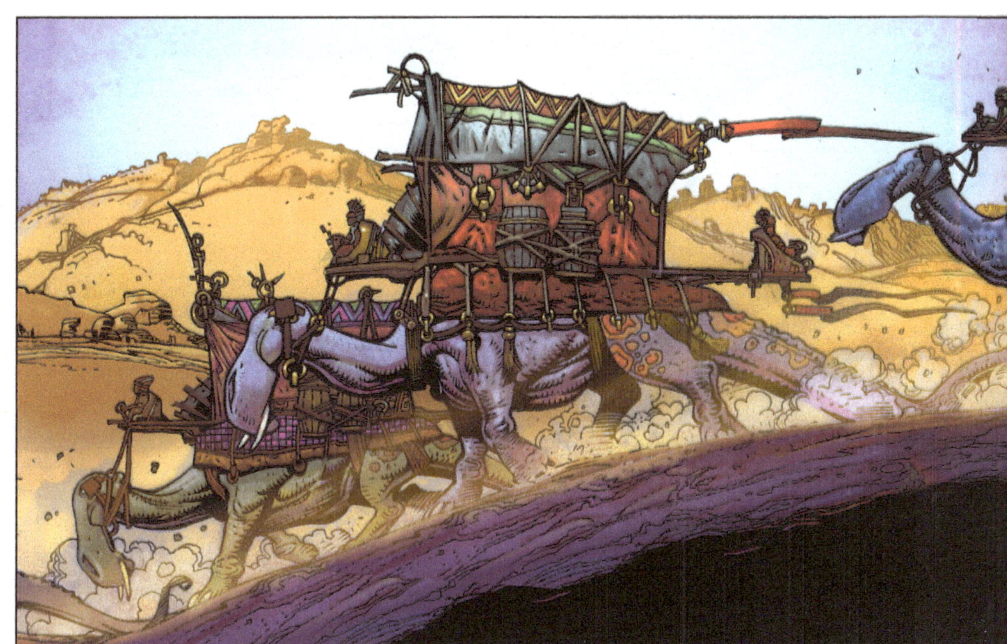

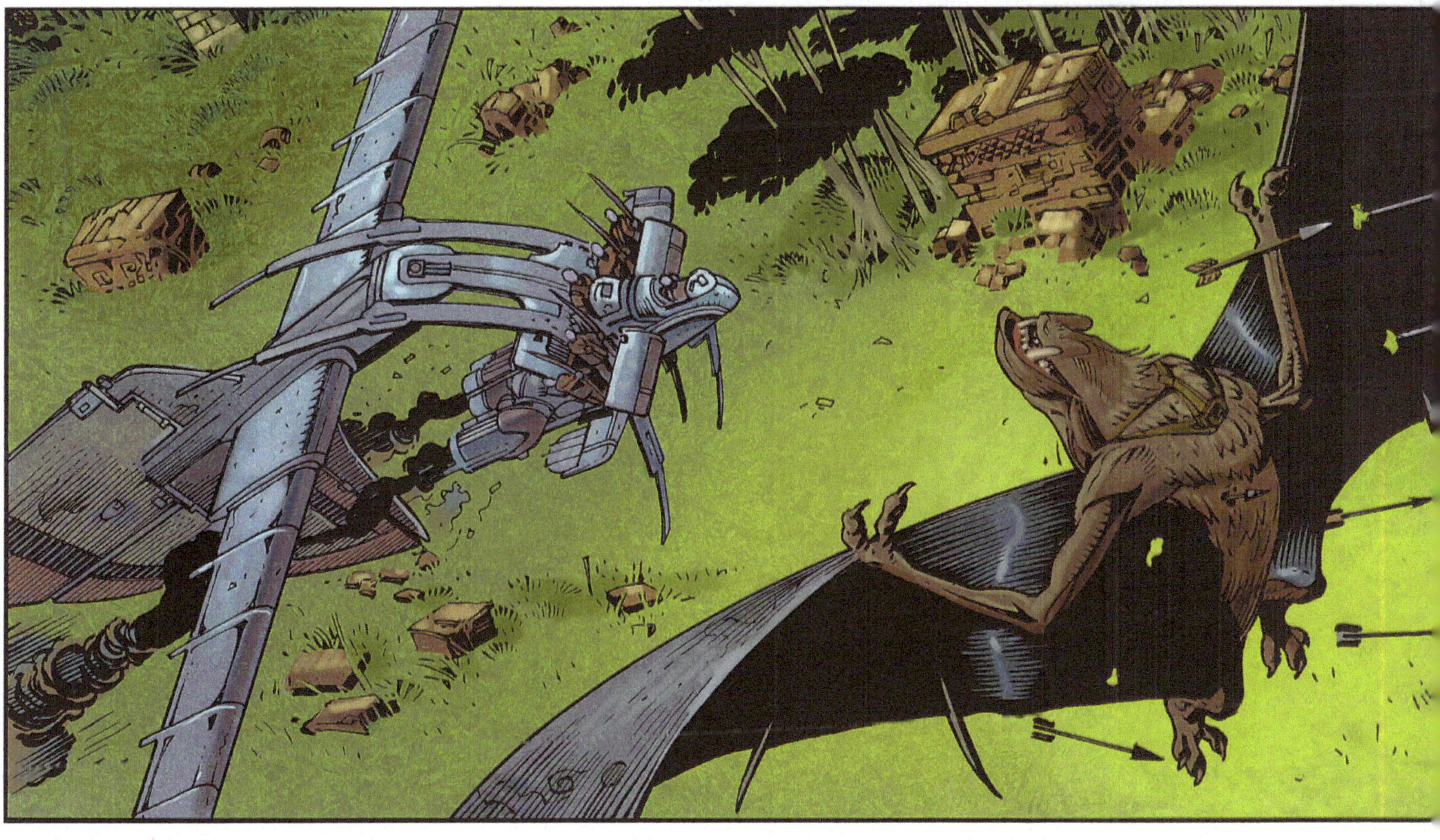

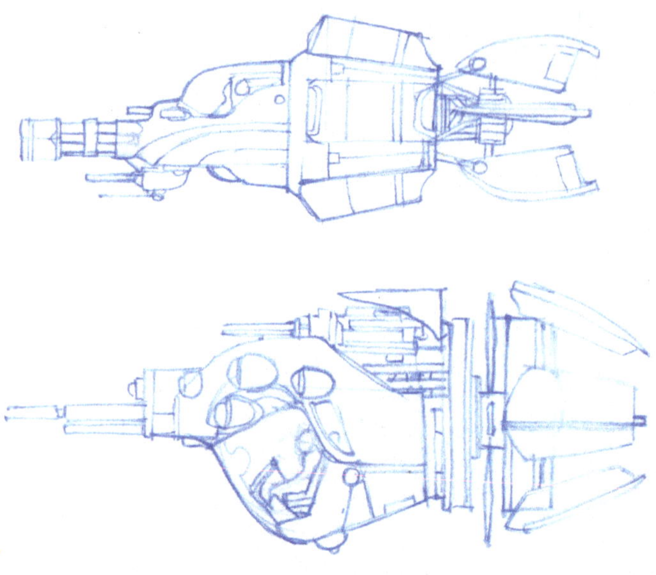

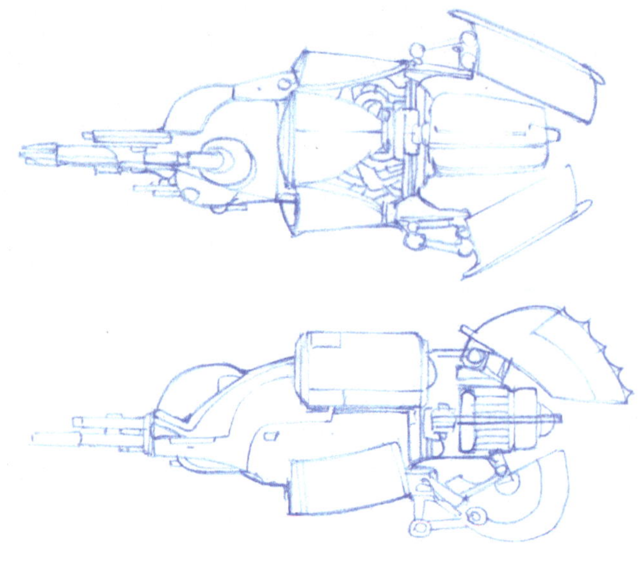

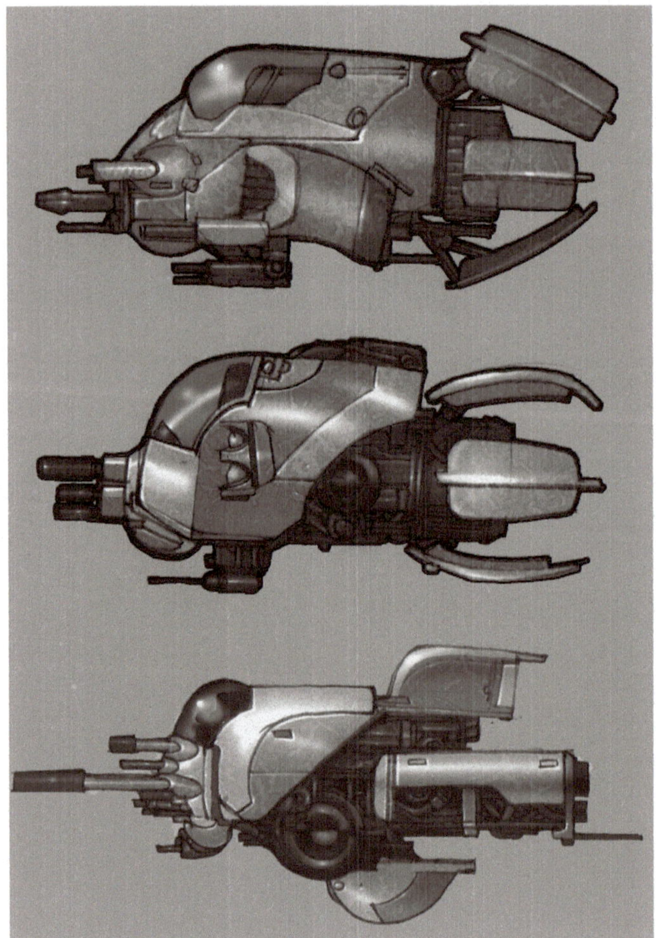

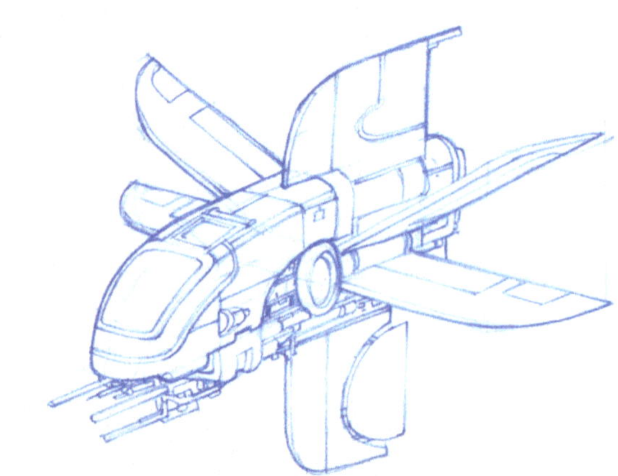

Here are some single-seater fighters: small ships designed for maneuverability in tight spaces. The tones were added to give them their overall value and texture.

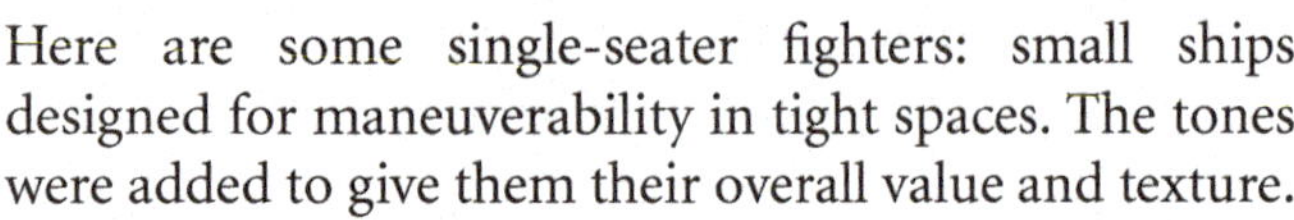

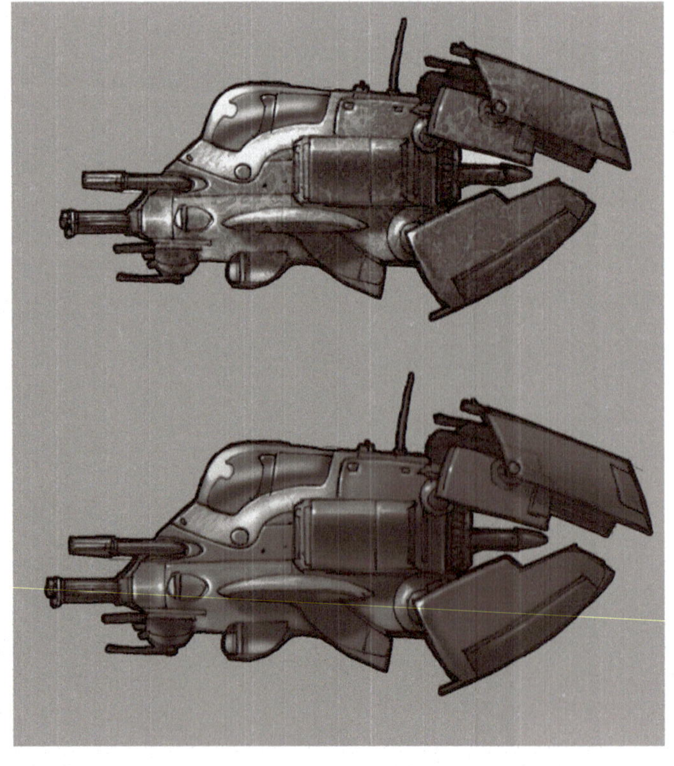

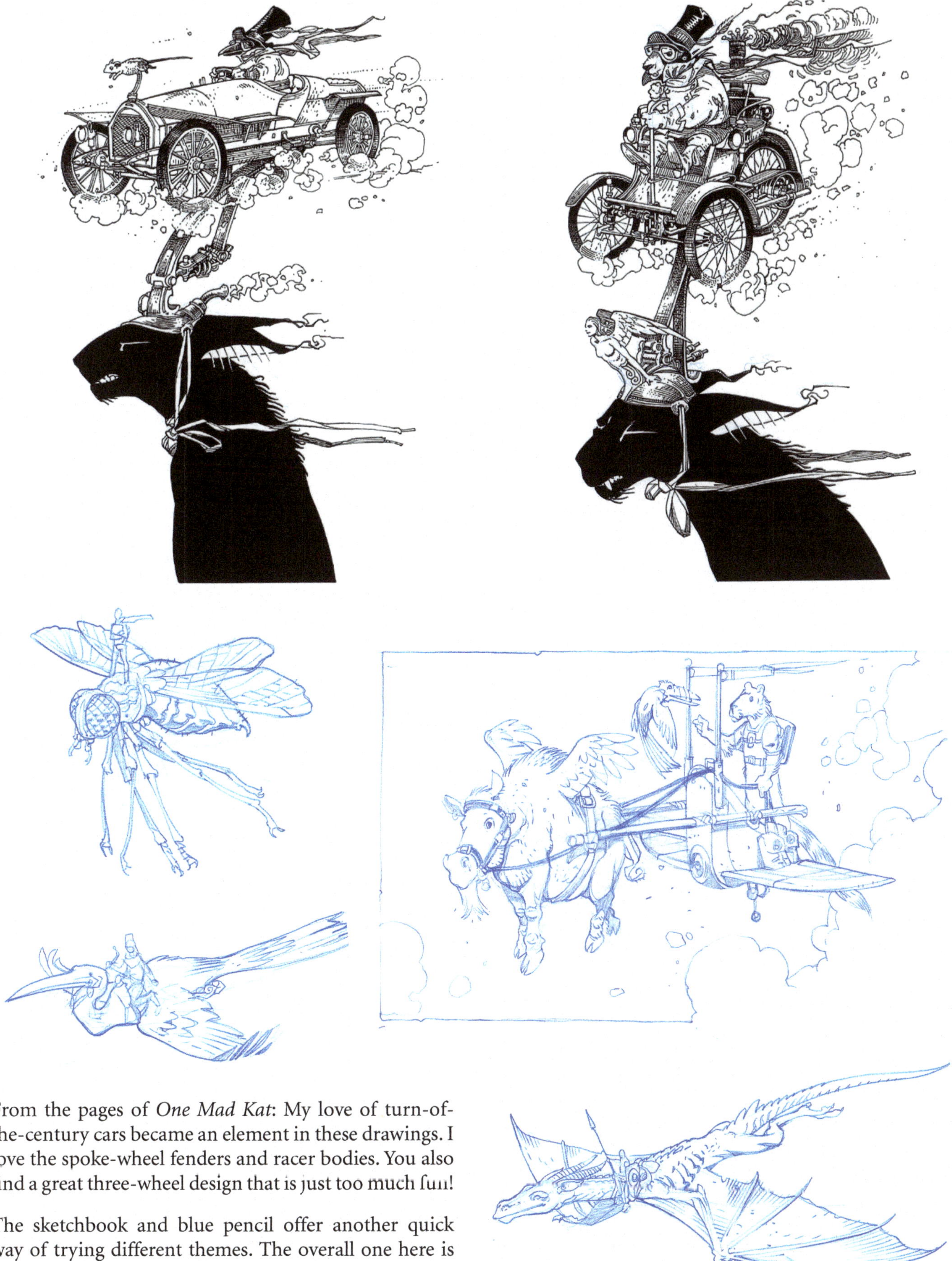

From the pages of *One Mad Kat*: My love of turn-of-the-century cars became an element in these drawings. I love the spoke-wheel fenders and racer bodies. You also find a great three-wheel design that is just too much fun!

The sketchbook and blue pencil offer another quick way of trying different themes. The overall one here is organic flight transport.

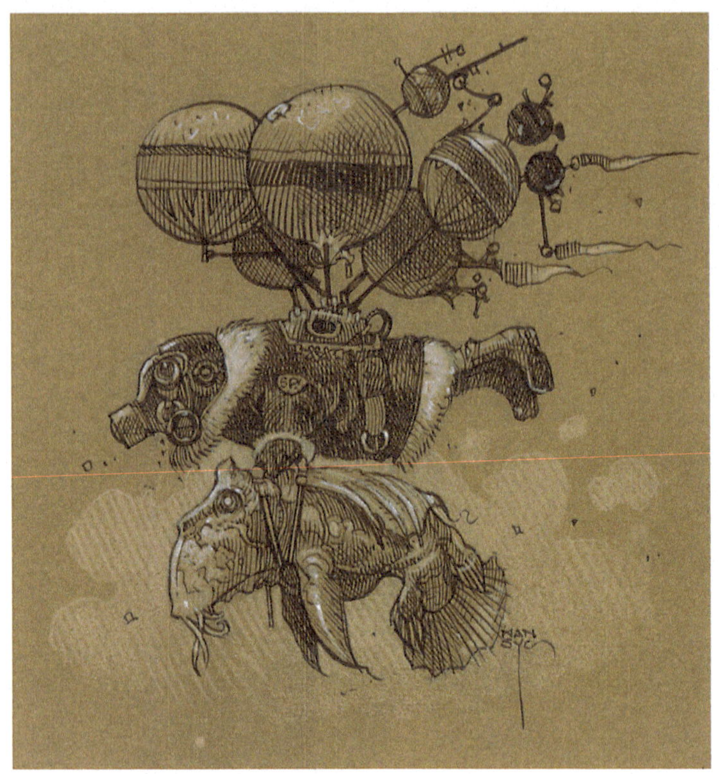

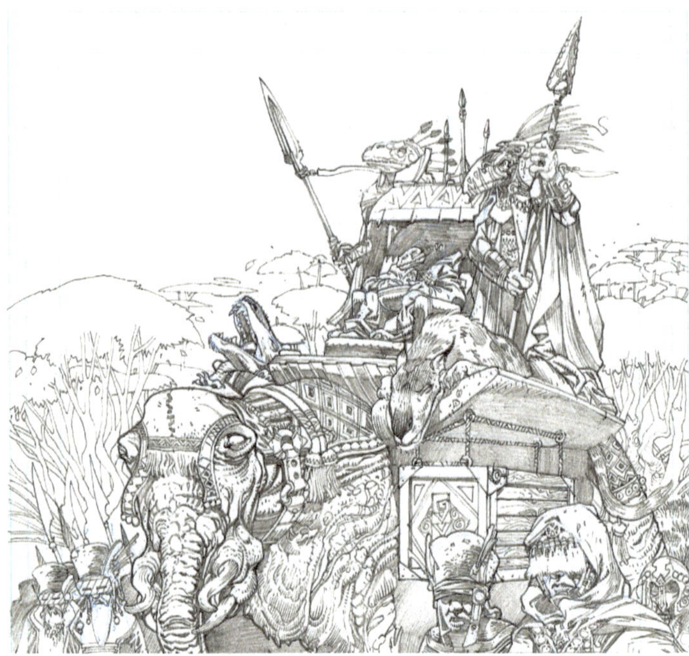

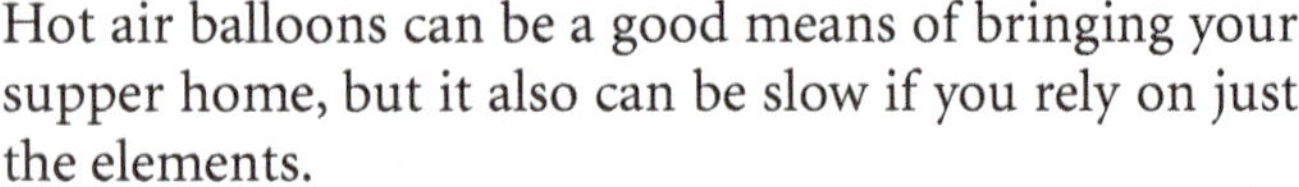

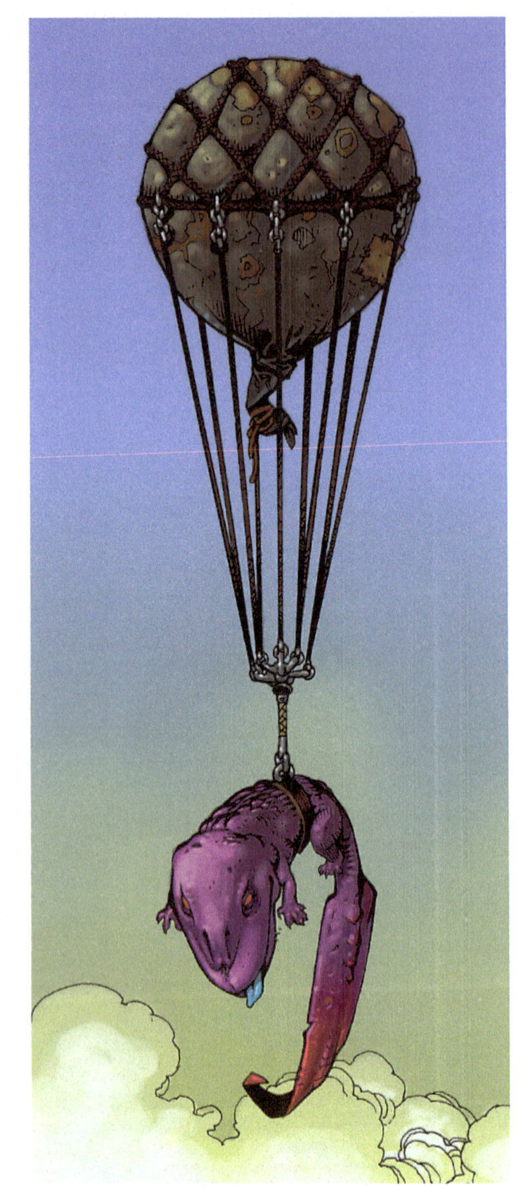

Hot air balloons can be a good means of bringing your supper home, but it also can be slow if you rely on just the elements.

The king can always travel in style on the back of a multitusked "phant," with his favorite hounds eating snacks in the shade of his canopy and guards all around.

The sketchbook also can push the ideas of a flying wing or birdlike flying pack.

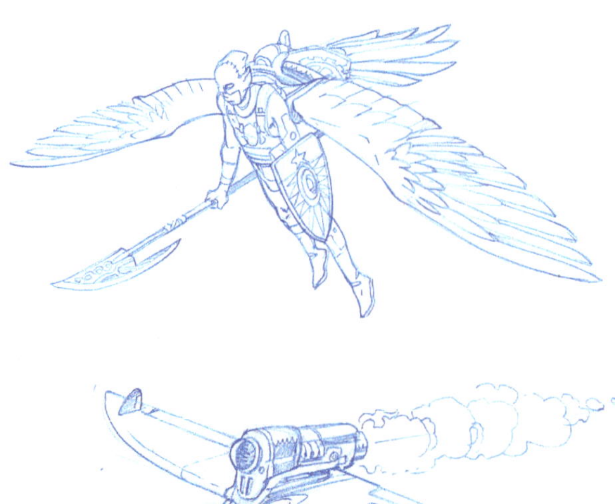

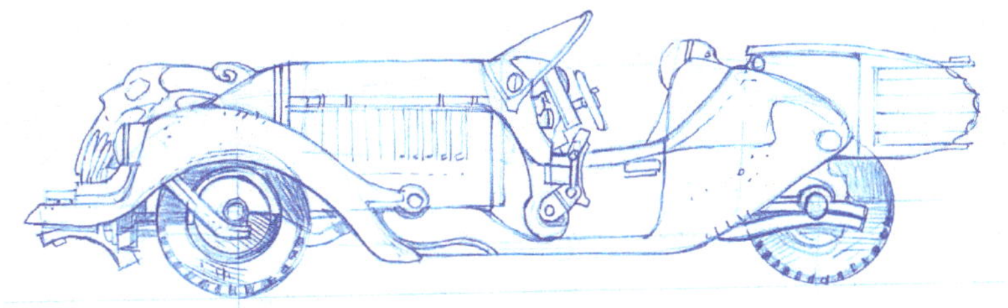

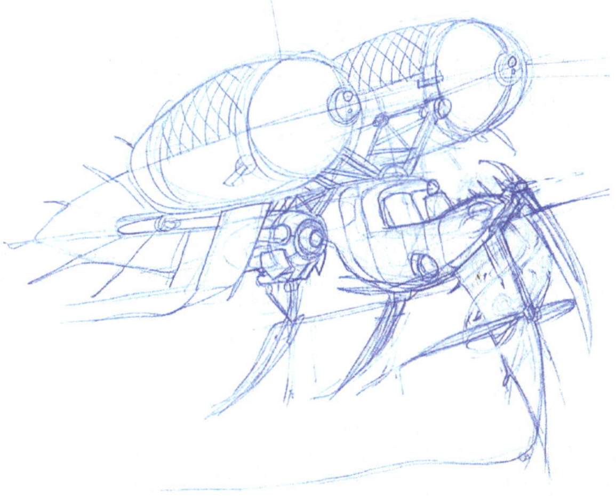

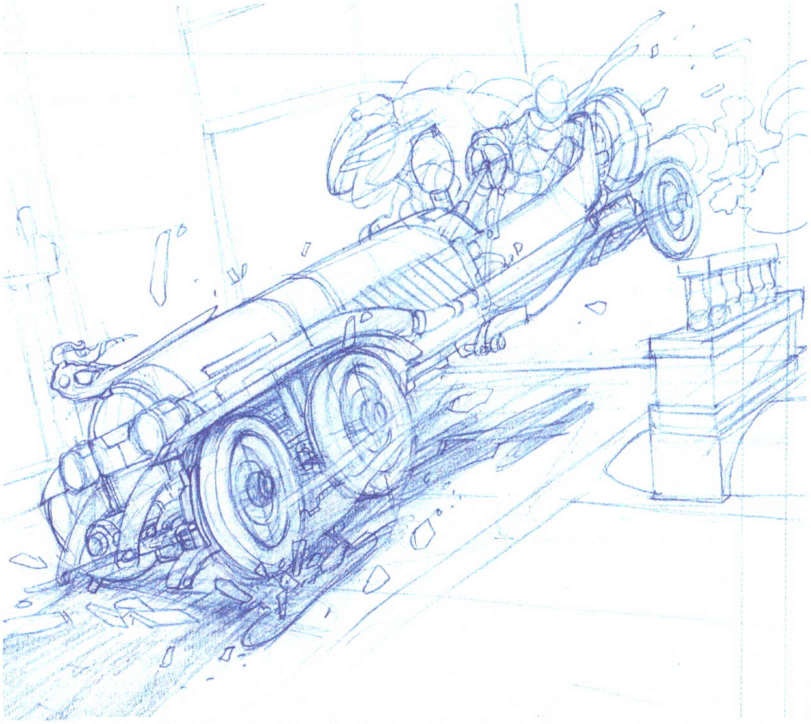

The roadster can be made from parts of other vehicles and start a new trend.

I was thinking of a very heavy engine balloon pack with a fin design to guide the direction of flight for this ship. You can have light metals, floating woods, and any other chemical reaction you want to bring this to life. Steampunk is a classic example of mixing the past and the future together.

The Bentley long-nose thirty-six-cylinder racer is a lot to handle when transporting the Chameleon Lord away from danger. This is how a story will sometimes start for me: creating a disaster and letting the narrative rise from the ashes.

If nothing else works, maybe your friend will carry you over the line.

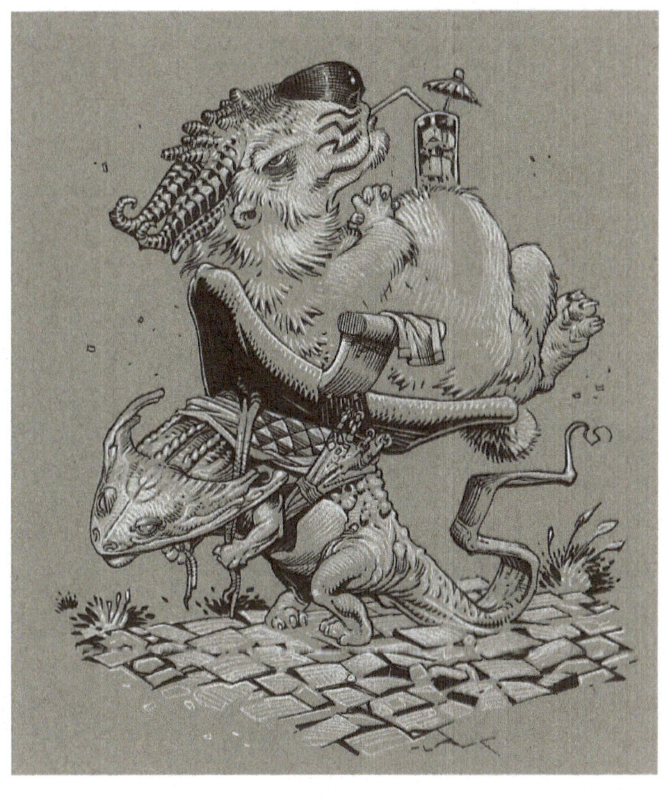

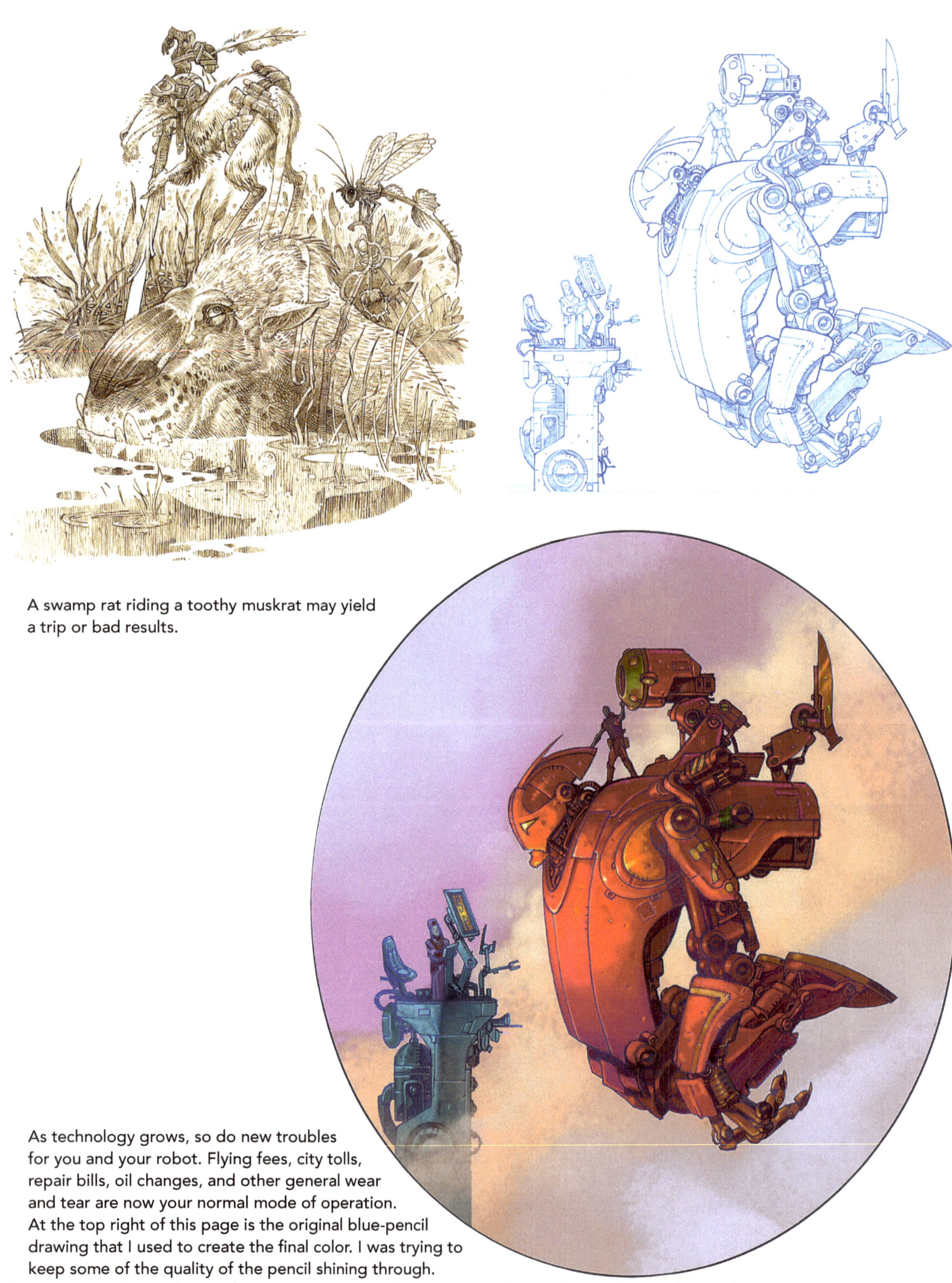

A swamp rat riding a toothy muskrat may yield a trip or bad results.

As technology grows, so do new troubles for you and your robot. Flying fees, city tolls, repair bills, oil changes, and other general wear and tear are now your normal mode of operation. At the top right of this page is the original blue-pencil drawing that I used to create the final color. I was trying to keep some of the quality of the pencil shining through.

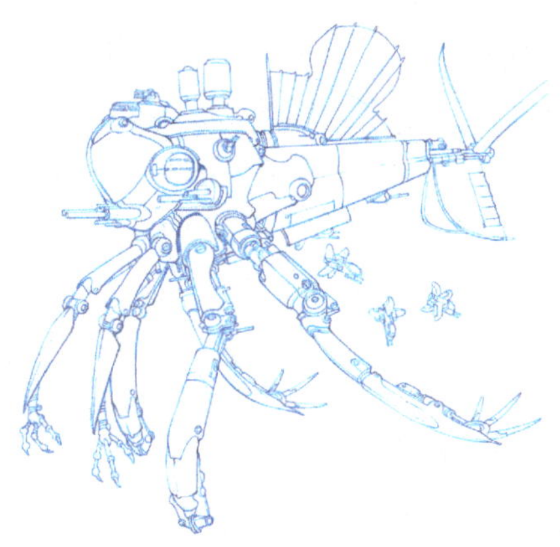

## MIXING IT UP

Here I had fun putting an insect, a fish, and high tech together. We have a large bomber transport that can deliver small fighters and take care of itself. The arms can be used for a multitude of things, from grasping to fighting, curling up, and protecting the belly. The fin can be used as a solar gatherer and droop down flat. It also is armed with side cannons and front and rear guns.

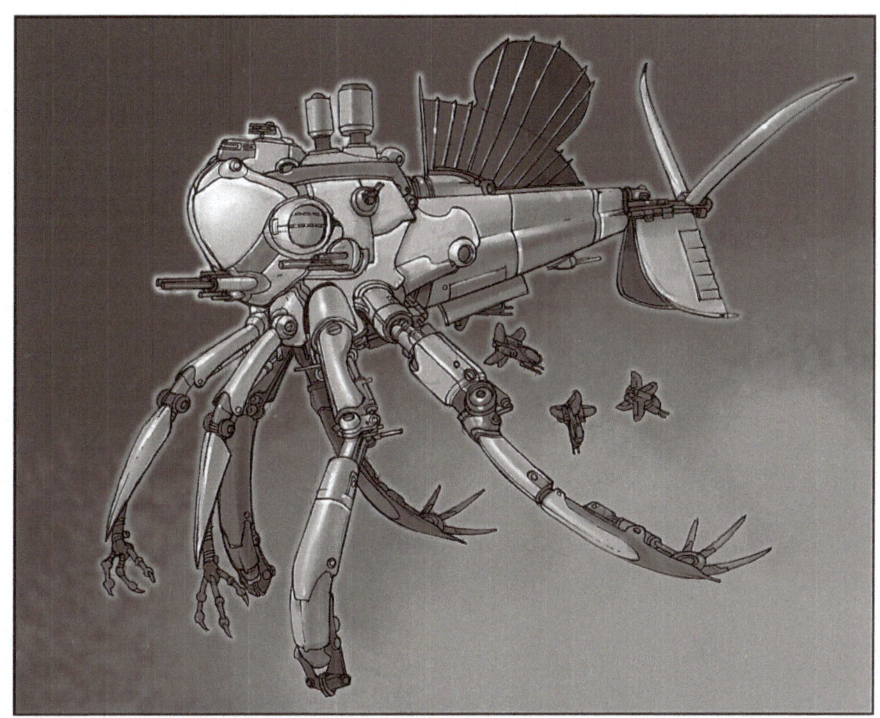

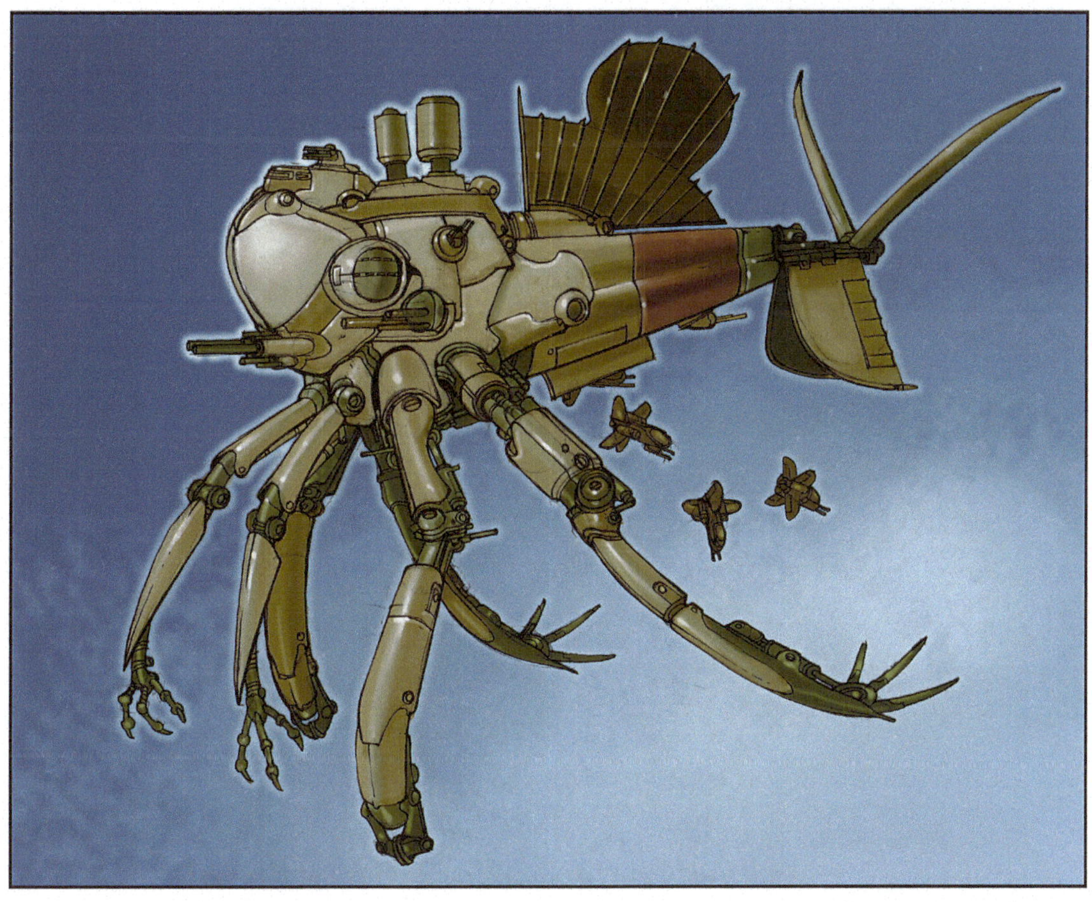

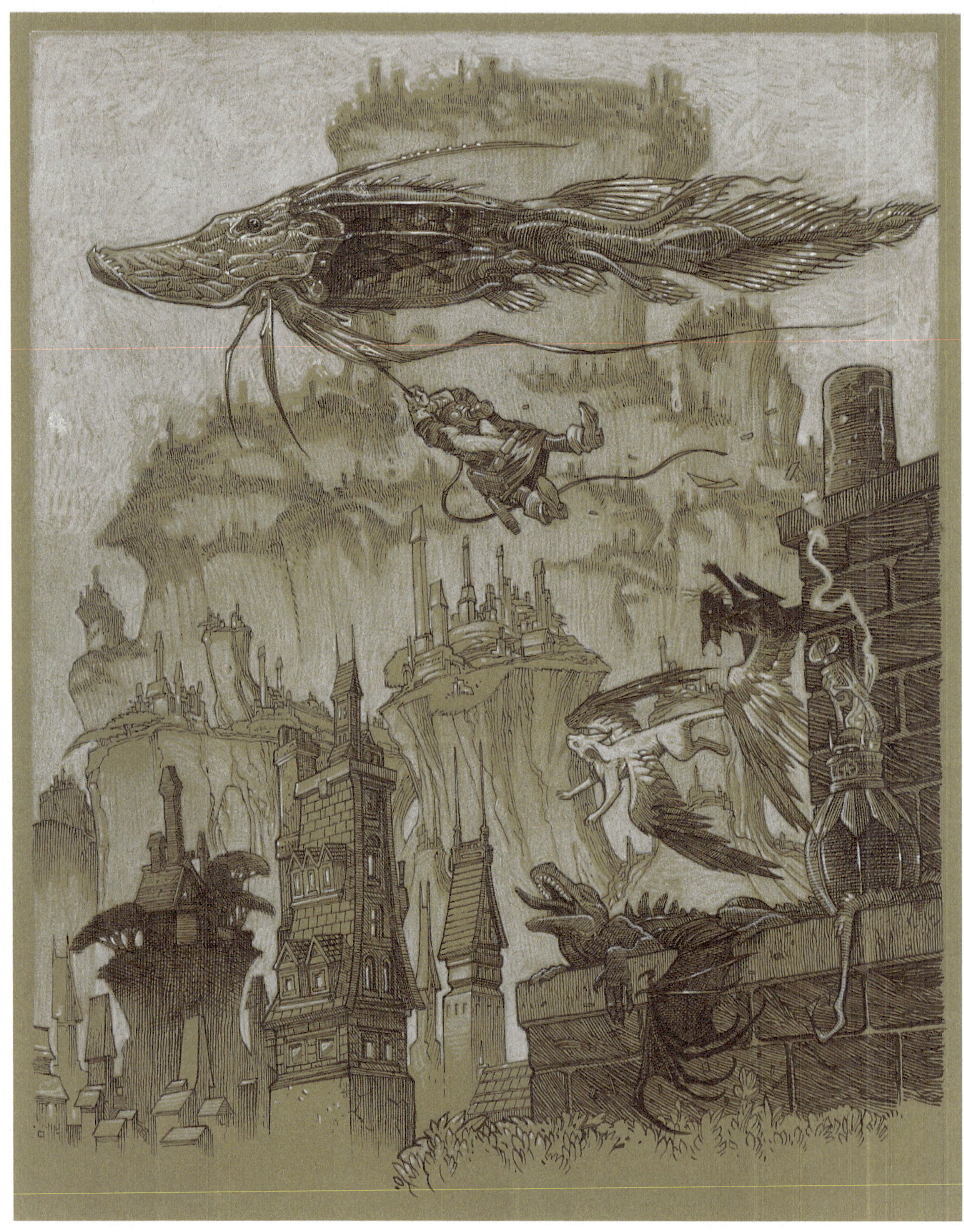

Here is perhaps the worst method of travel: hitching a ride on a variegated snaptooth. It does sail high enough, so you don't take out any chimneys, but it is known to take some detours that are not fun or healthy to the rider. Life in this city has its ups and downs.

# 15

# OTHERWORLDLY

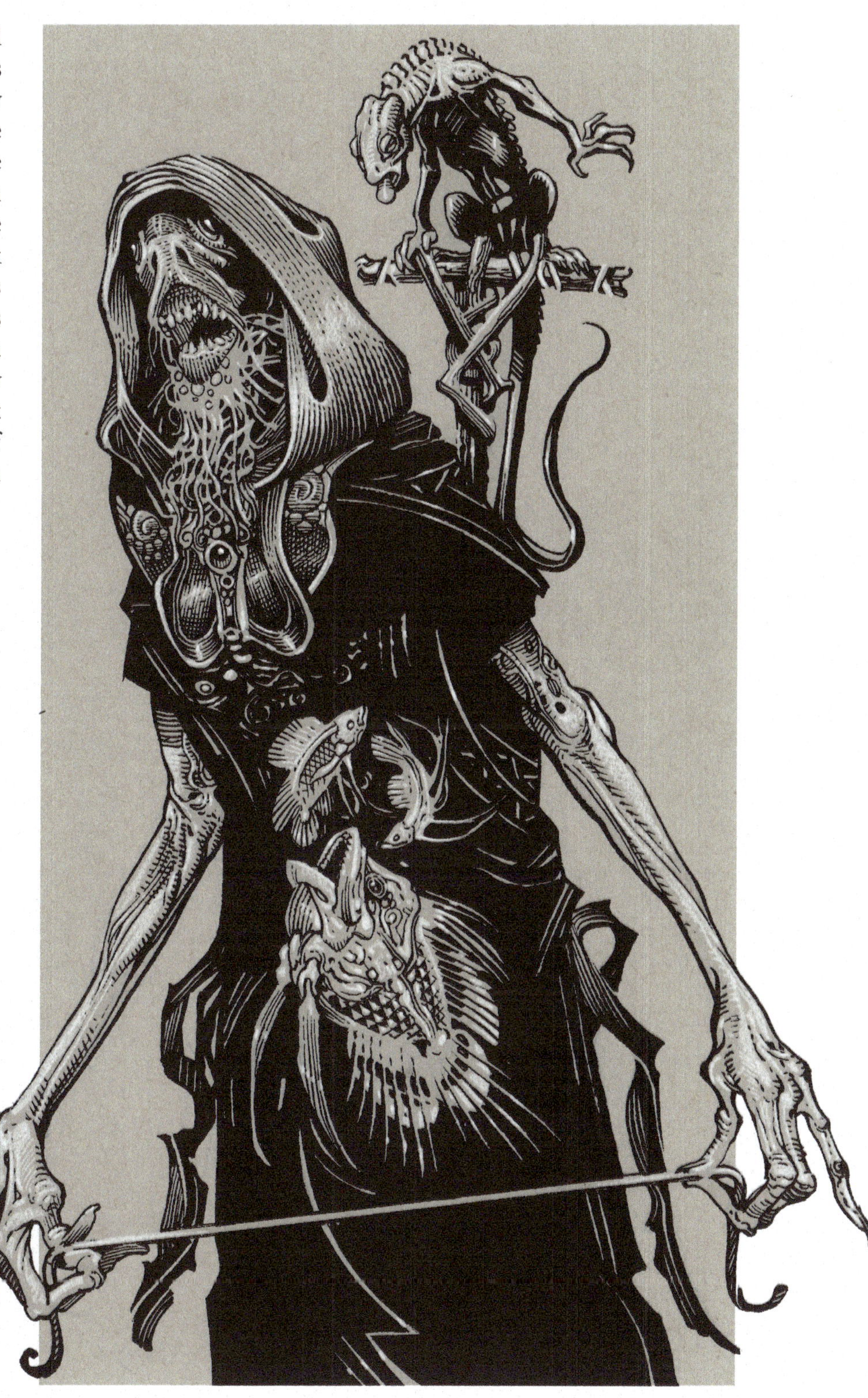

Here is where you can let it all run wild! I love different types of textures and surfaces. How do you contrast them against one another or with each other to create something new? Taking a stroll in their world of windblown shells are the Beast, the Beauty, and the Black Insect. This set of drawings was conceived as portraits of various creatures that were met along a journey in Vermilion Sands by J. V. Holbrook. When you look at historic portraits, there are a lot of different poses and attitudes you can bring into your characters.

A short sentence can add to the depth of a character. So sometimes when creating, I might add that dimension by saying it before I start. In this case: the shortest distance between two points is a straight line.

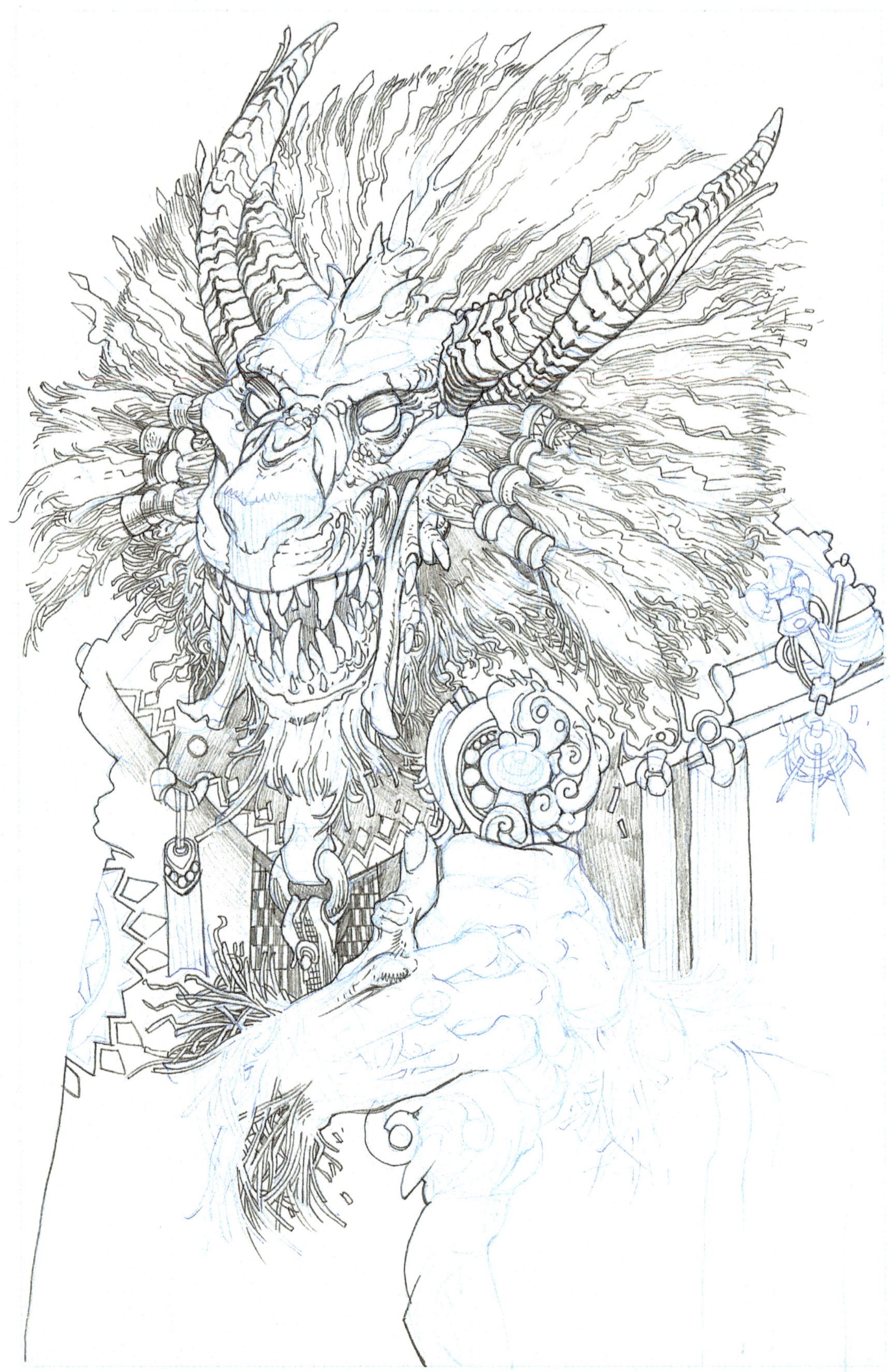

The idea of a maned creature having a bad hair day was the start for this drawing. Here's the pencil stage. For me, doing a tighter pencil will allow me to ink faster and be able to make adjustments more easily. I had fun with the types of hair.

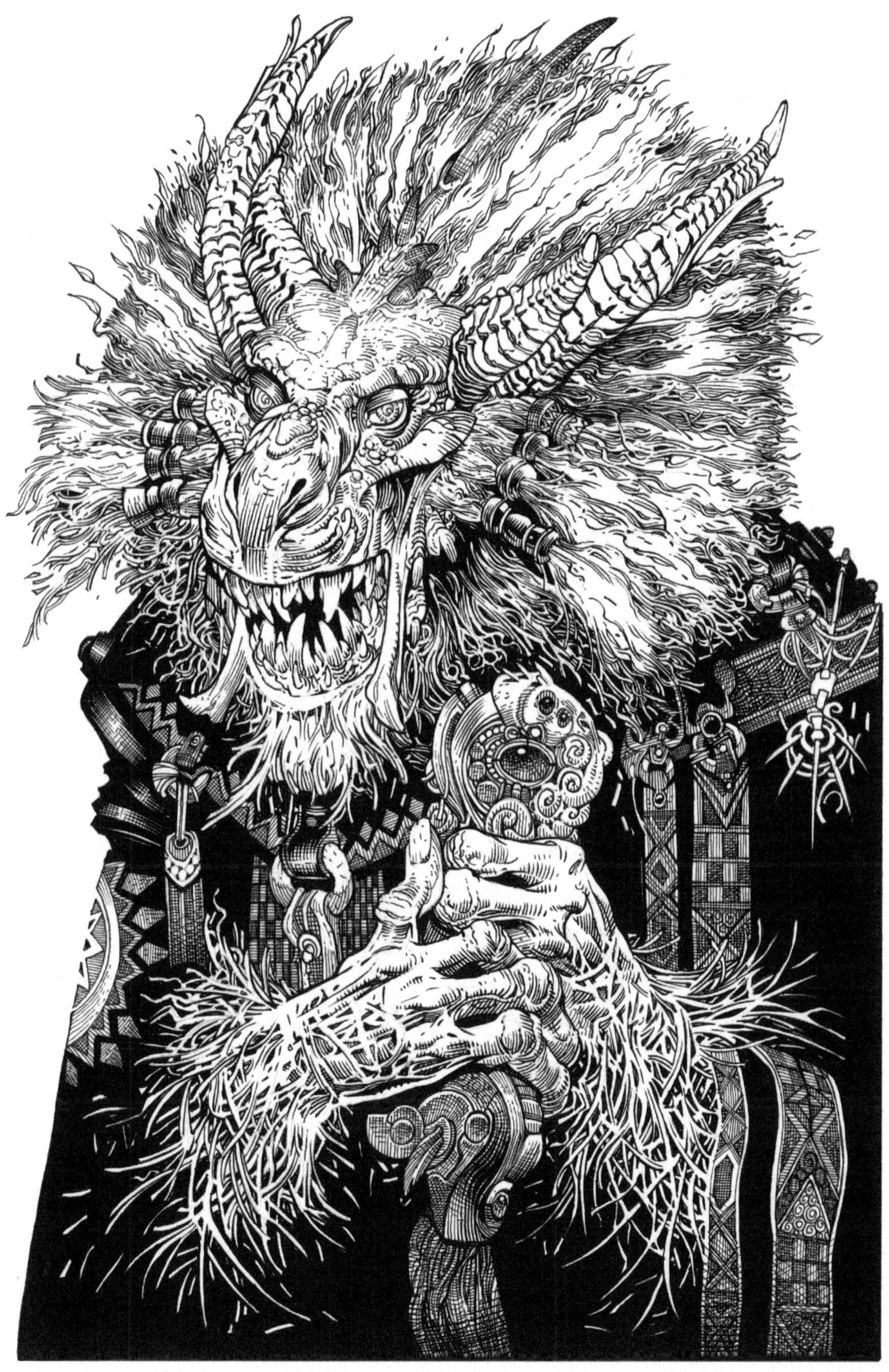

In the inks, the one element that I had the most fun with was the strawlike hair on the hands and upper arm. For some reason, Scarecrow from *The Wizard of Oz* kept coming back into my mind. This is an exercise in positive-negative overlapping lines.

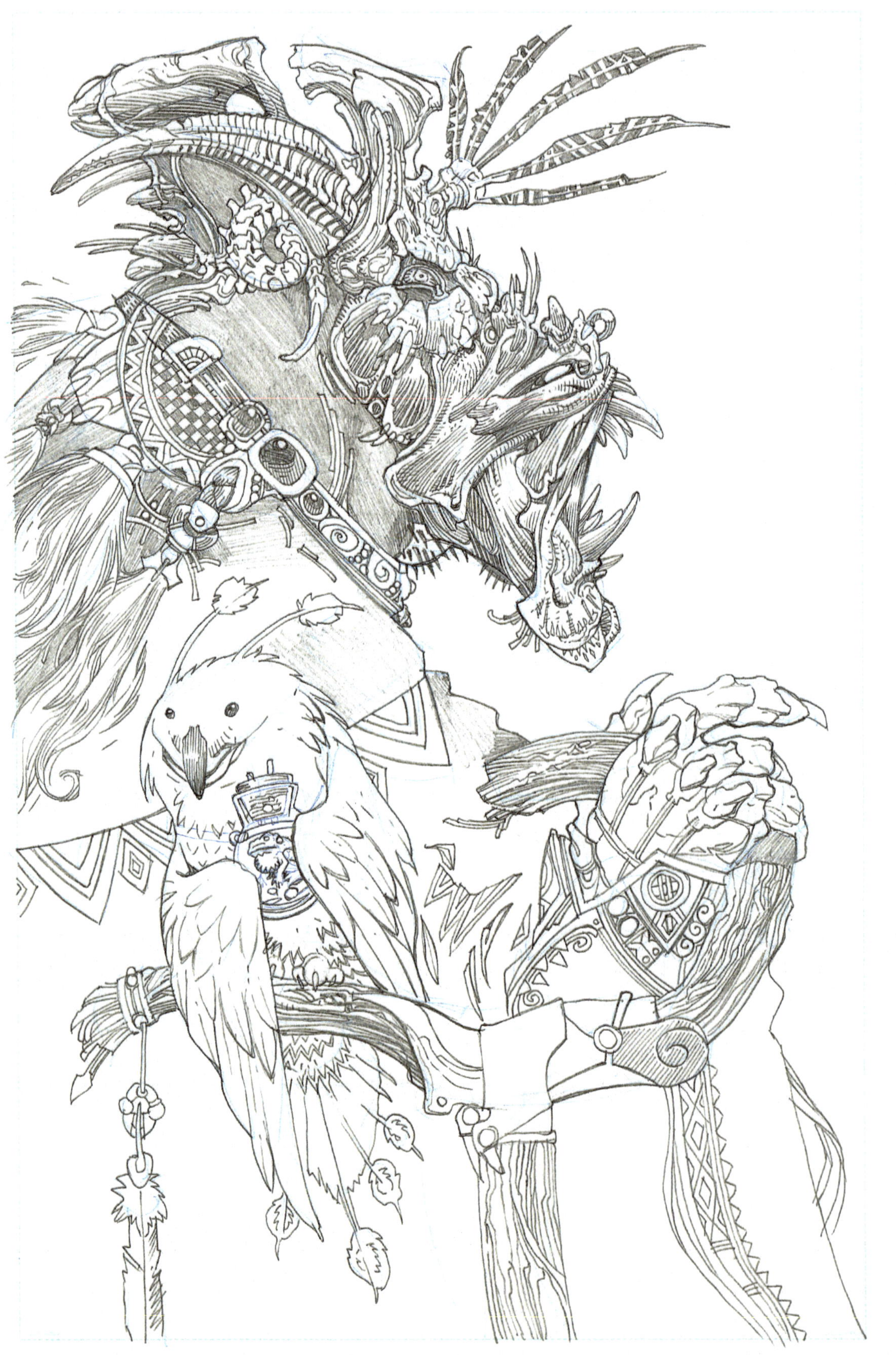

Sometimes an idea can start with a simple contrast: the white bird and the owner/friend/master. It also seems that our bird has a pet in the jar.

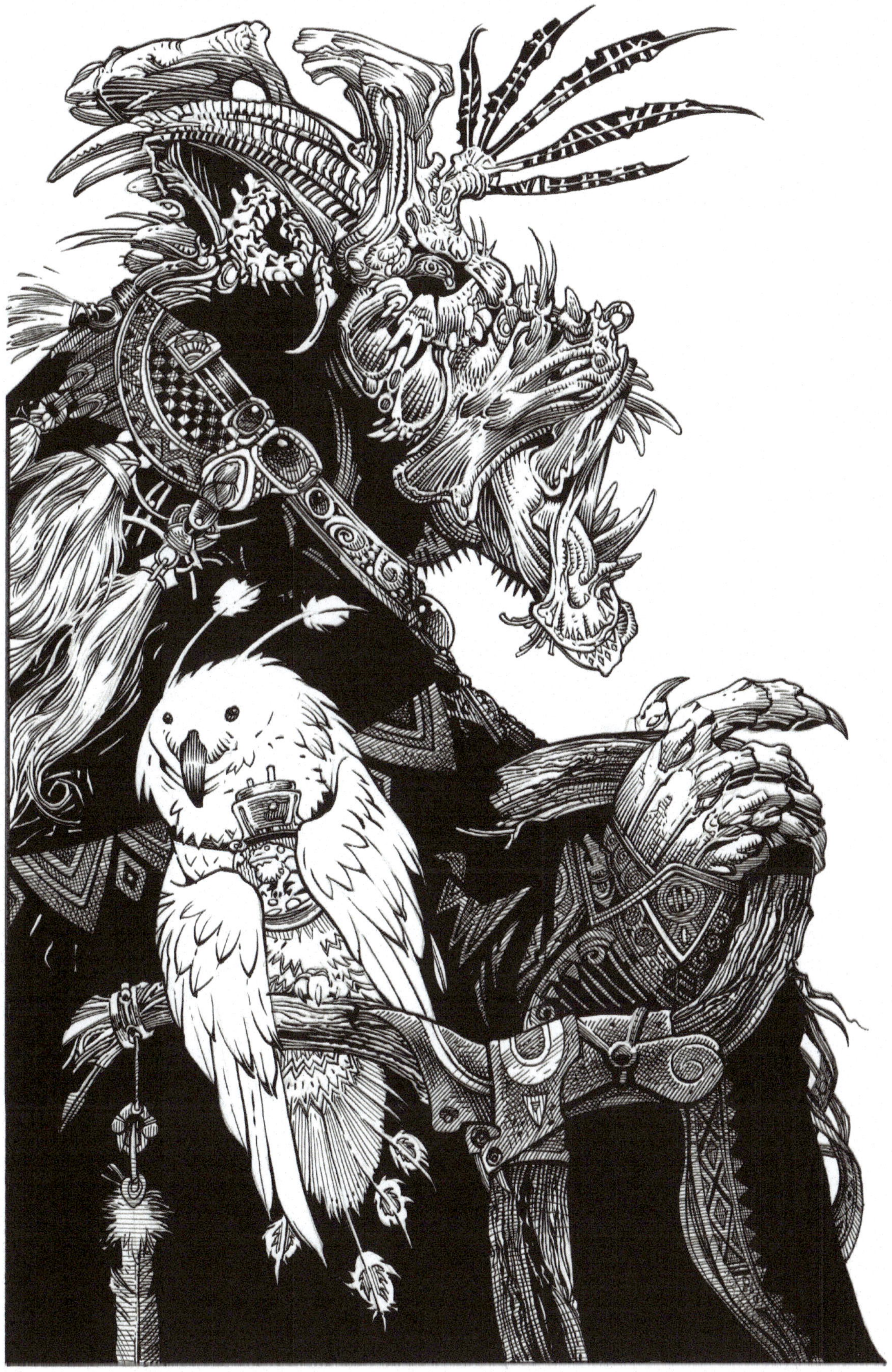

In the inks, the large dark areas make the white bird stand out. I did very little rendering on it to keep it this way. It is nice to contrast the different textures: the softness of the cloth with crosshatch versus the directional lines on the wood and the owner's hand.

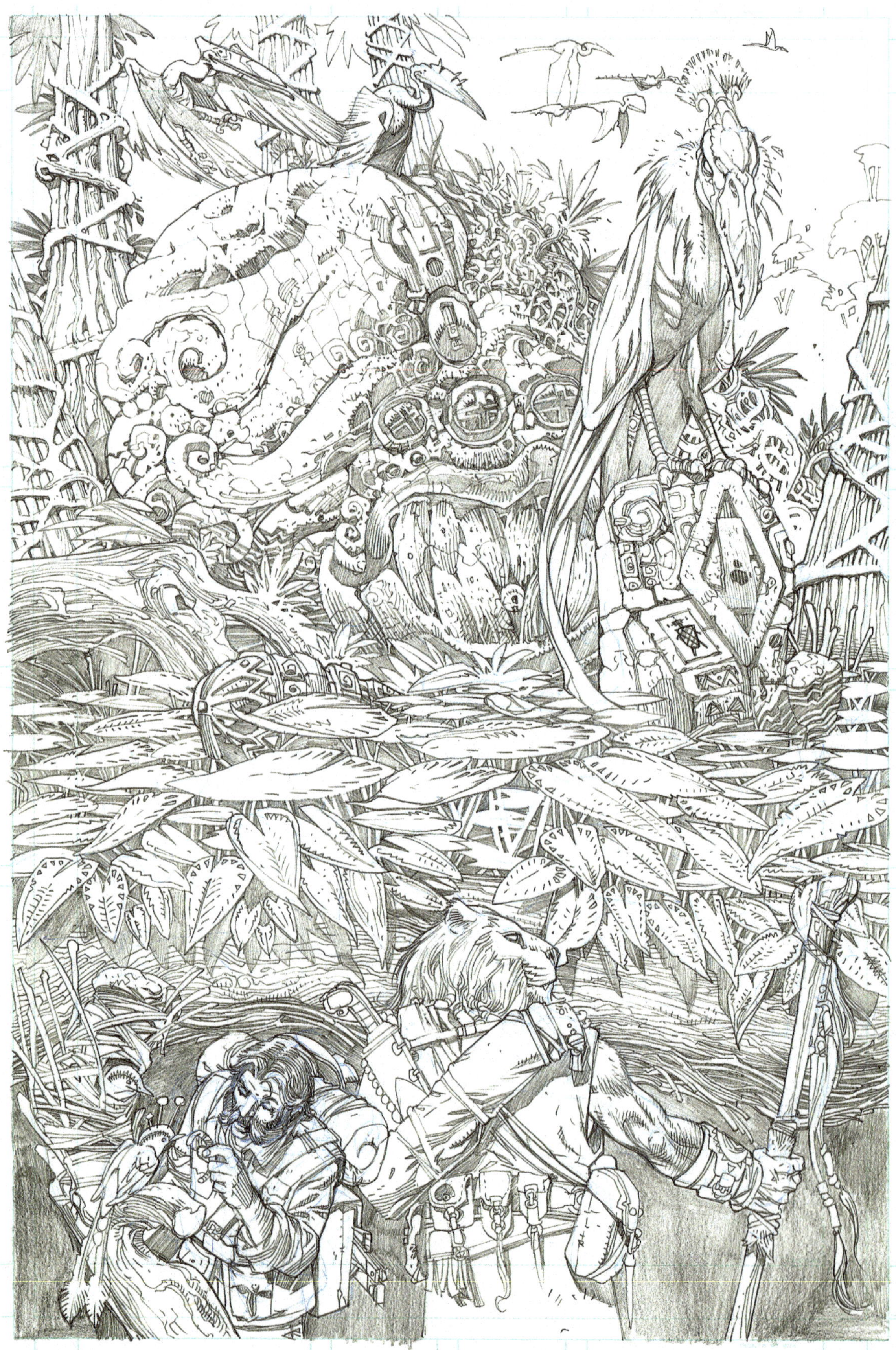

This portrait is of J. V. Holbrook and his guide as they travel through the back forests of Vermilion Sands. Holbrook is feeding a worm to a tri-billed flycatcher. He is always the naturalist and observational animal artist.

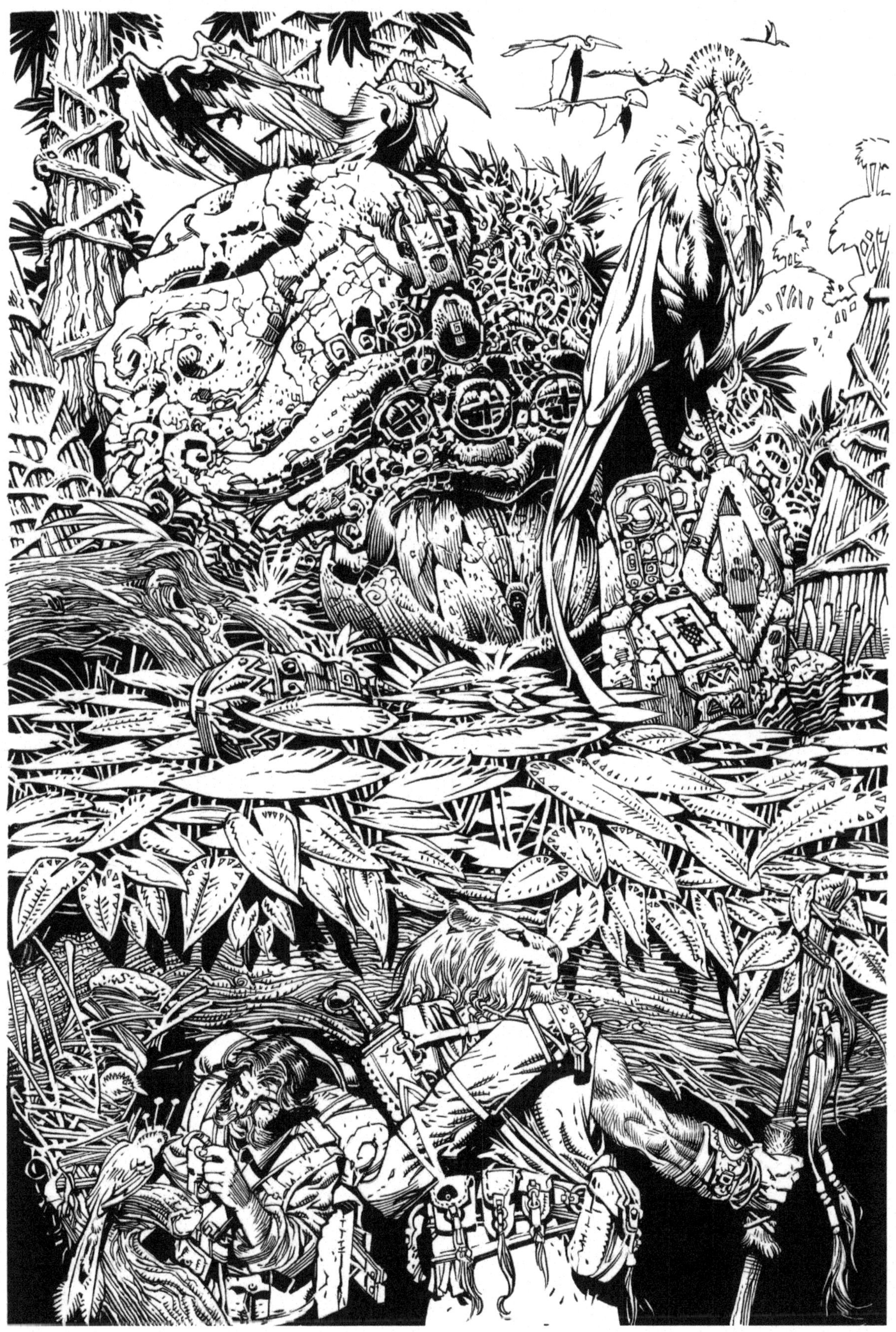

Ink gives you a very black-and-white image. The rich textural feel gives the drawing a more dense jungle quality. Things appear as if they have a little more weight, and the blacks are deeper, more mysterious holes.

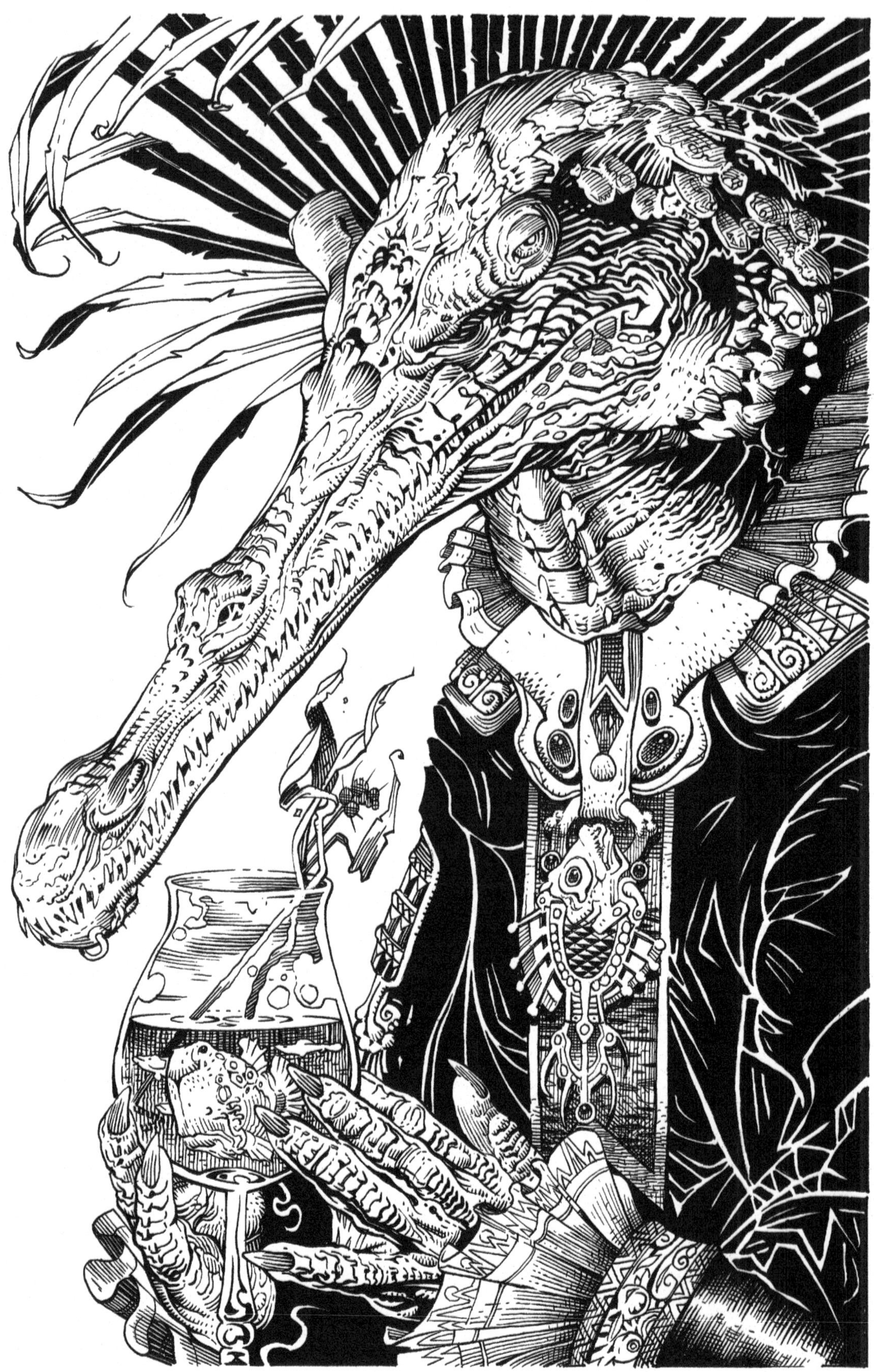

In this drawing, a giant reptilian is having a drink at the bar. How do you bring a sense of believability to all the elements found in this world? The drink, dress, jewelry, and body language all become elements to give the beginnings of understanding of your drinking mate.

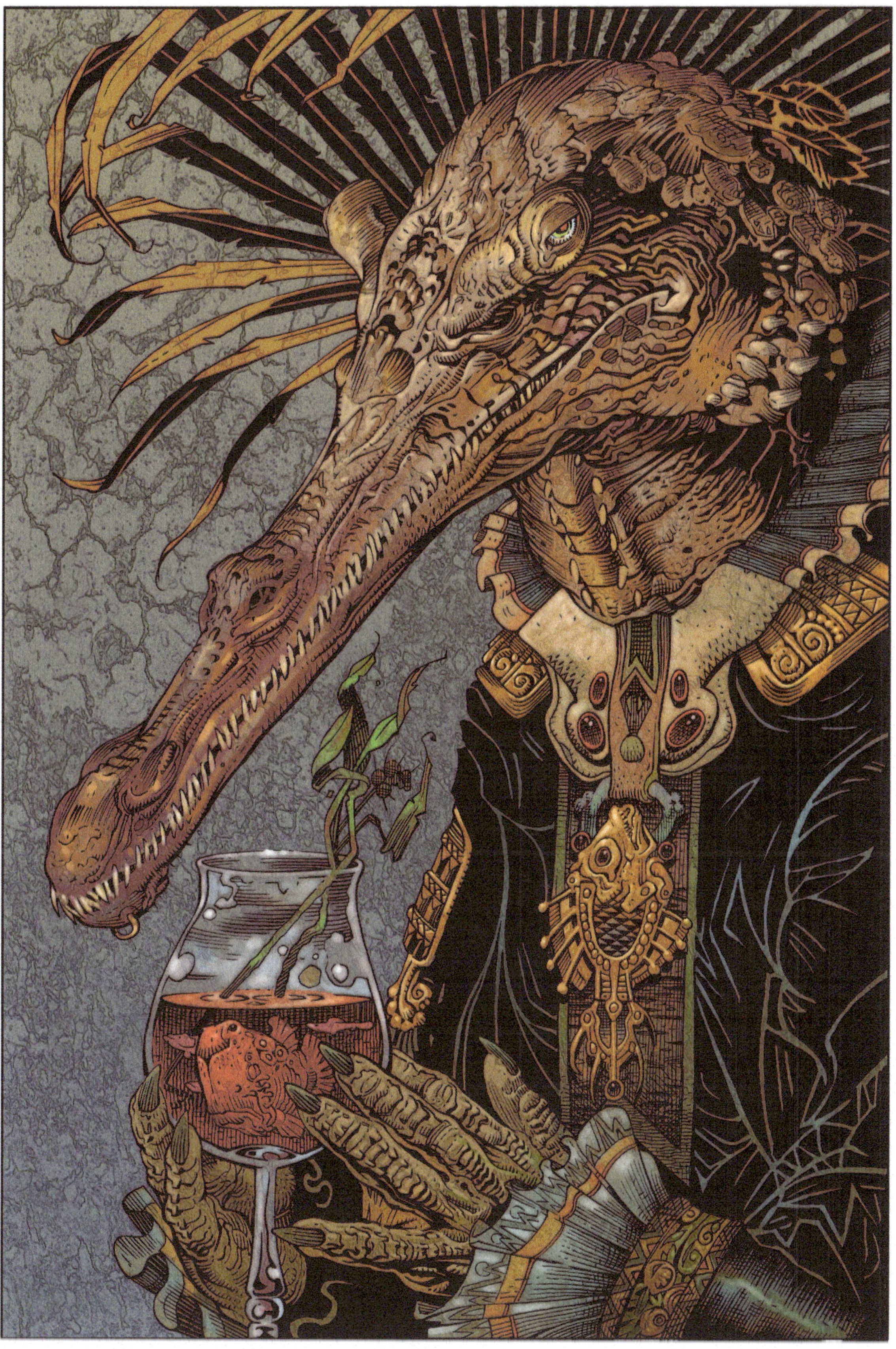

Color will change and give you another level to bring all these elements (drink, dress, jewelry, body language) into play. I tried to give a velvety feel to the jacket, with high collars and cuffs that are delicately colored, an elaborate design to the gold jewelry, and a sprig of garnish to the blood-red tide drink.

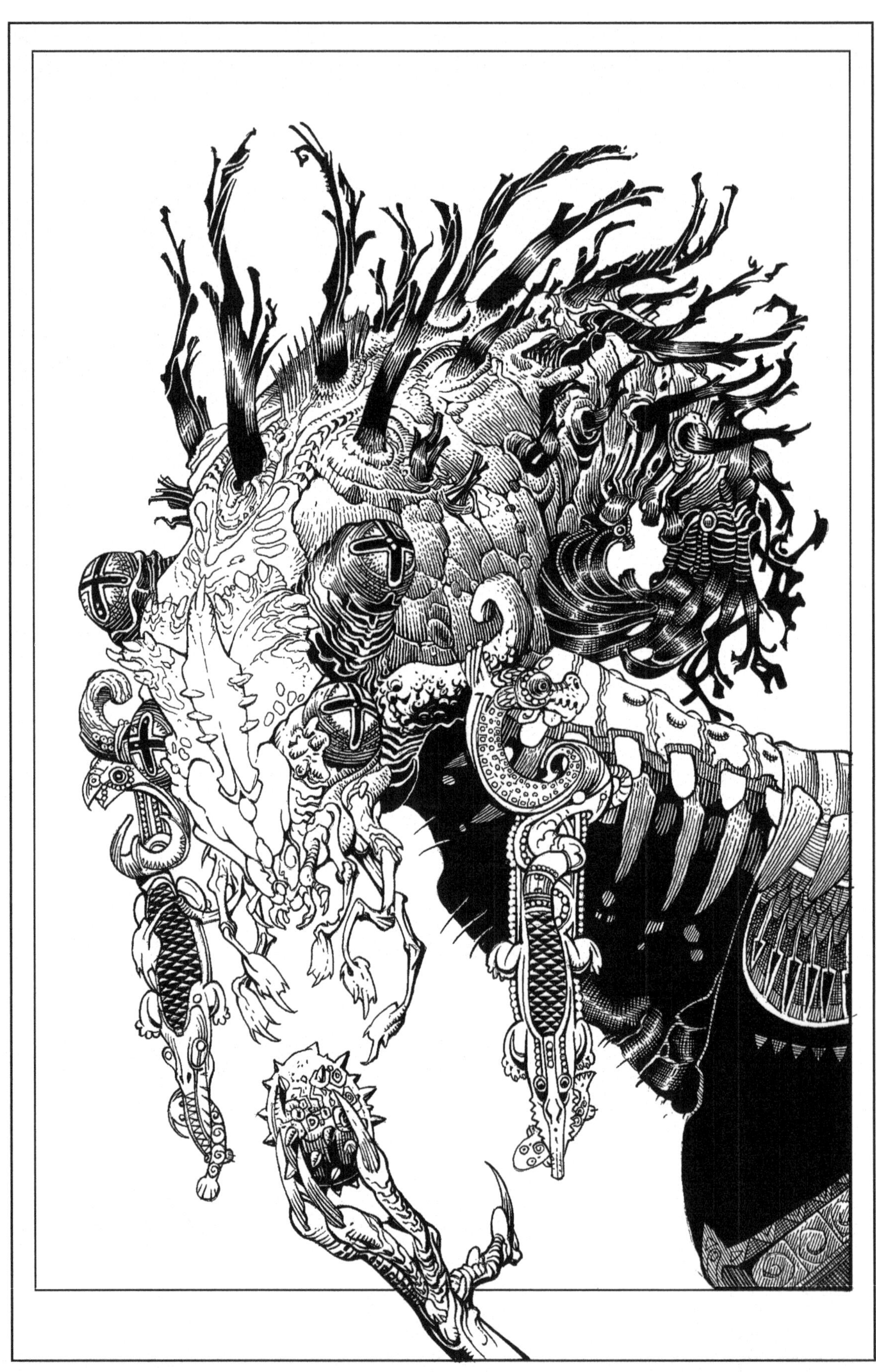

Three elements were blended to bring this character to the paper: a mantis, a sea shell, and my love of pre–Columbian jewelry.

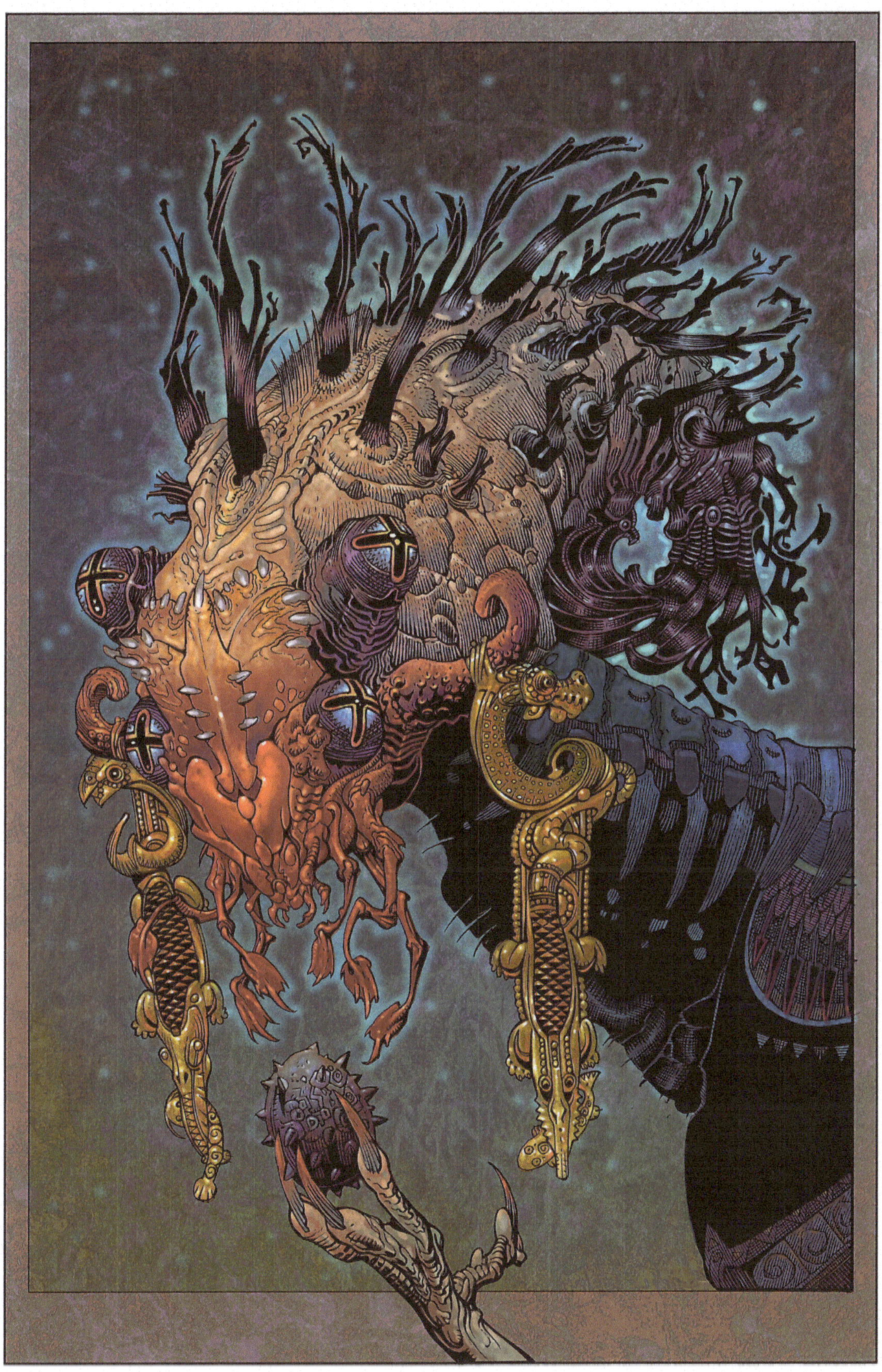

Insects have an incredible range of colors. Some of them are for camouflage. Some are iridescent and change in the light as they move. Some have dark and light patterns to blend into the surrounding world. Purple is a color that has historically been attached to royalty. It is a hard color, like red, to find as a pigment. Certain pigments have value because of their rarity.

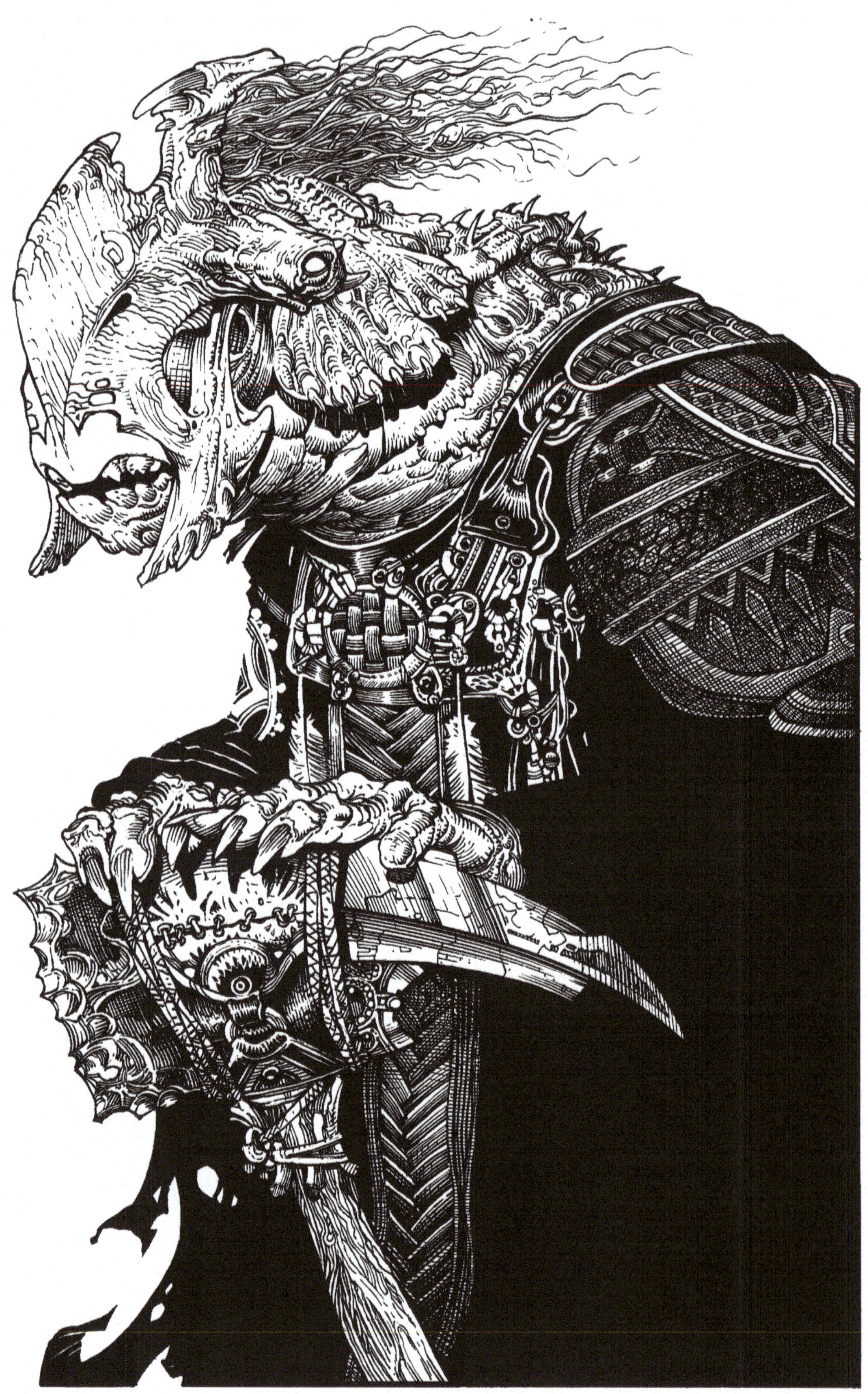

"Portrait of an Ax Guard." A guard is the product of an idea that can have many layers. Adornments: What kind of ceremonial dress would it have? Protective elements? A prized ax in its special holder? Type of ax? Materials the ax is made of? And some war wounds?

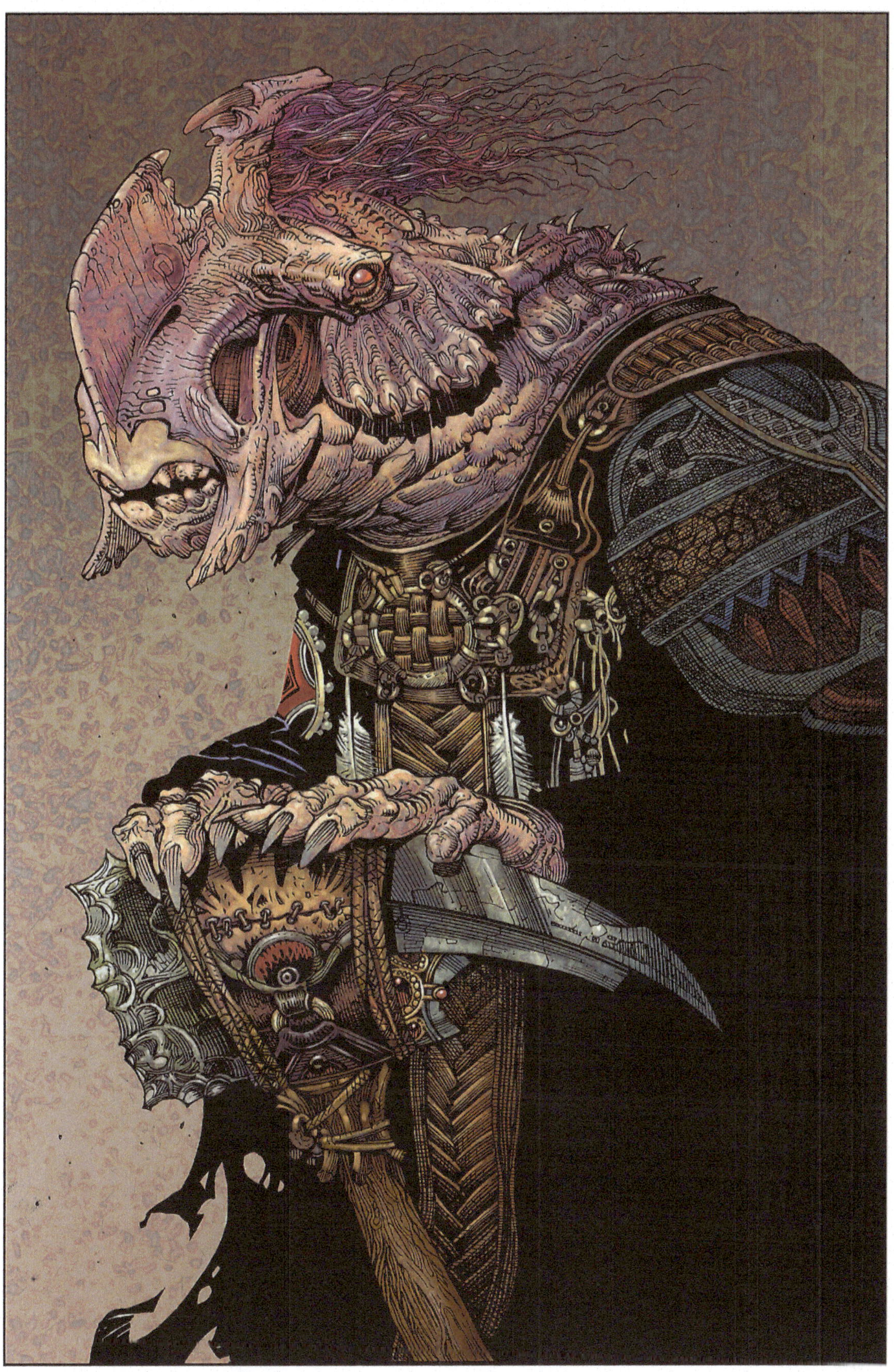

In coloring this piece, I wanted to keep the wardrobe softer and the lights in the ax guard's face and hands. The shoulder pads blend into the robe, and the chest has brighter colors on the ornamentation. The flesh has the ranges of bright and warm colors to draw the eye. I also tried to contrast the figure against a textural background with a completely different feel.

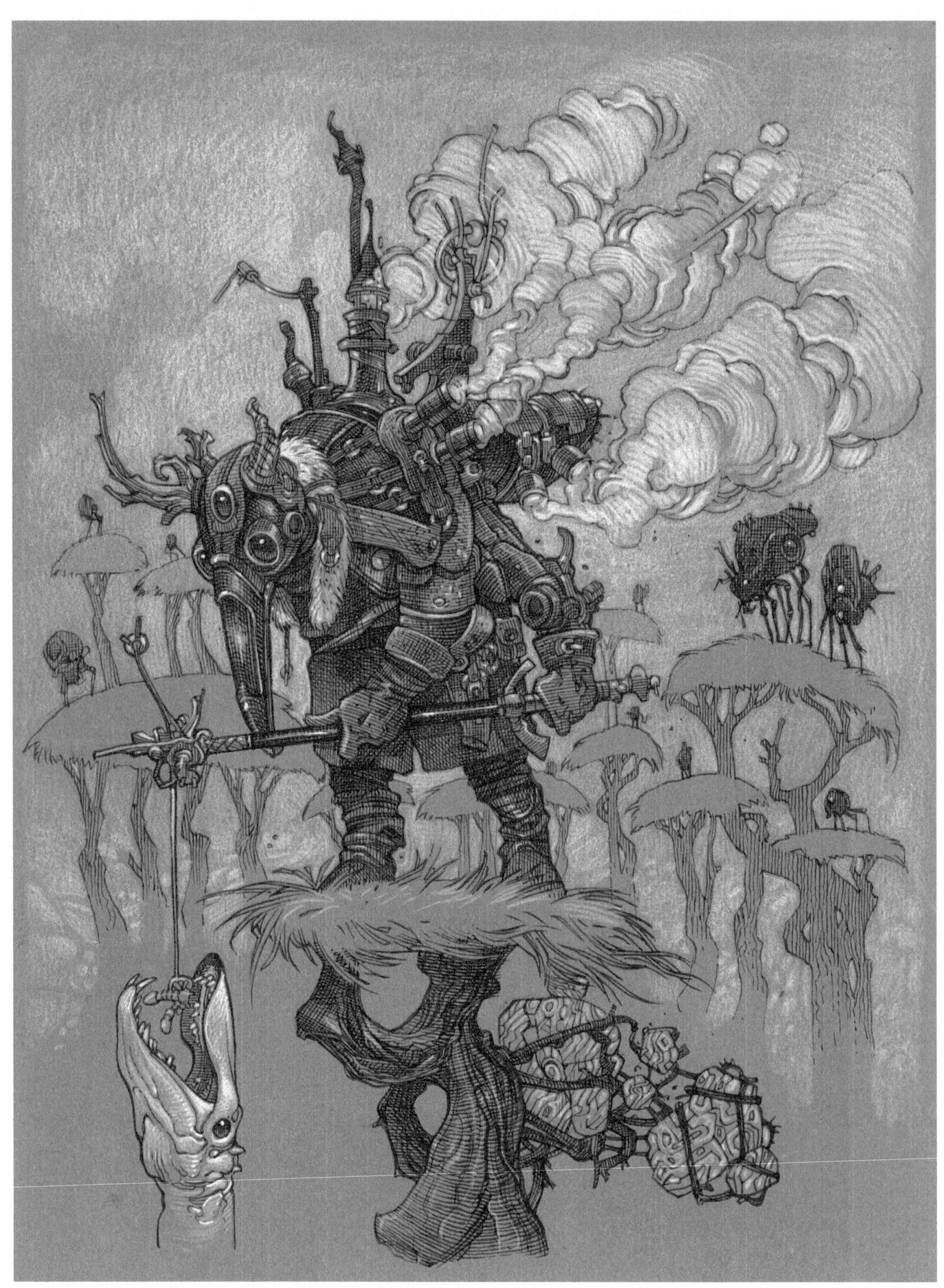

Sometimes your visual narrative easily tells the story to the viewer.

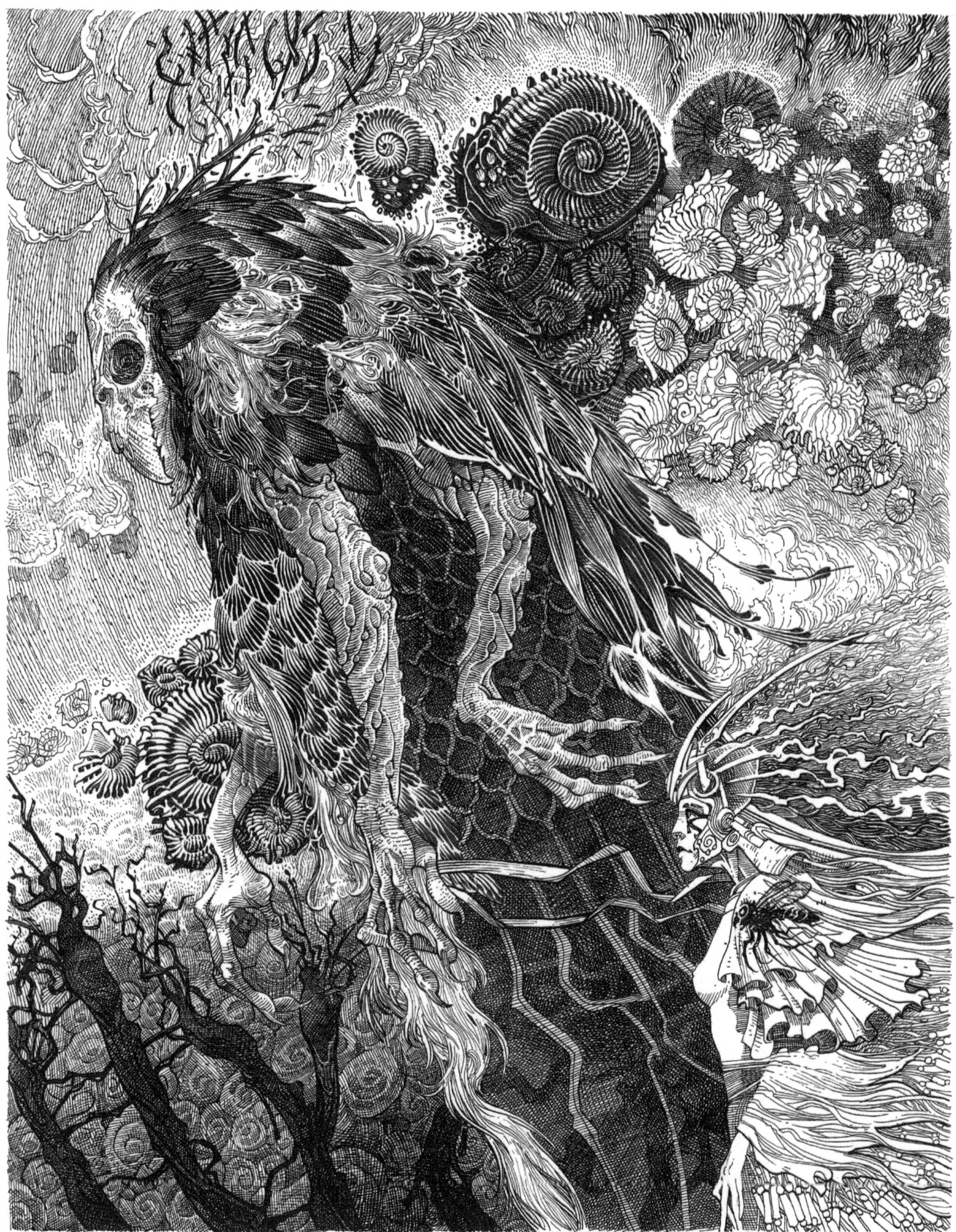

Other times the mystery of the story can be built by the viewer.

# 16
# PUTTING IT ALL TOGETHER

Sequential art adds another spin for the artist. Now you have to think about telling a story with panels of images. You are in control and have to deliver the whole story. In a pinup page, you can draw an object once. In a book, you have to draw many things over and over again and be aware of visual pacing, camera angle, and establishing the world you are in.

These thumbnails are rough six-by-nine-inch drawings. They are illustrated in proportion to the finished page, so if I am happy with them, I can blow up my thumbnails and transfer them to the finished paper. I still work on paper, though all this can be done on a computer and then printed out in blue lines for the inker. After all these years of working on paper, I am faster with layout this way.

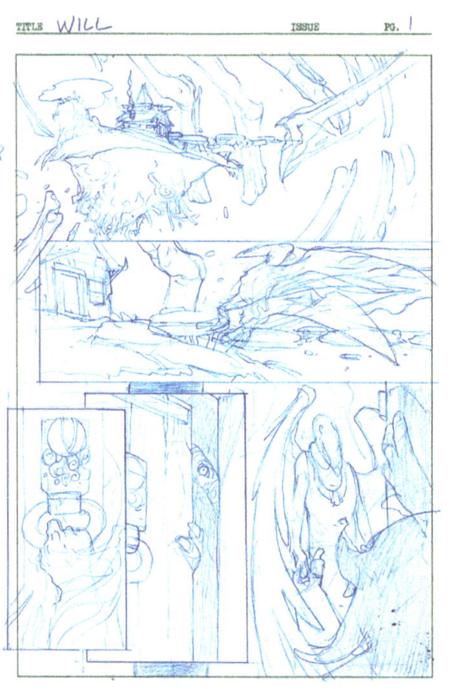


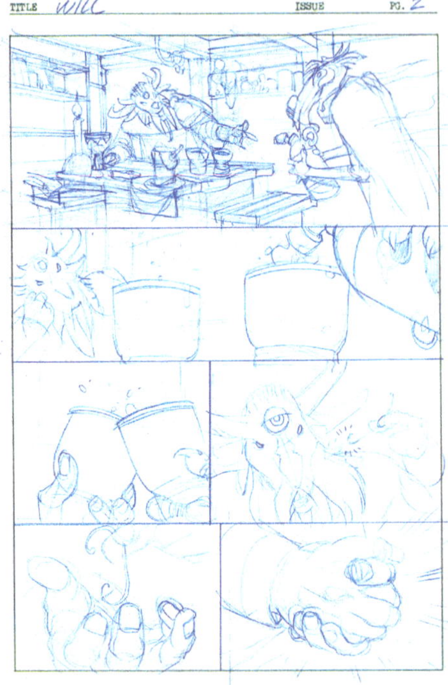


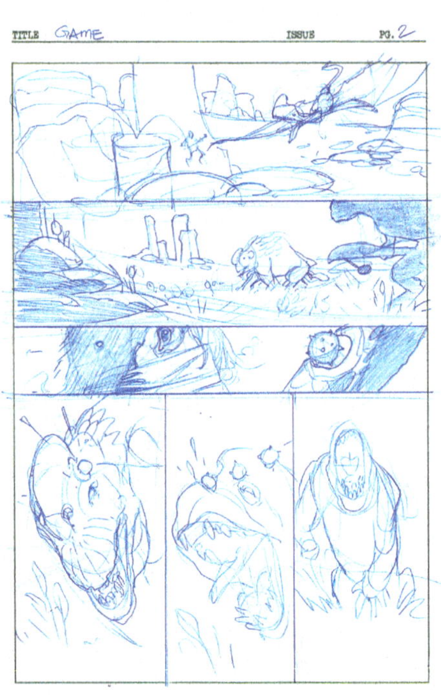


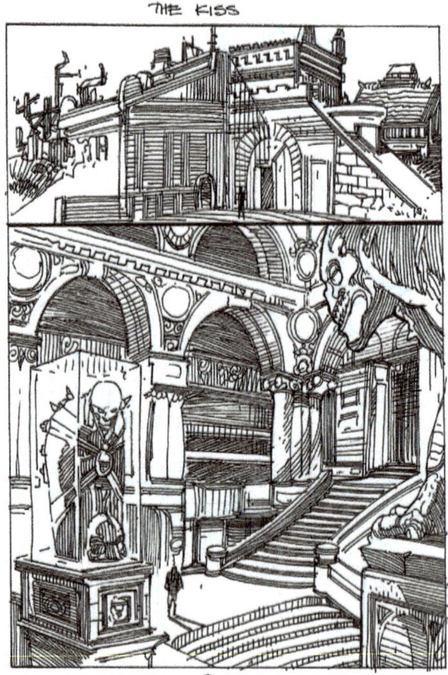

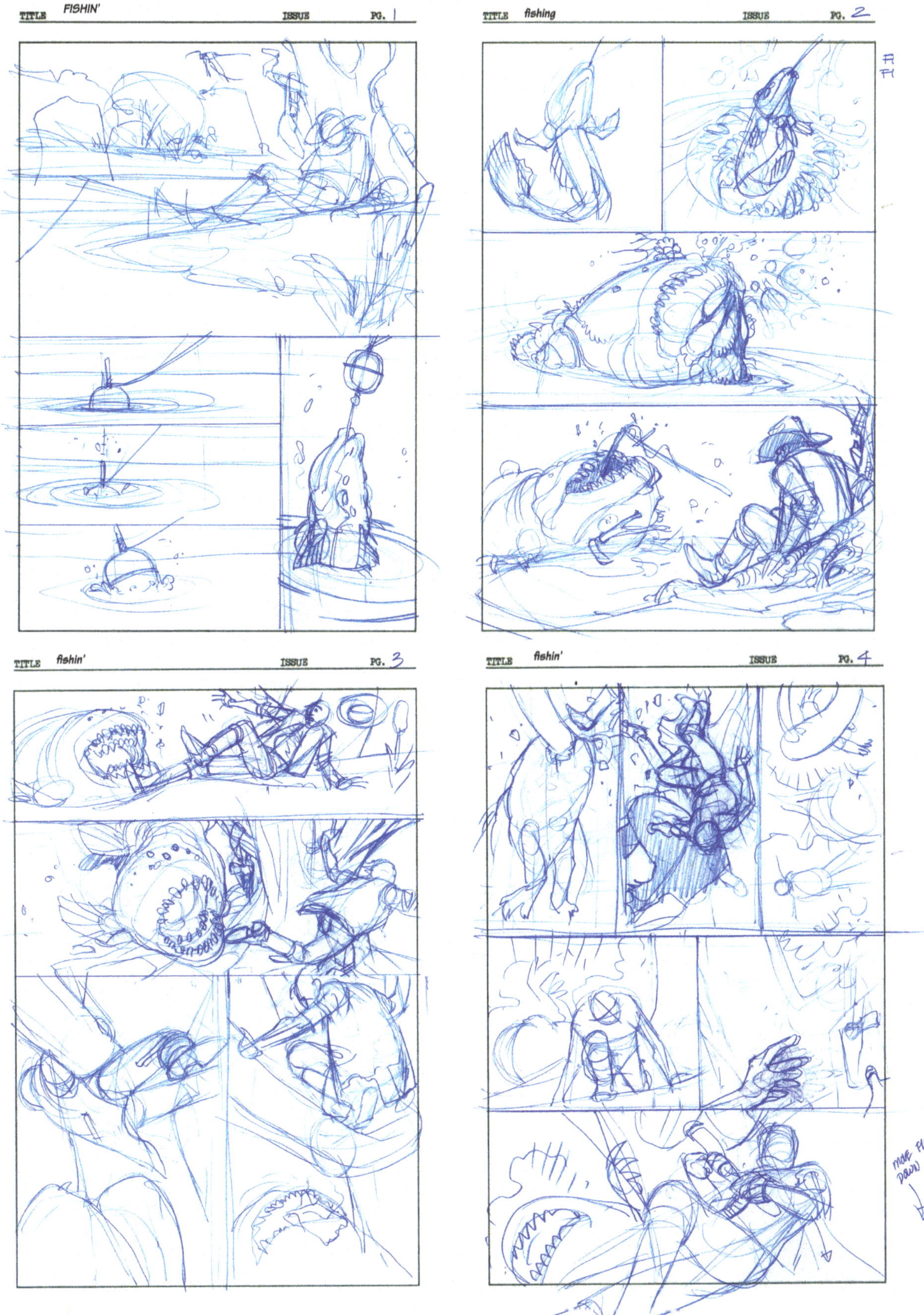



These are pages of continuity thumbnails for a short story called "Fishing." Here is where you are putting it all together and having to repeat elements to tell a tale. This also is a silent story for the first four pages, so everything has to be told visually.

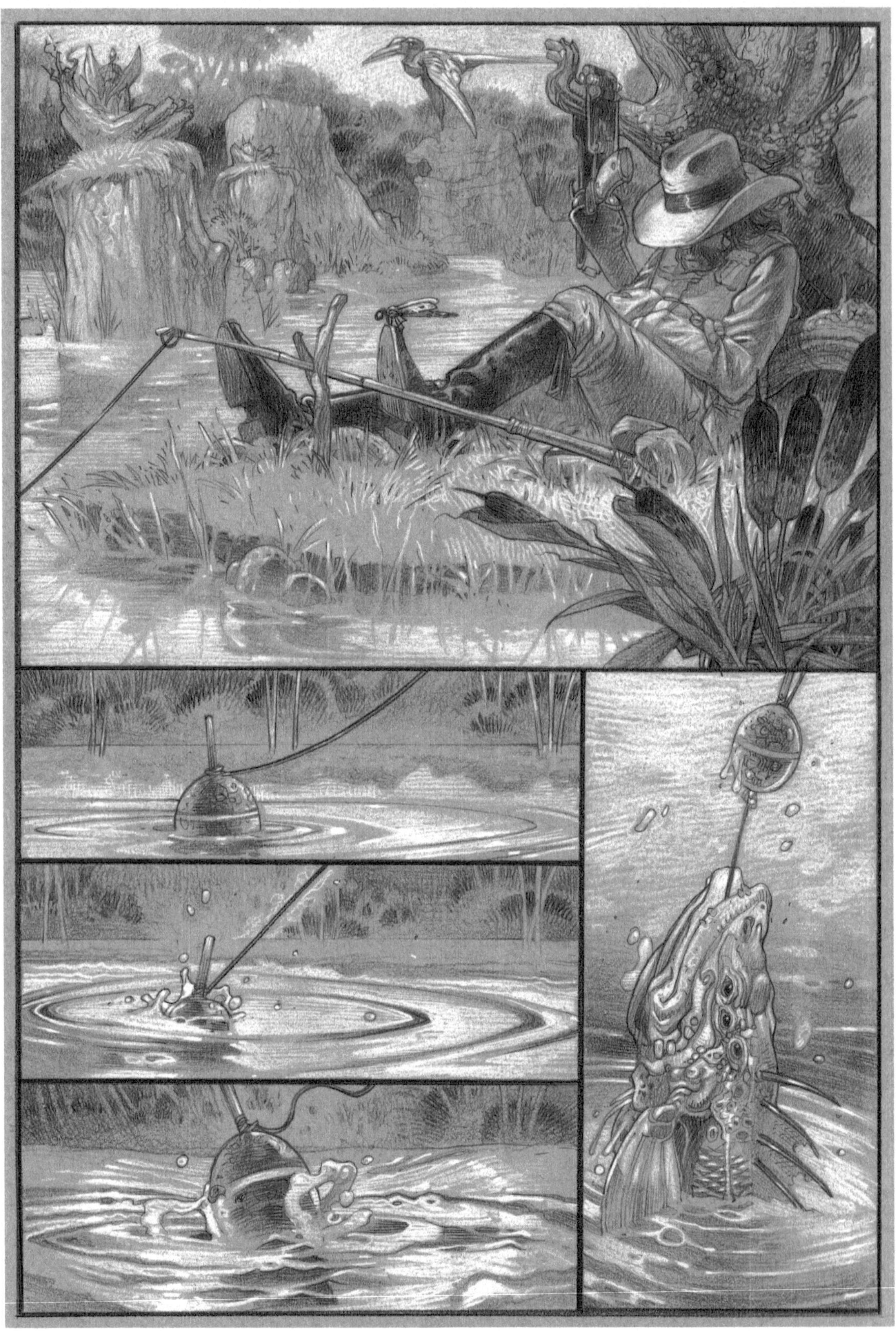

Page one is finished on gray paper with black and white pencils. The scene is set with a napping fisherman. So what does his world look like? What kinds of birds are flying through? A winged insect is resting on his boot, and the line is cast in the water. The fisherman will wait to see the bobber move and then yank the rod to set the hook and pull in our finned friend.

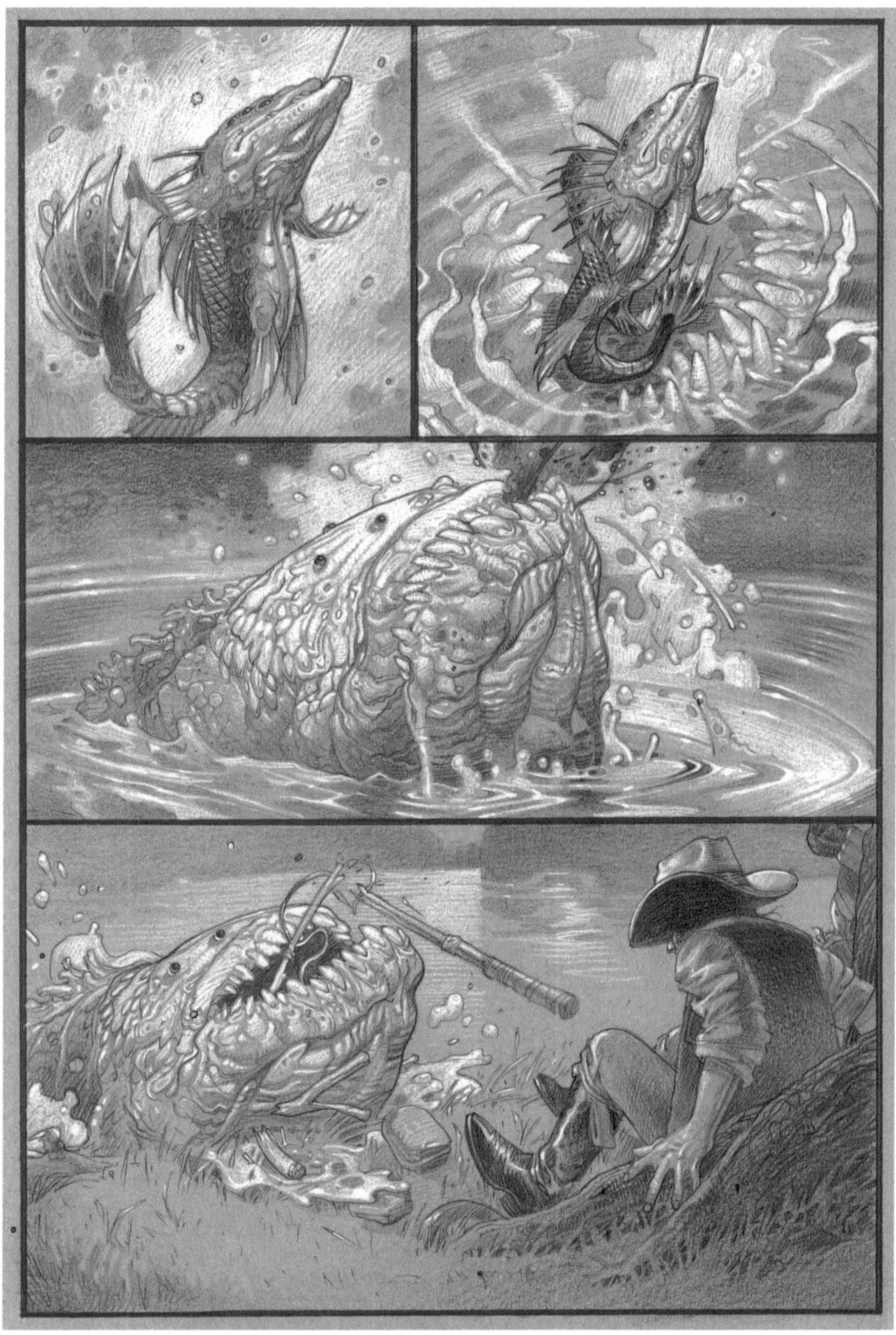

Because there is no reel, you have to yank in the fish. Of course, that sets up ripples and actions that will bring other fish to the area. In this case, much bigger fish!

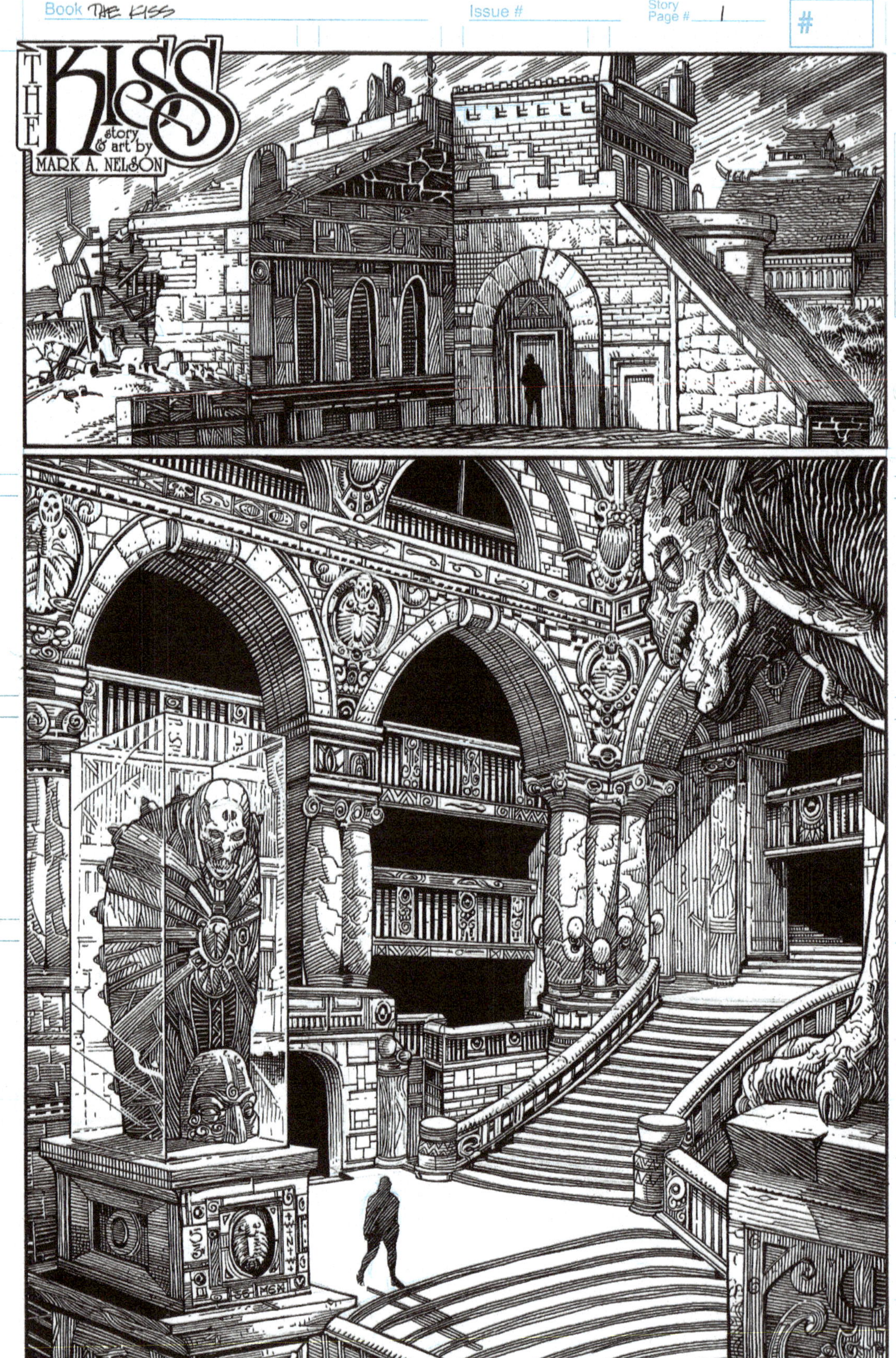


Here is a final inked page from the short story "The Kiss." The thumbnail can be seen on page 138. All the building studies and references pay off!

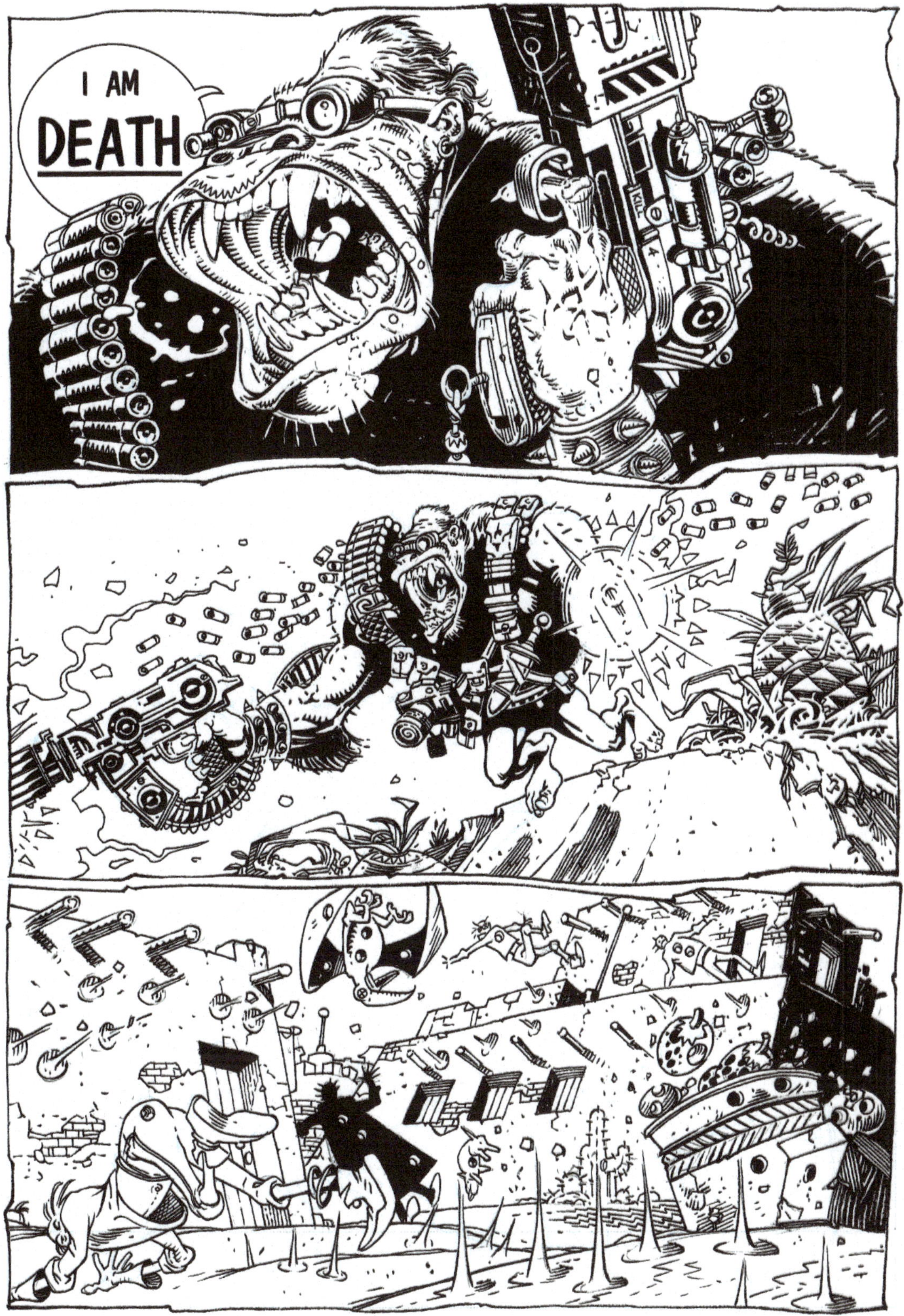

# CRAB BOY





*Crab Boy* was a humorous homage to superhero comics, where you never run out of bullets and other ammunition. This page introduces you to the bad guy and his style of carnage.

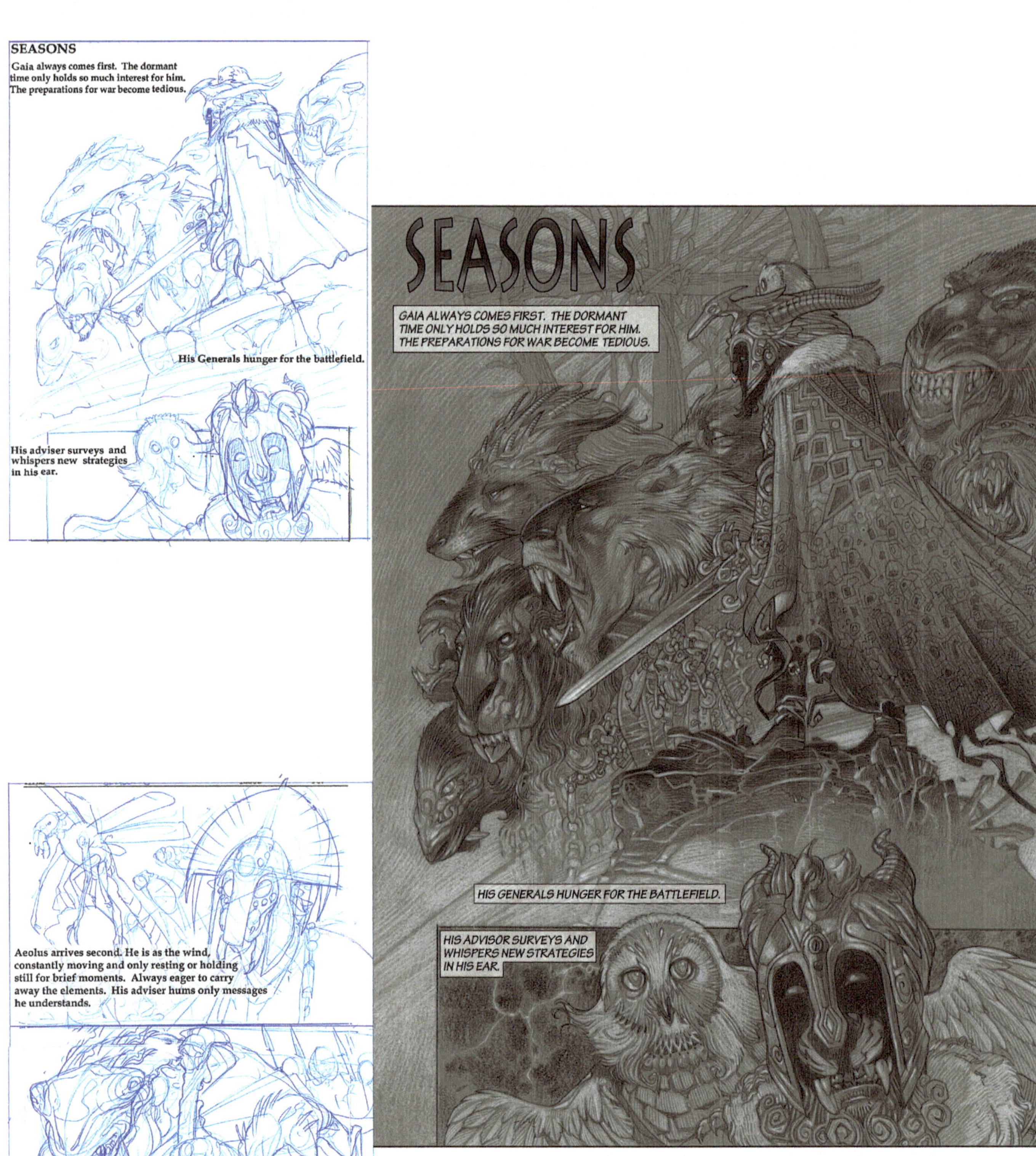


Thumbnails can be a help when placing the word balloons and text. I can make adjustments to the drawings before starting the finishes.

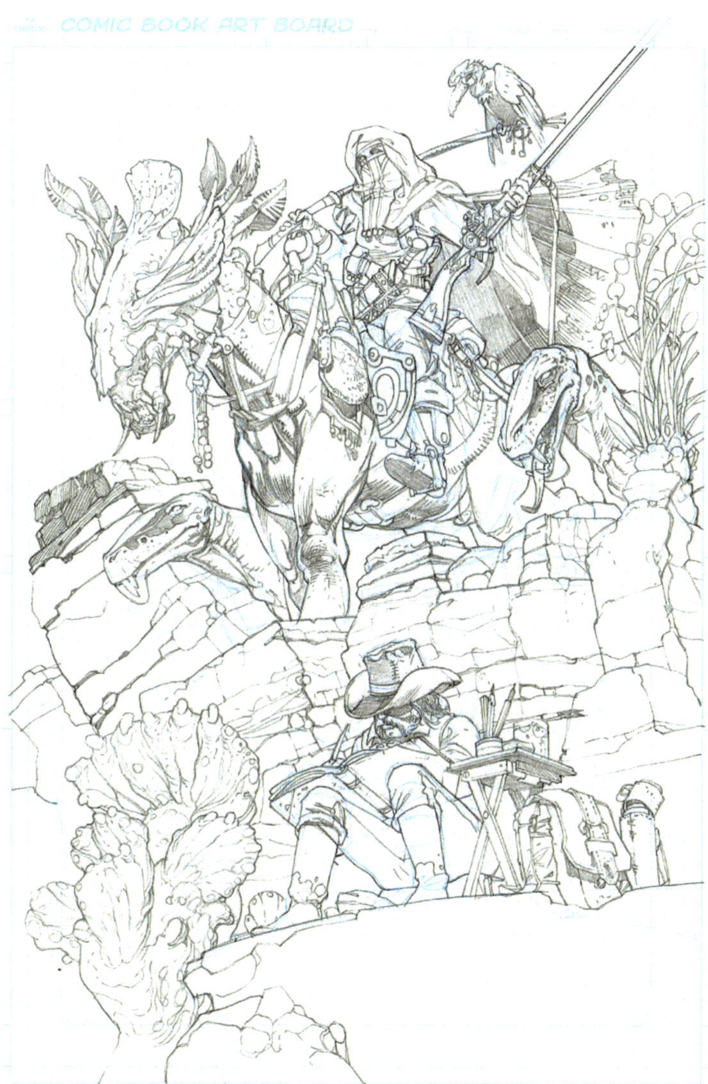

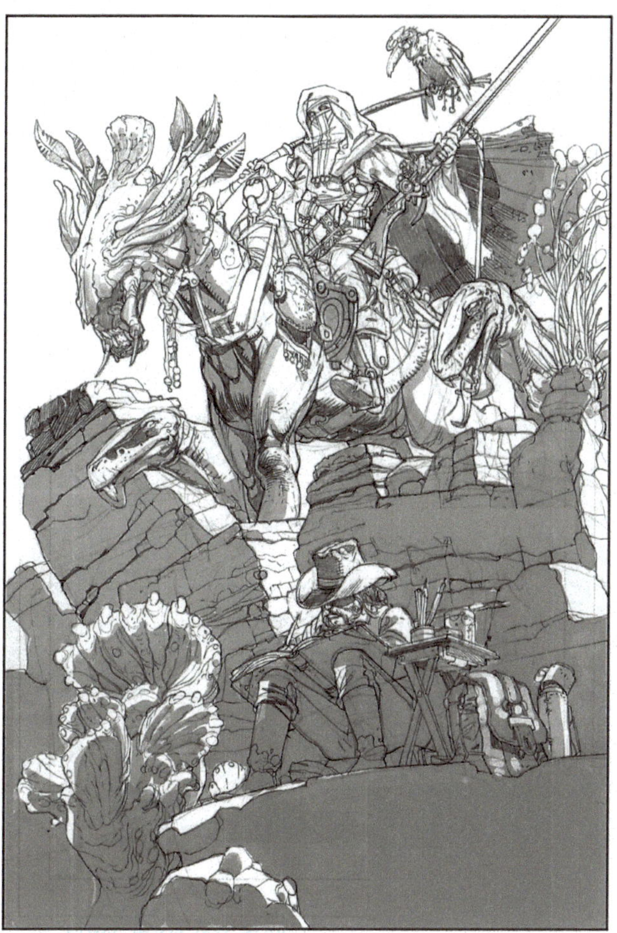

Here is the process I went through to do a cover piece. Most of the time I like to do more finished pencils because it makes it easier to ink, and you are not making as many decisions on the fly about the values. First is the pencil. Second, I took it into Photoshop and did a simple gray overlay in order to get the feel I wanted. Third, I began the inks with the rocks.

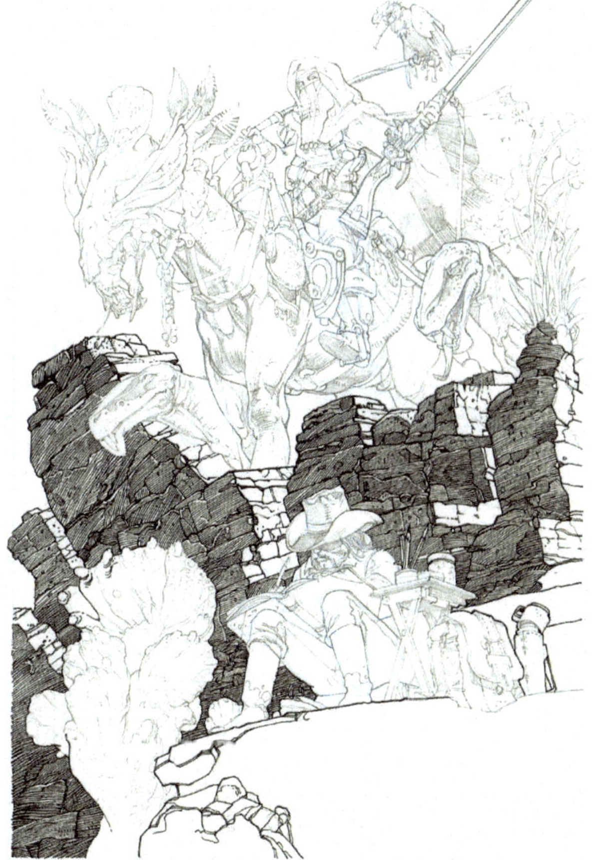

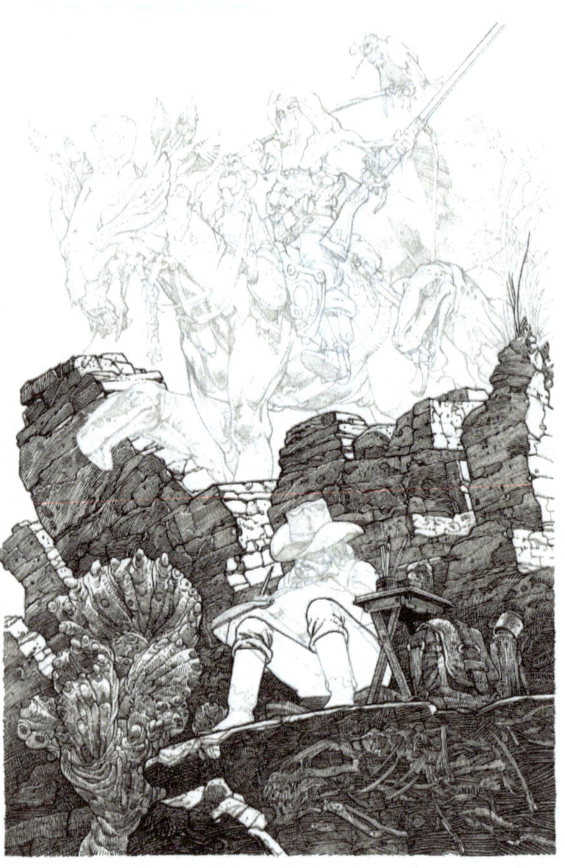

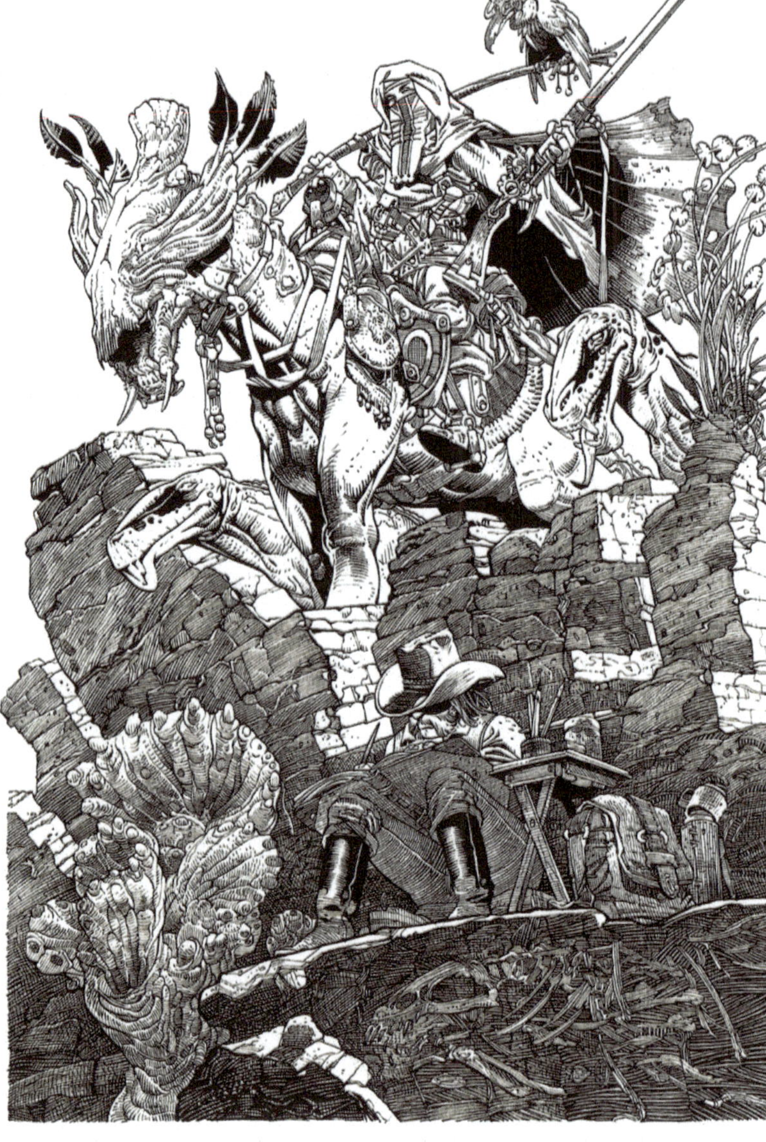

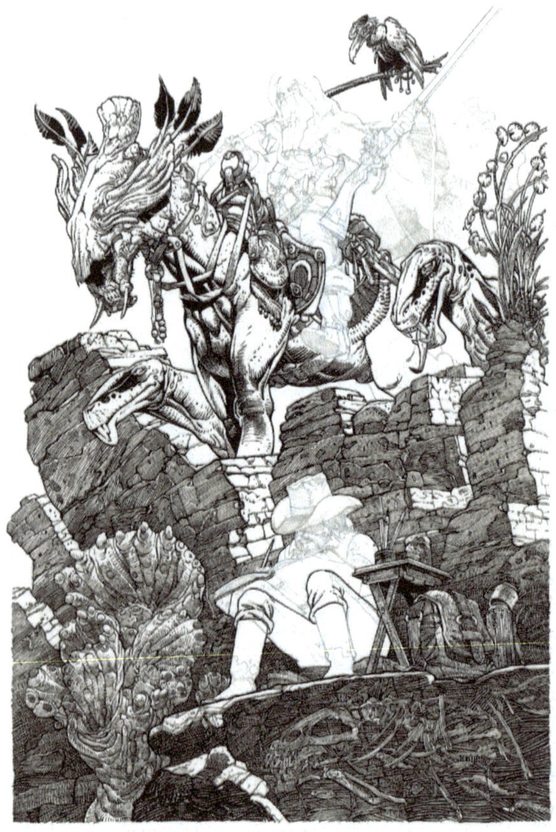

After inking the rocks, I did the large cactus and then moved on to the horse and the rider. I left the main figure for last. Part of this decision was because of a story I heard about Albrecht Dürer. It was said about one of his famous etchings that he left the figures of Adam and Eve for last, so he could charge up the environment they were in. (It also gives me another fun story to tell.)

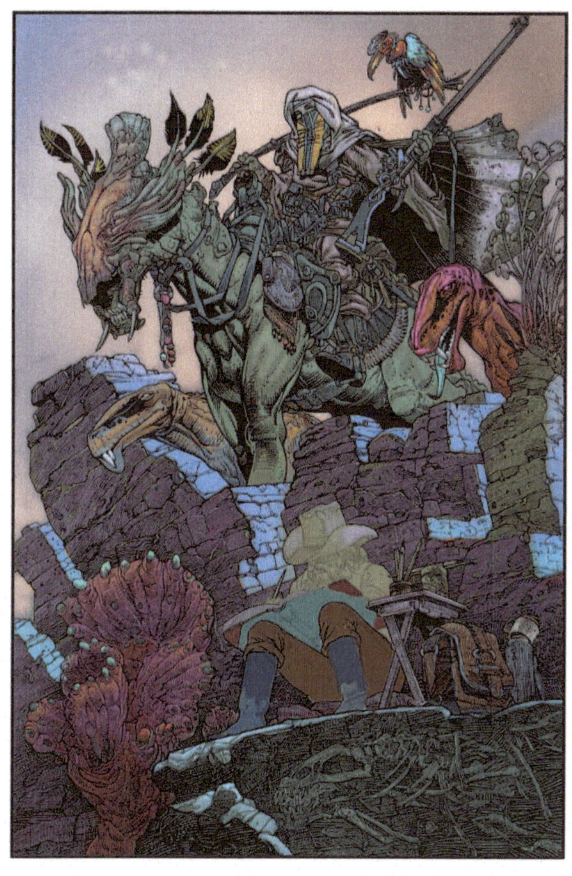

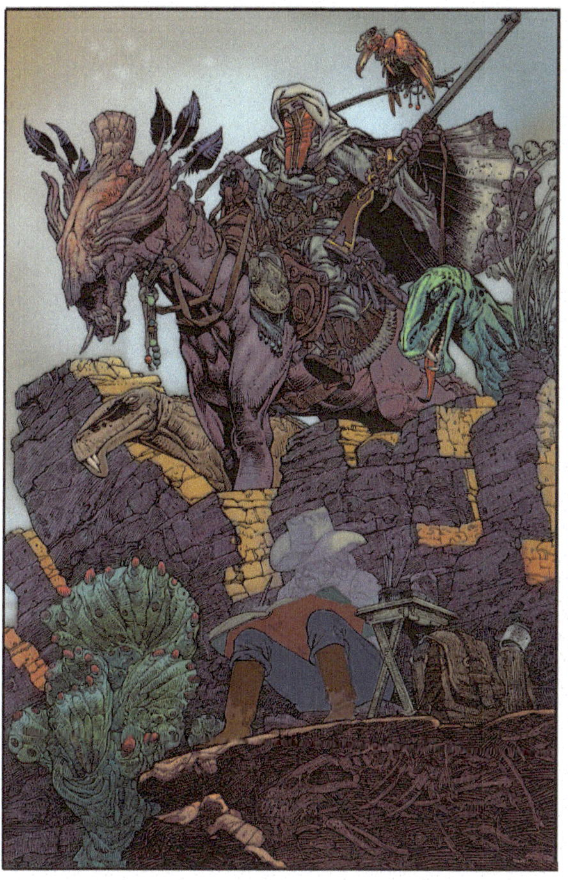

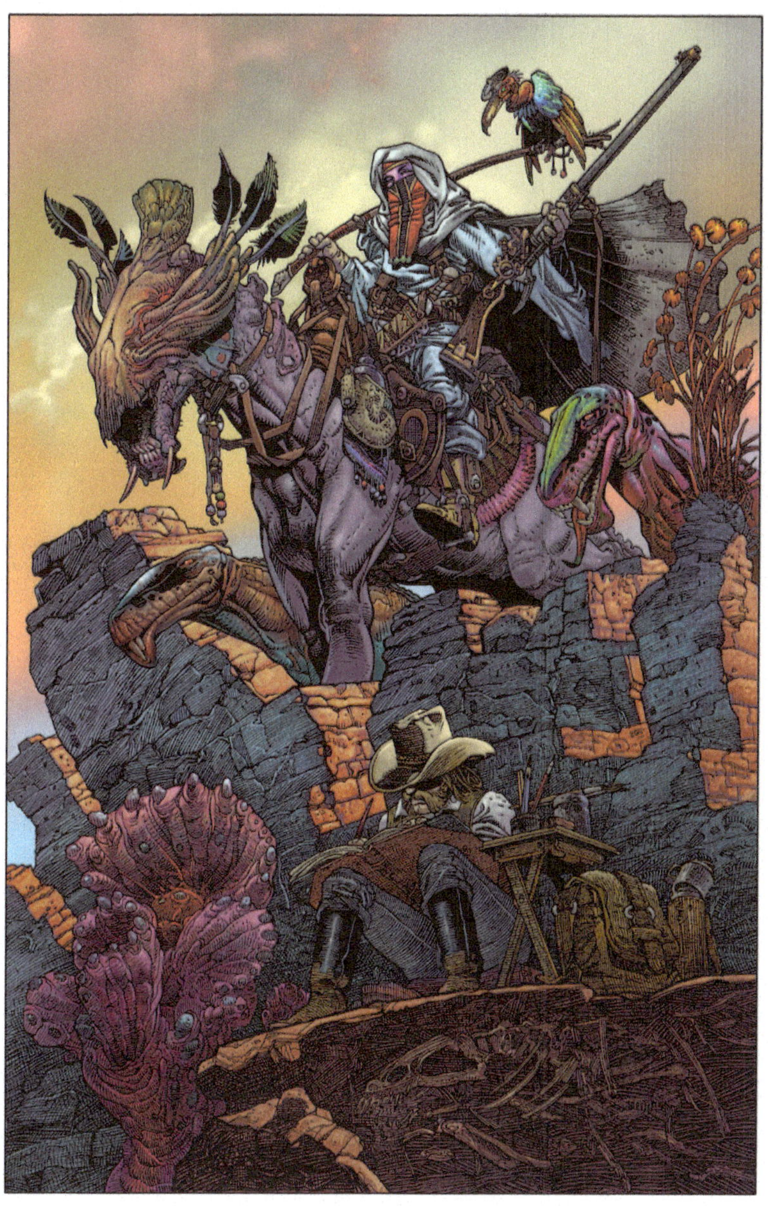

Color comps are a way of playing with different color choices. The two smaller images are quick comps that I did. I picked what I liked best out of each one to do the final (big image). You can see I did the comps before inking the last figure.

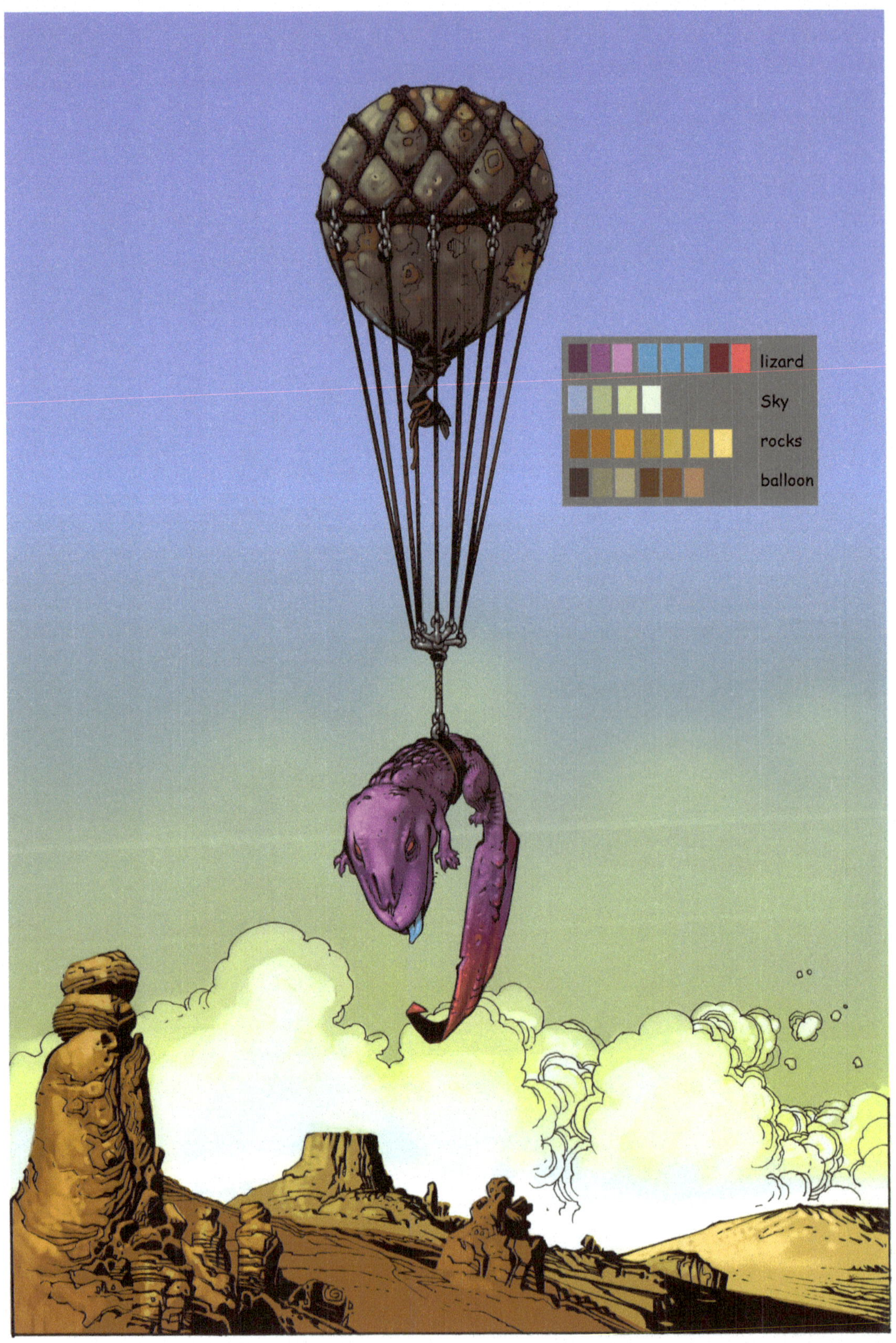



The way that I save my color palettes for the pages and characters is to do a layer with colors on a 50 percent gray or white background. The gray helps with the values of your colors. In print, I always count on a 10 percent dot gain. Everything will be 10 percent richer.

So a 90 percent black/gray will be 100 percent black. The 50 percent gray helps keep the colors up in a more printable range. Also, keep in mind that when you work on a computer, the image is projected with light, so everything looks brighter.

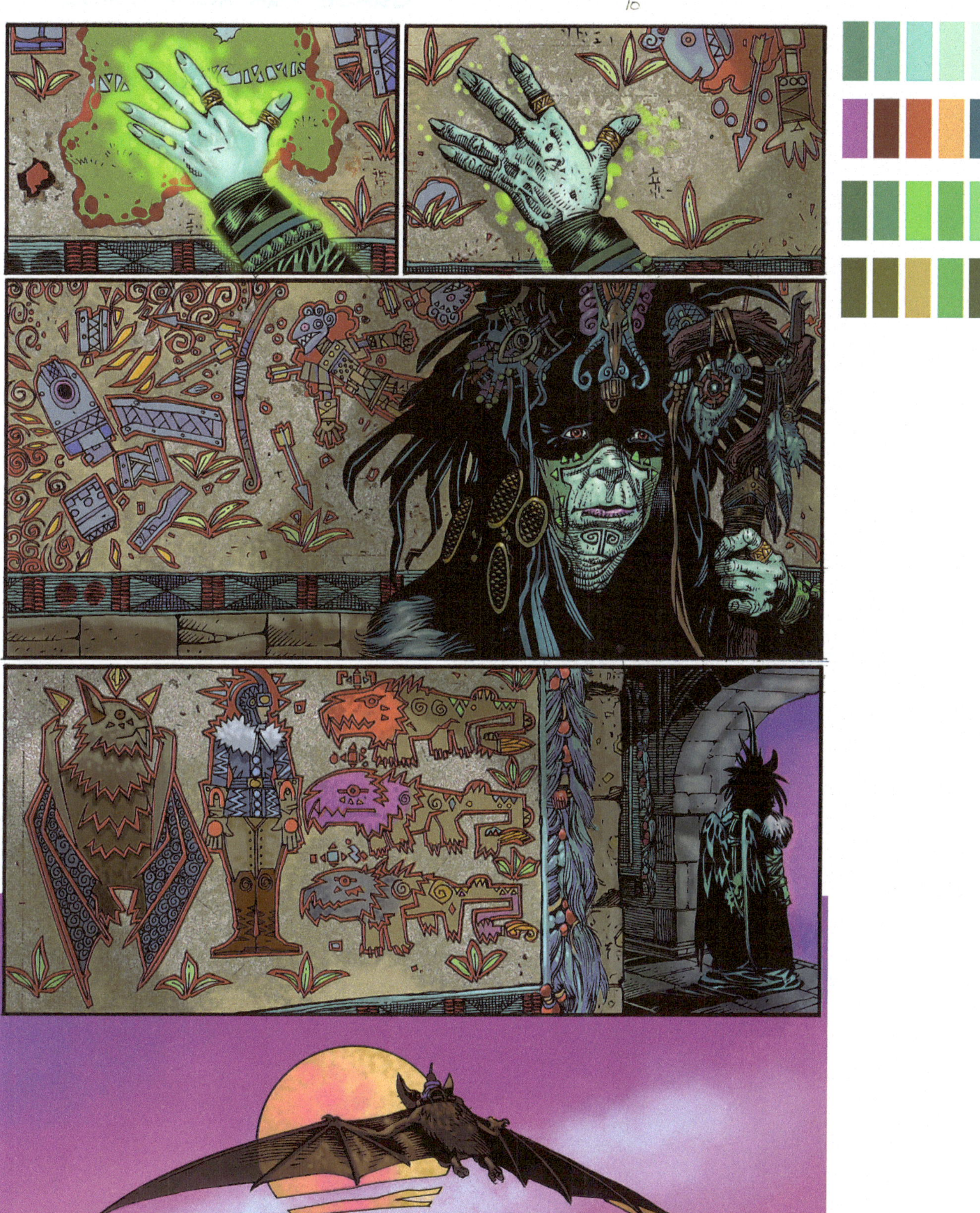

Here is the palette for the Priestess. You can see I also used it on the backgrounds to unify the colors throughout the panels and the page. This method will allow you to pick a type of harmony and flow to the range of your colors. That said, I just jumped in and started coloring from a toned background.

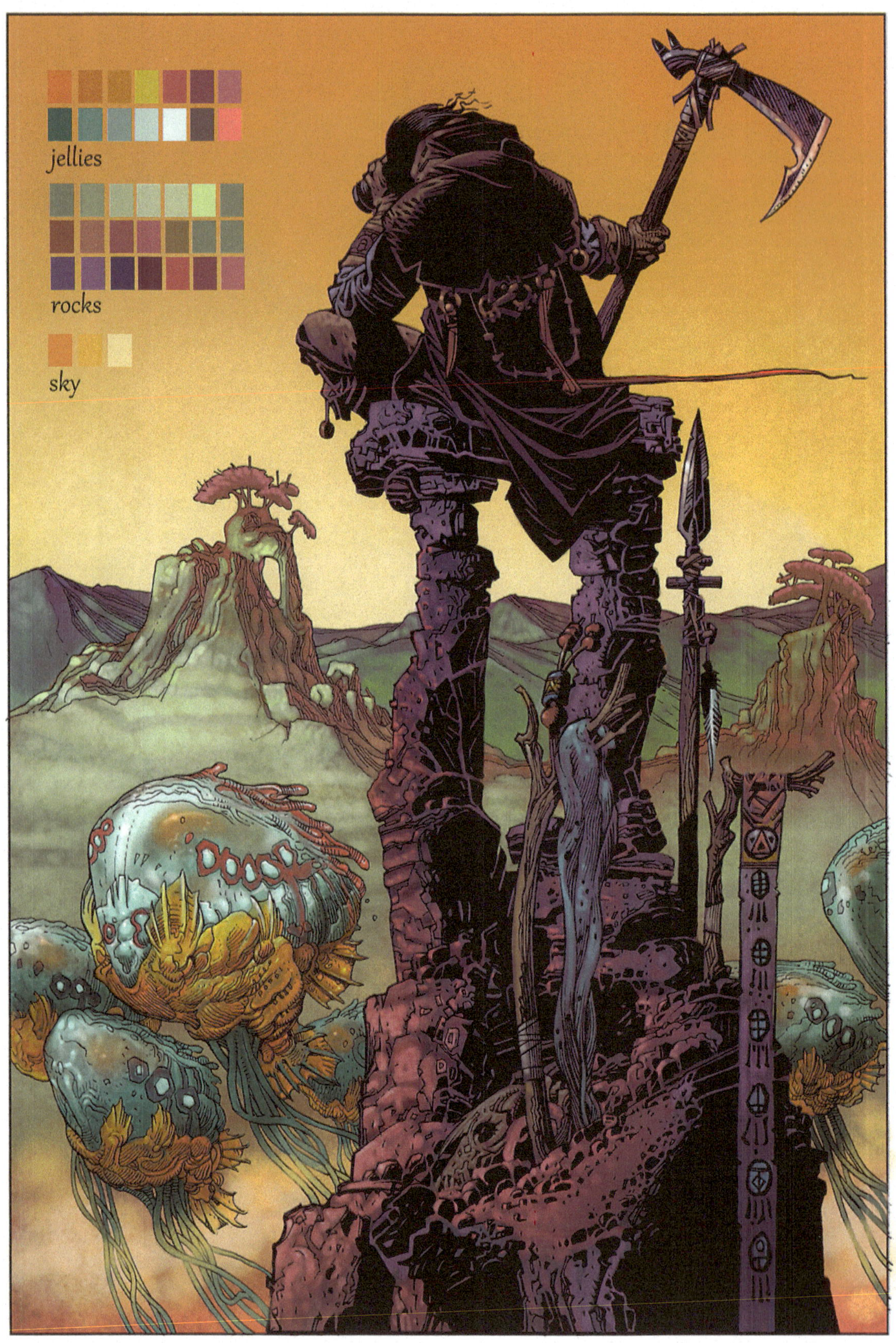

On the last page of color palettes, here is the first page of the Giant Jellyfish hunters. You've seen the development of their dress, some of their work habits, and now put all of it together.

# ACKNOWLEDGMENTS

I would like to thank Jeff Menges for his help and guidance, and Brian Ford, who made sure I "spell gud."

The list of artists who have influenced and will influence me would be too long. All I can say is "If you don't do it, who will? Get out there and make good art!"

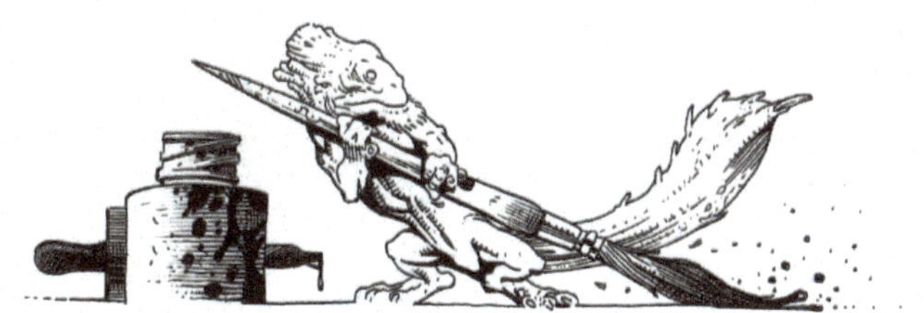

# ABOUT THE AUTHOR/ARTIST

Mark A. Nelson was born in Winnipeg, Canada, of American parents working aboard. From age two until college, he lived in Grand Forks, North Dakota. Here, his love of art, nature, and snow blossomed. The prairie is a subtle ecosystem with complex layers, where one has to observe and think. This is where the "what if" game started with friends, and it has been a stable building block in his creative process.

Nelson began his art training at Moorhead State College, moved on to the Cleveland Institute of Art for a BFA, and finally to the University of Michigan, Ann Arbor, for an MFA. On this artistic journey, he had many teachers who made him challenge his ideas, think about what he was trying to say, and develop the skills to do this.

As an artist, he enjoyed collaborating in the comics industry, including the Harvey–nominated *Aliens* with Mark Verheiden and *Blood and Shadows* with Joe R. Lansdale. As an inker, he worked on Marshal Law, Spider-Man, X-Men, Huntress, Airboy, and others. He wrote and illustrated "From Pencils to Inks," a how-to-draw comics column for *Hero Illustrated*.

Nelson was employed in the fantasy field with TSR, Wizards of the Coast, World of Warcraft, and others. He was art director and lead concept artist for video games at Pi Studios and senior concept artist at Raven Software. His illustrations have appeared in *Spectrum: The Best of Contemporary Fantasy Art, Aphrodisia—Art of the Female Form*, and *Aphrodisia II*, which won a Gold Award for its cover, and he served as a juror for *Spectrum 20*. There are two collected volumes of his work: *From Pencils to Inks and Visual Dialogues* and *Innsmouth, the Lost Drawings of Mannish Sycovia* (with Stephen Smith).

Nelson taught art at Northern Illinois University, Madison Area Technical College, Savannah College of Art and Design, and various workshops around the United States. He is currently a freelance artist at Grazing Dinosaur Press, and his labor of love is "Thunder Hunters," a story of epic proportions about an artist on a foreign planet.

www.grazingdinosaurpress.com
www.facebook.co/grazingdinosaurpress
www.deviantart.com/mansyc

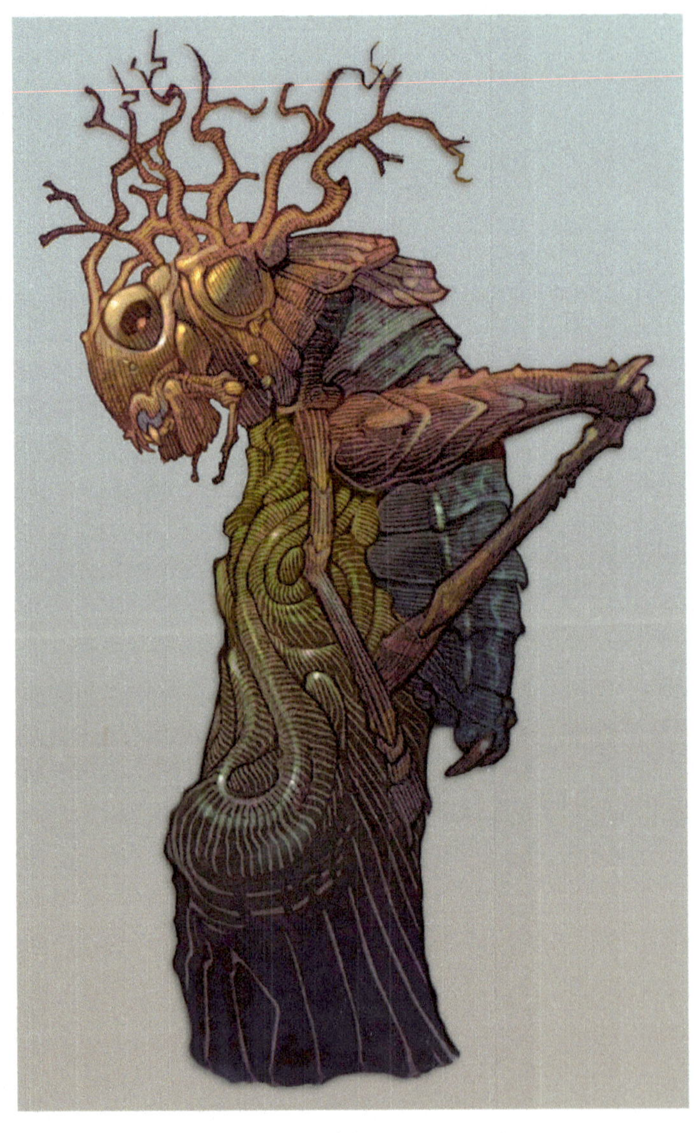